MAGAZINES
FOR
THE
MILLIONS

MAGAZINES
FOR
THE MILLIONS

Gender and Commerce in the
Ladies' Home Journal
and the
Saturday Evening Post
1880–1910

Helen Damon-Moore

State University of New York

Published by
State University of New York Press, Albany

©1994   State University of New York

Printed in the United States of America

For information, address the State University of New York Press,
State University Plaza, Albany, NY 12246

Production by Christine Lynch
Marketing by Dana E. Yanulavich.

Library of Congress Cataloging-in-Publication Data

Damon-Moore, Helen, 1958–
    Magazines for the millions : gender and commerce in the Ladies'
home journal and the Saturday evening post, 1880–1910 / Helen Damon
-Moore.
        p.   cm.
    Includes bibliographical references and index.
    ISBN 0-7914-2057-4 (CH). — ISBN 0-7914-2058-2 (PB)
    1. Women's periodicals, American—History—19th century.
2. Women's periodicals, American—History—20th century.   3. Sex
role in mass media.   4. Ladies' home journal.   5. Saturday evening
post (Philadelphia, Pa. : 1839)   I. Title.
PN4879.D36   1994
051'.082—dc20   93-33767
                                                                              CIP

10 9 8 7 6 5 4 3 2 1

In Memory of My Father,
Kenneth A. Damon
and
For My Mother, Lillian,
and My Husband, Dennis

TABLE OF CONTENTS

ACKNOWLEDGMENTS

I am grateful to the Spencer Foundation, whose grant helped to make the early stages of research on this project possible. Parts of the Epilogue have appeared elsewhere and were revised for this volume. They originally appeared in Carl F. Kaestle, Helen Damon-Moore, Lawrence C. Stedman, Katherine Tinsley, and William Vance Trollinger, Jr., *Literacy in the United States: Readers and Reading Since 1880* (Yale University Press, 1991), as Chapter 9, "Gender, Advertising, and Mass-Circulation Magazines." This material is adapted here by permission of the publisher.

Aiding my research in significant ways were the Steenbock Library staff at the University of Wisconsin, the Historical Society of Pennsylvania staff, and the Cornell College reference librarians, especially Sue Lifson and Alison Ames Galstad. I am indebted to A. Margaret Bok, daughter-in-law of Edward Bok, for her family reminiscences and for the information she shared with me pertaining to Louisa Knapp Curtis. Securing and reproducing illustration materials was made easier by Charles Scribner III of Charles Scribner's Sons Publishing, and by Susan LaLuzerne, Deborah Stewart, and Al Devine of the Wisconsin Center for Education Research. I have benefited from skillful support in preparing the manuscript for publication, and in this connection I should like to thank David Heesen, Ann Opatz, Carol Brokel, and Jackie Wallace.

Several scholars read an early, condensed version of this study; the constructive criticism I received from Lois Banner, James Baughman, Paul Boyer, David Paul Nord, Joy Rice, and Barbara Sicherman has been very much appreciated.

Several colleagues read the manuscript in its entirety, including Jan Cohn, Catherine Nickerson, and Rosalind Rosenberg. I am grateful to each of them for their intelligent, sympathetic and most useful commentaries. My greatest debt is to Carl Kaestle, whose study of readers and readership inspired my own concentration on magazines and magazine readers, and whose suggestions have strengthened my work in many ways. Carl has been an ideal mentor and colleague, and I can never thank him enough for all he has done.

Carola Sautter and Christine Lynch at SUNY Press have been gracious and helpful at every stage. It has truly been a pleasure to work with them.

I would also like to thank my friends and family for sustaining me through the long days of this project. Anne Durst, Catherine Burroughs, and Amy White discussed the book's themes with me and lifted my spirits when the going got rough, as did my sister, Cate Damon, and my brother, Ken Damon. My daughters Laura Damon-Moore and Stephanie Damon-Moore have given me great joy, and they have regularly reminded me that books and papers are not the most important things in life. Their caregivers—Shelley Cousin, Caryl Alberts, Marjorie Whitley, Elizabeth Harken and Joyce Harken—have provided critical support for my work, and I thank them all.

My father died long before this study was written, but the value he placed on education has contributed to it in very real ways. I am very grateful to my mother for carrying forward the parenting task on her own so energetically and so well. She is an inspiring role model. Finally, love and special thanks to my husband, Dennis. Our mutual interest in the study of gender has informed this project since its inception, and his unflagging enthusiasm for the study has contributed in significant ways to its shape and to its completion. Without his thorough reading of the manuscript the prose would have been weaker and the conceptualization less clear. I might have been able to do it without him, but it would have been much less fun. Again, my thanks.

Introduction

Early in the twentieth century a midwesterner named LaRue Brown, doubtless speaking for many young men of his day, commented disparagingly on the distance between reality and the images presented in contemporary popular media. He announced in a letter to his sweetheart, Dorothy Kirchway, that he "greatly preferred to marry a human woman and not an abstraction from the *Ladies' Home Journal*."[1] This sentiment certainly makes sense in its personal context. Who would choose to marry an abstraction? But probing beneath the surface of Brown's pronouncement reveals questions of fundamental importance in our culture today.

Is it indeed possible, for example, to make a clear distinction between a "human" or "real" person and the "abstractions" that media convey? What exactly is the content of the gender abstractions conveyed by magazines like the *Ladies' Home Journal*? How do commercial media images affect the gender construction of women and men in a given culture or time? Is gender construction a significantly different process for women than for men? Just how is gender construction negotiated in everyday life?

This study explores these complex and critical issues by attending first to a more straightforward question. Why would a young man like LaRue Brown refer specifically to the *Ladies' Home Journal* when bemoaning abstractions about womanhood? The answer is clear: the *Ladies' Home Journal,* founded by Cyrus Curtis and Louisa Knapp Curtis in 1883, was a magazine of undisputed importance from its earliest days. Originally conceived as a newspaper supplement designed to appeal to women, the *Journal* developed in a few short years into the largest-selling magazine in the United States. It served as a prototype for other commercial magazines with its low price and heavy reliance on advertising for revenue. In 1903 the *Journal* became the first magazine in the world to surpass a million in paid circulation. The magazine's producers estimated, not unfairly, that by the 1910s one in every five American women was reading the *Journal.*

LaRue Brown therefore in all likelihood singled out the *Ladies' Home Journal* for comment because it was a familiar and enormously popular periodical in his day. The *Journal*'s popularity takes on a larger meaning for the historian, since it served as a forerunner and prototype of the female-targeted mass-circulation magazines that continue to thrive today. Exploring the reasons for the success of the *Ladies' Home Journal* goes a long way toward explaining how female gender norms and commerce became entwined in the late nineteenth century.

But the story of the Curtis publishing enterprise is richer and more instructive than the *Journal*'s history alone reveals, because the Curtises were not content to rest with the success of their first magazine. In 1897 they purchased a second magazine, the *Saturday Evening Post*. They originally targeted the *Post* to men in order to parallel their successful women's periodical. Unexpectedly, the *Post* floundered as a magazine for men. The commercial milieu of the late nineteenth century—informed as it already was by an emphasis on the female consumer—demanded a broadening of the newer magazine to target women as well. The resulting family-oriented *Post* was much more successful than its earlier male-targeted incarnation. By 1910 the *Saturday Evening Post* too had surpassed a million in circulation, and it eventually outstripped even the *Journal* in both circulation and advertising revenue.

By the early 1900s, then, the *Journal* and the *Post* were both periodicals targeted to particular gendered audiences: the *Journal* to women, the *Post* to both women and men. They featured a blend of gendered material and commercial messages that producers of other periodicals were quick to imitate. The *Journal* and the *Post* thus exemplified and conveyed to their readers a powerful and mutually reinforcing mix of gender and commerce that had come to characterize a significant segment of American popular culture by the turn of the century.

This combination of gender and commerce is now so institutionalized that we take it for granted. As women and men in our consumer culture we are defined in large part by what we eat and drink, by what we wear, and by what we use: we are what we buy. Thus gender is commercialized. In turn and in concert with this pattern, commerce is highly gendered. Certain items are sold in certain forums to women, certain items in certain forums to men. Commercialized gender and gendered commerce are phenomena that are pervasive, mutually reinforcing, thoroughly embedded in capitalist culture, and appealing to many consumers as well as useful to producers of commercial goods. As such, they seem almost immutable to change.

In spite of this seeming immutability, some feminists and analysts of commercialism have criticized this gendered commercial milieu. Numerous studies detail and disparage sexism in advertising, and some analysts go further to suggest that gender stereotyping in the media at large is problematic.[2] While these critiques are plausible and important, the relationship between gender and commerce remains underanalyzed and undertheorized. My reading of the *Journal* and the *Post* suggests that the critique of the gendered commercial milieu can be deepened and broadened by tracing its early days. There certainly were significant problems with the turn-of-the-century junction of gender and commerce, and exploring how these phenomena developed and came to inform one another can provide a basis for conceiving a sophisticated critique of contemporary media and for formulating more positive alternatives.

I argue in this study that the *Ladies' Home Journal* and the *Saturday Evening Post* were prototypes that aided in the creation, development, and sustaining of the commercializing of gender and the gendering of commerce. They were conveyors of both gender messages and commercial messages, serving a new and central function in American popular culture.

These magazines were more than conveyors of messages, however. They were also commercial products produced by the publisher and editors, supported by revenues from advertisers, and read by millions of American women and men. I argue as well, therefore, that the magazines' producers, advertisers, and readers conspired, sometimes intentionally and sometimes unintentionally, in a process that helped to create a gendered commercial discourse and a commercial gender discourse. The magazines' producers—that is, the publisher and editors—were neither all-powerful nor all-knowing, and they relied on advertisers to buy space in their magazines and readers to buy the magazines and to attend at some level to their messages. Advertisers needed producers to convey their messages and readers to read their messages and act on them. Readers chose whether to buy the *Journal* and the *Post* or not, chose what to read within those magazines, and construed their own meaning from what they read and saw. In the biggest picture, however, the Curtis magazines' readers were constrained by the agenda-setting, circumscribing function of these magazines.

This hegemonic process, in which all parties were active though unequal players, is central to the story of the *Journal* and the *Post*.[3] The story of these magazines and of the early days of the union between gender and commerce calls for careful attention to the complexities of both gender construction and popular culture production and consumption. Making sense of these processes presents serious challenges to scholars, and their historical configurations are particularly daunting to fathom. But in order to understand contemporary society as well as the past we must attempt to sort them out. To do so, I believe an interdisciplinary approach that borrows from women's history, men's history, and cultural studies is necessary to represent as accurately as possible the complexities of gender and popular culture.

Theorizing gender development has prompted a great deal of recent discussion among social scientists, literary critics, and historians. Historians have given particular attention to the metaphor of separate spheres and to the larger issue of gender as a social construct. The separate spheres metaphor has dominated much women's history analysis, and at the outset of my research the *Journal* and the *Post* appeared to embody the metaphor perfectly: the *Journal* spoke to women and the *Post* spoke to men. However, it soon became clear that the separate spheres metaphor was of limited usefulness as an explanatory concept, for on the most immediate level the story of these two magazines was more complicated than the metaphor could represent or describe. The *Journal* was targeted to women, and its first editor was a woman; but its second editor was a man, which significantly altered the periodical's tone and content. The *Post* originally targeted men, but to succeed commercially it had to broaden its appeal to women. In terms of the magazines' producers and audience alone, therefore, the metaphor was inadequate.

In addition, as Linda Kerber notes, the language of separate spheres has been prone to "sloppy use" in which historians have referred, often interchangeably, to "an ideology *imposed on* women, a culture *created by* women, [and] a set of boundaries *expected to be observed by women*."[4] This last variation suggests a physical separation between women and men, with women relegated to the private, domestic sphere, and men operating more freely in the public, economic sphere. This has been, indeed, a popular conception of spheres. The metaphor once again proves limited, however, when put to the test of the actual experience of Curtis magazine producers and readers. For example, Louisa Knapp Curtis edited the *Journal* from her home; hence, one might assume that a female editorship was synonymous with the private sphere, a male editorship with the public sphere. But after Louisa's editorship her male successor, Edward Bok, made a point of the fact that he wrote his own editorial for the *Journal* each month at his home. In addition, the *Journal* assumed and its readers confirmed the fact of late nineteenth-century women's numerous activities outside the home and the private sphere. These activities included church attendance, club work, and, for a significant minority of women, work for pay outside the home.[5]

Finally, the metaphor of separate spheres is undercut by the overall mission and character of the *Journal* and the *Post* as commercial products. Targeted to women, the *Journal* was indeed centrally concerned with issues of home life. Targeted first to men and then to men and women, the *Post* was more concerned with issues of the public realm and of work. But both the *Journal* and the *Post* proclaimed and stood for the value of consuming, an activity that transcended the metaphor of separate spheres. Consuming—that is, choosing and buying commercial products and using them in the home—was an activity performed in part in public for the good of the family and the home. Consuming, in turn, rested on the capacity of adults, particularly male adults, to earn money. This was also an activity usually performed in public for the good of the family and the home. It becomes clear that the metaphor of separate spheres obscures rather than clarifies the story of the *Ladies' Home Journal* and the *Saturday Evening Post* and their contributions to gender construction.

It is also evident, however, that the magazine producers themselves were, in some circumstances, informed by the notion of separate spheres. The very creation of the *Ladies' Home Journal* and the *Saturday Evening Post* rested on the assumption that women and men have separate interests that can be packaged in separate commercial magazines. In addition, the magazine producers sometimes employed the metaphor explicitly as they tried to make sense of gender constructions and conventions of the day. Louisa Knapp Curtis employed the concept most directly, but she referred to it mainly to reject it. It behooves the historian, then, to employ the metaphor of separate spheres only to the extent that historical figures themselves have employed or have been clearly informed by it.

The metaphor of separate spheres has come in for criticism and rejection as a part of a larger criticism of dichotomous thinking and representation in general. Deconstructionists have catalogued the Western propensity for organizing ideas and behaviors into such diametrical oppositions as public–private, superior–inferior, dominant–submissive, and active–passive. For those interested in gender construction, the overarching dichotomy is, of course, male–female. Masculinity and femininity are traditionally defined as opposed and mutually exclusive categories. This traditional definition is deeply rooted and powerful. Exploring this definition and others, and examining rather than assuming their dichotomous character, becomes the major task of the gender historian.[6]

It is further necessary to historicize gender, to locate gender norms as carefully as possible in their context. As Joan Scott asserts, gender as a social construct

> can only be determined specifically, in the context of time and place. We can write the history of that process only if we recognize that "man" and "woman" are at once empty and over-flowing categories. Empty because they have no ultimate, transcendent meaning. Over-flowing because even when they appear to be fixed, they still contain within them alternative, denied, or suppressed definitions.[7]

Careful attention to the language of gender construction, however, must be tempered by rigorous examination of the historical structures within which the language is being employed. The study of gender lends itself to deconstructionist analysis because gender norms are conveyed through specific uses of the language. But as Bryan D. Palmer writes in his largely negative assessment of poststructuralist and deconstructionist theory, "language is not life."[8] While deconstruction is helpful in sensitizing historians to the importance of language in constructing identities, its emphasis on the supremacy of language downplays human agency and emphasizes social constraint.[9] Analytical social history that is rooted in the lives and experiences of real people can anchor the historian who is interested in linguistic constructions, preventing what Palmer calls the "descent into discourse."[10]

Analysis of the *Journal* and the *Post* reveals some of the complexity of gender construction, since we see real people negotiating their own gender identities and interpreting gender norms for their readers. We also see the producers and readers negotiating power relationships with surprisingly uneven results. The magazines' production and consumption involved many very real struggles for power and economic privilege, some across gender lines and some within.

As we push beyond the concept of separate spheres and its attendant simplistic dichotomies to examine the ways gender is constructed, we see complex interactions both between women and men and between concepts of femininity and masculinity. We see, for example, that gender construction varies spatially, from culture to culture; temporally, from one historical period to another; and longitudinally, over the course of the life cycle.[11] Thus gender is a fundamentally unstable construct, constantly changing.[12] Denise Riley captures this instability when she substitutes a new question for Sojourner Truth's classic, "Ain't I a woman?" Riley asks instead, "Ain't I a fluctuating identity?"[13] These fluctuating identities—female and male—are by nature difficult to capture, to characterize. In fact, the experiences of the Curtis publications' producers and the content of the magazines clearly demonstrate this difficulty. The producers faced the dilemma of what to include, what to exclude, what to emphasize, and what to de-emphasize with respect to gender norms in their magazines. The extent to which the magazines' messages are mixed internally reflects in part the challenge of trying to compartmentalize, much less to influence, gender norms in any given period.

It is helpful in this light to analyze each magazine as a whole. Most studies of magazines to date have focused on one segment or aspect of magazines, either their production (institutional histories/producer biographies) or their editorial matter, short stories, or advertising.[14] Analyzing each magazine in its entirety over a significant period of time reveals both a measurable amount of internal contradiction and a demonstrable evolution in gender-related content over time. Above all we see the "layers of internal inconsistencies and the coexistence of multiple gender meanings" that Elizabeth Fox-Genovese suggests are more realistic than the earlier historiographic view of gender as a "coherent system of male domination."[15] The magazines' gender-oriented content is instructive because their producers were attempting to sell huge numbers of magazines. It was not possible to do so by striking a single note; producers had to strike a chord with their gender messages that would appeal to as many readers as possible.[16]

The producers of the *Ladies' Home Journal* and the *Saturday Evening Post* were seeking a middle-class audience, and the evidence suggests that they succeeded. A class analysis of the turn-of-the-century media world reveals a stratification of the available materials. Newspapers and magazines targeted either the working or the middle class, and producers like Cyrus Curtis and his editors worked hard to earn the stamp of middle-class approval for their commercial publications. There was a shift from a producer to a consumer emphasis within turn-of-the-century publications that transcended class; working-class and middle-class publications alike were informed by this shift.[17]

The producers of the Curtis magazines were appealing primarily to members of the middle class to which they themselves belonged, simplifying their task to some extent. Studies show that gender definition differs by race, ethnicity, age, class, sexuality, and region.[18] Indeed, at any given time and in any given culture, many masculinities and femininities may coexist, peacefully or otherwise. As they spoke to white, upwardly-mobile, lower-middle-class and middle-class readers, the Curtis publication editors were communicating with people they considered to be essentially like themselves. To the extent that readers supported the magazines with their subscriptions, the messages of the magazines accordingly reflected a range of gender constructs acceptable to a certain segment of the late nineteenth-century white population.[19]

There were at the same time major differences between the two magazines that we must account for. The *Ladies' Home Journal* and the *Saturday Evening Post* were mass-circulation magazines produced by the same publisher, both intended for white middle-class readers. One might assume therefore that their rhetoric would be similar. But comparing the two magazines highlights two different discourses that the personalities of the editors alone cannot explain. We see from the earliest days of both magazines, for example, that the *Journal* was more highly "gendered" than the *Post*. The *Journal* was more openly targeted to women than the *Post* was to men, and it more consciously reflected upon matters of gender construction. The explicitly comparative approach afforded by the juxtaposition of these two magazines suggests that gender construction, at least as it was expressed on paper, was a significantly different process for women than it was for men.

This comparative approach also demonstrates that, while gender norms may have been presented differently in the two magazines, they were at the same time interactive. That is, norms regarding masculinity affected norms regarding femininity, and vice versa.[20] At some points in history, shifts in gendered expectations and their interactive effects have been profound. For example, when men left farms in order to work in factories with the onset of the Industrial Revolution, a whole set of complementary gendered expectations for women was established. One scholar suggests that we have yet to write the history of this complementary "Consumer Revolution."[21] The relationship between gender and commerce embodied by the *Journal* and the *Post* does, in fact, illuminate some of the contours of the "Consumer Revolution." The story of the *Ladies' Home Journal* and the *Saturday Evening Post* points clearly to a set of interactive norms that centered in large part on women's "new" role as consumer and men's "old" role as provider.

The comparative approach also highlights the fact that people are not highly gendered beings every moment of their lives; as Denise Riley notes, it is "not possible to live twenty-four hours a day soaked in the immediate awareness of one's sex."[22] This does not mean that the culture fails to designate some behaviors and attributes as womanly and some as manly. Nor does it mean that individuals never view themselves in gendered ways. It does mean, however, that historians must attend closely to exactly how women and men are being characterized by given commentators at given times, and to what purpose. Significantly, for example, the *Journal* and the *Post* both viewed women as quite constantly and continuously gendered beings. The *Journal*'s format and content revolved around this assumption, and much of the only explicitly gendered discussion in the *Post* centered on a conception of women as women that found no parallel for men. The reasons for this particular approach are twofold. First, as Simone de Beauvoir observed in the mid-twentieth century, woman is "other." Because the masculine is the norm, the feminine must be elaborated, signified, and explained. Second, women at the turn of the century were actively agitating for change, and they were altering their role in important ways. In contrast and in reaction, the major emphasis with regard to the male role was on preserving the status quo.

This emphasis on preserving the masculine status quo must, however, be examined rather than assumed. Steve Craig in *Men, Masculinity, and the Media* suggests that too many feminist analyses of the media accept the "masculine as norm" phenomenon without question, viewing portrayals of men in the media as unproblematic or even exemplary.[23] What we need are more studies that do precisely what these studies do not and the *Post* did not do—that is, examine the media treatment of men as men.

The comparison of the two magazines therefore yields important revelations, and it points to the need for more explicitly comparative works of gender history. Too many studies in women's history employ direct analysis of women's lives and ideas while resting on unexamined assumptions about men's lives and ideas. To the extent that the newer men's history parallels women's, some studies under that rubric have been similarly skewed. While studies that shine a light on women or men alone should not be abandoned, the attempt to understand gender as it has been defined historically calls for much more work that looks simultaneously and explicitly at constructs for both women and men. Only then will we begin to flesh out the complexities of gender's historical forms.

In sum, we benefit by examining each magazine as a whole, and then by comparing the two to each other. It is crucial as well to locate the texts—and their producers' creation of them—in the context of the larger culture. Similarly, it is central to the topic of gender construction and its relationship to commerce to consider the possible effects of the magazines' gendered and commercial messages on their readers. This is where methods germane to the examination of popular culture come to the fore.

Michael Schudson defines popular culture as "beliefs and practices, and the objects through which they are organized, that are widely shared among a population." The study of popular culture therefore includes analysis of (1) the production of cultural objects, such as newspapers, magazines, and television; (2) the content of the objects; and (3) the reception of objects and the meanings attributed to them by the general population or subpopulations.[24] The *Journal* and the *Post* are the objects of this study, and their production, content, and reception are all subjects of examination here.

The reception aspect of cultural study emphasizes the link between the reader and the text. Carl Kaestle, in an essay entitled "The History of Readers," traces various theoretical approaches to characterizing the reader–text connection. Analysts like Raymond Williams and Harold Innis have theorized on a grand scale, emphasizing the themes of centralization and consolidation, and the "subordination of cultural democratization to the needs of capitalism."[25] Other more intermediate theories have included the uses and gratifications approach, the psychological interactive reading model, and the reader-response approach. These theories, while they come from different disciplines—communication theory, cognitive psychology, and literary criticism—all feature an emphasis on reading as an interactive process.[26]

While these grand and intermediate theories have been useful at some levels, our theoretical conclusions vis-à-vis readers and texts are provisional at best. As Kaestle remarks, "the very phenomenon we wish to explore is both empirically elusive and conceptually complex."[27] Readers in history cannot be interviewed about their reading, and it is seldom possible to link actual readers with specific texts in the past. It is also very difficult to determine how reading was used by particular readers. Did people read for entertainment, edification, simple distraction, or some combination of these?[28] The study of reading requires a balance, not only between the reader and the text, but between the reader's act of making meaning and the social/historical context, and between cultural meaning and social function.[29]

Kaestle posits a model of reading that incorporates precisely this balance. He theorizes that readers act individually "to develop identities, choose allegiances, form beliefs, and conduct their day-to-day lives, but they do so within the constraints of cultural inheritances and economic relationships."[30] This model accounts for both agency and constraint in the world of reading. It accommodates as well the range of responses that is possible for any given text, and the fact that these responses will not be predictable in all cases. It also suggests, however, that we will see some patterns over time in reading and its uses.[31]

Kaestle et al. identify some general patterns that are relevant to this study. They suggest that literacy expanded impressively although unevenly over the course of the twentieth century; that reading materials increased in number and became increasingly standardized in this period; that the content of printed material was always contested, even as it became standardized; and finally, that literacy had plateaued by the late twentieth century.[32] While these larger patterns provide a useful backdrop to a study of magazines and readers, it is, in the end, the producer–text–reader relationship that is of most interest here.

In trying to represent the relationships among producers, texts, and readers, some researchers have turned to visual models. Robert Darnton offers a circuit model, for example, which begins with a book's author, then moves to connections between authors and publishers, publishers and printers, printers and shippers, shippers and booksellers, and booksellers and readers. He represents the important but uncertain connection between readers and authors with a dotted line, leaving the circuit only partially completed.[33]

Anthropologists have employed similar connective metaphors to describe culture in general, such as networks, structures, or what Clifford Geertz has called the "web of significance."[34] The web metaphor captures the complexity of the relationships among popular culture elements better than the circuit model because it is not linear in design. The web encompasses the producers of the magazine (including publishers, editors, writers, and advertisers), the textual content of the magazines, and the readers who bought the magazines and who may have purchased the products advertised in their pages.

A study of the *Journal* and the *Post* highlights these connections or the lack of them more clearly than studies of some other popular culture objects can, first, because the magazines had to sell themselves to advertisers in order to attract their advertisements, and, second, because they had to appeal to readers in order to attract their subscriptions.[35] Similarly, advertisers had to create messages that readers would believe, enjoy, and act on. These decisions were, after all, in the hands of readers. If they were interested in a magazine, they bought it and read it. If they were not interested, they did not even purchase it. Likewise, if they were interested in a product, they bought it, and if they were not interested, they did not.

Commercial markets were in fact expanding rapidly in the late 1800s, which gave rise to the need for advertising in the first place. One sign of this rapid expansion is the shift in commercial discourse from conceptualizing potential buyers as "customers" to describing them as "consumers."[36] The shift in language reflects the shift from face-to-face contact in local stores to the less personal contact between commercial messages and thousands of potential buyers. Advertisers faced the challenge of addressing and enticing thousands of consumers across the nation "personally."

Advertisers coped with this challenge by seeking out a gendered audience for their messages, and a gendered forum for those messages. If the advertisers could target a particular gender group with their messages, they could "personalize" them to a higher degree than if they were more inclusive or neutral. Advertisers were able to capitalize on shared meanings of gender to aim their messages more carefully at some people than at others. They sacrificed some breadth in their target audience in the hopes of making their connection with a smaller constituency deeper and more likely to yield positive results.

Producers of popular culture like Cyrus Curtis and Louisa Knapp Curtis responded to advertisers' demand for a gendered forum for their commercial messages. First, they gathered advertisements that they thought might interest women in particular around a few columns in their newspaper. As those female-targeted advertisements grew in number, and as women seemed to be responding positively, the Curtises provided more editorial material. Within a few months the magazine that became the *Ladies' Home Journal* had taken shape. Thus, the *Journal* was from the start an advertising-driven periodical intended especially for women. Even the *Post,* intended by the Curtis producers to be a magazine for men, would come to target women as well, for similar commercial reasons.

And middle-class women of the day responded, first to the *Journal* and later to the *Post.* Women bought the *Journal* and they also seem to have purchased the advertised products in sufficient numbers to keep the advertisers supporting these periodicals. A major reason for women's positive response is tied to observations I made earlier about the nature of middle-class female gender norms at the turn of the century.

Women were agitating for change in these years, in large part working to expand their breadth of acceptable activities. In this light we see that buying magazines and consuming commercial products—insofar as they involved choosing, making decisions, and at least some small measure of autonomy—represented an appealing expansion of activity for a number of lower-middle-class and middle-class women who had some expendable income. This was a relatively safe expansion of the female role, an expansion that built on tasks previously designated as womanly; that is, the products women began to consume were often products they or their mothers had produced in their homes earlier. Therefore, the shift to "consuming" these items, to buying and using them, did not involve an abrupt change for women.

One might assume that this shift would have threatened lower-middle- and middle-class men, but it does not appear to have done so. The magazines and the advertisements within them offered men their own attractive option. If men were, as I suggested earlier, trying to maintain the gendered status quo at this time, it was probably in middle-class men's interest to grant women a limited amount of autonomy in exchange for maintaining their own status as primary breadwinners. Men continued to bear the burden of providing for their families, but they retained virtually all of the power and privilege pertaining to this role.[37]

Producers, advertisers, and readers therefore colluded in the creation and development of a gendered commercial discourse and a commercial gender discourse. All parties believed at the time that they were striking a satisfactory bargain: producers and advertisers made a great deal of money, female readers gained some autonomy and control of the family purse strings, and male readers retained their privileged status. But this bargain, which in some ways further deepened the gender divide of the nineteenth century, proved in the long run to be completely positive only for advertisers. It would be limiting for both producers and readers.

The magazines' producers were unable to break the tie between femininity and commerce when it later suited them to do so; they were forced to target women even when they thought another tactic might be preferable. And, much more importantly, readers were locked into patterns that eventually proved to be problematic as well. Women's role as consumer meant not only that consumers were women, but also that women were consumers. Women since the turn of the century have been defined in the media largely in terms of this aspect of their role, portrayed as buying and using most of the products in the home for the good of the family and to improve themselves. This pattern helps to explain why late twentieth-century women who work in huge numbers outside the home continue to bear the major brunt of the work done inside the home, and continue to be defined by what they buy.[38] And men are locked into the provider role, making difficult any attempts to play a more nurturing role in the family.

These are critical patterns for us to understand today, and the negotiation of this hegemonic bargain constitutes the major portion of this study. As I have noted above, gender is a slippery concept and the reader–text connection is slippery as well. In attempting to examine the two as clearly and thoroughly as possible I have (1) looked for complexity, tension, and contradiction in each of the magazines as a whole; (2) explicitly compared female-centered and male-centered material; (3) located the producers, texts, and readers in their social context; and (4) looked at change over time. The themes emerging as most important from content analysis of the *Ladies' Home Journal* are housekeeping, male–female relations, women's rights, and consumerism; those from the *Saturday Evening Post* are work, male–female relations, and women's rights. I read the magazines as I thought readers might, giving roughly equal weight to all their features, including editorials, departments, fiction, advertisements, and reader letters. While this may run roughshod over differences among genres within the magazines, it does seem to approximate more closely the way a typical browsing, relatively nondiscriminating reader might have "consumed" each magazine.

The book as a whole is divided by basic historiographic approach. The odd-numbered chapters are informed mainly by social history and gender history themes and approaches. They focus on the activities of the magazines' producers and on the development of the magazines as social institutions. The even-numbered chapters are informed more by cultural history and, again, by gender history themes and techniques.[39] They feature close content analysis of each magazine as a whole, culminating in chapter eight with a comparison of the two magazines over the same span of years. The even-numbered chapters also include my speculations about the magazines' impact on their readers. I conclude with an Epilogue that discusses the ramifications of the Curtis publications' contours for the publishing world of the twentieth century.

In 1883 Cyrus Curtis and Louisa Knapp Curtis introduced a magazine that had once comprised a single newspaper column. Within twenty years the Curtises had built a magazine empire that reached millions of readers and earned millions of dollars. As prototypes of highly commercial mass-circulation magazines and as forerunners of other kinds of commercial media, the Curtis publications had a profound impact on American popular culture. They helped to promote a relationship between gender and commerce that has been complicated, long-lasting, and powerful.

1

A Man, a Woman, and a New Magazine: Cyrus Curtis and Louisa Knapp Curtis and the *Ladies' Home Journal,* 1883–1889

In 1883, Cyrus Curtis and Louisa Knapp Curtis decided to turn their newspaper column for women into a separate monthly supplement to their weekly newspaper. After Louisa had prepared the material for the first number of the supplement, Cyrus took it to the office to be set in type. Upon receiving the material, the composing-room manager asked Cyrus what he wanted to call the supplement. Legend has it that Cyrus answered, "Call it anything you like. It's sort of a ladies' journal." The composition manager carried this vague notion to an engraver, who drew a masthead for the supplement, using The Ladies' Journal as a title. To embellish the words the engraver added to the title a picture of a home, engraving the word "Home" under it. The first subscription request for the new magazine asked for "The Ladies' Home Journal," as did most subsequent orders, and thus an unknown engraver and its earliest subscribers named the first American mass-circulation magazine.[1]

The story of the *Ladies' Home Journal* name highlights the relatively unstructured nature of the 1880s world of magazine publishing, a world that this new magazine itself had a significant part in defining. With their "sort of a ladies' journal," as Cyrus described it, the Curtises established a model for an important genre of magazines in the United States. This genre has remained remarkably stable over the course of a century.

Even more importantly, Cyrus and Louisa helped to mediate the interaction of the growing consumer culture with notions about gender, providing in their magazine a forum for the intersection of these two significant cultural forces. Many elements combined to propel the *Journal* into the mass-circulation magazine ranks: the personal characteristics and relationship of the editor and publisher, the expansion of reading audiences, and commercial developments that included the rise of middle-class consumption and the demand for national advertising. Cyrus Curtis and Louisa Knapp Curtis were commercial pioneers who oversaw the intersection of gendered reading with the demand for a gendered advertising forum to create and develop the highly successful *Ladies' Home Journal.*

Cyrus Curtis was born in 1850 in Portland, Maine. The son of poor but cultured and loving parents, he took on the role of hard-headed businessman and

1.a. The Early *Journal* Masthead.

provider early in his life. His instinct for business and hard work as a newspaper boy paid off, and when he was fifteen the first issue of Curtis's first newspaper, *Young America,* appeared on the Portland scene. Curtis was soon selling 400 copies of his paper weekly, earning him the impressive sum of eight dollars per week. The next year, however, Curtis's printing operation was lost in a fire that also destroyed most of his family's belongings. The future publisher gave up hopes of further schooling. After several years of clerking in a general store, he left the town of Portland at nineteen to make his way in Boston.[2]

The young man held down a job in a dry-goods store, supplementing his income by soliciting newspaper advertisements for an advertising agency on his lunch hour. Though shy by nature, Curtis moved quite comfortably in the world of business. In 1872 he joined forces with a partner who put up the capital for a weekly, which they called *The People's Ledger.* Soon he was doing all the work on the paper, and within a year Cyrus had bought his partner out.[3]

Curtis's years in Boston saw a development more significant than the acquisition of a periodical, however. In 1874 he met Louisa Knapp, a woman a year younger than he, and the two soon fell in love.[4] Knapp was at the time serving as private secretary to Samuel Gridley Howe, a prominent Boston doctor and reformer and the husband of activist Julia Ward Howe. Louisa's work experience was unusual at a time when women constituted only about 14 percent of the labor force, and less than 3 percent of the clerical work force.[5] Given the fact that Knapp was the daughter of an established businessman, her work for pay was even more unusual, and it seems to have led her to a certain flexibility of attitude on the issue of paid work for women.[6]

Knapp's work experience also gave her a first-hand knowledge of the business world. Edward Bok, the second editor of the *Ladies' Home Journal* and son-in-law of the Curtises, wrote years later that "the workings of a man's mind

1.b. Cyrus H.K. Curtis. Courtesy Charles Scribner's Sons.

were not a new revelation to Mrs. Curtis," a fact that served her well in her subsequent partnership with Cyrus.[7]

Cyrus Curtis had a talent for recognizing and encouraging special abilities in others. Early in their relationship he sensed Louisa's business and editorial abilities and encouraged her to apply them. Louisa was a practical, down-to-earth extrovert, thereby complementing Curtis's shy demeanor at the same time that she reinforced his business acumen and drive. Her earlier work experience

1.c. Louisa Knapp Curtis. Courtesy Charles Scribner's Sons.

and her ongoing interest in public activity led her to work with her husband both on and off the company payroll. The strength of their partnership had a great deal to do with the success they were to achieve together.

They were married on March 10, 1875, and their first and only child, Mary Louise, was born in August of 1876, when Cyrus was twenty-six and Louisa twenty-five years old. Cyrus had long been interested in Philadelphia as a publishing city, and upon learning that he could publish the *People's Ledger* more cheaply there than in Boston, the Curtises decided to move to Philadelphia. The weekly newspaper field was very crowded, however. Curtis struggled with various publications until 1879, when his brother-in-law lent him two thousand dollars in order to establish the *Tribune and the Farmer,* a four-page weekly selling for fifty cents a year.[8] Cyrus edited the newspaper while Louisa served as business manager. The Curtises, employing an innovative approach, brought in an advertising manager who solicited advertisements for the paper and collected payment for them.

The Curtises' publishing breakthrough did not come, however, until they began running a "Women and Home" column in the *Tribune and the Farmer.* The new column was originally added largely out of expedience. One week in the late summer of 1883 Cyrus found his paper three columns short. Thinking of material that could be gathered quickly and easily from other sources, and that could be built around advertisements that might be of particular interest to women, Curtis proposed a "woman's department" to fill the space.[9] The column ran regularly thereafter, featuring odds and ends taken from various sources. This material was then surrounded by advertisements geared to women. Curtis clipped the items from what he believed were reliable newspaper columns and advice pamphlets.

But Louisa criticized the column, saying, "I don't want to make fun of you, but if you really knew how funny this material sounds to a woman, you would laugh, too."[10] As Cyrus Curtis's biographer later commented, "Mr. Curtis never dreamed for a moment that in his wife's laugh was hidden his first great success."[11] Louisa moved from the business to the editorial department of the *Tribune and the Farmer* on the grounds that she as a woman could produce higher quality reading matter for women. She replaced the old reprinted items with fresh material of her own, and the column soon grew to fill a page. Louisa's department for women began to stimulate a great deal of correspondence and to attract more support from advertisers. Consequently, the Curtises decided to publish a monthly women's supplement to the weekly *Tribune.* The first issue of that supplement, entitled the *Ladies' Journal,* edited by Louisa under her maiden name and published by Cyrus, appeared in December of 1883.[12]

The *Ladies' Home Journal* therefore evolved from a newspaper column to a department to a supplement, which quickly outstripped the original paper in popularity. While the practical details of this evolution are unremarkable, the cultural ramifications of the early *Journal*'s evolution are striking. The creation of the "Women and Home" column and its evolution into the early *Ladies' Home Journal* rested in part on the significant changes in the status of women as readers which were occurring in the mid-nineteenth century.

Reading was common among some groups of women much earlier than the mid-nineteenth century. Late seventeenth- and early eighteenth-century Puritan women, for example, were responsible for catechizing their children and hence for reading the Bible in the home.[13] By the 1780s educational opportunities for women beyond this group had begun to expand significantly. Between 1780 and 1830 women began increasingly to attend district schools and academies, and the justification for expanded literacy had broadened from the needs of Republican motherhood to the notion that reading was for women, as it was for men, "a necessity of life."[14]

Reading among elite groups may already have been differentiated by gender to some degree by the mid-eighteenth century. Men were said to read newspapers and history more often, while women were believed to use their inferior intellects more on the less rigorous fare of fiction and devotional literature.[15] But many American women did not read at all in the eighteenth century, and it was not until the first half of the nineteenth century that a large new reading public coalesced. By then, 90 percent of the American people were minimally literate, and technological advances in printing and paper making made literature accessible to more readers than ever before. *Harper's Magazine,* one of the new organs of middle-class culture, proclaimed that "literature has gone in pursuit of the million, penetrated highways and hedges, pressed its way into cottages, factories, omnibuses, and railroad cars, and become the most cosmopolitan thing of the century."[16]

Women were an important part of the new reading public. Magazines for women began to appear in the early to mid-nineteenth century, targeting mainly a well-to-do audience but signalling an important segmenting of reading by gender. The mid-nineteenth century also saw a notable increase in book sales among women of some means. It was good business to target women readers for magazine and book publishers alike. Women in the mid-nineteenth century were beginning to be regarded as a special interest group worthy of special attention. It was in these years as well that children's books were targeted by gender, reflecting both the emphasis on childhood as a distinct, discrete phase of life, and the notion that reading was an appropriate vehicle for gender-role socialization.[17]

The experience of one woman who would eventually write for the *Ladies' Home Journal* represents these important new trends in the reading of middle- to upper-class educated women in the nineteenth century. Marion Harland was born in 1830 and came of age in mid-century. She was a popular writer of advice books, novels, and magazine short stories and advice columns in the mid- to late nineteenth century. Harland's commentary on her family's reading is revealing:

> My sister and I read "The Spectator" aloud to our mother as she sat busy with fine needlework, and learned whole books of Cowper's "Task" and Thomson's "Seasons" . . . rushed through Plutarch's "Lives" with breathless energy no novelist could now provoke . . . and on Sundays pored over "Pilgrim's Progress," Pollock's "Course of Time," and Young's "Night Thoughts." Our

mother took "The New York Mirror" and "Graham," and "Godey," and the "Saturday Evening Courier." On winter nights my father relaxed his objections to light reading so far as to read aloud from these columns.[18]

In Harland's home, then, reading was an accepted, even a central activity for women. Though her father seems to have controlled much of the family's reading aloud, it was her mother who subscribed to several of the leading periodicals of the day, including newspapers. This agency on the part of women readers certainly goes well beyond catechizing children, and it is an important development in the evolution of women as readers.

Barbara Sicherman's case study of women's reading in late-Victorian America highlights precisely this sort of agency. She finds that by the late nineteenth century, women as a group were "integral to the culture of reading."[19] They had established reading clubs, literary societies, and libraries in community after community across the country. More importantly, she asserts that many individual women

> found in reading a way of apprehending the world that enabled them to overcome some of the confines of gender and class. Reading provided space—physical, temporal, and psychological—that permitted women to exempt themselves from traditional gender expectations, whether imposed by formal society or by family obligations.[20]

Women read, in other words, not only to escape, but also actively to reshape some of the constraints of their world.

One of the central questions for social historians of reading is whether reading was indeed a liberating or a constraining activity. Making such a judgment rests on situating a group of readers in a particular time period and evaluating their specific circumstances. For example, newly literate female readers in colonial America appear to have experienced a liberating effect from learning to read. Reading became one of the few activities available to such women that were in some measure private and performed for themselves.[21] For this group, as for Barbara Sicherman's upper-class Victorian women, reading appears to have been relatively liberating.

But the experience of another group of women tells a somewhat different story. Reading for the female readers of the eighteenth-century British magazine, the *Tatler,* was clearly less beneficial. It is the case that the male-edited *Tatler,* to the extent that it targeted women readers specifically, acknowledged women's importance as readers. It courted women and encouraged them to read. But the magazine's direct and indirect messages reinforced female subordination to patriarchal structures. In this instance, therefore, one might say that reading became a liability because the more women read the more exposure they had to the patriarchal status quo.[22]

Thus some women at some times seem to have experienced more benefits from reading, while other women at other times appear to have suffered more from the constraints of reading. On balance, then, reading would appear to be a mixed blessing. Literacy is certainly one of the keys to changing one's status, and in this light it is critical to women's struggle. But print material is on the whole more supportive of conformity than it is of change. Consequently, its effect on readers may be more limiting than it is liberating.[23] A close look at the readership of both the *Journal* and the *Post* in forthcoming chapters will feature careful consideration of this issue.

Some women of Marion Harland's generation became major producers of culture themselves. Harland, Harriet Beecher Stowe, and Rose Terry Cooke were among the first American women to become mainstream writers, and they dominated reading lists for much of the nineteenth century.[24] Marion Harland and her mother therefore illustrate the evolution from women as readers for the purpose of teaching children, to women as active pursuers of reading matter for themselves, to women as producers of reading matter for others.

Harland and others like her also represent an important broadening of the function of women's reading. Harland's mother, a fairly well-to-do woman with servants, was a member of the primary audience for which *Godey's Lady's Magazine* and similar periodicals were produced.[25] With its fashion plates, reprinted sheet music, and sentimental fiction, to say nothing of its two-dollar per year subscription price, *Godey's* was geared to an elite audience. The magazine had attained a circulation of one hundred and fifty thousand by 1860 and was the first major American women's magazine, but by the 1880s many mainstream women writers like Harland would be writing for a different kind of publication: the practical, cheaper, helpful-hints magazine.[26] Such magazines would soon eclipse elite magazines like *Godey's* in popularity.

These years also witnessed, therefore, a change in the function of reading for many women. Some women may have experienced an increase in leisure in the days of early industrialization, allowing for more reading for entertainment and general enlightenment. But for most women in the early nineteenth century new domestic chores simply took the place of old ones. As stoves replaced open fireplaces and products like flour were commercially produced, diets became more varied and cooking more complicated; as fabric was produced outside the home and paper patterns were made available for home use, wardrobes became more elaborate.[27]

These new tasks and others meant that there were larger gaps between the experiences of one generation of women and the next, a problem that was exacerbated in many cases by the physical separation of the generations resulting from migration.[28] In a culture where at least some women were undertaking new tasks, and where women were often separated from traditional sources of advice and information, helpful-hints literature was potentially more and more relevant to many women's everyday activities.

The nineteenth century thus saw an important broadening of the reading public to include more and more women, the increasing gender segregation of reading materials, and a broadening of the function of reading for women. These trends relied in part on the development of a cohesive middle class, or a "self-conscious socio-cultural group."[29] This group consisted mostly of native-born, Protestant, white collar, salaried business and professional men and their families. Their group identity was informed by a shared set of morals, values, and attitudes, and by a certain cluster of cultural features: the home and what went into it, residential location, child-rearing strategies, leisure activities, and levels and patterns of consumption.[30]

Men's class definition, since it rested in large part on occupation, was somewhat more direct than women's in the mid- to late nineteenth century. Most women's financial dependence on men tied their status to men's occupations. Yet women were responsible for many of the trappings of the middle-class: home, child-rearing strategies, leisure activities, and—to an increasing degree over the course of the nineteenth century—levels and patterns of consumption. Consequently, the Consumer Revolution that paralleled the Industrial Revolution seems to have been informed by gender concerns and assumptions from its earliest days.

The beginnings of the Consumer Revolution appear to be situated in the decades after 1830. These years saw the expansion of the production of goods intended for middle-class consumption, including furniture, carpeting, china, glassware, and elaborate fashions.[31] The consumer culture as we know it today took shape more firmly in the 1880s, when business expanded rapidly, transportation networks improved, and national markets grew.[32] Producers sought national markets when continuous-process machinery put out many more goods per unit than had been possible in the past. The decade of the 1880s saw the almost simultaneous invention of such machinery for making flour, breakfast cereals, soup and other canned products, matches, photographic film, and cigarettes.[33] American producers at this point chose to control neither output nor prices but sales, a development that made ever larger national markets crucial.[34] With the dramatic improvement of the nation's transportation and communications infrastructure, the stage was set for the rise of mass markets.

One of the businesses ancillary to the new large corporations' drive to create national markets was the advertising agency. Given their much higher output, companies like Campbell, Heinz, and Borden had to embark on massive advertising campaigns conducted with the help of these agencies.[35] In turn, advertising agents, along with publishers like Cyrus Curtis, had to convince manufacturers of the importance of advertising. Many business people were reluctant to advertise because advertising had been dominated for years by patent-medicine manufacturers, long viewed as charlatans in the business world. The new agents showed business people that respectable claims would do the sale of their products more good than harm. They also helped manufacturers to create advertisements that spoke directly to consumers, in an attempt to convince merchants to stock the product if they did not already do so.[36] And women were increasingly the targets of these advertisements.

Women had traditionally been responsible for making and/or using several of the products increasingly turned out by continuous-process machinery, a crucial fact in the history of consumption and advertising, and in the history of gender construction as well. Since a number of the earliest mass-produced items were assumed to be of interest to women, and since producers needed to move them and used advertising to do it, a significant proportion of early advertising was targeted specifically to women. By the late 1800s women were perceived to be at least potential consumers of a variety of products like clothing and entertainment items, and they were already viewed as the major consumers of household goods. One analyst calls this development the "feminization of American purchasing."[37] By 1895 a brochure for the advertising agency Lord and Thomas was asserting that

> She who "rocks the cradle" and "rules the world" is directly and indirectly head of the buying department of every home. The advertiser who makes a favorable impression with her may be sure of the patronage of the family.[38]

Gender provided an avenue through which advertisers could "personalize" their increasingly impersonal contacts with potential buyers. As markets became national, neither local nor regional product identifications were meaningful. Gender-related assumptions provided a discourse through which advertisers could reach a targeted yet national audience. We see very early in the history of advertising that advertisers sacrificed a possibly broader audience—that is, both women and men—for the narrower gender-targeted audience that was perceived to be reachable through a particular gender discourse. But this discourse would need a suitable conduit, a medium through which advertisers could reach out to middle-class women who had some money to spend.

Cyrus Curtis and Louisa Knapp Curtis were ready to capitalize. They saw that a magazine designed expressly for women that featured a practical emphasis could be an important forum for advertising. Edward Bok later noted the significance of the "Women and Home" column's commercial function: "It was a productive field, since, as woman was the purchasing power, it would benefit the newspaper enormously in its advertising if it could offer a feminine clientele."[39] Other women's magazines founded in this period also had explicit ties to commercialism. While each of these publications eventually became the broader product now known as a women's magazine, *McCall's* came from a flyer featuring dress patterns, and the *Woman's Home Companion* and *Good*

Housekeeping originated as mail-order journals.[40] The recognition of women's power to consume by the late 1800s thus led to the establishment of magazines for women that were highly identified with consumption.

These magazines were also established because of the sense that women's interests were easily addressed in one contained "package." Although mid- to late nineteenth-century women came from all walks of life, producers of books, newspapers, and magazines confidently offered reading material that could speak to many of women's interests in a relatively small space. Women with some expendable income were assumed to share a set of domestic and familial interests. And, if they were addressed at all in newspapers, women were addressed in a single column, page, or supplement. Similarly, producers believed that all of women's interests and all women of some means could be addressed in one magazine.

This trend toward packaging women's interests in a single publication parallels and is to some extent a product of the metaphor of separate spheres, which informed at least some thinking in the nineteenth century. Women, insofar as they were confined to the private sphere in such thinking, were allocated a separate, discrete space that was, metaphorically speaking, smaller and more limiting than men's space in the public sphere. Men's larger, more flexible sphere did not actually resemble a circumscribed sphere at all. The metaphor was therefore fundamentally flawed, since there was no men's sphere to correspond neatly to women's sphere. Applying the metaphor to the lives of both men and women also implied an equal division of labor that did not exist. Finally, it implied an equal division of income and economic power that did not exist. As we shall see, use of this flawed spheres metaphor had a critical impact on the development of both gender relationships and commerce at the turn of the century.

The currency of the spheres metaphor suggests the artificiality of the private/public dichotomy that also informed the development of commercial magazines in the late nineteenth century. For example, the *Ladies' Home Journal,* as published by Cyrus and edited by Louisa, was a public product, since it was created and printed in the business world, sent through the public mails, and financed by advertisers. But the magazine was read in people's homes, and it spoke to private issues such as establishing and maintaining a household, parenting, and marital relations. Similarly, advertising in the 1880s began to commodify needs and activities previously recognized as private, including cooking, eating, cleaning, dressing, bathing, and nursing.

As we shall see, the *Journal*'s producers were informed by and employed different variations on the private/public theme. At this point in the early stages of the *Journal*'s development, the distinction between private and public was quite purposely blurry, reflecting the editor's views on gender construction and her stance on women's issues. Future editors would employ the dichotomy more rigorously.

Women's magazines were not, of course, the only magazines on the market. The Curtises began publishing their *Journal* 142 years after the first American magazine was founded in 1741. But historically, magazines in the U.S. had not been a dominant medium. A major impetus to magazine founding on the national scale was the Postal Mailing Act of March 3, 1879, which established favorable mailing rates for periodicals. The Postal Mailing Act was enacted in an attempt to create a national press that might be the "mucilage" to hold the Northern and Southern states together.[41] Between 1865 and 1885 the number of periodicals increased more than fourfold, from 700 to 3,300.

The average citizen in these later years was still not a magazine reader, however. The magazine market was polarized, with quality monthlies like *Harper's* and *Scribner's* at one end of the spectrum, and cheap weeklies and story papers at the other end. In the mid-1880s things began to change; the next fifteen years would be a golden age of mass-circulation magazine founding. Many factors were influential, including technological advances in the printing trades, faster delivery possibilities by means of railroads and rural free delivery postal routes, businesses hungry to create national markets, and the shift from bulk to packaged merchandise. No one profited more from these developments than did Cyrus and Louisa Knapp Curtis.

The goal of publishers like Curtis was to sell as much advertising and as many magazines as possible. The business story of the early *Ladies' Home Journal* illustrates how a successful publisher went about doing so. The first issue of the supplement appeared in December of 1883, with Louisa Knapp as editor and Cyrus Curtis as publisher. Curtis from the start relied on advertising in order to supplement the six cents an issue he charged, but he used other devices to build the *Journal's* circulation as well. While the magazine's subscription price was fifty cents for a year, from the beginning club or group memberships at four for a dollar were offered. The *Journal* also offered premiums for new subscriptions. For one new subscriber a woman could "earn" a lace doily, for five a beaded purse, for fifty a desk, for seventy-five a piano. Curtis was consciously seeking a wide lower-middle-class to middle-class audience for the magazine, one to whom his advertisers could sell their new products.

The *Ladies' Home Journal* was a major prototype for all mass-circulation magazines. It sold cheaply to thousands of readers and relied heavily on advertising for making profits. In tandem with Louisa's editorial efforts, Cyrus's strategy worked amazingly well. The *Journal's* circulation was 25,000 at the end of its first year, double that in six more months, and by 1886 it had reached the impressive figure of 400,000. The Curtises were not content with this phenomenal growth, however, and in 1888 they engaged the N. W. Ayer Company to advertise their magazine in three other periodicals—at a total cost of four hundred dollars.

In fact, Cyrus Curtis's relationship during these years with the advertising agency N. W. Ayer illustrates the pivotal role Curtis played in the advertising world of the late nineteenth century. He first used the Ayer agency to place advertisements for the *Journal* in other magazines. Ayer then began to buy advertising space in the *Journal* for some of its clients. Curtis designed most of the advertisements himself, pioneering in the use of white space to make the advertisements more noticeable and appealing. In turn, in the late 1880s the Ayer Agency lent Curtis much of the $310,000 he spent in a massive advertising campaign that gave the *Journal* the unheard-of circulation figure of 452,000. His pioneering role in creating and employing effective advertisements is signaled by the fact that Cyrus Curtis, magazine publisher, was also known in his time as the "Father of Modern Advertising."[42] His greatest contribution in the long run was his advancement of the concept of selling directly to women.

By 1889 Curtis had decided to consolidate his gains. He increased his advertising rates and abolished cut-rate subscriptions to the magazine. This resulted in a short-term drop in circulation, but the *Journal* soon gained other subscriptions. Curtis had essentially raised the quality of both his advertisers and his audience to a truly middle-class level.

The *Ladies' Home Journal* had offices in New York and Chicago as well as in Philadelphia by this time, and in 1889 the magazine employed seven to ten people a day simply to open letters. After seeking as wide an audience as possible, and then firming up his subscription list by withdrawing cut-rate offers, Curtis in 1889 claimed to reach the best classes of American families.[43] He and Louisa decided that the July 1889 issue would double in size, becoming a thirty-two page magazine with a cover. In a few short years the magazine had evolved from a collection of helpful hints in a newspaper to a phenomenon in the publishing industry.

Hence Cyrus Curtis and Louisa Knapp Curtis presided over the union of reading, consuming, and advertising with gendered assumptions about middle-class women in their new magazine. One of the unintended results of their publishing venture was the print media's further institutionalization of gender difference in American popular culture. The *Ladies' Home Journal* was an influential contributor to the trend toward heightened gender differences in print matter that was gathering force in the late nineteenth century.

The Curtises were pioneers in the field of magazine publishing. They saw a need for a certain kind of publication and they worked to fill that need. The Curtises were certainly interested in realizing profits from their magazine. But

Louisa in particular desired as well to be of service to her late-nineteenth century peers. Editing the *Ladies' Home Journal* was also challenging and fulfilling work. We turn now to the messages conveyed in Louisa's *Journal,* messages that helped so much to define gendered commercialism and commercialized gender at the turn of the last century.

2

From Gendered Lives to a Gendered Magazine: The Content of the *Journal,* 1883–1889

The fact that Louisa Knapp's *Ladies' Home Journal* was a commercial product affected the magazine's mission from the start. It was critical that Knapp's magazine entertain as well as edify, and the *Journal* sought to engage its readers as well as to give them practical information. Knapp's *Journal* was a feminine text, produced primarily by women for women. Knapp and her staff viewed their readers as peers and they spoke to them and heard from them in what they considered to be a two-way exchange. Images of women in Knapp's *Journal* were varied, and flexibility was the magazine's general orientation with regard to women's roles.

Louisa Knapp commented freely in the *Journal* on the state of American women's lives as she perceived them in the 1880s. Her magazine sought to empower and free women, and Knapp and her contributors were not afraid to note obstacles blocking women's progress and to suggest a variety of solutions. However, one of the major solutions they recommended—increased consuming by women—was entirely compatible with and supportive of patriarchal capitalism. And readers responded positively to Louisa's and her staff's consumer-centered solutions. Together, then, *Journal* staffers and readers helped to lay the groundwork for an increasingly commercial gender discourse.

Gender construction was a thoughtful, relatively conscious process in the *Ladies' Home Journal* during Knapp's tenure. This construction took various forms. At one level the magazine simply embodied middle-class womanhood: its various features and departments corresponded to perceived interests in women's lives, and its overall tone bespoke middle-class femininity. But gender was represented more concretely in images of women that the magazine presented in fiction and feature articles, and in its direct reflection on gender matters in editorials.

We see evidence of active gender construction in Louisa's own life as well. Louisa Knapp needed to resolve the contradiction between the domestic orientation of her magazine and the fact of its thoroughly commercial nature and its success as a product on the market. How could a woman who espoused domesticity and touted its importance edit what was fast becoming a national, mass-circulation magazine? The way in which Louisa resolved this contradiction helps to illuminate the process of gender construction for women.

One analyst of gender theorizes that attempts to reconcile the old and the new are at the heart of gender construction, at least for women.[1] This dialectical model of the construction of the female gender role suggests that the gender ideology with which a woman grows up is the thesis of her feminine ideology; her life experience sometimes contradicts this feminine ideology, becoming the antithesis of her inherited script; and the woman then forms a synthesis, a new altered script that incorporates both the old and the new.[2] Each generation then repeats this process.

To move beyond the individual construction of femininity, we must characterize the major gender ideologies, life circumstances, and experiences that a generational cohort of women encountered, and then examine their attempts to resolve or synthesize these sets of realities.[3] This type of analysis can illuminate the construction of gender by the *Journal*'s producers in their own lives, the *Journal*'s attempt to construct gender in its pages, and the possible process of gender construction for individual readers.

Louisa and her cohort of writers were a small, relatively homogeneous group of middle-class women who shared certain life experiences that affected the magazine they produced. Born in the late 1840s and 1850s, they were coming to maturity in the 1880s, still in the early stages of marriage (or having been widowed early), and mothering small children. These women had graduated from high school but not college and they all brought office or freelance writing experience to their work at the *Journal*. The staff consisted of Louisa as editor, Mrs. Emma C. Hewitt as associate editor, and Mrs. Mary E. Lambert as head of the fashion department.

Emma Hewitt (b. 1850) was a domestic writer of note in her day who in 1884 "became regularly associated with the *Daily Evening Reporter* of Burlington, New Jersey, though her name never appeared in its columns."[4] In 1885 she began writing a highly popular general column for the *Journal* called "Scribbler's Letters to Gustavus," and in 1886 she joined the editorial staff, serving as associate editor of the magazine for fifteen years. Mary E. Lambert (b. 1849) began her writing career under the "stern impulse of necessity," when she found herself widowed and forced to support her children as well as "other dependent ones."[5]

The broader circle of *Journal* contributors featured some of the most prominent names of the day, among them Louisa May Alcott, Harriet Beecher Stowe, and Julia Ward Howe; and Cyrus Curtis took full advantage of each prominent contributor in promoting the magazine. Obtaining these famous writers for this as yet unknown magazine was not easy, but Curtis was resourceful. Anticipating Alcott's reluctance he offered to pay $100 to her favorite charity if she would submit an article, and she could not refuse.[6] But most of the early contributors to the magazine, while well-known in the late nineteenth century, have now been forgotten. These women included Marion Harland, who wrote both domestic advice articles and short stories for the *Journal.* Harland was one of the best-loved writers of her day, and procuring her services was a real coup for the Curtises. Cyrus quickly parlayed her hiring into dollars for the magazine. He convinced the manufacturer of a new egg-beater, whom Cyrus knew was an admirer of Harland, to advertise his product in the *Journal.* Harland then endorsed the egg-beater in a *Journal* article. Joining Harland in supplying the early *Ladies' Home Journal* with much of its fiction were Rose Terry Cooke, a prolific contributor to many magazines of the day, and Elizabeth Stuart Phelps, who was among the most advanced of the early *Journal* writers in speaking about women's rights.

It is Phelps who once held up to a school friend a thimble in one hand and a paint-brush in the other, saying: "It is a choice between the two."[7] She is perhaps the exception that proves the rule in this cohort of editors and writers, however, since most of these women were notable for the degree to which they did not see their choices as polarized. To the extent that they did, they found ways to transcend that polarization, or even to make it work for them. Louisa Knapp and her staff took their work seriously, and together they produced an enormously successful commercial magazine for women. Equally important, they were forging for themselves life models that enabled them, at least for a time, creatively to combine domesticity and paid work.

Studies of women aspiring to professional status in the late nineteenth century suggest that the central tenets of "professionalism" were ambition, intelligence, and the willingness to work hard. In addition, according to these studies, such women had to value scientific training highly, and to subject themselves to endless striving, just as their brothers and fathers did. By these lights, Louisa and her cohort appear to be pre- or even unprofessional.[8]

To dismiss these women in this way, however, would be to obscure an alternative set of creative life models. For in contrast to the certainty, clarity, and long-term commitment of male professionals, Louisa Knapp, Emma Hewitt, Mary Lambert, and their colleagues were united by their juggling of domesticity and work, by the disjointed and interrupted nature of their work experiences, and by the sense that their work, while it was important, was not all-important. The lives of these magazine producers embodied a flexibility not often associated with Victorian America. And as Mary Catherine Bateson writes in connection with more contemporary women's lives:

> These are not lives without commitment, but rather lives in which commitments are continually refocused and redefined. We must invest time and passion in specific goals and yet at the same time acknowledge that these are mutable. The circumstances of women's lives now and in the past provide examples for new ways of thinking about the lives of both men and women. What are the possible transfers of learning when life is a collage of different tasks? How does creativity flourish on distraction? What insights arise from

the experience of multiplicity and ambiguity? And at what point does desperate improvisation become significant achievement?[9]

We certainly see in Louisa and her staff "new ways of thinking about the lives of both men and women," in particular an attempt to balance domestic and professional life. Hence Emma Hewitt was described to readers as a highly energetic and capable woman who contributed to at least a dozen other periodicals at the same time that she helped to edit the *Journal,* and yet her "articles on domestic topics are not based on theories in any way, but are the result of experience."[10] Similarly, Mary Lambert's literary skills were praised, but it was carefully noted that "she is never too busy, however, to give attention to her interesting family and her beautiful home."[11]

The commentary in the *Ladies' Home Journal* about Louisa's work vis-à-vis home is instructive about the way that gender is constructed. Women and men negotiate their lives on a day-to-day basis, navigating through a sea of possibly contradictory tasks and demands. Louisa's old script called for her to be centrally defined as a wife and mother, with her tasks revolving around the concerns of the home. She believed in the value of these features of the female role, and they informed much of the magazine that she edited.

The new script Louisa embraced centered on her position of leadership in the world of mass-circulation magazines. As I have noted, the *Journal* under Knapp's editorship rapidly became the largest selling and most lucrative magazine in the nation. To resolve the contradiction between her old and her new script, Louisa edited the *Ladies' Home Journal* out of her home, and this fact was revealed self-consciously in the pages of her magazine.

The major source for this revelation was an article appearing originally in the New York newspaper, the *Journalist,* which was reprinted in the February 1887 issue of the *Ladies' Home Journal.* By this time the *Journal* had a circulation of over three hundred thousand. Knapp was a very capable editor of this rapidly growing magazine, and the *Journalist* characterized her in these terms. But we can see Knapp creating her feminine persona as well, in the details she allowed the newspaper to reveal. The article described her, for example, as a "very domestic woman" who did her editorial work in "her own library, where she has every convenience and the best reference books of the day. Every morning she devotes two or three hours to the *Ladies' Home Journal.* She keeps up telephonic communication with the publisher but seldom visits his offices."[12] This "telephonic communication" was unusual in these years. Indeed, Louisa and Cyrus purchased one of the first telephones in Philadelphia in order to facilitate this special arrangement.

On one level, then, we see the compromise that allowed Louisa to resolve the contradiction between her old script and her new. But the emphasis on her domesticity and her strict, even physical separation from the business side of the magazine suggests that, on another level, Knapp was constructing a script

2.a. Portion of the 1887 *Journalist* article.

[*From the New York Journalist, Oct. 22, 1887.*]

THE LADIES' HOME JOURNAL.

Pen Pictures Of Its Founder And Publisher — His Enterprise, Push And Sagacity. —The Accomplished Editor And Her Capable Women Associates.

CYRUS H. K. CURTIS.

In no other country in the world has there been such a marvelous growth of type products as in the United States. It has, for many years, worn, because it merited, the laurel, as being the land of bright, well-conducted newspapers, and essentially a field for good and cheap illustrated periodicals. Its magazine adornment, artistic and literary, has received unstinted encomiums from the ablest critics in England, Germany and France. Of all American business proverbs the most characteristic, as a popular acceptanc of truth, is that laconic, full-of-meaning phrase: "*Success is success!*"

To CYRUS H. K. CURTIS, of Philadelphia, hundreds of thousands of this favored land's gratified and satisfied readers are indebted for the most successful of rapidly-prospering monthlies. It is a publication, at once unique and phenomenal. We refer to "THE LADIES' HOME JOURNAL AND PRACTICAL HOUSEKEEPER," now just four years old, the aggregate yearly issue of which exceeds six millions copies, mailed direct to the subscribers! Here is a success that beats all rivalry, and we propose to tell something of the stout hearts and willing, active hands that produced such astonishing results in so brief a space of time.

First, the founder and publisher. Mr. Curtis is a native of Portland, Maine; a typical, energetic, restless Down Easter. He is thirty-seven and a half years old. He began his newspaper career in 1862—war days, when "Extras" were chronic and in great demand. At the age of twelve he put his treasured Fourth-of-July money into local *Evening Couriers* and quickly tripled his capital. This was a good start, and he faltered not in the race. Before another year had rolled away or Gettysburg had been fought and won, young Curtis, in partnership with an ambitious schoolmate, owned a four-page, six by four paper, which exhausted the partner before its third number was issued. Curtis held on to *Young America* and newspaper selling for three years. In 1868, he went to Boston, where two years later, associated with a printer-editor, named Farrar, he boomed *The Indenendent* for a whole year. When that paper became dependent, he gracefully killed it and began publishing *The People's Ledger*, which in 1876 he carried to Philadelphia, run it there, with varying recompense, for two years, sold it to his printers and started *The Tribune and Farmer*. This cheap, yet really excellent weekly reached forty-six thousand circulation (all paid-up subscribers) in four years. Then, in December 1883, Philadelphia's best advertisement, THE LADIES' HOME JOURNAL, was established. A wonderful history, speedily made, and its narration will be often and graphically repeated in type-praise.

Physically there is not much to speculate upon when we look at Cyrus H. K. Curtis. He is a little under medium height, dark eyes and hair, beginning to show a sprinkling of gray, and weighs about 125 pounds. That is his bodily avordupois, but his brain must out-weigh a coal-merchant's ton, being so full of golden ideas. His father, Cyrus L. Curtis, was "a whole-souled, generous, pious, genial, story-telling, joke-loving man, of fine musical and artistic talent; a great favorite in Portland." The elder Curtis never had an enemy and his boy Cyrus has never had the spare time to make one. For his purity of life, the whole town loved the senior Curtis, and a once happy home was desolate when he died. The son inherited a strong natural talent for music. His mother (still living) is a diminutive, one-hundred-pound Yankee woman of "faculty," full of get up and go, vigorous and remarkably chipper. She will tackle anything, and never lets an unfinished bit of work pass from her fingers. Lovable, as conscientious, she always denied herself for the sake of her children, who now call her blessed. From her, Cyrus H. K. Curtis inherited his sterling qualities of mind and heart, steel wires for nerves, quickness of action and never-walk-slow gait.

THE LADIES' HOME JOURNAL keeps five power presses running steadily, ten hours per day, each month, and these presses in four weeks use up six thousand dollars' worth of white paper. All the folding is done by improved machinery and thirty thousand copies per day are turned out by the patent folder. Over fifty girls are employed to keep the subscription books during each day and a dozen others come to work at 6 P. M. and remain three hours every night. This extra work is necessary because there is not sufficient room in the present building to accommodate a full quota of day operatives. THE LADIES' HOME JOURNAL receives the largest daily mail at the Philadelphia post-office, from five thousand to eleven thousand subscriptions in a single day. The daily average for September, 1887, exceeded five thousand and the actual net cash receipts during that month, for subscriptions were $22988.34. About twenty young men are kept busy mailing these papers every business day of the month.

Knowing from experience the great value of printers' ink, when nationally and rationally distributed, Mr. Curtis expended $20,000 last September in pictorial advertising. The leading dailies, weeklies, and monthlies, throughout the United States were utilized and the result has been daily visible in an avalanche of orders for THE LADIES' HOME JOURNAL. He says he is determined to push its circulation to the highest possible point, this year, and to the attainment of that end caused the large and showy advertisement to be inserted in all the best mediums for reaching the people. He admits that THE LADIES' HOME JOURNAL might be brought to the attention of a million women by mailing them sample copies. But he does not believe in the free sample copy method of conducting the publishing business. "I want," he says, "every woman who reads the JOURNAL to PAY for it, then she will value it, look for it, and read it."

That which is free is seldom valued. Sample copies of publications particularly, seem to create an antagonism, and the recipient looks upon it with suspicion, as though expecting a bill for a year's subscription, if he or she takes it from the post-office.

The business principles of Cyrus H. K. Curtis are admirably exhibited in the unparalleled success of that periodical which he has jealously watched day and night, since its inception. He has one price and no deviation. Two dollars per agate line for all advertisements; no deduction. The exact truth is told about circulation; the figures being verified by office books and accounts carefully kept and sworn to. Everything he buys for the paper is paid for, cash on the nail. He has no notes coming due, because he never gives them. His freedom from debt is exemption from worry. He has no debts created by buying what cannot be paid for. The subscription price of THE LADIES' HOME JOURNAL is placed at a small profit, and the handsome monthly's prosperity is therefore not dependent on advertisers or agency sharks.

What are the figures to be within another six months? Who can name a limit to the success of a periodical so sagaciously edited and managed? Best and cheapest of the illustrated monthlies, THE LADIES' HOME JOURNAL carries to every PRACTICAL HOUSEKEEPER in America, fifty dollars' worth of education for fifty cents a year!

MRS. LOUSIA KNAPP.

Mrs Lousia Knapp, who is editor of THE LADIES' HOME JOURNAL, receives an annual salary of ten thousand dollars! This is a larger sum than has ever been previously paid in this country to any woman journalist for similar work. The cultured and eminently practical lady who earns it, is a native of Boston, where she was born in 1851. She has been a newspaper man's wife and helpmate for twelve years. Her first editorial labor was on the household department of *The Tribune And Farmer* already noticed. She has a light complexion, blue eyes, which sparkle through gold-rimmed glasses, and one hundred and thirty pounds of plumpness to her scale credit. When in earnest she talks quickly, and becomes very earnest where her interest is awakened. Mrs. Knapp is a very domestic woman; good-natured, benevolent, and a judicious nurser of warm friendships. Her only daughter is eleven years old; a beautiful, carefully-educated, charming girl. Their home is in Camden, New Jersey, where Mrs. Knapp is a member of the First Presbyterian Church; active in good works, faithful to the word and deed of Christianity. Her home life is a realization of affection circled by all the graces of true womanhood.

The editorial work of Mrs. Knapp is done in her own library, where she has every convenience and the best reference books of the day. Every morning she devotes two or three hours to THE LADIES' HOME JOURNAL. She keeps up telephonic communication with the publisher, but seldom visits his offices. Firmly believing that some hours of each day ought to be spent in the open air, she may be seen almost any afternoon driving a pony phaeton through the quieter streets of Camden. She takes pleasure in giving outings to sick and poor neighbors, who are usually denied the healthful luxury of carriage riding.

Mrs. Knapp has a rare intuition. She knows to a nicety what interests and moves women, and appreciating their needs, anticipates their reasonable demands. Not a line is allowed to go into the LADIES' HOME JOURNAL until it has been carefully scrutinized and edited. Although strongly in love with her professional work, and eminently successful in it, as we have already shown, her duties as a housekeeper, a wife and mother claim her first attention. Here it may be noted that her disinclination for newspaper publicity, or to be known as an editor, has caused her to hide her real name under a *nom de plume*, and as most of her friends and neighbors are subscribers to the LADIES' HOME JOURNAL, it is a great source of amusement to her and the immediate family whe[...]
their delightful home, to list[...]gy hair.
and comments freely [...]out the house
which that home is [...] greatest care.
Louisa Knapp is real[...]dows or your doors
just yet! The *Journ*[...] will dare,
fore it can and will [...]y's in the hall."

MRS. EMMA C. HEWITT.

Mrs. Emma C. Hewitt, who is immediately associated with Mrs. Lousia Knapp in the editorial direction of THE LADIES' HOME JOURNAL, was born in New Orleans, Louisiana, February 1850. At three years of age, she came North with her parents who settled on a farm in Rahway, moving later to Burlington New Jersey, where she has resided ever since until a year ago, when she moved to Camden, N. J.

In 1868, she graduated from a prominent female seminary. About fifteen years ago, she began writing for different publications which vocation she pursued in the interests of household economy and the training of her sex. In 1884, Mrs. Hewitt became regularly associated with the *Daily Evening Reporter* of Burlington, N. J., though her name never appeared in its columns. She continued with that publication until its management was changed, a period of twelve months. It was in 1885 when she began writing for THE LADIES' HOME JOURNAL a series of bright articles, under the attractive title of "Scribbler's Letters To Gustavus." It was in August of that year that these special articles first appeared. Mrs Hewitt entered upon her duties in the publication house of the great periodical, March 29th 1886, from which date she devoted herself only to literary pursuits, contributing, in connection with her exacting brain-and-hand labor on THE LADIES' HOME JOURNAL, constantly to at least a dozen other periodicals of standing, sketches, stories, and articles on domestic economy. Her articles on domestic topics are not based on theories in any way, but are the result of experience. She comes of what is known as "a mighty smart family." Personally she is a little under medium height, dark-eyed, energetic, and quick as a flash at repartee. Like Mrs. Knapp, she wears glasses and sees through them a great deal of the practical side of life. She is unusually well educated and has vocal command of French with a knowledge of several other modern languages. Her children are a son and daughter of 12 and 14 years, respectively. Mrs. Hewitt's editorials and occasional and regular literary contributions to the LADIES' HOME JOURNAL are very popular.

HENRY CLAY LUKENS.

MRS. JAMES H. LAMBERT.

Of women who wield a fluent pen, with profit to themslves and to their readers, few have a wider or more justly earned popularity than Mrs. Mary E. Lambert or as she is better known Mrs. James H. Lambert. Mrs. Lambert is of Northern parentage. Her maiden name was Perine. She was born in Cahaba, Ala., where her father, who went thither from Staten Island, was a prominent merchant and planter of the old regime. When quite young she married a Southerner and lived in Georgia until after Sherman's march to the sea, where, having lost everything, she had to go to work to buy bread for her children and other dependent ones. Her literary career, began, under the stern impulse of necessity, with the contribution of pathetic and humorous articles on "The Progress of Reconstruction" to the New York *Tribune*. Pleased with the originalty and spirit of these sketches, Mr. Greely encouraged her to continue writing and to come North, where she might find a ready market for her literary wares. Thenceforward her pen was kept busy with book reviews and articles on live topics for literary papers, children's stories and poems for the magazines, and poetry and sketches for Mr. Bonner's *Ledger*. It was not long, however, be-[...]fore she struck a better paying vein in fashion
throu[...]ting, a field of newspaper work then compara-
A P[...]untilled but now thronged with busy and
flecked wi[...]orkers. She was engaged on the editor-
border, and [...]e *New York Weekly* for ten years,
tiny gilt speck[...]e to time was a regular contributor
In the upper [...]rk *Democrat*, *Our Society*, *The*

for herself that was suitable for public consumption. It is revealing that the commentary on Knapp's editorial arrangements came from a reprinted article. Through this third-party endorsement, Knapp could assure her readers that she was indeed a domestic woman of the 1880s without appearing to be self-promoting. Her magazine's content and the tone she employed embodied this domesticity, but the article allowed her to comment more directly on her devotion to things private. What was not revealed in this article was the fact that Knapp had earlier served as the business manager of the newspaper she and Cyrus had owned, and that she had moved quite comfortably for years in the world of business.

Knapp's representation of self in the magazine is not a case of hypocrisy. Rather, it illuminates two central facts about gender construction. First, gender is to some extent a performative act.[13] To return to the metaphor of the script, women resolve old and new experiences of womanhood to create their own sense of what it means to be a real or good woman. While they are sincere in these attempts to define themselves, they are also performing, that is, acting the part of a woman.[14] In the pages of the *Journal* Louisa represented her fit with the mission of her magazine—which was crafted to embody the appropriate gender norms of the day—as carefully as possible. She was, at one level, therefore, actor, playwright, and director, who played the part of an accomplished middle-class woman even as she wrote and helped others to learn the role.

The gender-as-performance metaphor is also applicable since Louisa used what was, in effect, a "stage name." She edited the *Journal* under her maiden name, Louisa Knapp, and her "real" identity as the wife of the magazine's publisher was never revealed in the *Journal*'s pages. Knapp could not have hoped to achieve a fully separate identity: as Mrs. Cyrus Curtis and as a member herself of Philadelphia's publishing community, there was simply no way for her to keep her personal identity truly secret. Using her maiden name professionally, however, allowed Louisa to compartmentalize her life. It quite possibly also allowed her to achieve a sense of autonomy in her partnership with Cyrus.

In addition to the performing aspects of gender construction, Louisa's representation of herself in the magazine illustrates a second feature of gender construction: definitions of gender may contain suppressed meanings in addition to those that are approved. The approved role for Louisa as she understood it was to put husband, child, and domestic life first. This understanding did not prevent her, however, from actively pursuing a very different kind of endeavor. She found a way to define herself that incorporated both the domestic and the professional aspects of her life. As we shall see, she also defined her magazine in ways that simultaneously reflected both approved and suppressed definitions of womanhood.

Female readers responded favorably to both the content of the magazine and the fact that it was produced by women. Many readers' letters commented on the *Journal*'s female staff. One representative letter from the West proclaimed: "Never was a paper born which so fittingly filled a vacancy, and so satisfied a long-felt want in our homes and families, or so flourished and grew as this *Ladies' Home Journal*. Truly, 'none know it but to love it, or name it but to praise'—and its editors *are women!*"[15] Similarly, Mrs. Willis T. Jackson wrote in 1884: "I saw your offer in *Demorest's* for May to send your paper on trial for three months. . . . I am sure it is excellent; how can it be otherwise, edited by a woman, its articles contributed by women—don't they understand a woman's needs? Please send a copy immediately."[16]

And women indeed produced the *Journal*. The first issue of the magazine consisted of contributions exclusively from women, and for five of Knapp's six years as editor women contributed 95 percent of the content of her magazine. During Knapp's last year of editorship, 1889, the percentage of contributions from men increased from about 5 to 15 percent, and a greater number of contributors were identified only by initials (perhaps to hide the fact that more men were contributing).[17] Therefore, even when the most men possible—if all those using initials are counted as male—were writing for Knapp's *Journal,* it is safe to say that the magazine still consisted of at least 80 percent material from women. Moreover, the men who wrote for the *Journal* in these years were completely affirming of women. Contributions from men like Robert J. Burdette and Will Carleton were among the *Journal*'s most progressive articles or were limited to short columns on gardening or reviews of books, and they were relegated to the less important pages in the back of the magazine. Women wrote the short stories (which always appeared early in the magazine), and women contributed the editorial material, the special features, and the household hints departments that were the backbone of the periodical.

The *Ladies' Home Journal* under Louisa Knapp's editorship was not much to look at. The supplement consisted of eight newsprint pages with small, fuzzy print, presented in the large and awkward folio format, 11 1/2 x 16 1/2 inches. The early magazine was made up of between twelve and twenty features and departments, each ranging from 200 to 750 words in length. The first issue of the *Journal* contained 25 percent advertising, and during Knapp's tenure the advertising share hovered around 30 percent. The format of the *Journal* largely reflected traditional domestic concerns, as its "Practical Housekeeper" subtitle signalled. A typical issue in 1884 contained five articles or departments about the household, four articles regarding child-rearing, and two columns on cooking. But three additional features of the early *Journal* suggest that it was not

2.b. Early first page.

THE LADIES' HOME JOURNAL AND PRACTICAL HOUSEKEEPER.

FIVE CENTS PER COPY. PHILADELPHIA, FEBRUARY, 1884. FIFTY CENTS PER·YEAR.

Jeremiah Jones's Housekeeping.

BY HELEN M. WINSLOW.

I DUNNO when I've had a spell before—not for a good many years, anyway; but the other day I was so beat out I was glad to take my bed, and let my pardner run the "housekeeping."

This was the way it happened. We'd had company for a number of days, right along—my relations from Freedom, and Jeremiah's from the flats—till it did seem as if there wasn't no let up to it. And after my brother and his wife and three children, Sister Tryphena and her daughter and grandchildren and dead husband's sister, and my brother's mother-in-law, had every one of 'em been and made us a good visit, it did seem a little too much when Jeremiah's two cousins from Bungtown, with their wives and five children, come right upon us without a word of warnin'; and nothin'—not so much as a ginger-snap—cooked in the house. Now, I don't hold to runnin' down your pardner's relations; but after we'd got the house fairly cleaned of cousins, sisters, aunts, babies, mother-in laws, etsettery, to see mother Jones and brother 'Hial drive up to the door early in the forenoon, with all the seven children tucked into every available corner of the wagon, was a little too much for female human natur', and I said to Jeremiah, when I went out to call him in from the oat-field, that it seemed to me this company-business was about played out.

Then Jeremiah came in and sat down to rub his rheumaticky knee, while his folks was a-gitting settled comfortably in the spare-room, and to pacify me, if he could, while I tried to snatch a few minutes to finish my ironing before his relations should have to be fed.

Now that man worships me, if ever a man worshipped a pardner; but it kind o' maddened him to have me speak so of his relations, and he snapped out:

"Wal, I'd like to know if a man's relations can't come a-visitin' once in a while without bein' reviled and backbit. I dunno but my relation's just as good as anybody else's relations."

I see I'd stroked his fur the wrong way, and I began to think of smoothin' of it down.

"Yes, Jeremiah, they be," says I; "only I'm tired to death of my own relations, to say nothing of anybody else's. I dunno what folks want to form themselves into battalions, and charge upon their family connections, and eat 'em out o' house 'n' home for—jest 'cause they *be* relations. But come, you catch the old rooster on your way up, and wring his neck, and we'll have a good dinner for 'em, if we do have to sacrifice old Boniface."

For I was bound not to give his relations a chance to say I wa'n't as good a hand to get up a dinner as any of the Joneses—not if the old rooster could help it. And so all our hens were widdered by one turn of fortune's hand—or my pardner's—and go in the weeds to-day that his relations should have a good dinner.

I had to go cookin' and work over the hot stove all that roastin' day—though it's against my principles to do housework afternoons—and I never got round to visit a word—only as some of 'em tagged me into the buttery and kept gettin' under foot—till after supper. But jest as I'd got round to set down and take some comfort visitin' with 'em, 'Hial up and says, "We shall have to be goin' home, for I 'xpect old Toby over to look at the speckled cow to-night. Mebbe he'll buy her." And all I and my pardner could say wouldn't keep 'em a minute.

After they went, Jeremiah and me bein' all alone, we said we'd go to bed early and get a good night's rest; for we didn't know what a day might bring forth in the way of company, and if our third and fourth cousins should all take a notion to give us a surprise-party the next day, we should need all the rest we could get.

I had got partly undressed and got my night-cap on, and Jeremiah had got down to his overalls, when we heard a noise in the cellar.

"What's that?" says Jeremiah.

"It's the cat," says I.

"That ain't no *cat*," says he, though he hadn't no theory in particular about it, only the desire to be contrary.

"That's the cat," says I again, more firmly, as the noise sounded the second time. "She's after the remains of old Bony that I set on the swinging shelf."

"That ain't no *cat*, I say," says Jeremiah. "I tell you it's somethin' wuss 'n cats. *I* believe the burglars a-burglin' round here." And he began to look pale.

"Burglars!" says I. "Pshaw! Who'd be burglin' round here this time o' night?"

"I say 'tis," says he, adding, as he slipped off his pants, "I wish you'd jest step to the cellar-door, Flavilly, an' see. I've all undressed."

"If you really think it's burglars," says I, "*I* should think you'd rather be a man, take down your father's old blunderbuss, and go yourself. How'd you feel to see the wife of your bosom brought back to you a mangled and bloody corpse?"

"Don't, Flavilly!" says he, his teeth almost chatterin'. "What kind of a condition be I in to go to the cellar-door? Say, how'd I look confrontin' burglars in this rig? An' mabbe it's some o' the neighbors, or—or—"

"Most likely 'tis," says I, in tones that ought to have froze him—but didn't, quite. "Probably it's the Elder come over to call, and come in through the gangway."

JEREMIAH JONES'S HOUSEKEEPING.—"BUT IT KIND O' MADDENED HIM TO HAVE ME SPEAK SO OF HIS RELATIONS."

And taking up the candle, I passed as majestically as circumstances (and my night-cap) would permit out to the cellar-door, went down the stairs, drove out the kittens and old Tabby, fastened the gangway tight, and started up-stairs again, intendin' to say some very cuttin' things to my lawful and beloved pardner.

But would that every time a woman thinks of some pesky mean thing to say to her pardner, Providence might stop it as effectually! The bottom cellar-stair was made of an old door-stone, and was dreadful uneven; so jest as I stepped on it, my foot slipped, and down I went with a crash.

Jeremiah heard it, and rushed to the door without considering his wardrobe this time.

"*Be* you hurt?" says he, addin', in a whisper, "Is it burglars?"

"No," says I, "it ain't, and yes, I be;" and then tryin to get up, I suddenly set back, with a groan.

Men may love to hector their pardners, be they ever so faithful, and be they ever so good cooks; but when they hear them groanin' in pain, then they're all tenderness.

Such a groan as I give then convinced my pardner that I was seriously hurt, and he came down the stairs as if his life and mine depended on it. I believe his only thought was for me. In fact, he owned up next mornin' that his one thought as he flew over those cellar-stairs was, "Who will get my dinner now?"

But to make a long story short, we soon found out that my ankle had a bad sprain on it, and do what we could, there was no dodgin' that. I couldn't step on it a minute, nor think of such a thing, so how I was to get up them stairs was more than I knew, or Jeremiah either. Says he:

"I shall have to take and carry you up, Flavilla."

And bad as my ankle ached, and fast as it was swellin', I laughed and laughed. For my weight is over two hundred pounds, and my pardner can't come up to one hundred and twenty-five by the stillyards, anyhow.

"Couldn't you wait here," says he, pretty soon, "till I could fix up a derrick, and h'ist you up with that?"

"Mebbe I *could*," says I, "but I ain't a-goin' to. You come here." And he came; and steadyin' myself on his manly shoulders, I managed, with the aid of the cellar-wall and a good many groans, to get up-stairs again and to bed. Then Jeremiah, he got the arnicky, and we rubbed it and did it up—the ankle, not the arnicky.

My pardner done nobly that night—I'll say that for him; he done everything—got bandages, rubbed arnicky, done it up so it looked like a very large roll of sausages, and even offered to go for the doctor. But it didn't do much good. I didn't sleep none with it, and what with so much company and all, I was about sick in the mornin', to say nothin' of the ankle, which had swelled and swelled till it was a sight to behold.

So Jeremiah, bein' still in a noble and generous frame of mind, declared I shouldn't get up at all, but lay abed, and he'd do the work. And as there was nobody else to do it, and I couldn't get up, I lay a-bed and let him try the housekeepin' department. Mebbe it was mean in me, but I thought there—on a bed o' sufferin'—I thought to myself:

"Now, for years and years, my pardner ain't known what it was to have me away from home or laid up in bed; *now* mebbe he'll begin to see what women are worth—for men, be they ever so good, get careless, and come to think women and women's work ain't, as you might say, the chief spoke in the wheel; but let that spoke drop out even for a day, and the whole domestic machinery is demoralized." But I'm moralizin', and not tellin' stories; or what I should be tellin' stories, and not moralizin'.

Jeremiah, he got up and built a fire and put on the potatoes to boil, and then started off to the barn and went to milkin'.

When he come in with the milk, the fire had all gone out, and he set down his pails in the middle of the floor and went for the fire. But he had to go out and split up some kindlin'-wood, and by the time he come in, the old cat and kittens had appeared on the scene again. They see the pails, and thinkin' it was their breakfast—and honesty bein' foreign to the nature of cats—they began to help themselves; but the Maltese one couldn't wait till the other one could get out of the way, and in his hurry he scrambled over him, and first I knew he was flounderin' around in the strainin'-pail. I could see it all from the bedroom where I lay.

Jeremiah, comin' in, see the kitten splashin' the milk all over the kitchen floor, and he dropped his kindlin' and picked up the kitten.

"Plague take these cats!" says he, shakin' the milk off the Maltese, and then tossin' him out into the wood-shed. "There! Go out there and dry up! What in tunket a woman wants of so many cats is more'n I know. What be I goin' to do, Flavilly?" says he, in a appealin' tone.

"First I should mop up the milk from the floor, so to not track it all round," says I. "Then I should start the fire. Then, when I got the potatoes to boilin', I should go into the milk-room and strain the milk for the calves. Then I should come out and fix the fire, for bein' made of soft wood, it needs constant tendin'. Then I should go down cellar and cut off a couple of slices of pork to fry, and bring up the butter and the pie. Then I should make the coffee. Then I should set the table and toast the bread. Then, if there was a minute to spare before the potatoes was done, I—"

"There won't be, Flavilly!" put in my pardner, solemnly. "The potatoes will have time to boil several times over before I get all that done. And I've got to finish milkin' and feed the calves first, too. What's that in that pan, Flavilly?" says he, pointin' to the table.

"That?" says I, cranin' my neck round tryin' to see, till it almost ached. "Oh, that's the bread I put to sponge last night. You want to keep watch of it, and not let it get riz too much."

"Sakes alive!" says he. "How does it happen, Flavilly, that *you* don't never have anywhere near so much to do before breakfast as there is this mornin'?"

"On the *contrary*," says I, not without a certain triumph in the thought, "I always have jest as much and often more to do than there is this mornin'. But I'm used to it, and there's nothin' like bein' used to a thing. But don't stop to talk, or you won't have breakfast till noon." And my pardner turned up the damper to the stove—lookin' as if he'd had one turned down on him somewhere—and started for the barn again.

In about twenty minutes he finished milkin' and came in. Then he went down cellar and got the salt pork. He forgot the butter, of course. Puttin' the meat to fry, he said he guessed he'd skim the milk next, addin' that he liked to do housework first-rate.

"Wish I'd known it before," says I, but he'd got into the buttery and shut the door.

In a few minutes I smelled the fat burnin', but I'd made up my mind to lay abed for two reasons; one was that you can't heal a sprained ankle by walkin' round on it, the other was that now was a good time to teach my pardner a lesson. The best of men need trainin' occasionally; and hard as it might be for both of us, it was for his good—and mine—that I was to give him one that mornin'.

Where I lay I couldn't see the kitchen stove, but the fat smelled worse and worse, and the air was soon as blue as the cloud that surrounds our old smoker. I tried to call Jeremiah, but my voice rang out through the room without makin' a bit of impression on my pardner, for he had shut the buttery door and passed on into the milk-room. The consequence was that when he came back finally, the meat was burned and the water all boiled out of the potatoes.

"Halloo!" says he, "here's the meat all burned to a crisp, and the 'taters too. What'd you let 'em do that for?"

"How could I help it?" says I, in calm tones; for I knew how natural it is at such times to want to lay the blame off on to somebody. "I'll get up, if you say so, Jeremiah."

"No, you won't, nuther," says he. "You're goin' to stay in bed, where you b'long; and, dummit, what's that stuff runnin' over the edge of the table?"

"It ain't the bread, is it?" says I.

"I should smile if it wasn't!" says he. "What shall I do with the pesky stuff, anyway? I want to set the table—throw it in the swill-barrel?"

"No, no," says I, tryin' not to laugh. "If it's clean, scrape up the top of it and put it in the pan. You'll have to mould up the bread the first thing you do, I guess."

"Wal, I sh'd like my breakfast *some* time," says he. "Leastway, to get out of the way in time for dinner. Can't the bread wait till to-morrow?"

simply a technical, how-to publication that corresponded only to the perfunctory aspects of woman's role.

First, short stories were a central feature of the supplement from the beginning. The inclusion of fiction in the *Journal* reflects the notion that reading as a "necessity of life" for women included reading for pleasure. Short stories in the early *Journal* were intended to provide a respite for women from the realities of their work-filled days. They were also a conduit for gender norms that was more subtle than nonfiction.

Second, the *Journal* brought news to its readers. Women's magazines have frequently been accused of avoiding truly newsworthy or controversial ideas or happenings, and it is the case that politics and business were not the main focus of Knapp's *Journal*.[18] However, Knapp's magazine included features that, viewed in the light of many women's concerns, did constitute "news": biographical sketches of famous women of the day alluded to the new activities of prominent women and highlighted various causes; and features pertaining to social life regularly considered such matters as poverty, temperance, club work, education, and even the workings of government.[19]

Finally, the *Ladies' Home Journal,* beginning with its very first issue, considered regularly and thoughtfully questions related to gender. This aspect of women's magazines has performed a critical function in our culture, and it has been taken for granted in the past and is still taken for granted and devalued today. The *Journal* was a pioneer in reflecting upon gender roles, creating a forum that continues to this day to foster the popular representation of and discussion of gender issues. In fact, the assumed propensity of women to seek to understand their lives, especially in relation to men, actually informed almost every feature of the early *Journal*—its general advice articles, short stories, editorial comments and homilies, letters from readers, and even its advertising.[20] The need to consider gender issues reveals the extent to which female meant "other" in late nineteenth-century culture. It also suggests the extent to which the *Journal* embodied the process of gender construction. Women in the *Journal*'s pages were always in the making.

The contours of the magazine's rapidly growing audience as well as its importance in their lives are suggested by several readers' letters. A woman from Vancouver, Wyoming Territory, testified to the value of her *Journal* reading, as well as to the geographic spread of the magazine's list of subscribers:

> Is there room in the *Journal* for another western sister? If so I will be glad to enter. . . . Your little monthly messenger has helped me to while away many an otherwise lonely hour, and as the cold winter is nearly here I thought my time would be well employed if I got a few subscribers for you, and at the same time, gave my friends a little useful reading matter.[21]

Florence B., a young girl, wrote movingly about the *Journal* as a guide and a "friend":

You are my "mother's paper" . . . but I have wanted to write to you for a long time to tell you what a comfort you are to *me*—though you didn't intend to be. I read you through from beginning to end, some parts two or three times, and then "we girls" read you over and talk you over and then feel that we "know what to do" better than we did before. . . . When I get lonesome I like to read it because it makes me feel there *is* a good deal of real sympathy and love in the world after all.[22]

Even men responded. "Martha's husband" wrote that "I seldom read the paper myself, but busy bustling Martha reads aloud and we discuss whatever is interesting to the male intellect."[23] The circulation of the *Journal* in the West, and the fact that daughters and husbands of *Journal* readers found at least parts of the magazine interesting, suggest the possible breadth of the magazine's audience and the important role it seems to have played in the lives of various groups of people.

The main audience for the *Journal* in these early years, however, seems to have been the one for which it was expressly targeted: white lower-middle-class to middle-class women from all over the country, women increasingly likely to live in towns and cities with populations of over ten thousand.[24] Cyrus pioneered the use of marketing research for magazines, and quite early and thenceforth regularly he and his staff studied the neighborhoods where the *Journal* was widely read. Cyrus felt comfortable later, in the 1890s, characterizing the *Ladies' Home Journal*'s readers as people who lived in the suburbs of large cities and who were respected church-attenders; he also believed that the *Journal*'s small-town readers belonged to the professional ranks in their communities.[25]

Cyrus and Louisa were quite explicit in their desire to reach such an audience, which appeared to be the fastest growing segment of consumers with some expendable income. The *Journal* was intended from the start to reach a national audience, since it was central to its mission to provide a national forum for advertising. And women were always viewed as its primary readers.

The enormous popularity of the magazine from its earliest days and the relative lack of reader objection to specific articles supports the conclusion that many readers were finding the *Journal* of interest and relevant to their lives. Knapp and her staff assumed that they and their readers were interested in the same things, that is, in the details of domestic life, in women's increasing activity outside the home, and in negotiating successful relations with others. The ideology that most closely corresponds to the ideals promoted by Knapp's *Journal* in these years is the ideology of Real Womanhood, described by historian Frances Cogan in *All-American Girl*. Cogan, using advice literature and domestic novels as her main sources, delineates an important alternative to Barbara Welter's Cult of True Womanhood. As opposed to the piety, purity, submissiveness, and exclusively domestic emphasis of the latter, the ideology of

Real Womanhood encompassed a set of attributes adding up to survival for many lower-middle-class to middle-class women. These attributes included intelligence, physical fitness and health, self-sufficiency, economic self-reliance, and careful marriage choice.[26] It was woman's duty, according to this ideal, to make the most she could of herself, intellectually, physically, and financially, as well as emotionally. This model resembles the *Journal*'s quite closely, with one important difference. Cogan suggests that Real Womanhood adherents were traditional in their tenacious hold to the concept of separate spheres.

The *Journal*'s single comment about spheres between 1883 and 1889 signals its position as an advocate for flexibility regarding gender issues. Louisa Knapp asked in an 1886 editorial "and what is woman's sphere? Decidedly, in the present day, it is a very undecided thing."[27] In light of this cultural uncertainty Knapp and her writers were trying to help women come to terms with the changes they and their families were experiencing. Knapp went on to say that "every few weeks some new writer comes to the front and endeavors to establish a fixed standard [regarding woman's role]. But 'thus far shall thou go and no farther' does not seem to have the desired effect upon constantly advancing woman."[28] Consistent with this progressive view is the fact that—even as Knapp's *Journal* attempted to establish its own set of images of middle-class womanhood—the magazine generally took advanced and flexible positions with regard to women's expanding activity.

Indeed, at the end of her editorial, Louisa Knapp collapsed the sphere metaphor altogether, effectively dismissing it:

> Taking all the facts into consideration, we think "woman's sphere" is the same as that of man, i.e. to do cheerfully and well the work that comes to her hand, whether it be with a pen, a surgeon's knife, a dentist's drill, a pair of scissors or a broom.[29]

Here and in the *Journal* in general Louisa was irreverent in her approach to spheres. She also refrained from speaking in terms of a definite division between public and private, since that division served mainly to limit women's activity.

Her flexible and affirming tone was borne out repeatedly in the *Journal*'s treatment of various women's issues, including education, suffrage, club work, and work outside of the home. The messages were less confident and progressive regarding housework and male-female relations, reflecting ambivalence and an inability or unwillingness to confront some harsh realities.

The earliest *Journal* concerned itself with a girl's right to a high school education: Knapp asked in 1884, "Why should we not educate our girls, as well as our boys, to be self-supporting?"[30] This was a progressive view, since

2.c. An Early Knapp Editorial Page.

THE LADIES' HOME JOURNAL

AND

PRACTICAL HOUSEKEEPER.

A NATIONAL ILLUSTRATED FAMILY JOURNAL.

CONDUCTED BY MRS. LOUISA KNAPP.

Published Monthly at 441 Chestnut St.,

PHILADELPHIA, PA.

THE CURTIS PUBLISHING COMP'Y,

Publishers.

Terms: 50 cents per year, 25 cents for six months. In clubs of four or more, only 25 cents per year.

Advertising rates 50 cents per agate line each insertion. Address,

LADIES' HOME JOURNAL,
PHILADELPHIA, PA.

Renewals can be sent now, no matter when the subscription expires, and the time will be added to that to which the subscription is already entitled.

Notice is always sent of expiration of subscription. If not renewed it is immediately discontinued. No notice is required to stop the paper, and no bill will be sent for extra numbers.

Receipts.—The fact that you receive the paper is a proof that we have received your remittance correctly. If you do not receive the paper promptly, write us that we may see that your address is correct.

Errors.—We make them; so does every one, and we will cheerfully correct them if you will write to us. Try to write us good-naturedly, but if you cannot, then write to us any way. Do not complain to any one else or let it pass. We want an early opportunity to make right any injustice that we may do.

Philadelphia, December, 1885.

CURRENT NOTES.

The best mind cure is to make up one's mind to.

If you have built air castles, put foundations under them.

This number is enlarged to 16 pages to accommodate our premium list.

A Boston woman who invented a corset has made $50,000 in three years.

Promises made in the time of affliction, require a better memory than people commonly possess.

Colds are more frequently the results of overeating and a disordered digestion than of exposure.

A man who, sometime ago, married "an angel" says it is about as complete a faith cure as anything he has heard of.

In walking, the weaker of two persons takes the arm of the stronger. This is why dudes always take ladies' arms.

Men of genius are often dull and inert in society; as the blazing meteor, when it descends to the earth, is only a stone.

Chicago Socialists drank 300 kegs of beer at a public picnic where a conspicuous motto was "Our Children Cry for Bread."

The JOURNAL for 1886 will contain not less than 12 pages, same as last month, cut, pasted, and trimmed, and the price kept at 25 cents per year in clubs of four or more.

The antiquated cups and saucers are no longer in the demand which constitutes a "craze," but old silver to decorate the five o'clock tea-table has become the object of search by the fashionable public.

Miss Cleveland writes to a friend in Washington that she has been paid $7,250 thus far as her share of the profits upon her book. The sale keeps up fairly well, and her profits will aggregate not less than $25,000.

A well-known English clergyman, who had preached, one morning, in a magnificent New York church, watched the congregation defiling out of the aisles.

"Do American ladies, then, go to some place of amusement after church?" he asked. "They are dressed for the theater."

☞ If you cannot raise a club yourself, have you not a son, daughter, niece, nephew, or grandchild, who would be glad to earn for themselves some of the premiums we offer? Boys and girls make the best of club raisers, and easily secure large clubs with but little effort, at the extremely low price for the LADIES' HOME JOURNAL—only 25 cents per year.

If you are so situated that you cannot secure a small club, we suggest that you send us fifty cents extra with your own renewal, thus sending us an even dollar bill, which as per club rates will entitle you to four yearly subscriptions, and a premium. You make a present of a yearly subscription to three of your friends, and thus get a premium worth $1.00 and your subscription for only fifty cents more than your own single subscription would cost.

☞ 100,000 SUBSCRIBERS.

One year ago, we closed our first year, with 25,000 actual paid subscribers, and six months later, last July, we had 50,000. Just doubled in six months. In our August number we said "Can we double it again in six months? We can with your help,—not without it."

Our friends have given us a generous and hearty support and enabled us to close our second year with a full hundred thousand paid subscribers. Now, dear readers, can you accomplish for us the object of our present desire—A CIRCULATION OF 200,000 COPIES.

With such a constituency how important and responsible are the duties laid upon us! We desire to discharge these duties honestly, honorably and conscientiously, and we shall be glad at any time to receive aid from any of our subscribers to this end.

We enclose a club blank with the request that you kindly send it back well filled with new subscribers. There need be no trouble in filling it if you will, but tell your neighbors what a helpful little gem the JOURNAL is, for only twenty-five cents a year.

SCRIBBLER'S LETTERS TO GUSTAVUS.

NO. V.

BY MRS. EMMA C. HEWITT.

The day I received your last letter, Gustavus, I also received one from Julia.

That poor woman must have been pretty hard pushed before she wrote to me, for women are much less apt to talk of their husband's faults than men of their wives. It may be a species of pride and vanity; I'll deny that; it may arise from the feeling that they would rather nobody should know that they had not been wise enough to see all this before they were married, and thus save themselves from having to put up with it. Whatever the cause, the effect is the same. To answer your letter I shall quote to you Julia's letter to me, or some of it:

"Oh, cousin Scribbler," she writes, I wish you'd give me some advice. Gustavus just thinks I'm awful, I know he does. But just let me explain. The baby is teething now, you know, and I do get so tired holding him, and so hot and hoarse singing to him; and if I'm up half the night with him and walking half the next day I'm just good for nothing by the time the next night comes. So, for the last few days, I've just felt I didn't care how I looked, and when Gustavus came in at night I must confess I hadn't even had my dress changed; but, indeed, I hardly have time to comb my hair and clean my teeth, though I do struggle religiously every day. Well, Gustavus didn't say anything, he only looked, but I pretended not to see, I don't suppose I even cared so much as I ought to have done, but I was so dead tired, Cousin Scribbler, I have felt for three days as if there was but one thing in the world I wanted—to go to sleep and never wake up.

But this afternoon things came to a climax. Last night baby was just awful, and, as Gustavus says he can't afford to lose his sleep because he has to be at the store the next day, and that I can make mine up through the day, he went up into the third story and slept, away from the noise. Well, breakfast time came, and oh, Cousin Scribbler, I did want to sleep, for baby was real quiet then.

You don't know anything about it, but this tired feeling is dreadful. (She's wrong there, Gustavus, for once upon a time, when you were a cantankerous teething infant of six months, I was wild enough to offer to keep you all night when your mother went home to see her sick father. I think I slept for pretty nearly a week after that experience). Gustavus don't like it though, if I don't come down and pour out his coffee, so I come. I don't presume I looked very fresh. Then, after he was gone, Mary burned her hand, and, as it was ironing day, and Gustavus would want a clean pair of white pantaloons, I had to iron them. (The other two pairs in wash I left for another day). When five o'clock came I had the baby just nicely asleep again, in for a good long nap, I thought, and I was just going to take a little nap myself, when who should come in but Gustavus, an hour earlier than I expected him. I do love Gustavus, indeed I do, but I did wish he hadn't come so soon. So he took off his coat, put on his wrapper and slippers, and then what do you think he did? Waked baby up to have a romp with her! Cousin Scribbler it was very foolish, I know, but I cried. I just couldn't help it, my nerves were all unstrung, and I knew in fifteen minutes she'd fret again, poor little soul, and I'd have it all to go over again. Gustavus didn't say much, except, 'Julia, my dear (in the most cutting way), if you only knew how exceedingly unbecoming it is to you to cry, you'd stop it. It might have been comparatively becoming to you when you were younger and fresher,' and then he added, in an injured tone, 'what you're crying for, I can't see. I think it a great pity a man can't enjoy his child's society a little while, (that was the trouble, he would enjoy it such a little while) without causing a rumpus in the family. I'm sure, goodness knows, I see little enough of her, away at business as I am all day (if he only could keep awake at night he'd see plenty of her) and, besides this is the time of day for her to be out, when it is nice and cool.' So I didn't say anything, I found it wasn't any use. But thoroughly disheartened, I got ready for dinner. My crowning iniquity was in the evening.

Gustavus has been called upon to make a speech on the Fourth of July, and, while he was reading it to me I actually went to sleep. Indeed I couldn't help it. He was so angry, and talked about a man staying at home and trying to make himself agreeable, and finding very poor encouragement, etc., and so on, till I was utterly wretched. What shall I do?"

There now, Gustavas, that's all I'm going to quote. I shall write to her and tell her one thing though, I think, and that is when things go wrong not to cry (there were several big tear splashes on the paper when I received it) but to whistle and swear a little and see if that is any relief.

Men seem to extract an immense amount of comfort out of it. Now see here, Gustavus, what you do the first thing when you come home? Put on your wrapper and slippers (don't you?) nicely adjust your balance on the two hind legs of your chair, seize the newspaper and place your feet on the mantelpiece. You're very tired, no doubt, and all this rests you. But when Julia is tired at the end of the day what do you expect her to do—assume a fatigue suit like you and place her small slippers beside your small ones upon the mantelpiece? Not much. You expect her to starch herself up in her good clothes and sit beside you decorously on a chair. I don't deny that Julia has grown a little careless in her personal appearance, more than is exactly warrantable under the circumstances, and I shall tell her so; but a baby crawling from arm to arm and pulling at one's hair and stuffing one's ribbon in its mouth, does dislocate one's habits of neatness dreadfully, to say nothing of spoiling one's good clothes. I must say I quite agree with Julia in her liking for print dresses, there is nothing more suitable to take care of a baby in—and as you won't let her wear a large white apron ("too much like a nurse," you say, and pray isn't she your nurse? Provide another one for her and I dare say she will willingly hand over the aprons to the substitute) her nice clothes would soon be one perfect mess. Why, I saw that baby of yours pick up a corner of her mother's green silk overdress one day and stuff a whole handful of it in her mouth, to the ruination of the dress and the imminent danger of poisoning herself. She might have chewed calico until she was black in the face and it would not have permanently injured her or the dress either. And remember this, that though your mother brought up three or four little children without any nurse, she had an old maid sister or two to help; beside, your father, who always shared the care of the children, because he maintained that a woman had to work just as hard as a man, and needed just as much sleep. You see he'd been at home a good deal and saw just how things work; for your grandfather, Gustavus, was a good deal such a man as you are, and he not only "allowed it was woman's place to take care of the children" but allowed them to do so, and your father was a great help to your grandmother—he was an older son and felt and knew all his mother had to contend with. I think when you take your month's vacation, Gustavus, if you'll keep your eyes open to see what Julia really has to accomplish, and your ears open to hear how often that baby cries for its mother, and your hand open to pay for such outside service as Julia needs, and you can afford, and your heart and mouth open to feed and say pleasant words whenever you can, you will have spent the best month of your life.

Remember that there is a kindness which speaks in words that pour a blessed balm on many a bruise given by contact with the hard world. There is a kindness not expressed in bread and butter and shoes. Any man, if he be anything of a man, provides food and raiment for his household, but they don't all provide loving words, the tender smiles of conversation absolutely necessary to a hungry heart, and when a heart dies of hunger, Gustavus, it does it so quietly that no one but its owner knows it is dead. But it is dead, all the same, and like any other dead thing, it can never be revived by offering the food which was withheld till too late.

SCRIBBLER.

P. S. I forgot to give you a piece of information. It takes nearly an hour to iron one pair of nice white pantaloons, can you calculate what time it takes to iron three? and after you have calculated so much, can you imagine how much time there is left in the morning to iron the baby's clothes and the rest of the general wash, and can you not form some idea as to why Julia gave up wearing white dresses, much to your displeasure. Don't you see that by the time your three pairs of pantaloons are ironed and Julia's two dresses (for she can't get along with less than two with the baby crawling all over her) ironing day is pretty well filled. I think if I were you I'd send my white pants to the laundry to be done up, and, if I wanted to be particularly generous, I'd insist on Julia's doing the same thing with her dresses.

THE FAULT-FINDER.

Why should an old woman say she is too old to learn. That is a ridiculous statement. No woman can ever "know it all."

What in the world do you want to live in the kitchen for? Fix up your sitting-room and get away from the stove awhile.

Why do you always figure on a money basis in speaking of improvement or other farm interests? There is something besides money in it. You can get more good for yourself out of a better looking home and farm than most people ever can get out of a mile of "art gallery."

You ought to be ashamed of yourself to sell that faithful old horse that has been like a member of the family so long. They will probably wear his life out on the stage. Of course, he hasn't got much speed, but he has been a good friend. Do you want people to get rid of you when your usefulness goes?

The ordinary house-cleaning is an era of bad meals, ill temper and general inconvenience. It puts the whole family out of joint for a week. Can't you have the cleanings more frequent and less violent?

Don't expect too much of that boy. "An old head on young shoulders," is an abnormal development of brain. You don't want any monstrosities in your family.

I read in a paper recently that bloody milk is due to a disorganized condition of liver. Don't be too sure of that. A kick from a hired man's boot will produce it, too.

Don't try to kill rats with "Rough on Rats," or any other poison; these mixtures all contain arsenic. Get a good cat and let it earn its own living.

THE DANGERS OF FLIRTING.

Whatever idea the young girls who practice street flirting may entertain of their seemingly innocent pastime, it may be set down as a certainty that when a respectable young man desires the acquaintance of one who may some day become his wife, he does not go out on the street and seek her acquaintance through a flirtation. But, on the other hand, the flirt of the street, no matter how innocent and fair her intentions may be, is the last person he would seek as his life's companion. The young lady who engages in this kind of pastime should bear in mind that she not only endangers her reputation and leaves a stain upon her good name, but that her name is a by-word among those with whom she flirts, to be bandied about on the street corners, fastening on her otherwise fair name a stigma or stain that will follow her years after she sees her folly and attempts to mend her ways.

CIRCUMSTANCES ALTER CASES.

Not long ago as an elderly couple were out walking, a lady on the opposite side of the street tripped and fell down. The old gentleman rushed across the street, raised his hat and offered to assist her in any possible way. His wife followed him across at a slow pace, and witnessing his devotion to the stranger, she got mad, and shook her fist at him.

"It's all right—it's all right," he whispered.

"Yes, I know it is," she hotly exclaimed: "here an unknown woman hurts her toe, and you plow across the street to eat her up with kindness. The other day when I fell down stairs, you stood and laughed and wanted to know if I was practising for a circus."

MARRIAGES—OLD FOOLS.

"If marriage is good for the young," says the Chicago Herald, "it is good for the old."

Accordingly, that journal protests against the prevailing disposition of people who make fun of old men who marry, and bespeaks for them admiration instead of ridicule arguing that the capacity for affection grows rather than diminishes with advancing years.

If old men would only be content to marry women of middle age, there would not be so much criticism of their conduct. The world, however, has never been satisfied to see December wedded to May. People always have talked and always will talk when a man chooses a bride young enough to be his daughter.

The more you say, the less people remember.

CORRESPONDENCE.

M. H. P.—We have not the space to devote to exchanges.—[ED.

VERY MANY READERS:—We do not recommend the Hudson Manufacturing Co.

Mrs. John Cleverley can use the sulphur without any fear of injuring the furniture.

Nellie Lincoln Rossiter, New Lisbon, N. J., will be pleased to answer all questions on silk culture.

"Brownie."—Next Feb. 14 hang a healthy female bird in room for a few days with male, then put them together, rest depends upon mutual fancy. BUFFALO.

"Jessie Farrar, Carthage" asks for back numbers of L. H. J. from August 1884 through August 1885. If she will tell the sisters what State she resides in some one may be able to grant her request.

For bee stings Mrs. Nettie Hays recommends the following: Take a cabbage leaf and bind the under side of it on the wound. As it gets heated apply a cool fresh leaf, and the cure is effected in a few minutes.

DEAR EDITRESS:—If any of the readers chickens are troubled with lice, grease them. Close the hen house, set a pail of live coals in, and sprinkle sulphur over them. Give a good smoking.

GRANGER, IND. MRS. J. T. L.

"Blue Eyes" wants a remedy for a troublesome corn—something to permanently remove it. Also something to take off the tan from her face.

The editress would advise her to let the healthy brown look wear off, and never trouble any of the many advertised cosmetics that only injure the complexion.

Bessie Wood:—If your friend has ability he must succeed in time—but until he is sufficiently established to earn a comfortable living—do not marry. Remember love alone is not very filling—though it may help digest the nourishing food his active brain and your willing hands may provide. Are you willing to deny yourself the many things his present scanty means cannot supply? After all you must answer your own question.

DEAR EDITRESS:—In the September number I offered to send a sample of feather-edge braid collar on receipt of stamp, meaning those who had tried my directions in the March number without success. I have received numerous letters requesting samples, and most of them have not even seen the original directions. I shall be obliged to withdraw that offer now, as I have commenced my school duties and have not time to make any more samples.

Yours respectfully, ANNIE BELLE.

BUFFALO, Sept 15, 1885.

"Pearl, of Silverton, Col."—If your wheezing canary has not sung since moulting, such has been produced by taking cold hanging in a draft. Birds condition at such time similar to a person having measles, pores open. Give your bird flaxseed pounded if he will not crack such, and a drop of linseed oil every day, also a lump of sugar with a few drops of wine, plenty of sun but not too warm a room from fire. Hope he bathes every day. The wheezing (asthma) is a bad symptom.

EDITRESS HOME JOURNAL:—Tell "Louie" who asks in the Oct. JOURNAL about removing black heads to get ten cents worth of gum benzoin from a druggist, put it in a pint of alcohol, and when it is dissolved add about a tablespoonful to the water she washes her face in, rub with towel quite hard, and at night put cold cream on her face, and her black heads will all disappear. But never under any circumstances try to squeeze them out, it ruins the skin. The above remedy was given to a friend by a noted physician, and can not injure the skin in any way. A great many ladies use it as a toilet wash on general principles, it preserves and freshens the skin.

SUBSCRIBER.

FREEHOLD, N. J., Oct., 19th, '85.

EDITRESS OF LADIES' HOME JOURNAL:—Dear Madam.—When making formal calls and some of the family receive you at the door, is it etiquette when leaving to leave your visiting card, or does custom differ? Please answer, and oblige an old subscriber. E.

[Etiquette is but polite custom, and as this varies in different places, we can give you no general rule. Many people when leaving do quietly lay their card in a conspicuous place where you will not fail to see it if admitted to your house by a member of the family with whom they were acquainted.—ED.]

ART P. O., IND.

DEAR JOURNAL:—You have been visiting me now for nearly a year, and really I do not know how I could possibly get along without you, and now I come to you for the first time for a little information.

Will some of the good JOURNAL sisters tell me how to prevent ferns and autumn leaves from curling up when pressed and made into bouquets? I have tried several times but they always curl up and do not look pretty.

I have some ribbons and silk ties which would do for patchwork but are soiled by my hair. How can I cleanse them without injury to the fabric? M. H. P.

[Silk ribbons can be satisfactorily cleansed by washing if care is taken to lay a clean cloth over the ribbon while ironing.—EDITRESS.]

MARYVILLE, MO., Oct., 15, '85.

EDITRESS HOME JOURNAL:—I would like to ask some of the sisters to tell me where I can obtain the full size designs for stamping so I can copy them, and can they give directions so I can enlarge the small ones to the proper size; there must be some way; a pantograph is not satisfactory. I would like the instructions for landscape painting and also painting on china. Has it been given in the back numbers, and, if so, how can I obtain them? I just commenced to take the JOURNAL. Have any of the sisters with little children ever tried knitting the foot part of the stocking the usual way up to the shoe top and then making the top of it star stitch (though I make it different from description in last number, it makes a closer stitch). I find them prettier, quicker done, takes less material, and when worn over the knee can be ravelled down, and knit over in less time than darned, and I think looks better. I am sure you will like it.

MRS. M. B. COOPER.

[Any enquiry you may wish to make concerning painting, should be addressed to Miss Lida Clarkson, Pleasant Valley, Dutchess Co., N. Y.—ED. JOURNAL.]

in 1885 only about 3 percent of American women were high school graduates.[31] Knapp's *Journal* went beyond championing a high school education also to defend a college education for women. Again, the number of women who were actually experiencing college in those years was very small: only 1.9 percent of women 18–21 years old.[32] References to high school training either took the desirability of a high school education for granted or were framed in terms of equal rights; early references to college for women, in contrast, took care to emphasize the way a college education could serve traditional activities. We see here, perhaps, the insecurity of women who were encouraging girls to go further in schooling than they themselves had. Such advancement was acceptable for Knapp and her staffers as long as the female role was not altered too dramatically.

In 1887, Will Carleton, who regularly wrote poetry for the *Journal,* proclaimed the compatibility of higher education and domesticity. As the announcement of the poem read:

[Will Carleton's "Worried about Katherine"] is an able argument against the theory, grown only too popular, that the *brain* of women is educated at the expense of home affections and capabilities. He takes the ground that the development of the mind tends to the development of the affections, and in proportion to the degree of 'book-learnin,' is the heart keener to feel, the mind more able to appreciate all that a hearty, pure home life means. He contends that the 'ologies' and the 'isms' do not spoil the housekeeper, nor does a knowledge of Greek and Latin affect in any way the living relations existing between children and parents.[33]

Similarly, Frances Dyer in an article entitled "Shall We Send Our Girls to College?" noted that working with children requires "the balance of character resulting from the discipline of a university life."[34] In sum, Knapp's *Journal* concluded that college would help women run sound homes, train children, and live exemplary lives. It also noted regularly that health objections to women's college attendance had been refuted by scientific studies, thus consciously avoiding the hysteria associated with books like Edward Clarke's *Sex in Education,* which had earlier concluded that the female brain and body could not survive higher education.[35]

References to suffrage and to women's rights generally were characterized by the same mix of progress and tradition. The first mention of suffrage was made in a biographical sketch of Frances Willard, who after "long consideration" was led to "advocate Woman's Suffrage, a privelege [sic] essential to their full usefulness in society."[36] Sketches of Isabella Beecher Hooker and Julia Ward Howe were unrestrained in praising the suffragists' work for the advancement of women. And Louisa herself wrote: "Mrs. Harriet Stanton Blatch crowds a great deal of truth into a nutshell when she says 'women are not too ignorant to vote, but men are too ignorant to grant them the vote.'"[37] While the phrase "woman's rights" saw occasional use, the early *Journal* never advocated blanket rights for women, and it never saw itself as a "feminist" periodical. The magazine and its producers were too moderate for that. Knapp's moderate and generally progressive *Journal* was, however, a consistent supporter of suffrage, suggesting the breadth of that movement's support.

The *Journal* also supported club work for women, a major arena for the expansion of middle-class women's activity in those years. Knapp herself not only participated in various organizations, she also took leadership. "When she joined a woman's club, a literary society or a church organization," her daughter later wrote proudly, "she invariably became its president in a short time."[38] The *Journal*'s support for women's club activity was largely implicit, expressed in adulatory reports of club work and biographical sketches of club women. The magazine in 1887 ran an article on "Sorosis," the first official women's club, which was founded in New York City in 1869. "We take such organizations for granted now," Knapp wrote, "organizations such as W.C.T.U., societies for organizing charity, visiting hospitals, distributing books and flowers, musical guilds, cooking and tennis clubs, Shakespeare classes, and the Boston and Chautauqua circles for home-study." Knapp concluded that "Sorosis has demonstrated that it is possible for women to meet and work together, rising above the petty jealousies of which they are so often accused, and aiming for continual advancement."[39] The *Journal* under Knapp regularly affirmed the importance of the specific work accomplished by women's clubs as well.

In a similar vein, "continual advancement" regarding woman's work for pay was a major theme in the *Journal*'s discussion between 1883 and 1889. References to woman's paid work differed in character by categories, but the *Journal* under Knapp supported work among young women, professional women, women of the lower classes, and, to some extent, even married middle-class women who aspired to both domesticity and work for pay.

The *Ladies' Home Journal* frequently urged the training of young women for self-support. Contributors suggested first, that work experience before marriage would be beneficial; second, that some women might never marry and should therefore know a trade; and third, that even married women should be trained for employment in case they were left alone with a family to support. While the fiction of Knapp's *Journal* contained few references to education and no mention of suffrage or clubs, short stories in these six years fairly often referred to the necessity for young women to work (see Methodological Note). Five stories featured a heroine who was forced to work for pay as a result of the death of a parent or some other family misfortune. "Uncle Gerald," in a story called "Hernecourt Pride," spoke for other fictional observers of such young women when he said, "Certainly I have only admiration for a young lady who has pluck and self-respect enough to save herself by honest work, honestly done, from the quagmire of debt which has engulfed so many of her race."[40]

2.d. Jenny June Croly, Journalist and Founding Member of "Sorosis."

[FOR THE LADIES' HOME JOURNAL.]
DISTINGUISHED AMERICAN WOMEN.

"Jenny June." The Successful Journalist, the Founder of Sorosis. Ten Years its President, and a Prominent Member of Several Literary and Art Societies.

The "Distinguished American Women" column, which ran throughout Knapp's tenure, often focused on the wives or daughters of famous men, but even more frequently it took professional women for its subjects. The column detailed and praised the work of women ministers, doctors, lecturers, lawyers, and even bee-keepers. And the modeling of Knapp and her staff was clearly a powerful statement in and of itself.

A striking exception to the *Journal*'s flexible stance regarding work demonstrates that any magazine is likely at some points to contain inconsistent and even contradictory messages; it also demonstrates that readers will respond to messages that offend them or that seem inconsistent with the rest of the mag-

2.e. Another Example of the "Distinguished American Woman" column.

[For THE LADIES' HOME JOURNAL.]
DISTINGUISHED AMERICAN WOMEN.

Frances E. Willard, President of the W. C.
T. U. Her Life, Work, Methods, and
Domestic Environment.

azine. The March 1887 issue of the *Journal* featured an article called "Woman and Work," by Rose Clark. Clark, not a regular contributor to Knapp's magazine, was very concerned that

> working for wages is not only offered as a universal remedy for the ills of domestic drudgery and dependence, but it is regarded by many as the one great means for developing woman's talents and enabling her to become, in the highest sense of the word—useful. . . . Girls who would help their mothers or be their "father's comfort" feel pressure to work, and worse, some married women do. . . . [In addition] when women having natural protectors work for wages, they usurp places which belong to the really needy. . . . Finally a woman who permits herself to become thoroughly imbued with a

moneymaking spirit almost inevitably grows sordid, grasping, narrow and unwomanly.[41]

This piece touched a nerve in Knapp's readers. The article provoked numerous angry responses, and the letters selected for publication ran in regular feature columns instead of the editorial page, as if in direct response to the article. Claire Alix from Los Angeles, California, wrote that she was dissatisfied with the "moderate living" that her husband provided. "I have a real or fancied ability for business; I combine domestic duties with money-making employment. But I deny that either my home or business life is a failure, or that my husband is rendered contemptible by my work or that the spark of manliness is extinguished within him." Alix went on to suggest that working for a future home signaled not contempt but reverence for the home life. In addition, the Californian argued, she was gaining valuable experience for a day when she might be left alone without her husband and his financial support. Alix concluded by asserting, "I do not believe that business life endangers your modesty, or subjects you to the temptation to shirk and lie."[42]

A reader from the other coast agreed. Mrs. C. S. D. from Gardiner, Maine, wrote, "I have always since married, worked, not because I 'would turn my wages into fine raiments and showy adornments,' but because I feel it is my duty . . . to help my husband." For Mrs. C. S. D., money for the necessities of life was more fundamental than working for personal fulfillment. She asserted that it takes a great deal of money to be "father's comfort," and that "those with wealth in abundance," presumably including Rose Clark, "know little of the struggle in this world for existence."[43]

The reaction to Clark in these and other letters suggests that at least some members of the *Ladies' Home Journal* audience may not have had as much expendable income as the producers assumed. It also suggests the nature of the transitional culture of the late 1880s: expectations of marriage and of financial security were rising, and the solution for at least some couples was for both spouses to work.[44] Working women were regularly profiled in the *Journal*, the magazine ran a column beginning in 1885 called "Hints on Money-Making," and several features during Knapp's tenure highlighted new business opportunities for women. Knapp's *Journal* was, on the whole, quite supportive of women's choice to work for pay.

The producers of the *Ladies' Home Journal* were flexible on the issue of work for pay, but at the same time they still subscribed in large part to the domestic ideology of the day. A woman's role was defined by tasks in the home, which included cooking, cleaning, and caring for children. Tension was very much in evidence in the early *Journal*'s discussion of housekeeping, however.

The *Journal*'s commentary demonstrates the conflict between traditional domestic ideology and newer commitments to expanded opportunity for women, running parallel to and reflecting Louisa Knapp's more personal conflict. The magazine's resolution of that conflict was both a reflection of the old domestic ideology and a harbinger of the new consumer culture that the magazine would help to shape.

The *Ladies' Home Journal* began as a column of domestic advice, and Louisa's magazine was the embodiment of domesticity. During Knapp's tenure every issue contained departments on cooking, cleaning, artistic needlework, interior decoration, and the care of flowers and house plants. Thus to a large extent the magazine *was* housekeeping, and the *Journal* certainly symbolized the notion that housekeeping, with its various specific duties, was important and central to women's lives. Nonetheless, in the 1880s, the *Journal* began to consider the housekeeping aspect of women's role in light of several social concerns.

The first of these related to training young women for their domestic role. In April of 1884 the *Ladies' Home Journal* reported that a "census of a Philadelphia boarding school of forty-eight girls showed that one could make bread, one knew how to fry oysters, three knew how to broil beefsteak, forty-eight could embroider, and forty-seven dance."[45] The *Journal* bemoaned this sort of "training" as frivolous. Fashionable training and mothers' neglect meant that a whole group of young women were substandard housekeepers. This fact was especially disturbing because housekeeping was considered to be one of woman's most fulfilling and health-giving undertakings. Louisa's *Journal,* like the ideology of Real Womanhood, suggested that genteel lassitude and ill-health were best cured by hard work and a no-nonsense attitude. An 1884 editorial noted that one "Chicago lady says she never knew what true happiness was until her husband lost his last dollar and she had to do her own housework," and also that "Abernathy, the celebrated physician" had recently suggested to a "nervous, dyspeptic woman: 'Dismiss your servants and make your own beds.'"[46]

This combination of glorifying housework and downgrading the keeping of servants reflects a certain social reality of the time: by 1870 only one in seven white families in America had a servant, and by 1900 the number had dropped to one in ten.[47] But the suggestion that women with servants were indolent and that housework was refreshing did not reflect the reality of most women's lives. Even the lives of middle-class women often revolved around backbreaking and/or heavily time-consuming work.[48] This pattern in the *Journal* may well have represented its staffers' effort to rationalize the least appealing part of women's work.

Even as it sang the praises of housework as an invigorating and worthwhile pursuit, however, the *Journal* began openly to discuss some negative aspects of women's domestic work, including physical debilitation and lack of free time. A letter to the "editress" of the *Ladies' Home Journal* in 1885 offered the possibility that less might be more, noting that

> if the art of writing consists in knowing what to leave unwritten, may it not be asserted that the art of successful living is in knowing what to leave undone? Studying the career of successful men, we see that they win the world, not by attempting a great number of things, but by excelling in a few. Is not the same true of woman? Much is said about her and her work. Is it not the greatest ill for her, that she attempts so many things [that] success is almost an impossibility?[49]

This reader went on to urge women to buy (instead of sew) underwear for their families, and to wear plain clothes and cook plain meals.

The reader highlights one of the central challenges late nineteenth-century women faced, the challenge of adapting to rising standards of living. For example, the availability of flour led to increased consumption of elaborate baked goods that took longer to prepare. Such baking required more fuel for the stove and dirtied more dishes, which for many nineteenth-century women meant hauling more water with which to wash. Therefore as life improved it also got more complicated for many women.[50]

But going backwards to a simpler life, as the reader proposed, was an unacceptable solution in the eyes of the *Journal*'s producers. Simplifying daily life stood in stark contrast to the commercial mission of the magazine. Instead, Knapp and her staff suggested that "a woman has a right to expect, and demand, if need be, the purchase of labor-saving contrivances for lightening her domestic work."[51] In other words, the answer to many of life's complicated problems was for women to become more self-conscious and accomplished consumers.

Knapp and her staff genuinely viewed the expansion of women's consumer interests as a liberating and broadening force. Consuming, they believed, would lighten the domestic load and would give women increased autonomy and authority in their lives. In other words, asserting one's role as consumer was viewed as an effective and legitimate way for women to broaden their base of power. And the *Journal*'s discussion of male–female relations between 1883 and 1889 demonstrates that the producers believed strongly that women needed to expand that base of power. In its consideration of gender relations the *Journal* emphasized conflict between women and men, and issues of power were central to that conflict.

While their relationships were often fraught with tension, nineteenth-century men and women willingly courted, married, and maintained intimate relationships with each other. Historian Karen Lystra, in her book *Searching the Heart,* appropriately emphasizes the flexibility that usually informed these gender transactions:

[The] modification of an elaborate Victorian gender gap is . . . strongly supported by displays of gender ideology in everyday life, for sex roles are not only defined but transacted. A role, therefore, can be seen not just as a reified essence contained in a binary structure of conformity or nonconformity, but rather as a dynamic and contextually fluid relationship between people. Based upon a learned set of values, beliefs, images and rules, male and female roles may be understood, not as static essences to be possessed, but as a complex repertoire drawn upon in male-female interactions in a dynamic and creative fashion.[52]

Men and women in the nineteenth century were attempting to interact in satisfactory ways, and the various strategies they employed reflected the particular circumstances of the time as well as the personalities and experiences of the individuals involved.

Knapp and her staff valued marriage and male–female intimacy highly. They assumed that women would marry, and they believed that it was in women's best interests to do so. The nature of much of the *Journal*'s commentary on gender relations is striking in this light, because that commentary was largely negative and adversarial. Specifically, Knapp and her contributors noted the trends toward more divorces and fewer marriages, and laid the blame for both squarely at the feet of men. "One reason why divorces are so common now," wrote Knapp, "is because a want of love and praise on the part of husbands drives their loving wives from their sacred home."[53] The year 1885 saw the publication of an article entitled "Why They Do Not Marry: A Young Woman Explains a Social Problem," which advanced the notion that many young men of the day were lazy and inefficient. This perception was the main reason that the author and several of her friends were preparing for professional careers; a profession, she wrote, "could supply a woman with both interest and support, two roles in which husbands just now fail. . . . I have always thought that if I could find a man at all like my father I could love and marry him; but that school of men has vanished from the younger ranks."[54] In short, the author and other *Journal* contributors declared, men were not working hard enough.

But the *Journal* also chastised men for working too hard. *Journal* readers and staffers alike worried about men working to the point of excluding all other activities. "Dear Mrs. Knapp," wrote Fanny M. T. from Detroit. "My husband is generally getting into the habit of . . . getting his supper downtown, offering as an excuse that he is very busy at the office and cannot spare the time to come home. . . . He seems to grow more and more impatient at my efforts to keep him home evenings."[55] Knapp responded by reassuring Fanny that she was not the only American wife encountering such difficulties, and she urged Fanny to confront her husband directly about this problem. An 1887 article, "The Strain for Wealth," suggested that even good faith men could be led astray by the temptations to overwork. Man's role as breadwinner was natural and laudable, the article noted, but the pursuit of money beyond the necessary amounts was coming between wives and husbands and weakening home life.[56]

Consideration of men as marital partners and as workers in Knapp's *Journal* was almost always negative. In fact, most discussion of gender relations in general was negative in the pages of the *Ladies' Home Journal* in the 1880s. Yet the magazine's producers and readers believed in marriage and they loved individual men. Why, then, the tendency to cast male–female relations in a negative light? This tendency could be seen perhaps simply as an adversarial public discourse, a journalistic battle of the sexes of sorts. Emphasizing to young women the crucial nature of the marital choice was more than this, however. It represented an early call to arms in a world where gender roles were changing, but where most women were still economically dependent on men. And the *Journal* went even farther than the marital choice in its attempt to secure more power for women.

The *Ladies' Home Journal* in the 1880s embodied the comparatively new late nineteenth-century tension between the ideals of love-based, companionate marriage on the one hand, and the more pragmatic and often problematic realities of living in a cash-based society on the other. Possible tensions had been more easily resolved in earlier years. Eleanor Roosevelt's biographer notes, for example, that as late as the 1870s Eleanor's grandfather would not let his wife handle money or go shopping in public.[57] The rise of department stores, female-targeted commercial publications, and advertising, along with the development of the companionate ideal in marriage seems to have heightened the importance of money matters for many couples in the 1880s. The *Journal* sensed this tension in the culture, and it urged couples to work together on these complicated issues. As Knapp asserted in 1887, "there is a crying need of a right mutual understanding with respect to the ownership of the family income."[58] Not surprisingly, one of the major solutions to difficult money problems, the magazine suggested, was for women to control at least some discretionary income.

But men would continue to provide the income for the family, and therein lies the key to the fact that the expansion of consumption for women was a relatively safe form of change in the culture of the late nineteenth century. Increased consuming on the part of middle-class women did not challenge in any meaningful way the gender hierarchy of the day, nor did it undermine the capitalistic organization of the economy. Indeed, designating consuming as women's work and urging women to do it more often actually shored up capitalism and aided in the further development of national markets. Women's expanded consumption also masked critical gender inequalities, including the fact that men were paid for their work in public while women were not paid for their work in private. Interestingly, the *Ladies' Home Journal* suggested in 1887 that women should be paid for their work in the home.[59] This suggestion came out of the recognition that women's economic contribution, to the family unit and to the society at large, was lost in the pay arrangement of the nineteenth century—a pattern which, as we are well aware, continues to this day.[60]

The *Journal*'s suggestion was grounded in a potentially radical critique, the recognition that women were being discriminated against in a most pervasive and pernicious way. This critique was overshadowed, however, by the *Journal*'s much more regular and assertive calls for increased and more sophisticated consumption on the part of women.

The magazine's producers exhorted women to consume. They also urged women to read advertisements in order to perform their enlarged and improved role well. Both the call to consume and the encouragement for reading advertisements clearly served the commercial *Journal* and the magazine's advertisers. But Knapp and her staff also sincerely believed that reading advertisements would support women's modified role, which would be, in their view, strengthened and broadened by consumption. Knapp, in a revealing 1886 editorial, asserted that

> men always twit women with reading all the ads, even if they are not in need of anything. 'Not in need of anything!' When does the time come when the head of a household is 'not in need' of something! If not for her children, her house, or herself, at least for her husband.[61]

The female reader/consumer, defined here as the "head of a household," suggests just how far Knapp thought the consuming role could take women. Women, according to Knapp, bought for the home and for everyone in the family, a far-ranging definition of woman's purchasing power.

Accordingly, the *Journal* took an increasingly aggressive part in showing women the value of reading advertisements. Readers were assured that the *Journal* could vouch for its advertising and that it offered substantial "Protection for Subscribers." In March of 1888, Cyrus, in a rare personal column, took seven paragraphs to assert that " 'The Journal' is independent (and that is what advertisers don't like) and can be published at a fair profit without one line of advertising. I am *not* dependent on advertising, and *will lose every line of my advertising patronage* before I will allow my readers to be gulled."[62] This assertion, of course, was more bluster than it was bite; the *Journal* relied heavily on advertising to make a "fair profit," although the definition of "fair profit" could perhaps be manipulated. Curtis only anticipated here the larger trend in commercial discourse as he made bold statements that were virtually lies. Curtis's pronouncement foreshadowed the condescending approach that advertisers would come to take in their pitches. "Trust us," Curtis and future advertisers would intone.

The *Journal* also emphasized what readers would miss if they neglected reading advertisements. Advertising was interesting and informative, the magazine declared. The *Journal* "revealed" in 1887, for example, that Frank R. Stockton, author of such stories as "The Lady and the Tiger," had once been forbidden by doctors to read for several months. When he was finally permitted to read for half an hour a day, Stockton was said to have demanded, "Give me some advertisements. Yes, I'm pining for ads."[63] Readers would be left behind if they did not read advertisements, Louisa editorialized: "You cannot keep posted on what is going on in the world unless you notice advertising as well as reading columns."[64] In order to be safe, the magazine opined, readers should simply read every page of the magazine and should keep each issue for future reference. "Advanced subscribers read their paper clear through," staffers asserted, "advertising and all, and . . . would not lose a copy for anything."[65]

Thus readers were urged to read advertisements. In addition, advertisements often featured endorsements from well-known *Journal* writers. An 1888 advertisement for Royal Baking Powder quoted Marion Harland:

> I regard the Royal Baking Powder as the best manufactured and in the market, so far as I have any experience in the use of such compounds . . . use no other. . . . It is an act of simple justice and also a pleasure to recommend it to American housewives.[66]

This blurred distinction between editorial and advertising content characterized most early commercial magazines, and it strengthened the commercialism of the magazines and the consumer-identity of their readers.

The *Journal* would soon run large quantities of national, brand-name advertisements, but that type of advertising was just beginning to emerge in the 1880s. Many of the *Journal*'s earliest advertisements touted books and magazines and a variety of cheap miscellaneous goods. The first issue of the *Journal* included eight ads for chromo cards (pictures for collecting) and collectors' stamps, four for agents to sell books and magazines, one for the "Marvelous Webber Singing Doll," one for ladies' underwear, one for a "toilet knife," one for a book on oxygen treatments, and one for bug spray.[67] Thus miscellaneous entertainment items headed the list. The advertisements were very small for the most part, and they generally included the name of the product, a brief description, and the address of the company.

By the late 1880s, however, advertisements were more sophisticated, and the household products later generally associated with women's magazines began to outnumber advertisements related to entertainment. The messages of these advertisements followed two related lines: that new products could help women in the home, and that smart consumers bought certain products. An advertisement picturing a smiling, energetic woman read, "Mopping Made Easy,

2.f. Marvelous Webber Singing Doll.

2.g. Dr. Scott's Electric Curler, Tooth Brush.

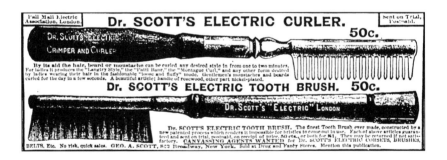

A Task No Longer. The Problem Solved By the Triumph Wringer."[68] Another washer manufacturer urged women to "Buy the Wringer that Saves the Most Labor."[69] And one medicine company suggested the wisdom of a lifelong commitment to buying its product:

THE LADIES' JOURNAL AND PRACTICAL HOME HOUSEKEEPER.

PREMIUM SUPPLEMENT.

☞ If you cannot raise a club yourself, have you not a son, daughter, niece, nephew, or grandchild, who would be glad to earn for themselves some of the premiums we offer? Boys and girls make the best of club raisers, and easily secure large clubs with but little effort, at the extremely low price for THE LADIES' HOME JOURNAL—only 25 cents per year.

BEAUTIFUL DOLLS

Given for a club of 20 new subscribers. These dolls will delight the little girls. You need not be afraid to bump their heads together, or drop them on the floor; they will not break, as their heads cannot be broken. Their hair and eyes are beautiful, and their complexion indicates perfect health. Any little girl would be happy with one or both of these dolls to care for and educate. The face, neck and shoulders are wax. The eyes are bright and beautiful. This Doll has already grown to be fifteen inches tall. Any little girl can easily secure this doll by getting 20 neighbors or friends to subscribe for the LADIES' HOME JOURNAL. Price, $1.30. Postage paid.

PHOTOGRAPH ALBUM,
Given for 20 new members.

This Album is bound in fine leather, has bevelled edges and is ornamented in black and gold, as seen in the cut. It contains places for 40 pictures; part of the openings are oval and part square. The pages are lined with gold. The book has gilt edges and nickel clasp. Size, 6½ x5½ inches.—Given for twenty new subscribers at 25 cents each year.

LADIES' SHOPPING BAGS.

This is a very popular shopping bag with ladies, and is a very convenient arrangement for carrying purse, handkerchief, and other such small articles when on the street or shopping. It has nickel trimmings and is made of fine leather. The style is shape is constantly changing, and we will send the latest shape or style at time it is ordered. Given as a premium for 10 subscribers at 25 cents each. Price, including one year's subscription, 50 cents. Given for a club of 12 subscribers and 75 cents extra

OUR TABLE-WARE PRESENTS.

Spoons and Forks, Silver-Plated on Finest Steel.

We want to tell our readers that these Tea, Dessert and Table Spoons and Forks, although they are sold at a low price, are very serviceable. We have tested them. They are silver-plated on the finest steel, and will wear a long time.

Handsome Sugar Shell, Given for Four New Subscribers.

A new, handsome, neat and stylish pattern, triple-plated, on finest English white steel. Will wear for years. Almost as good as solid silver. All the objectionable qualities of German Silver and brass, which are known to have a disagreeable taste, and use, when a little worn, poisonous, will be avoided in the use of these goods. They are also stronger, and of greater durability than any goods produced.

Butter Knife given for only 4 new subscribers. Price 50 cents.
Set of Six Tea Spoons given for 12 new subscribers. Price $1.00.
Set of Six Table Forks given for 20 new subscribers. Price $2.00.

For a club of 30 new subscribers we will send the Sugar Shell, Butter Knife, Tea Spoons and Forks, a good, serviceable present for a young housekeeper. Price $3.00 for the Set

A SILVER-PLATED TEA SET.

Tea Sets. Three Pieces. This is one of the latest and most elegant tea sets ever made. It is quadruple plate and beautifully ornamented on the sides, leaving a place for monogram. Each piece is finely engraved and chased, and the Cream Pitcher is gold-lined. The pattern is one of the prettiest we could select out of a hundred, at the factory where they are made. We can guarantee this set to last a lifetime.

Price, $18.00, or given to anyone who will send in 200 new subscribers, or for new subscribers and $5.00. Express to be paid by receiver.

As a Christmas, wedding or birthday present, hardly anything would please a wife or mother more. Certainly these goods cannot be purchased at any retail store at so low a price, and the pattern is much prettier than can be found outside of the largest cities. We know this set would please you.

SPECIAL TERMS:
This splendid Tea Set will be given for 100 new subscribers at 25 cents per year each, or given for 200 new subscribers in cash, or given for 50 new subscribers and $2.50 extra in cash, or given for 25 new subscribers and $3.75 extra in cash.

A HAMMOCK FREE

To any one sending us 25 new subscribers at 25 cents per year, each and 25 cents extra. The Union Hammock is are stronger and more durable than other styles. Each mesh is strengthened by means of a safety knot. If a strand should break, it will be impossible for it to pull out, as the case with the imported hammocks.

Style B B is eleven feet long, and has a good foot bed. It is variegated in color, has nickel-plated rings and is very handsome. It can be safely used, by persons weighing 150 pounds, as it is capable of sustaining 500 pounds dead weight. Given for 20 new names and 25 cents extra. Postage and packing, 25 cents. We offer it for sale, including the payment of postage by us, for $1.25.

A First-Class Parlor Organ.

This splendid premium can be easily earned in a short time by any bright boy or girl or young lady in want of a good instrument. See the special, easy terms, on which this Organ can be secured, printed below. With the aid of a few of the required number of subscribers could be secured in a week. Many ladies have secured as high as 4 subscribers in a single day to The Ladies' Home Journal. You can do as well if you but try.

Miraculous—Height, 70 in., Depth, 24 in., Length, 48 in.

Patterson Organ, Five Stops, Five Octaves, Sub Bass and Coupler, handsomely ornamented. A splendid parlor furniture, as well as sweet-toned musical instrument. Has Two Sets of Reeds, Two and one-half Octaves of Diapason Reeds, and Two and one-half Octaves of Diapason Reeds, with Tremulant Catalogue price $160. Manufactured by James T. Patterson, Rockport, Conn.

SPECIAL TERMS.

We have made special arrangements with the manufacturer for this Organ for our subscribers, and they have made such easy terms as to put it within the reach of the clubs of families who could not afford it at the regular price. This Organ will be given for 600 new subscribers at 25 cents each

Or given for 550 new subscribers and $10 or each extra
Or " 500 " " $20 " "
Or " 450 " " $30 " "
Or " 400 " " $40 " "
Or " 350 " " $50 " "

☞ This is one of our Best Premiums.☜

A FIRST-CLASS RELIABLE WATCH AND CHAIN

A Splendid Present easily earned by any bright boy in a few hours

THE WATERBURY WATCH

Now this is an offer which certainly should be improved by all wishing to own a beautiful, reliable and durable watch at very little cost.

On account of the very low price of this watch many people suppose that it is a toy. Now as we have had four years of experience with this wonderful watch, we can speak from actual knowledge of the facts. For accuracy, beauty and durability it is superior to many watches costing from $10 to $12.

Tens of thousands of these watches are in constant use by all classes of people, from boys to bankers, and are keeping as good time as watches costing high prices.

ANOTHER OFFER.

We will give this watch for a club of 50 subscribers and $1.00 extra in cash, or we will give it for a club of 40 subscribers and $2.00 extra in cash. Sent, securely packed in a Satin-Lined Case, postpaid.

> When Baby was sick, we gave her Castoria,
> When she was a child, she cried for Castoria,
> When she became Mrs., she clung to Castoria,
> When she had children, she gave them Castoria.[70]

Hence advertisers began to join the *Journal* producers in trying to encourage a lifelong pattern of consuming for women.

How might the *Journal* have affected its readers in these years? We can only speculate, but it is important to do so. Otherwise, we are left analyzing a text in a vacuum, a text that had no significance since it had no audience. And the *Ladies' Home Journal* certainly had an audience. It is important, however, to avoid conceptualizing *Journal* readers or the readers of any other magazine as a unified, cohesive group. While such readers may have shared some characteristics, they were certainly not all alike in temperament or in life circumstances.[71] Nor did any reader define herself centrally as a *Journal* reader; reading the *Journal* was but one in any particular reader's array of activities.

It would be simplistic, therefore, to assume that *Journal* readers absorbed each issue of the magazine, made it part of themselves, and thereafter modeled their behavior and beliefs entirely on the *Journal*'s example. It is the case that the 1880s media world was much less varied than the contemporary media world. Magazines like the *Journal* were the only national medium available, and newspapers and magazines were the only kind of media available at all. Even in this context, however, it is necessary to avoid assuming simple direct effects from the magazine's messages on its readers.

Analysis of the effects of advertising on readers suggests that there is both a superstructure and an infrastructure of consumption.[72] The superstructure of consumption is a set of images that helps to make a given product, or consuming in general, seem normal, appropriate, convenient, and popular.[73] Cyrus Curtis and Louisa Knapp Curtis provided a consumer-oriented vehicle for this superstructure, and advertisers began to build it up with their commercial messages. The 1880s, then, saw the early elaboration of the superstructure of consumption on the cultural level when media producers and advertisers joined forces to promote consumption as a way of life.

In contrast, the infrastructure of consumption is a set of social conditions that predisposes an individual or group of individuals toward certain patterns of consuming. The decade of the 1880s appears also to have been a time when the infrastructure of consumption was ripe for development. A number of women were actively seeking to expand their roles, but many of them were still economically dependent on men. As I have suggested, traditional sources of advice were often removed, and more and more products previously made by women were available commercially. Knapp and her staff believed that increased consuming was a concrete way for women to expand their activity and gain some autonomy that could be satisfying and even fun. Hearing no objection from readers to their initial promotion of consumption, and reinforced by rapidly escalating circulation figures, Knapp and her staff continued to encourage women's consuming. And women, every time they bought the *Journal,* renewed their subscription, or purchased a product advertised in the magazine's pages, colluded with the *Journal* producers and advertisers in the process of creating a gendered consumer culture.

This collusion is poignant in the case of the *Ladies' Home Journal* because most of the magazine's producers as well as its readers were women. Knapp and her staff consistently employed a sisterly, peer-to-peer tone in the magazine, and they identified closely with their readers. *Journal* producers and readers alike seemed to believe that women's activity should be expanded, particularly in the areas of education, suffrage, club work, and work for pay. But without a thoroughgoing critique of the gendered division of labor and unequal economic positions of men and women, the call for expanded activity was muted. Thus the magazine's producers and readers tacitly agreed to a critical compromise—that women would become more active and autonomous consumers in a societal structure that was pervasively biased against them. This compromise soon took on a life of its own. The resolution of the conflict between the old and the new middle-class feminine script therefore came at a high price.

As I have noted, Knapp's working arrangement represented a similar compromise between the old and the new, and the limited span of her tenure illustrates the exigencies of that compromise. In 1889 the Curtises decided to make improvements on the *Journal* beyond those they had made a year earlier. The June issue of 1889 announced that the next issue would double in size to thirty-two pages and that it would also sport an important new addition—a cover.[74] Behind this expansion lay a great deal of additional editorial work. Knapp had managed her dual role for six years, but the momentum of big business finally seemed to be too much at odds with her domestic life. Her daughter later reported: "I have heard her tell that her reason for giving up this work was that I, then aged thirteen, came to her one day and said, 'Oh, mamma, whenever I want you, you have a pen in your hand.'"[75] Edward Bok, Knapp's successor as editor, later expanded:

[A] growing sense of her maternal duty . . . led her to realize that her daughter's welfare must be her sole thought. Fortunately, this conviction came when her husband was well along the path of his success, and then as expeditiously and fully as she had undertaken her joint responsibilities with her husband, she relinquished them to devote herself to her daughter.[76]

Louisa Knapp contributed a column to the *Journal* in subsequent years, but her central role in the magazine's production was over. The transition cannot have been as easy for her as Bok suggests it was; the *Journal* had been a major part of Louisa's life for years and she had loved her work. It is entirely possible that she was tired of balancing such demanding work with domestic and child-rearing responsibilities; but this does not mean that she necessarily gave up the *Journal* happily. She made the "choice" that Cyrus Curtis did not have to make so directly, that is, the choice between working for pay and parenting her child. However this "choice" to leave her position as editor made her feel, Louisa was once again actively creating herself in the context of her current situation.

It is quite likely the case, then, that women's limited choices prompted at least some conscious reflection about their gendered lives. Louisa Knapp appears to have been answering the question for herself that she regularly addressed in her magazine: what does a good woman look like, and how can I best approximate that ideal? At the end of her editorship Louisa asked again the questions of role definition she had first posed when she presented herself in the pages of the *Journal* as the editor who works from home. It is possible that, insofar as they faced difficult choices and decisions in their own lives, *Journal* readers went through similar deliberations about their femininity. Can a good wife work for pay? Can a good daughter go to college? Can a good wife be a bad cook? There were quite possibly as many different variations in answering such questions as there were middle-class women in the United States at the turn of the century. Later comparisons with Bok's *Journal* and Lorimer's *Post* will indicate that masculine construction was never this conscious and reflective.

We can only speculate about whether reading the *Ladies' Home Journal* during these years was a liberating or a constraining activity for women. To the extent that the magazine pointed out problematic features of American life for women and encouraged them to act to change them, it had the potential to liberate. It was also liberating since it presented women with a range of images and opportunities. But to the extent that it channelled women's frustrations into the avenue of increased consuming, it constrained readers. The magazine quite likely had different effects on different readers, effects we can never measure directly. We can see, however, that Knapp's intent was to affirm and liberate women within the framework of patriarchal capitalism that encompassed her work and life. Her readers as well as the publishing world suffered a significant loss when she left her position as *Journal* editor.

In October of 1889, almost six years after she had begun, Knapp turned the editorship of the *Ladies' Home Journal* over to Edward Bok, who came to the position by way of his syndicated newspaper column for women. Ironically, it was Knapp herself who was largely responsible for engaging the self-aggran-

2.i. Bok Contributed a Literary Column Before Becoming the *Journal*'s Editor.

dizing and publicity-seeking Bok as her successor. Bok would speak in the *Journal* of the magazine's first editor only when she died many years later; this fact, combined with her own modesty, relegated Knapp to virtual obscurity in publishing history, with her critical contribution evaporating almost completely. Her case illustrates an all-too-common scenario in nineteenth-century America. Women created and launched various institutions, including schools, orphanages, libraries, and parks, generally in voluntary groups with little money and relatively little structure. Once they were established and thriving, men took an interest, and women gave the institutions over to men to run. And women's initial contributions were erased from the collective cultural memory.

This was the case with several mass-circulation magazines in this era. While the early 1800s saw a number of active women editors, among them Sarah Josepha Hale, female editors became less and less common as the century wore on. By the late nineteenth century, when producing magazines like the *Ladies' Home Journal* had become big business, there were virtually no female editors of major mass-circulation magazines in the United States. This pattern persisted with few exceptions until the 1960s, three quarters of a century later.[77]

Knapp's very success, therefore, eventually led to what she viewed as an unbridgeable gap between her professional and her domestic life. Knapp's experience highlights the tension inherent in the early *Journal*'s promotion of expanded activity for women along with its emphasis on the importance of homemaking. Given the demands of an increasingly complex commercial culture, Knapp's informal arrangement was extremely difficult to maintain, and big business considerations would dominate American magazine publishing ever after. Similarly, as we shall see, as long as critiques of the commercial culture were based on a traditional gendered division of labor, the power relations status quo would remain firm.

Louisa was not a passive victim of her culture. The "choices" in the patriarchal, capitalist culture of the 1880s were very limited, but Louisa made the choice to leave the editorship, just as her readers made the choice to become ever more active consumers.

Edward Bok would take this consumer "choice" and make it the centerpiece and an irrevocably integral part of the *Ladies' Home Journal* of the 1890s. We turn, now, to a consideration of Edward Bok's early editorship.

3

A New Editor and a New Voice: Edward Bok Transforms the *Journal,* 1890–1900

As I have shown, the *Ladies' Home Journal* between 1883 and 1889 was a highly gendered, feminine text. The magazine regularly pronounced in these years that Louisa Knapp's gender particularly suited her to addressing the needs of her female readers. This emphasis meant that the magazine had to rational-ize Edward Bok's ascension to the editorship. In January of 1890 the *Journal* announced that Edward Bok was the magazine's new editor-in-chief. "With the fullest appreciation of the needs of a representative woman's periodical," the announcement read, "a tried experience, and the liveliest sympathy with every-thing appertaining to the elevation and instruction of woman-kind, Mr. Bok en-ters upon his duties thoroughly equipped for the position."[1]

According to the *Journal* during this transitional period, Bok was the next best thing to a female editor: he was sympathetic to women, and his syndicated "Woman's Page" had given him some familiarity with editing a woman's pe-riodical. Bok had a special understanding of feminine needs, the *Journal* reas-sured readers, that allowed him to both cater to and speak for women. As Mrs. Lyman Abbott declared in her new department, "Just Among Ourselves," "Dear Mr. Bok! I like him so much. I wish all the *Journal* sisters knew him. You would hardly believe that a man could know so well what we women want most. But he does, and he is so kind and willing!"[2] Likewise, Bok at the time described himself as "the mouthpiece of hearts and minds of your own sex be-hind me."[3]

The Curtises certainly hired Bok because he had already worked on a lim-ited basis with print materials targeting women, but the fact is that they valued his business experience even more highly. Bok had proven himself to be an adept businessman with a sure feel for late nineteenth-century middle-class tastes. The Curtises did not necessarily believe that a man would by definition be superior to a woman in editing a magazine. The always arrogant and often defensive Bok, however, believed in the natural superiority of male editors. In his autobiography Bok explained why men had come to dominate the ranks of mass-circulation magazine editors:

> We may well ponder whether the full editorial authority and direction of a
> modern magazine, either essentially feminine in its appeal or not, can safely
> be entrusted to a woman when one considers how largely executive is the na-
> ture of such a position, and how thoroughly sensitive the modern editor must
> be to the 101 practical business matters which enter into and form so large a

3.a. The Column Announcing the Editorial Transition.

LADIES' HOME JOURNAL

A NATIONAL ILLUSTRATED FAMILY JOURNAL.

Published Monthly by the

CURTIS PUBLISHING CO.,

At 433-435 Arch Street, Philadelphia.

Edited by

EDWARD W. BOK,

Assisted by Emma C. Hewitt

Subscription Rates: $1.00 per year, 50 cents for six months; singly or in clubs. Single copies, 10 cents.
Advertising Rates: Two Dollars per Agate line, each insertion. Reading notices, Four Dollars per line, Nonpareil measurement.

Subscriptions must begin with the number current when subscription was received. We do not date back, even upon the most urgent request.

Renewals can be sent now, no matter when the subscription expires, and the time will be added to that to which the subscription is already entitled.

Expiration Notices are always sent at end of subscription. If not renewed, it is immediately discontinued. No notice is required to stop the paper, and no bill will be sent for extra numbers.

Receipts.—The fact that you receive the paper is a proof that we have received your remittance correctly. If you do not receive the paper promptly, write us, that we may see that your address is correct.

When Renewing, desiring change of address, entering complaint, or in fact communicating in any way in regard to Journal, or premium, **be sure to enclose the yellow slip from your wrapper,** as by this means investigation is much facilitated.

Errors.—We make them; so does every one, and we will cheerfully correct them if you will write to us. Try to write us good naturedly, but if you cannot, then write to us any way. Do not complain to any one else, or let it pass. We want an early opportunity to make right any injustice that we may do.

New York Office: 38 Park Row, Potter Building.

W. S. NILES, MANAGER.

Our New York Office is for the transaction of business with New York advertisers. Subscribers should not address any letters to that office.

Chicago Office: No. 541 "The Rookery."

RICHARD S. THAIN, MANAGER.

Our Chicago Office is for the convenience of Chicago advertisers. Subscribers should not address the Chicago office.

Boston Office: 13 School St., Hunnewell Building.

B. T. HENRY, MANAGER.

Our Boston Office is for the accommodation of Boston advertisers. Therefore do not send subscriptions to the Boston office.

Philadelphia, January, 1890.

AN EDITORIAL CHANGE.

With this issue of The Ladies' Home Journal, the editorial management of the periodical passes from the hands of Mrs. Louisa Knapp to those of Mr. Edward W. Bok.

The retirement of Mrs. Knapp is rendered necessary by increasing domestic duties, incompatible with the editorial demands of a growing publication. While her direct editorial connection will be severed, her hearty interest and sympathy in all that appertains to the success of the Journal remains undimmed.

Mrs. Knapp has been prevailed upon to continue her successful management of "The Practical Housekeeper" department, and this feature will henceforth be under her direct personal supervision. Enabled to concentrate her undivided attention to this department, it is safe to predict for it the most unqualified success.

In the capacity of Mr. Bok to continue the work so auspiciously begun and carried out under Mrs. Knapp's direction, the management has every confidence. With the fullest appreciation of the needs of a representative woman's periodical, a tried experience, and the liveliest sympathy with everything appertaining to the elevation and instruction of womankind, Mr. Bok enters upon his duties thoroughly equipped for the position.

In the general policy of The Ladies' Home Journal no changes will be effected. The thorough approval constantly evidenced by our readers indicates that the present lines followed are satisfactory to them.

The new editorial management will, therefore, devote its attention more to the improvement of established lines, so that each department of the magazine may prove, even more than now, a distinct and valuable feature in itself. These improvements, and new attractions, will make themselves manifest in due time.

THE CURTIS PUBLISHING COMPANY.

3.b. Edward W. Bok. Courtesy Charles Scribner's Sons.

part of the editorial duties. . . . Then, again, it is absolutely essential in the conduct of a magazine with a feminine or home appeal to have on the editorial staff women who are experts in their line; and the truth is that women will work infinitely better under the direction of a man than of a woman.[4]

Bok believed that the complicated business needs of a late nineteenth-century mass-circulation magazine were more important than any feminine rapport might be. It is the case, however, that Bok's *Journal* of the 1890s was built in large part on the strong foundation that Knapp had laid. Knapp's *Journal* had blended a sisterly, down-to-earth tone with regular exhortations to consume. The Bok-Curtis *Journal* would refine this blend to create an approach that continues to characterize popular women's magazines today. Bok's magazine featured (1) a self-consciously intimate tone, (2) frequent consideration of gender-related matters, (3) far-ranging advice to readers about living their lives well, and (4) pervasive references to the commercial culture, in both editorial and advertising material.

Bok's editorship had a profound impact on the turn-of-the-century magazine. Because he was a man, Bok believed that he had to work especially hard to foster connections between his magazine and his readers. Because he was a relatively insecure man, Bok was very nervous about the advancement of middle-class women in the late nineteenth century. The combination of these attributes would lead Bok to transform the *Ladies' Home Journal* into a "helping" magazine, thereby aiding in the institutionalization of the condescending tone that continues to characterize women's magazines today.[5]

But the condescending and prescriptive messages of Bok's *Journal* would be mixed and moderated by the magazine's commercial nature. As the magazine expanded its service departments and carried more modern advertising campaigns, it featured several different, sometimes contradictory messages regarding woman's role. Under Bok's early editorship the *Ladies' Home Journal* became a more thoroughly commercial magazine, a development that both modified Bok's message and gave it a wider and wider hearing.

Much of what we know about Edward Bok comes from his autobiography and his memoirs. His autobiography, *The Americanization of Edward Bok,* was published in 1923, and it won the Pulitzer Prize. It is a relentlessly cheerful, moralistic, and prescriptive reflection on success, and it is written, in a most mannered way, in the third person. His book of memoirs, *Twice Thirty,* was published just two years later, in 1925. It is equally prescriptive, but it is more cynical and pessimistic. Bok continued to employ his arrogant and critical tone, but he seemed to be less sure in this second book that people would or could take his advice.

Bok was born in Helder, the Netherlands, in 1863. His family was well-to-do, but his father's unwise investments and the family's subsequent struggles led them to seek a new beginning in America in 1870. Bok was the younger of two sons. His older brother, William, was eight-and-a-half when the family immigrated, while Bok turned seven soon after they settled in Brooklyn. Bok seems to have harbored some ill will toward his father, who had a difficult time providing for his family. His later writings are full of references to the brothers' need to earn money from young ages, and to the hardship that poverty presented for his mother, whose "Americanization experiment was to compel her, for the first time in her life, to become a housekeeper without domestic help."[6] In order to contribute to the family's earnings, Bok quit school at the age of thirteen to become an office boy at the Western Union Telegraph Company. He took evening classes in stenography, employing this skill first at Henry Holt and Company. Two years later, in 1884, he moved to Charles Scribner's Sons, where he soon rose to the position of advertising manager for the house journal and highbrow publication, *Scribner's Magazine.*

In addition to his work at Scribner's, Bok organized in 1886 the Bok Syndicate Press. He had earlier formed a friendship with Henry Ward Beecher. As he was wont to do, he found a way to make money and to generate publicity for himself through that association. Bok began to send a weekly letter composed by Beecher to a few newspapers, and soon he was regularly supplying a number of papers with the conservative minister's wisdom. He then began to compose his own "literary letter," consisting of advice on reading materials and gossip about popular writers. In 1886 he decided to broaden his syndicated material to reach out to women. He first syndicated a weekly gossip column from the *New York Star* called "Bab's Babble," later expanding the column to a page by including weekly commentary from Ella Wheeler Wilcox and other nonfiction materials on women's topics from female and male writers alike. "It was commercial, if you will," Bok later wrote characteristically, "but it was a commercial editing that had a distinct educational value to a large public."[7]

Cyrus Curtis and Louisa Knapp Curtis found these twin perspectives of commerce and education appealing. Bok's "Literary Leaves" column began to run in the *Journal* in 1889, and by the summer of that year the Curtises had offered Bok the editorship. Bok's route to the *Journal* bears some resemblance to Cyrus Curtis's: in editing a more general publication, Curtis stumbled on to a column for women that proved to be highly popular. Cyrus had quickly turned over the editorial function to Louisa, however, handling only the business affairs of the magazine himself. But Bok, as the prospective editor of the *Journal,* was being asked to go much farther—to occupy himself with women's concerns, to write for women, and to manage the work of staff members and contributors, a substantial number of whom were women. Bok reports that he, his mother, and his friends all questioned the wisdom of his accepting the Curtises' offer.[8] Why then did he do so?

Bok's autobiographical comments and the content of his *Journal* suggest several reasonable explanations. One is Bok's clear recognition that publications for women were becoming a big business, and that the *Ladies' Home Journal* was the biggest of them all. He was a sharp businessman who recognized in Cyrus Curtis a kindred spirit. The editorship of the *Journal,* therefore, was an appealing commercial proposition.

Another, related reason for Bok's interest in the editorship was his proud but somewhat defensive membership as an adult in the American middle class. The fact that Bok's immigrant family had lost status upon immigration to the

United States drove him to do everything in his power to regain the American version of that status. Once he had attained middle-class standing, Bok became more middle-class—and American—than many of his peers who had been born in the United States. He felt compelled to interpret membership in the American middle class to others, and the *Ladies' Home Journal* was a perfect medium through which to convey his interpretation to a large audience.

Finally, Bok by personality and mission was a preacher. Pedantic, opinionated, and moralistic, Bok delighted in the prospect of reaching and influencing huge numbers of Americans with his observations and advice. A congregation consisting mainly of women was perhaps the most appealing group to try to reach, since the "woman question" was a major topic of the day, and since preaching and lecturing were common and approved styles of public discourse with women.[9] Bok joined many late nineteenth-century ministers, physicians, and politicians in their defensive and adamant condemnation of women's "progress."[10]

These interests and attributes suited Edward Bok to the editorship of a major women's magazine. But the fact remains that he was engaging in an enterprise that many held in low esteem, since it was grounded in the relatively low status of its female audience and since the *Journal* was a middlebrow rather than highbrow publication. Bok appears to have coped with this reality by separating his true persona from his role as editor. Distinguishing between Editor Bok and the real Bok, he later wrote in his second autobiography: " 'Give the people what they want,' was his slogan. 'Give the people what they ought to have and don't know they want,' was mine."[11] These two impulses were clearly contradictory, and analysis of the content of Bok's *Journal* demonstrates that they both indeed informed the magazine's message.

Thus Bok coped by compartmentalizing. It is fair to ask also how his audience coped with his preaching and moralizing. Why was Bok's *Ladies' Home Journal* successful? First, it is the case that Bok was building on the solid base established by Knapp; he inherited a successful, expanding publication. Second, while Bok preached and prescribed to his audience, he also conveyed the sincere message that the late nineteenth century was a complicated time for women as well as for men. Innovation and change were exciting and sometimes in order, but they also brought with them, Bok recognized, confusion and tension. Third, Bok was a savvy businessman: he consulted readers on their desires and tastes regularly, and he responded to readers' ideas whenever he felt he could. Finally, Bok's voice was not the only one heard in his magazine, and the blend of voices in the *Journal* of the 1890s seems to have been compelling to thousands of late nineteenth-century middle-class women.

Bok was part of the "new breed" of editor-publisher operating in the late nineteenth century, a group that also included S. S. McClure, Frank Munsey, Walter Hines Page, George Horace Lorimer, and Peter Fenton Collier. The gentleman editor of the Gilded Age was being supplanted by enterprising young men who came from humbler backgrounds.[12] Several of these men grew up in poverty; several of them, including Bok, were also immigrants. Many came to the magazine business via newspaper stints of some kind; they all had experience with the developing sales and service economy, where communication was more direct and where "impression management" was paramount.[13] They worked long hours and were driven to succeed—to reach more people, to wield more influence, to make more money.

This group produced profound changes in the very idea of what a magazine should be. They did not simply take old magazines and add more and more advertising and recruit more and more subscribers. Under the leadership of these new editor-publishers, magazines were conceived as active agents that could influence readers' lives; editorial voices became much more personal, direct, and forceful; anticipatory production, that is, soliciting articles and stories from designated writers, became the norm; and both readers and advertisers were pursued more aggressively than ever before.[14]

By the time Bok came to the editorship of the *Journal,* Curtis had already instituted several of these changes in the business side of the magazine's operation. The contrast between Bok's editorial style and Knapp's earlier approach, however, suggests just how much Bok himself brought to the magazine. Bok's *Journal* exemplified virtually all of the new magazine characteristics identified above. Bok himself later claimed that his magazine had not "remained an inanimate printed thing, but had become a vital need in the personal lives of its readers."[15] Anticipatory production was the only way to run a modern magazine, Bok believed. His vision for the *Journal* made a coherent, quite controlled set of contributions absolutely necessary. In addition, Bok reinforced all of Curtis's efforts to recruit both readers and advertisers. He urged women to convince their neighbors of the advantages of *Journal* reading, and he regularly boasted about the quality and size of the *Journal* audience. It was Bok's editorial voice, however, that distinguished his *Journal* most clearly from Knapp's magazine.

As we have seen, Louisa Knapp made a conscious effort to avoid being identified as an editorial personality, editing the *Journal* under her maiden name and shunning publicity. Her rather haphazard editorial page consisted of brief reflections delivered in a straightforward style, as if coming from a peer, and of letters from readers accompanied by her responses. The rest of the magazine was characterized by the standard removed and genteel editorial style of the Gilded Age. Bok consciously rebelled against this style, which he found outdated. He explained his stance later:

> The method of editorial expression in the magazines of 1889 was also distinctly vague and prohibitively impersonal. The public knew the name of scarcely a single editor of a magazine: there was no personality that stood out

in the mind: the accepted editorial expression was the indefinite "we"; no one ventured to use the first person singular and talk intimately to the reader. . . . He [Bok] felt the time had come . . . for the editor of some magazine to project his personality through the printed page and to convince the public that he was not an oracle removed from the people, but a real human being who could talk and not merely write on paper.[16]

Bok made changes at all levels. Within several months he had made the editorial page very much his own, featuring signed editorials that were organized the same way each month. While making his name more prominent in the pages of the *Journal,* Bok also published collections of his articles, and he spoke regularly on the lecture circuit. He reasoned that "through the medium of the rostrum he might come in closer contact with the American people personally, and secure some first-hand criticism of his work."[17]

Bok wrote in the first person from the start at the *Journal,* and he went even farther to address his readers directly. In April of 1890 Bok wrote: "Nine months ago you, my present readers, and I were strangers. To-day it seems as if I knew you all."[18] Bok went on to encourage "his" readers to help him create the *Journal*'s "large family circle." In 1891 he told readers that he always wrote his editorial from his home (as Knapp had), thinking of it as a personal letter to them. He also regularly solicited opinions from readers regarding the *Journal.* He asked them which features pleased them most and least, whether they would prefer more or less fiction, and if there were special subjects that they would like covered.

Bok was reflective about the role the *Journal* played in his readers' lives, and he occasionally shared those reflections in the pages of the magazine. In August of 1895 he noted that many readers did not know or care about the conduct, policy, or purpose of any magazine they read. Others—and this was the group that obviously had his approval—found a magazine to be a friend, and responded by writing to the *Journal* with criticism, praise, or questions. These readers theoretically became actively engaged in the life of the magazine, a relationship that Bok always strove to make reciprocal. "A magazine's greatest value," he declared, "lies in its ability to enter directly into the lives of its readers."[19] Bok proudly reported later that

so intimate had become this relation, so efficient was the service rendered, that [*Journal*] readers could not be pried loose from it; where women were willing and ready, when the domestic pinch came, to let go of other reading matter, they explained to their husbands and fathers that the *Ladies' Home Journal* was a necessity—they did not feel that they could do without it.[20]

Did this make *Journal*-reading a passive activity manipulated by the editor? Some historians argue that turn-of-the-century magazines like the *Ladies' Home Journal* changed the reading process to make it thoroughly passive by emphasizing trust, reader participation, and proprietorship.[21] While this is not

THE LADIES' HOME JOURNAL

An Illustrated Family Journal with the Largest Circulation of any Magazine in the World.

Published Monthly by

THE CURTIS PUBLISHING COMPANY,

At 433-435 Arch Street, Philadelphia, Pa.

Edited by

EDWARD W. BOK

In association with

MRS. LYMAN ABBOTT
MISS RUTH ASHMORE
MARGARET BOTTOME
KATE UPSON CLARK
EMMA M. HOOPER
MRS. LOUISA KNAPP
MARY F. KNAPP
ISABEL A. MALLON
EBEN E. REXFORD
ELIZABETH ROBINSON SCOVIL
REV. T. DE WITT TALMAGE, D. D.
KATE TANNATT WOODS

Advisory and Contributing Editors.

With editorial representatives at London and Paris.

Subscription Rates — One dollar per year; fifty cents for six months, payable in advance. Single copies ten cents.

Advertising Rates — Three dollars per Agate line each insertion before (this) editorial page; two dollars and fifty cents per Agate line on succeeding pages. Reading Notices, five dollars per Nonpareil line.

BRANCH OFFICES:

New York: Potter Building, 38 Park Row
Boston: Hunnewell Building, 13 School Street
Chicago: 226 and 228 La Salle Street
San Francisco: Chronicle Building

Philadelphia, February, 1891

AT HOME WITH THE EDITOR

O write in a busy editorial office, where each moment offers a fresh interruption, is not conducive to that domestic and sympathetic spirit which I am ever anxious shall pervade the JOURNAL pages. And so the thought has come to reserve "The Editorial Desk" in the future more for the busy daily routine of an editor's life, while these pleasantly familiar talks, which monthly I enjoy on this page with my readers, shall come from within the precincts of my own home. There, by my own fireside, I shall be better able to imagine myself seated at your hearthstone. There, in my favorite chair, cheered by the glow of the evening home lamp, and with those around me who are man's best friends, I know I shall feel closer in sympathy with your interests and thoughts. Since home is the watchword of our JOURNAL, why is not the editor's home the best place from which he should talk to his readers?

AND during these past three or four months I have felt particularly at home with the JOURNAL readers. For ever since the invitation to write to me was printed in the October and December numbers under the title "Will you Favor the Editor?" I have become better and more personally acquainted with many. Several thousands of these letters have come from every part of our own great land, from across the seas, and from countries with which heretofore I have had only a geographical knowledge. Have I read them all, you ask? Every line you have written. Evening after evening have I sat within my family circle reading—often aloud—your messages of good cheer, your suggestions and your criticisms. All have been welcome. They have cheered far beyond your power to imagine. A greater pleasure has never been experienced by an editor than that which I have felt in reading what you have so generously written. The temptation was often strong to reply, and I began to lay many of the letters aside to send a hearty thank you, but they came too fast, your kindness was too great. And so here, to each and all, I tender my most grateful acknowledgments. Your encouraging words have had their effect; your suggestions, many of them, were excellent, and will be largely carried out. Several articles in the January issue, and more in the present number, will doubtless be recognized by many of you, and rightfully claimed. And more will follow. Certain special features, at once recognized as helpful when they were suggested, are now being prepared by the most skillful hands which knowledge and money can obtain. Outside editorial connections have been formed, and while these special wants of our readers are being brought into shape, the regular editorial staff of the JOURNAL will be busy in adding strength to the work under their charge. And thus will the JOURNAL show the sincerity of its one great aim to please its readers. Over two hundred suggestions have come to us which we shall adopt; and our only wish is that our readers may send us two hundred more. The willingness to please you in all respects is ever with us: it is simply an indication of your wishes that we ask. The JOURNAL is made for you, and this fact I would always ask you to bear in mind. What you want in your JOURNAL you shall have, always provided it is feasible.

the simple case of manipulation and control that Bok implies—get the readers to interact with the magazine and they are subscribers for life—there is evidence that this shift in tone and approach initiated by Bok was an important and largely negative one. Readers were active agents who chose whether to buy the magazine, what to read in it, and what to believe of what they read. But the shift over which Bok presided significantly altered the nature of the text–reader interaction. Readers were no longer being addressed by a peer as they had been under Knapp's tenure. Instead they were being addressed by a condescending man who often patronized them. In addition, the readers' voice was weakened in the magazine since their letters and opinions were increasingly controlled by the structures of the magazine. Finally, as the *Journal* shifted from sharing to instructing, the notion that women need help was institutionalized. This message would be emphasized in all subsequent women's magazines, and it continues to distinguish most popular women's magazines from most popular men's magazines.[22]

Therefore, readers were regarded and addressed in very different ways in Bok's *Journal* than they had been in Knapp's. The effects of this change on readers were probably uneven. For example, Bok's editorials were openly pedantic and prescriptive. Judging by reader letters, at least some readers disagreed with Bok and were offended both by his patronizing air and his conservative ideas. In other words, Bok's blunt expression of the idea that "women need help" was easy to confront if one felt so inclined. But the way in which this message came to inform service departments in the magazine was much more subtle. Tracing the development of these departments highlights this pattern.

Household departments had been part of the very early "Woman and Home" page and had remained the backbone of Knapp's *Journal*. But Bok took the concept and made it a reflection both of his desire for interaction with readers and his drive to secure more *Journal* readers. As he wrote later:

> The editor had come to see that the power of a magazine might lie more securely behind the printed page than in it. He had begun to accustom his readers to writing to his editors upon all conceivable problems. This he decided to encourage. He employed an expert in each line of feminine endeavor, upon the distinct understanding that the most scrupulous attention should be given to her correspondence: that every letter, no matter how inconsequential, should be answered quickly, fully, and courteously, with the questioner always encouraged to come again if any problem of whatever nature came to her.[23]

Bok put the *Journal*'s money where his mouth was. He hired a sizable staff of thirty-five editors to handle as many as twenty-five different service departments. He proclaimed in the magazine his editors' willingness to answer immediately any questions by mail. And he "encouraged and cajoled his readers to form the habit of looking upon his magazine as a great clearinghouse of information."[24]

Bok's service departments were more numerous and more specialized than Knapp's had been. One general column in Knapp's *Journal,* "All About the Home," became four in Bok's, on cooking, cleaning, decorating, and fancy needlework. Knapp and her staff had taken these columns for granted, viewing them as the natural outgrowth of women's practical interests. Bok, however, saw them as a vehicle for recruiting readers. Moreover, to the extent that readers had interacted with Knapp's service departments, that interaction was spontaneous, unstructured, and characterized by a sense of sharing. There was a genuine respect in Knapp's *Journal* for the opinions of readers, and there was a real give-and-take relationship between the magazine and its audience.

Bok's service departments, in contrast, came to focus more exclusively on answering reader questions. Bok not only took traditional service departments on housekeeping and made them into advice-dispensing columns; he also expanded the notion of service by creating specialized advice columns on living well in general. The first of these columns was "Side-Talks with Girls." Bok conceived the idea for the column as soon as he took over the *Journal,* in light of the "fact" that "in thousands of cases the American mother was not the confidante of her daughter."[25] He convinced Isabel Mallon, the "Bab" of his earlier syndicated letter, to write the column "Side-Talks with Girls," which she did, under the name Ruth Ashmore, for sixteen years.[26]

The evolution of the "Side-Talks" column is instructive. While the column addressed young women's most intimate questions about courtship, marriage, and young wifehood, it also quickly became removed and impersonal in its attempt to speak to as many concerns as possible. It soon gave short answers to questions that were not even printed in the magazine. An 1895 column, for example, ran fifty answers to unprinted questions, answers which included the following:

> To Rina—I think you are doing very wrong to meet the young man away from your home when your parents object to him so positively;
>
> To A. B.—It is quite proper to take a young man's arm after dark; and
>
> To J. F. B.—If your hair comes out and seems dead I should advise your having it shaved; in my experience this seems the one method of giving it new life.[27]

One senses the possible richness and pathos of the letters themselves.

Yet even as the column grew less and less personal, the *Journal* took increasing responsibility, behind the scenes, for at least some readers' problems. Bok claimed later that

SIDE TALKS WITH GIRLS

WHAT YOU WANT ✴ ✴ TO KNOW ✴ ✴

EDITED BY RUTH ASHMORE

This Department is conducted and edited by RUTH ASHMORE, who cheerfully invites questions touching any topic upon which her young women readers may desire help or information. Address all letters to RUTH ASHMORE, care of THE LADIES' HOME JOURNAL, Philadelphia, Pa.

IT was not that she did not know the absolute rules of deportment, but she wrote to ask what she should do under certain circumstances. Yet she wanted to be a polite girl and a considerate one, and she knew that it was the little courtesies that go to make up life as it should be. Now, I advise her in the first place, to ignore all rudeness. To the man who speaks impolitely to her or neglects to reply to her civil "good morning," an absolute and continued silence will be found the most desirable course to pursue. Usually people are taught gentleness by seeing it reflected; but when this is a young man who is so rude to you, then what I advise will be found most efficacious.

A FEW POLITE SUGGESTIONS

WHEN she is at a reception, or calling on a friend, it is not necessary to rise for an introduction to strangers, unless indeed one of them should be a very old lady, in which case age demands the acknowledgment of rising. And then, my dear girl, just remember that rushing around getting acquainted here, there and everywhere is neither refined nor polite; that a great eagerness for new friends usually suggests that, not being able to keep old friends, you are forced to search for new. It is all right for you to like to meet pleasant people; but it is all wrong for you to choose that the last new acquaintance shall be your most intimate friend. Then just trouble yourself a little not only to be thankful, but to express it in words, when any courtesy is shown you. A few "thank you's" will do more to make men and women like you, and the people who do service to you respect you, than almost anything else. Of course, you know that it is not necessary to introduce to each other people who happen to meet on the street, and neither is it necessary when you are in a parlor where there are a great many people, to make everybody known to everybody else, given a few judicious introductions and then let people take care of themselves. It is rather rude to conclude that nobody is capable of amusing him or herself unless you are to the fore; and no, brush that idea, with a number of other cobwebs, out of your brain. Scolding? Not a bit. Only just answering the questions you asked me, which another girl asked me, and two or three other girls asked me. I am making of them all, what might in Eastern countries, be called "A lump of delight."

THE FRIENDLESS GIRL

I DON'T mean by this the girl who is alone in the world, but I mean the girl who thinks that she cannot make friends, and who has become morbid and unhappy about it. In the first place friends are not blocked out like caramels; you may have no end of acquaintances—pleasant ones—but friends come with years. The two weeks' acquaintance is not the one with whom it is wise to be confidential, nor should you count upon her eternal fidelity. My dear girl, in this busy world so many people have so much to do that they cannot form many close friendships, and they choose the people they prefer. If you are absolutely friendless, in the sense that I mean, the fault must lie a little with you. Probably you are a wee bit selfish, and selfishness and friendship, like oil and water, do not mingle well. You claim that you love everybody. Now love is too precious a thing to give to every one. Suppose I tell you a little story: There were once two beautiful fox-terriers; when a tramp came to the house where they lived one of them rushed to meet the visitor, and waived caresses upon her, and quickly coiled itself in a most comfortable position on her lap. The other dog stood quietly by; if it were asked for a paw, it gave it, but always retreated and sat down beside its master; somebody said one day, speaking of the first: "How different this dog is from the other one; it is so much more affectionate!" "Oh, no," said their master, "you are very much mistaken; the dog who is so affectionate with you, gives its affection to every stranger it meets, the other one waits until it knows you well and then from that time on it is your friend, and is ready to greet you and show signs of its friendship. When I was ill, the dog that won out the affection were preferred to stay with strangers; the other one rested at he foot of my bed and refused to stir. When my sister sat there crying because of some trouble that had come to her, the dog that loved everybody went into another room, but the dog that went up to her, licked the tear-stained hands, looked up in her face with its soft brown eyes as if he were trying to say 'I'm your friend, don't worry.' This was a little bit of moral, and it means that while you can have plenty of pleasant acquaintances you will find that a few friends are best worth having; and that—I must repeat

SOMEBODY'S SWEETHEART

SHE is going to be married! She told me so the other day, and she said there were a good many things she did not know that I might tell her about. Bless her! I am sure she is somebody's sweet heart, and he is to be congratulated. She wants to know how she shall tell people she is engaged to be married. Well, if I were in her place I would have a little entertainment of some sort—a tea or an afternoon at-home—and, as my little lady stands by her mother's side, her mother can say "You must wish Dorothy all happiness. She is engaged to be married to Mr. Charles Brown." Then, if this is too much trouble let her mother write a few letters to her friends telling them of her engagement, and not imposing any secrecy, and just give Charlie permission to say to one or two men, "I am sure you will be glad to know that Miss Dorothy Vernon has promised to be my wife." And after you have taken either of these methods of announcing the engagement there will be no danger whatever of the whole town in which you live not hearing about it. Then, too, Dorothy wants to know—you see she is a wise little woman—is going to make a home for herself—how she shall mark her napery. The prettiest way is to duplicate her own method of writing her initials, in letters about two inches high, with white cotton. On the sheets these go just in the middle, below the upper hem; on the pillow slips they should be in the centre of the upper side, in the middle beyond the hem. On the napkins their placing depends very much on the size. They must be so placed that when the napkin is ironed out, folded to a large square, and then folded over to a long shape, the initials will be just in the centre. The same rule applies to their placing on the table-cloth, that is about the position. Spread the table-cloth on the table and let the initials come where they would be just beyond the hostess' plate. I have answered all of Dorothy's questions, I hope to her satisfaction. And now that I am all through I want to say to her " Dear girl, I trust that you will be happy with a home, a something that you will never be, however, unless you make the man you have married a happy husband, and, for this you must work and pray. God bless you and teach you to do what is right."

THE GIRL TO BE AVOIDED

SHE is the girl who takes you off in one corner and tells you things that you wouldn't repeat to your mother. She is the girl who is anxious to have you join a party, which is to be "a dead secret"; and at which, because people are very free and easy, you are uncomfortable and wish you were at home. She is the girl who tries to induce you, "just for fun," to smoke a cigarette, or to take a glass of wine, and you don't know, and possibly she doesn't, that many of the sinners of to-day committed their first sins "just for fun." She is the girl who persuades you that to stay at home and dare and love your own, to help mother and to have your pleasures at home and where the home people can see them, is stupid and tiresome; and that spending the afternoon walking up and down the street, looking at the windows and the people, is "just delightful." She is the girl who persuades you that slang is witty, that a loud dress that attracts attention is "stylish," and that your own modest gowns are dowdy and undesirable. She doesn't know, nor do you, how many women have gone to destruction because of their love for fine clothes. She is the girl who persuades you that to be on very familiar terms with three or four young men is an evidence of your charms and fascination, instead of looking upon it as an outward visible sign of your perfect folly. She is the girl who persuades you that it is a very smart thing to be referred to as "a gay girl." She is very, very much mistaken. And of all others she is the girl who, no matter how hard she may try to make you believe in her, is the girl to be avoided.

FOR THE MUSICAL GIRL

THE girl who is going to win the prize for music is interested in knowing about some desirable books on music. So a kindly woman, thoughtful of my girls, has sent me a list of good books on music and musicians. They are: "Music and Morals," by H. R. Haweis, and "My Musical Memories," by the same author. Then there is the "Life of Chopin," by Liszt. "Music Study in Germany," by Amy Fay, will tell how the girls who went abroad to study music, worked and succeeded. The "Life of Mendelssohn" by F. Hiller; "Mendelssohn's Letters" and "The Mendelssohn Family," by Sebastian Hensel, are all interesting books; and, of course, Fillmore's "History of Pianoforte Music," as well as the "Autobiography of Rubenstein," will be found at once useful and pleasant reading. There's a list of musical books that ought to delight the music-loving girl. And

[o]ut of the work of Ruth Ashmore . . . there grew a class of cases of the most confidential nature. These cases, distributed all over the country, called for special investigation and personal contact. Bok selected Mrs. Lyman Abbott for this piece of delicate work, and through the wide acquaintance of her husband, she was enabled to reach, personally, every case in every locality, and bring personal help to bear on it. These cases mounted into the hundreds, and the good accomplished through this quiet channel cannot be overestimated.[28]

Bok and his staff were genuinely concerned about their readers, but Bok's concern clearly went beyond helpful to become didactic and intervening. The idea that a magazine could and should take responsibility for actually solving the personal problems of its readers suggests the extent to which Bok thought the *Journal* could help.

This "quiet channel" of intervention is the most extreme example of Bok's paternalistic ethos, but it underscores the fact that advice to all *Journal* readers was becoming increasingly direct and prescriptive. And this advice was not limited to the youngest *Journal* readers. Older women were given spiritual counsel in a column called "Heart to Heart Talks." Ministers and former U.S. presidents were engaged to lecture women about their role. And Bok's editorials frequently bordered on dogmatic.

Bok was pedantic no matter whom he addressed: his wide range of writings published outside the *Journal,* speaking to men and women, young and old, rich and poor alike, featured without exception the same patronizing tone. And Bok would continue to employ in the *Journal* the same didactic approach he used with women even as he increasingly addressed men. If Bok's preachiness was not consciously sexist, however, it set a tone for the *Journal* that eventually made the magazine a sexist publication. One editorial alone, for example, included the following pronouncements:

> What are often considered indignities suffered by women are nothing more nor less than the natural results of their own behavior. . . . We receive just what we invite in this world;

> The married woman's Platonic friend should be her husband, it is unfair to him to have any other assume or hold the position that is his by right; and

> It seems to me that if some of our American women would trouble themselves less about municipal and suffrage problems, which men will take care of, and devote their much-flaunted capabilities for municipal executive ability toward the solution of the servant-girl problem, which is theirs and theirs only, it would be better for our American life.[29]

Bok lectured, scolded, and patronized women. We will explore this pattern further when we look at the content of Bok's *Journal* more thoroughly in chapter 4.

THE LADIES' HOME JOURNAL

complete.

Vol. VII, No. 1.   PHILADELPHIA, DECEMBER, 1889.   Yearly Subscription One Dollar.
Single Copies 10 Cents.

Contents

Dark night her tent once more unfurled, on Power's first-century
home,
Upon the marble heart of the world—the great, grand city of Rome.
And hushed at last were the chariot-tires, and still the sandalled feet,
And dimmed the palace window-fires, on many a noble street.
And to a roof a maiden came, with eyes as angels love;
And looked up as the spheres of flame that softly gleamed above.

The voice of the star she understood; its glorious meaning knew;
And all her dreams of woman's good, seemed likely to come true.
And when again the twilight gray was brightened by the morn,
Within a manger far away, the infant Christ was born.

· CURTIS · PUBLISHING · COMPANY · PHILADELPHIA ·

The magazine to which Bok came was stable and editorially well-established. He inherited 440,000 full-paying subscribers. This was a significant figure in an era when many publishers were still using cut-rates and free copies to move their magazines. As noted in chapter 2, Louisa and Cyrus Curtis were especially eager to have an experienced businessman at the helm, since they had just doubled the magazine's price as well as its size and added a cover. Bok and Curtis had their work cut out for them in their attempt to push circulation figures even higher. The price-doubling led to a drop in subscriptions. Curtis had incurred huge debts in promoting the *Journal,* debts exceeding $300,000 per year. Curtis invested all he had in advertising his "new" magazine, and then he borrowed from banks in order to invest more.

The *Journal* under Bok grew bigger and more complicated in every way. Curtis's drive for increased circulation and advertising revenues intensified during the first years of his partnership with Bok. He continued to work to expand subscriptions within the *Journal*'s traditional audience, married middle-class women with children, adding an integrated, national network of some thirty thousand subscription solicitors to his regular massive advertising campaigns.[30] Curtis tried to broaden the audience at the same time, however, trying to attract some upper-middle-class readers as well. For example, in 1891 he sent the prospectus for the coming year's *Journal* to all the names listed in the social registers of San Francisco, Boston, and Milwaukee.[31]

An early advertising textbook testifies to some success in promoting the image of the *Journal* as a quality magazine. The textbook contrasted two displays for women's stationery. Crane's better letter paper, for women of "taste and refinement," was advertised in a group of magazines including *Scribner's,* the *Atlantic,* and the *Ladies' Home Journal,* while Eaton's lower-grade, "self-respecting paper" display appeared in *Good Housekeeping* and the *Woman's Home Companion.*[32]

An analysis of Curtis record books reveals that by the early twentieth century the *Journal* was mainly directed at families having moderate middle-class incomes from $1200 to $2500. Some attention in addition was given to the higher class with incomes from $2500 to $5000.[33] In his customarily direct manner, Bok testified in one of his early issues of the *Journal* that he was writing to two classes, "the rich and the . . . great majority," the latter referring to the middle class. Bok noted with little regret that the *Journal* could not reach the poor, remarking with characteristic confidence that "other men are helping them."[34] One can reasonably conclude that the magazine was written for the middle classes, with a nod given to upper-middle-class tastes and interests.[35]

The *Journal* nodded at the upper middle class, but it pursued younger and male readers unequivocally. While Curtis took the initiative for broadening the *Journal*'s class base, Bok was in large part responsible for encouraging younger women and men of all ages to take advantage of what the *Journal* offered. As noted earlier, Bok's second issue of the *Journal* featured "Side-Talks," a column just for girls. After that the magazine regularly spoke to six-teen- to twenty-five-year-old women in this and other forums.

Bok's most striking attempt to broaden the audience, however, involved not women but men. A letter quoted in chapter 1, from the husband of "busy, bustling Martha," suggests that some men may have been acquainted with the *Ladies' Home Journal* during Knapp's tenure, but she and her staff made no serious attempt to reach out to them. As early as June of 1891, in contrast, Bok testified that men were reading the *Journal,* and he thereafter regularly referred to the growing numbers of male *Journal* readers.[36] The *Journal* in these years did receive a significant amount of mail from women and men of all ages. The "Side-Talks" column attracted thousands of letters from girls and women each year, and Bok regularly responded to letters from boys and men in his editorial column. He even instituted three letter-answering columns for boys and men between 1890 and 1900: "Side-Talks with Boys," "Problems of Young Men," and "What Men are Asking."[37]

Cause and effect are not easy to determine here. Bok testifies that younger women and men began to write to the *Journal* for help, and that the *Journal* responded accordingly. As demonstrated earlier, however, it was characteristic of Bok to stress helping, in order to build a larger and more loyal circle of *Journal* readers. It certainly seems likely that Bok saw younger readers and male readers as two new groups that could broaden the *Journal* audience. He capitalized on that potential by instituting new columns targeted specifically for them.

And the *Journal*'s audience grew. In 1891 a three-month campaign to in-crease circulation yielded more than two hundred thousand new subscribers. This brought circulation to more than six hundred thousand and overloaded the *Journal* operation to the point where it had to stop encouraging new subscrip-tions in order to catch up.[38] By July of 1893 the *Journal* had over five hundred thousand regular subscribers and, in addition, sold almost three hundred thou-sand newsstand copies every month.[39]

The staff for the *Journal* grew accordingly between 1890 and 1900. Knapp had led an editorial staff of three during most of her tenure. By October of 1890 Bok was editing the *Journal* in association with a staff of sixteen, including Mrs. Lyman Abbott, Ruth Ashmore (Isabel Mallon), Margaret Bottome, Kate Upson Clarke, Emma M. Hooper, Mrs. Louisa Knapp, Mary L. Knapp, Eben E. Rexford, Elizabeth Robinson Scovil, Reverend T. DeWitt Talmadge, and Kate Tannatt Woods.[40] It is interesting to note that the Mary L. Knapp in this list is the Curtises' daughter and Bok's wife. Mary Louise Curtis Bok chose to write under her mother's maiden name, Knapp, which was not a name she used otherwise. She thereby identified with her mother rather than her husband or her father in this professional setting. By 1892 Bok's staff had expanded to

WHAT MEN  ARE ASKING

BY WALTER GERMAIN

All inquiries must give full name and address of the writer. Correspondents inclosing stamp or addressed stamped envelope will be answered by mail.

LAWRENCE—Dinner Invitations should always be promptly acknowledged and addressed to the hostess.

T. W. B.—Proper Dress for Funerals. If possible always wear black at a funeral, or dark colors.

WEST RIVER—The Plaid in Your Necktie, which you describe as blue and black with a narrow red stripe running both ways, is the "Elliot" plaid.

G.—Cleaning Gloves. The unpleasant odor of benzine from your freshly-cleaned gloves will disappear if you place them in the air for a while.

G. R. S.—Introductions. The gentleman should be introduced to the lady in some such form as the following: "Mrs. ——, will you allow me to present my friend, Mr. ——?"

MASTER L.—The Eton Jacket is usually considered the dress coat for a very young boy. It is worn with black waistcoat and long trousers, white dress shirt and small black tie.

T. F. C.—A Christmas Gift from a young man to a young girl should consist of nothing beyond a book, some flowers, a basket of fruit or a box of candy. In books select some edition of a work which you are sure she does not possess—a volume of her favorite poet, for instance.

PEQUOD—Fashion in Evening Coats. The notch, and not the shawl, collar continues the fashion this winter. The material for dress suits is still the diagonal and unfinished worsted. Stripes or braid may be used on the trousers. The velvet collar on the evening coat has gone out of style.

F. B. G.—Marking Wedding Presents. Silver wedding presents are marked with the initials of the bride. Wedding presents should always be sent to the bride. It makes no difference, even though you should never have met the bride-elect. The sending of a present to her is the highest compliment you can pay her future husband, your friend.

L. A. D.—White Waistcoats will be worn this winter with evening dress, and for all formal occasions after dark, such as balls, dances, dinners, etc. They will be double-breasted and cut low in a U shape. Black dress waistcoats will be worn as much as ever, except by men who wish to vary the monotony of the prevailing fashion in evening attire.

J. L. B.—Gloves are usually worn by men on the street and in church. In making a call it is now customary to remove one glove, that on the right hand, before entering the drawing-room. At a formal entertainment, however, gloves are kept on. If your hostess is gloved you should be gloved, and if not you should remove your right glove before offering to shake hands with her.

E. J.—Breaking Engagements. Engagements are very serious matters, and should not be entered upon lightly. Mere lovers' differences should not be the cause of breaking off an engagement, although if both the young man and the young woman find that it is impossible to live in harmony, and that an unhappy married life is likely to result, the sooner the engagement is broken the better.

G. R.—Etiquette of Letters. You should begin a letter to a young lady, "My Dear Miss Browne," and not "Dear Miss Browne." And you should address the letter, "Miss Clara Alden Browne," unless she is the eldest sister, when "Miss Browne" would suffice. Writing-paper should be plain, smaller in size than the sample sent.

F. E. N.—Attire for a Clergyman. A clergyman, no matter what his denomination, should always be neatly attired in black. Evening dress for a clergyman consists of the regulation clerical frock coat, an ordinary frock coat or a black cutaway, with waistcoat and trousers to match. If he is High Church he wears the clerical stock and collar; otherwise a plain, white lawn tie, arranged in a simple bow. He may wear a watch-chain, but no other jewelry.

EXETER—Ballroom Etiquette. A man should not ask a girl to dance unless he has first been presented to her. He may ask his hostess, or a patroness (if it be a large public or semi-public affair), or a mutual friend to make the introduction. It is usually the custom for those who have gone down to dinner together to be partners in the first dance, but there is no fixed rule on the subject. As to the other dances, one is at liberty to choose one's partners.

J. W. J.—Cutaway and Sack Coats. The black cutaway, single-breasted, four-buttoned coat will continue to be fashionable this winter. Rough materials in check goods are preferable to diagonals. In colored tweeds and Scotch materials the cutaway is called a morning coat. It is becoming to thin men, but will not be used as much this season for business and every-day wear as the sack coat. Sack suits in gray cheviot and Scotch goods are preferred to those of brown in the same materials.

INQUIRER—No Wedding Cards. You say that you cannot afford to issue wedding cards. As you will have read in the September issue of THE LADIES' HOME JOURNAL, in the article on "The Groom's Part in the Wedding," it is the family of the bride who should bear the expense of invitations, etc. But in order to avoid this outlay for them you and your fiancée might say to any friends you may meet, "We are to be married at the Church of ——, on such a day and hour. There are no invitations, but we would like you to be there." And to those whom you do not happen to meet send word, or even write if you are anxious to have them present at the ceremony.

H. L. M.—Shaving. Every man should learn to shave himself. A very fair razor may be purchased for one dollar, and an excellent one for one dollar and a half. The best strop is the plain leather, rough on one side and smooth on the other. A shaving-stick of soap, which will cost little, will last nearly a year. In stropping a razor be careful to keep the back of it to the strop. Razors should be stropped before and after using, and they should never be put away until quite dry and absolutely clean. Always shave with the grain of the skin, and not against it. Luke-warm water is better than either very hot or cold. The lather should be well spread over the face and well rubbed in before the shaving is begun. A little cologne water will be found refreshing to bathe the face with after shaving.

F. A. D.—Etiquette of Calling. A man calls by invitation on a young married couple. The first call, which is naturally more or less formal, should never last more than fifteen minutes. When you know people well you may make longer visits. In the country, where distances are considerable, even a first call is much less formal, and you may, with propriety, stay a longer time, but never stay too long. Always manage to leave when you are making yourself most agreeable. It will be a compliment to your new friends if you ask them to allow your mother to call on them. With a young lady suggest your sisters before your mother, as the latter request might seem as if you had matrimonial intentions, which may not be the case. If these people, without reason, should not return your mother's or sisters' calls I would keep away from them. (2) Recognition on the Street. A woman has the privilege of acknowledging or disclaiming acquaintances. She should bow first. If a male friend of yours is with a lady whom you do not know, and you should meet them on the street or in a public place, it is his duty to bow to you.

THE PRACTICAL HOUSEKEEPER

—EDITED ᴬⁿᵈ CONDUCTED—
ᵇʸ Mᴿˢ LOUISA KNAPP

SOME RELIABLE RECIPES.

GATHERED FROM THE NOTE-BOOKS OF EXPERI-ENCED HOUSE-WIVES FOR THE BENEFIT OF THE JOURNAL SISTERS.

PRESERVED ORANGE PEEL.

Weigh the oranges whole, and add sugar pound for pound. Peel the oranges neatly and cut the rind into narrow shreds. Boil until tender, changing the water twice, and re-plenishing with hot from the kettle. Squeeze the strained juice of the oranges over the sugar; let this heat to a boil; put in the shreds and boil twenty minutes.

Lemon peel can be preserved in the same way, allowing more sugar.
MARION HARLAND.

A VERY GOOD SPONGE CAKE.

Four eggs, one cup of flour (sifted), one cup of sugar (granulated), the juice of half a large lemon, or that of a small one; the grated rind of a lemon. Beat the whites of the eggs until they are stiff and dry, then add the sugar, beating well: then add the well-beaten yolks, then the rind and juice of the lemon; then stir in, very lightly, the sifted flour. Bake in a moderate oven.
MRS. STEPHEN DEE.

DAINTY COOKIES.

Two cups sugar, one cup butter, one cup cold water, pinch of soda dissolved in water, one teaspoonful vanilla, rolled thin as possible.

NUTRITIOUS CORN CAKE.

One and three-quarters cup of Indian meal, one pint of sour milk, one teaspoonful of soda, a little salt, one tablespoonful of sugar, one egg beaten light. Soda dissolved in sour milk, beaten until it foams, and baked in two shallow pans; quick oven. MRS. NATHAN D.

AUNT BETSEY'S GRAHAM PUDDING.

Two and one-half cups of graham flour, one-half cup of water or milk, one cup of molasses, one egg, a little salt, one heaping teaspoonful soda. Steam two hours. Eat with a sauce.

CORNA'S WHITE CAKE.

One and a half-cup of sugar, one-half cup of butter, one-half cup of sweet milk, two cups of flour, whites of five eggs, two teaspoonfuls baking powder.

BLACK CAKE.

One cup of sugar, one cup of butter, one-half cup of molasses, one-half cup of butter-milk or sour milk, one cup of raisins or English currants; all kinds of spices to taste; two eggs, one teaspoonful soda; flour enough to make it stiff like cake.

GRAHAM GEMS.

One cupful of graham flour, one tablespoon-ful of butter, one tablespoonful of sugar, two-thirds cup of buttermilk, one egg well beaten, scant teaspoonful soda; beat well; grease tins and have them hot when you add the batter. Bake in a quick oven.

SANDWICH CAKE.

Two cups of sugar, three-fourths cup of butter, one cup of sweet milk, two teaspoonfuls cream tartar, one teaspoon soda, two and a half cups of flour, whites of five eggs.

Take out four tablespoonfuls of the mixture, add one-half cup of molasses, one-half cup of flour, one-half cup of raisins; citron, and figs and spice to taste. Bake in square tins. One layer of the dark, two of the light, put together like jelly cake. M. B. E.

SOME PRACTICAL DISHES.

BEAN SOUP.

One small beef soup-bone, one quart of white beans soaked over night, four medium size onions, two heads of celery, four quarts of water; salt and pepper; simmer all together for five or six hours, then strain through a course sieve. Return to the stove until hot. Serve.

TOMATO SOUP.

One quart of tomatoes fresh or canned equal quantity of water; cook until soft, then strain; butter the size of an egg, salt and pepper, one-half cup of rice well cooked.

BAKED VEAL CUTLET.

One and half pound veal cutlet laid in a well-buttered roasting pan, with a cup of water to prevent burning, over which spread a dressing made as follows: two cupfuls of bread crumbs, two onions chopped fine, two well beaten eggs, butter size of an egg, salt and pepper; mix well, lay a tin cover on top and bake half an hour, remove the lid and allow it to brown.

FRIED OYSTERS.

Lay oysters in linen cloth for two hours; dip them in egg and then in wheat flour; fry brown in lard and bacon; don't float them.

CORN OYSTERS.

One pint of corn, one egg well beaten, one small teacup of flour, one-half gill cream, one teaspoon salt. Fry brown like pan-cakes; to be served with tomato catsup.

RACHEL'S SUET PUDDING.

One cup of chopped suet, one cup of raisins, one cup of sweet milk, one teaspoonful soda; stir stiff with flour. Steam three hours.

ORANGE CAKE.

Beat the whites of three and the yolks of five eggs, separately. Stir to a cream two cups of sugar, and one-half cup of butter, then add beaten eggs, one-half cup of cold water, two and one-half cups of flour, two teaspoon-fuls of baking powder, grated rind of one orange and all the juice, except one table-spoonful. Bake in two large square biscuit tins.

Filling for Orange Cake.—Whites of two eggs saved from the cake, one tablespoonful of orange juice, two small cups of pulverized sugar.

FIG CAKE.

One cup of sugar, one-half cup of butter, two eggs, one-half cup of milk, two table-spoonfuls of baking powder, two cups of flour; this makes three layers.

Filling.—One pound of figs, one cup of water; stew gently until soft, then chop fine, add two tablespoonfuls of pulverized sugar, spread between layers and frost the top.

Frosting.—White of one egg, two table-spoonfuls of cold water, one-half teaspoonful of vanilla, pulverized sugar stirred in until stiff; do not beat the egg.
LOUISE M. KNIGHT.

Five beautiful Baby faces are artistically grouped in a charming Albertype that will delight every woman who loves babies or loves a good picture. Send a 2-cent stamp to Wells Richardson & Co.. Burlington, Vt., and get this beautiful picture to adorn your home.

A USEFUL INVENTION.

Read the advertisement of the Family Buttonhole Attachment.

twenty-five, and by 1900 a staff of thirty-eight edited and headed various departments of the *Journal.* Knapp's stable of contributors had ranged from twelve to forty-five writers a year during her six years as editor. Bok, in contrast, oversaw the contributions of an average of one hundred different writers a year between 1890 and 1900.

Bok's list of contributing writers featured more of a gender mix than had Knapp's. The number of women writers for the magazine under Bok declined from seventy-two in 1890 to sixty-three in 1900, while the number of male contributors increased from twenty-four to thirty-four. In addition, the gender composition of the magazine's staff changed significantly. In contrast to Knapp's arrangement, Bok's "female experts" tended to edit standard service columns and household departments, while men contributed the up-front, livelier features. Service departments were the backbone of the magazine, and they set an important tone for the *Journal* as an advice-giving institution. But it was in the magazine's feature articles that opinions were most frequently offered on issues of broader interest to *Journal* readers. The fact that men wrote more and more of these features, although certainly not all of them, meant that men were increasingly addressing *Journal* readers on substantive questions, and that Bok's *Journal* did not have the gender homogeneity that Knapp's had featured. As we shall see in chapter 4, the resulting "gendered" aspect of the magazine as a text had a significant impact on its tone and, in turn, on its relationship with its readers.

The editorial staff was not the only group in the *Journal* organization that saw expansion during these years; by the time of the magazine's tenth birthday in 1893 the Curtis-Bok operation employed over four hundred workers.[41] Many of these were employees who performed various clerical and technical tasks for the company. In 1892 Curtis took a step that signaled the *Journal*'s development into a modern business enterprise. He hired John Adams Thayer, a typography expert, to serve as general advertising manager for the magazine. Thayer oversaw the work of advertising solicitors as well as that of an advertising copywriter and an artist. The copywriter and artist were responsible for creating advertisements that Curtis and his solicitors could submit to advertisers for approval.[42] This meant that Curtis's staff could join him in setting standards for the larger new enterprise of national advertising. *Journal* advertisements were soon noted for their generous use of white space, and by 1899 about half of the magazine's advertisements were illustrated. In November of 1893 Bok reported that the *Journal* turned away up to a dozen columns of advertising per month due to its own strict standards of quality.[43] Curtis and Bok's *Journal* had become a powerhouse in the industry, employing its own group of experts and placing advertisements in its pages only on its own terms.

By June of 1891 the operation was stable enough to support the creation of the Curtis Publishing Company, which was organized on the basis of a stock

3.h. Mary Louise Curtis Bok. Courtesy Charles Scribner's Sons.

capital of $500,000. Curtis retained nine-tenths of the stock. The remainder was held by company employees. By February of 1892 Bok owned the second largest amount of Curtis stock and was vice-president of the company. In the spring of that year the Publishing Company expanded into a new building on Arch Street in Philadelphia. The new building housed the *Journal*'s own eighteen printing presses, allowing for cheaper but higher quality printing of the magazine. By 1900, when the *Journal* operation had expanded yet again into a new building, the magazine was no longer an uncertain journalistic enterprise. Knapp, Curtis, and Bok had made the *Ladies' Home Journal* into an integrated, independent, big business.

The Curtises and Bok had joined forces in a personal way as well. Despite the fact that Mary Louise Curtis was only thirteen years old when her mother decided to leave the magazine's editorship, there is some evidence that the Curtises hired Edward Bok with the hope that someday he would become their daughter's suitor, as well as the new editor. It is indeed the case that, six years later, when Mary Louise was nineteen years old, she married Edward, who was fourteen years her senior.[44] The marriage was not a happy one, but it did serve to keep the Curtis Publishing Company in the Curtis family for many years.

Edward Bok thereby established himself as editor and the *Ladies' Home Journal* as an ever more lucrative publication in quick order. As I have shown, Bok instituted in these years the condescending message that "women need help." The tone and specific character of this message would help to further the mutually reinforcing relationship of the gendering of commerce and the commercialization of gender. But Bok would not be in full control of his readers and their reading of his magazine. Nor would he ever be in full control of the messages of his magazine. Let us turn now to those specific messages.

4

Mixed Messages in a Commercial Package: The Content of the *Journal,* 1890–1900

Perhaps the most difficult of all the tasks facing both Louisa Knapp and Edward Bok—who were, of course, products of their own particular gender socialization and ideology—was interpreting gender norms and gender relations to others, their readers. Bok and Knapp had to present, in a popular forum, images of femininity and masculinity with which a large number of readers could identify. Their task was to translate social behaviors and attitudes into a set of resonant cultural images, for, as one analyst writes, "our culture consists of the meanings we make of our social experience and of our social relations, and therefore the sense we have of our 'selves.' "[1] Although the *Journal* represented only one forum for making and presenting cultural meaning, it was a critical one. While gendered cultural meanings were produced for and by individuals in their families of origin, peer relationships, and marital relationships, and in their homes, schools, workplaces, neighborhoods, and communities, the gendered meanings conveyed in the *Journal* were important in a different way. They were published, and published in a national periodical.

Comparing them reveals that Bok's views were more conservative than Knapp's. But given the complexity of the gender issues at hand, even Bok's *Journal* featured a relatively broad range of views. Bok later described the magazine he had hoped to mold at the outset of his editorial tenure:

> [It was to be] a magazine that would be an authoritative clearing-house for all the problems confronting women in the home, that brought itself closely into contact with those problems and tried to solve them in an entertaining and efficient way; and yet a magazine of uplift and inspiration: a magazine, in other words, that would give light and leading in the woman's world.[2]

But Bok's *Ladies' Home Journal* was much more a reflector of its culture than it was a magazine of "light and leading." The magazine is more accurately characterized as a commercial package that included some images and views and excluded others.

There are several reasons for this characterization. First, Bok was the consummate businessman. Always a pragmatist as well as an idealist, Bok knew that if the magazine was to sell it had to combine the "give them what they ought to hear" and "give them what they want to hear" orientations. Second, in contrast to Knapp's magazine, where the messages were relatively cohesive, messages in Bok's magazine were more mixed, since he was a man speaking to women, and since his contributors were a more heterogeneous group than hers. In addition, where Knapp had approved of many of the changes middle-class women were undergoing, Bok did not. Finally, cultural definitions of femininity were clearly contested in these years, and it was not easy to choose among the ideologies and images of True Womanhood, Real Womanhood, and New Womanhood.[3]

These circumstances and the fact that it was Bok who was the editor, made the *Journal* a gendered text of a particular kind. Its messages, which had to be modern as well as traditional if the magazine was to sell, were mixed to the point of contradiction at times. These contradictions highlight some major gaps between Bok's views and those of many of his readers. These gaps in turn raise the question of the relationship between Bok's *Journal* and the gender construction of his readers. While the magazine does not appear to have influenced readers in the direct way Bok hoped it might, a fundamental shift in the definition of womanhood during his early tenure would prove to be critical to middle-class women's gender construction in the long run.

Edward Bok's *Ladies' Home Journal* was "modern." The technology used to produce the magazine had become increasingly sophisticated. The *Journal* doubled in size in 1889 from sixteen to thirty-two pages, and it averaged fifty pages by 1900. It sported a cover for the first time in 1889; later, these covers, along with art layouts and advertisements, would feature color to great effect. Advertisements in the magazine became more modern as they touted national trademarked brands. Much of the rest of the magazine's content was distinctly modern, as well. Bok and his contributors encouraged readers to educate themselves for domesticity, to use labor-saving devices, to take control of family finances, and to be good shoppers. In short, women were to make themselves into modern domestic professionals.

But "modern" did not mean "advanced." This was a crucial distinction for Bok. Modern women learned new things in order to improve their domestic sphere. Advanced women simply tried to escape it. Modern women went into the public sphere only as their moral influence was required. Advanced women claimed the public sphere as their own, aggressively seeking new opportunities to selfishly gratify their own whims. One of Bok's early editorials paid lip service to women's progress, citing some new educational and business opportunities. But Bok went on more characteristically to describe women's truly impressive achievements in the nineteenth century, the "first century of woman":

> She has created the home, and it is her monument. She has refined man, and her influence, through him, has permeated every industry, art and profession. Woman's power is now felt in almost every great movement or reform where

home, morals and education are affected. . . . Men in public life are turning more and more to the women of their firesides for counsel. And it is in her position by the hearthstone where lies woman's greatest mission. As she has established the home and fireside, so let her maintain them, their brightness, their purity and their resulting influences. The realm of domestic statesmanship is hers.[4]

Bok neatly summarizes here the ideology of separate spheres and the attendant Cult of True Womanhood, to which he largely subscribed. In Bok's scheme the two spheres were clearly demarcated, and separate from each other, with women assigned to the private and men to the public. Knapp, as we saw in chapter 2, had collapsed the sphere metaphor completely, and she and her writers subscribed mainly to the more progressive ideology of Real Womanhood. Bok, on the other hand, consciously reverted to the separate sphere, private versus public configuration. Bok did not fight progress altogether, but he supported only those new activities that would enable women to improve themselves within the parameters of the middle-class women's role, which, as noted above, Bok defined as "domestic statesmanship."

Building on Bok's reverence for domesticity, and on his anxiety about changes in some middle-class women's lives, the *Journal* of the 1890s featured an elaborate, extensive discussion about women's role. Most *Journal* writers during Bok's early tenure agreed that it was a time of restlessness and discontent among middle-class women. Bok asserted early in his editorship that he supported women's advancement, but he worried that women might be advancing in the wrong way:

> I am an ardent believer in woman's progress, in her advancement toward the highest position in life which she is capable of adorning, and I yield to no one in my admiration for woman's onward march. But sometimes I begin to wonder if woman is not progressing in the wrong direction, if she is not drifting away from that home anchorage for which God intended her. There is no mission so great or urgent which justifies a woman from leaving a home in which is her husband and her children.[5]

Rutherford B. Hayes, by then out of the presidency for ten years, noted in 1891 with the same regret that "in America the opportunity and influence of women grows wider and wider. Whether we like this tendency or not, we cannot fail to see it."[6]

Robert J. Burdette, who had also written for Knapp's *Journal,* was one of the few *Journal* writers in Bok's time to view middle-class women's expanded activity positively. He opened an 1892 column entitled "Woman Yesterday and Today" by observing that women earlier had been considered a race of beings altogether different from men, but now, they could do anything they tried.[7] Woman had lost something through this process, Burdette admit-

4.a. Humorist and *Journal* Contributor Robert J. Burdette.

ted, most notably a measure of solicitousness from men. But never would she exchange her independence for deference and helplessness. Burdette closed his column by citing the concept of spheres as irreverently as Knapp had in the *Journal* earlier. " 'Woman's sphere,' whatever that was," he wrote, "has almost disappeared."[8]

Bok and most other *Journal* writers were threatened by just such notions, and they regularly felt compelled to assert the basis for traditional gender roles. In 1895 the Reverend DeWitt Talmadge, in his "Under the Study Lamp" column asserted the holiness of the sexual division of labor. "Male and Female Created He Them," Talmadge intoned. The Reverend Charles Parkhurst, a prominent conservative minister and a regular presence on the late nineteenth-century lecture circuit, carried Talmadge's notion farther. Parkhurst preached that God had not only created men and women to operate in different spheres, but to operate in spheres as different from the other's as possible. The whole point of parental and societal nurture and discipline, in Parkhurst's view, was to make the differences between manhood and womanhood greater, not lesser. Some "rights women," Parkhurst declared, had become "Andromaniacs" who wished to "minimize distinctions by which manhood and womanhood

4.b. Talmadge's Column for the *Journal.*

are differentiated," and who demonstrated an "easy-going inappreciation of differences."[9]

Thus Bok marshalled religious forces in his magazine, calling on ministers to assert the God-ordained basis of traditional gender roles, and to chastise women who dared to challenge God's plan. In so doing Bok harkened back to the Cult of True Womanhood with its emphasis on women's piety, purity, submissiveness, and domesticity. Also evident is the fact that these "natural" roles required extensive elaboration and careful socialization in order to ensure their continuation. Bok and many of his contributors were very nervous about the cracks they were seeing in the ideology of True Womanhood. Bok's *Journal* featured much more religious and moral commentary than Knapp's, and that commentary focused almost exclusively on keeping women in their place.

Ruth Ashmore (Isabel Mallon) employed religious arguments as well when she addressed for the *Journal* in these years another major topic, "The Restlessness of the Age." Ashmore stressed the religious foundation of sex roles, writing that "when the good God was arranging the human pegs into their abiding places, He did not put the round ones in the square holes, but when a woman rushes away from the work that is laid out for her, she finds that she is wrongly situated, and she wears herself out worrying over this. Then she is old and tired when she should be young and fresh."[10] Thus, restlessness in Ashmore's view was the result of women trying too hard to change.

Restlessness among women was a regular theme in magazines of the day, and it is an area that underscores gaps between at least some *Journal* readers, on the one hand, and Bok and his contributors on the other. Early in the 1890s a reader introduced the possibility that restlessness among women caused, rather than resulted from, changes women were experiencing. Mrs. Smith, a former "school ma'am" from Michigan, testified to this different kind of restlessness in a moving letter to the "Just Among Ourselves" column in 1891:

> Fate—and John Smith—seem to have relegated me to a very uncongenial sphere of life, that of housekeeper. I want more time to cultivate my own mind for the sake of my husband and children. I do not want them to grow away from me, and yet I want them to have all the advantages possible to grow— physically, mentally, morally, and spiritually; but oh, I can't bear to be sacrificed, body and soul, in order to bring about these desirable things, and yet, it seems as though I must. Are any of you situated as I am? And, if so, do you sometimes get rebellious? I dream . . . that I am prostrate on the floor of my kitchen. My arms are pinioned to my sides by flat-irons; on my head is a skillet; my largest and heaviest iron kettle nearly crushes the breath out of my breast, while the poker, shovel, tongs, and carving knives dance around me like demons threatening to stab my eyes out.[11]

In response after response to this moving testimony, other readers assured Mrs. Smith that "we all get restless." Letters referring to Mrs. Smith's unhappy situation were printed over a period of ten months, and readers offered many solutions to the problems Mrs. Smith had cited. One suggested that she trade child care with another mother, hence gaining some time to pursue her own interests. This suggestion prompted the editor of the column in turn to propose the development of a visiting nurse profession. Such nurses could go into the home to relieve women of responsibility for their children occasionally, Mrs. Lyman Abbott suggested.[12]

Bok and most *Journal* writers viewed restlessness as the result of change rather than of tradition, however, and they reacted in two ways. One was to assert that women needed to limit their activities, to lower their expectations, and to return to the supposed calm of their mothers' and grandmothers' lives. This view was based on the recognition that women's lives had changed rather substantially and that such change was disruptive and produced strain for women.

The second response undercut the first. Despite regular references to thoroughgoing change for women, and to the pervasiveness of a restless feeling among middle-class women, Bok and some of his writers occasionally used the rhetorical device of intimating that actually women were not restless at all. When a reader asked Bok in 1895 if she was correct in inferring that he had "no sympathy with the 'new woman,' the woman who is restless," Bok replied that he could not be sympathetic because "there is no 'new woman.' "[13] Bok may have hoped that this rhetoric would be effective in turning women away from change. But the rest of his *Journal* commentary in the 1890s testified to the fact that he did indeed believe that there was a "new woman"—and that he saw her as a distinct threat to his vision of the American middle-class, gender-polarized way of life.

Bok's answer to this threat was to emphasize the benefits of professional domesticity. He and many of his contributors discussed education, suffrage, and women's work for pay in terms of women's traditional role. One such contributor was the Reverend Charles Parkhurst, who was a regular columnist for the *Journal* throughout the 1890s. In 1895 Parkhurst set the tone for the *Journal*'s general discussion of education, specifying that since the true mission of woman was to bear and train children, it was important that she be educated. Parkhurst thereby framed his argument in terms that emphasized the nurturing aspect of women's role: "There is no . . . completeness of college training that will unsex her," he wrote, "provided that such possessions and acquisitions are dominated by the feminine instinct and mortgaged to maternal ends and purposes."[14] Parkhurst's emphasis on tradition stands in direct contrast to Knapp's discussion of women's higher education, which was much more open. College training for women was viewed in Knapp's *Journal* as compatible with domesticity, but such an education did not necessarily have to be "mortgaged to maternal ends."[15]

Parkhurst and Bok were also more highly prescriptive than Knapp had been about the content of women's higher education. In 1900 Bok congratulated "3000 Sensible Girls":

> [w]hen over 3000 girls voluntarily come to their senses, and deliberately elect to know something of browning as well as Browning, it is a very fair indication that all American girls are not quite so silly and heedless of the true elements which constitute a woman's life as some would have us believe.[16]

In effect, Bok advocated college-taught domestic science as professional training for the domestic sphere.

He was challenged, however, by his own readers' testimony. One reader wrote in 1894:

> I have a college education (including domestic science courses) and have rejoiced and gloried in it. But I married a young man with his fortune yet to make, and I found trouble. I could do housework, though not with skill and speed. . . . My education, so far, seems to make me not a better mother, but a worse, because an overly intellectual and preoccupied one. My husband is kind, but, like myself sees and chafes at my unfitness for my sphere.[17]

Five reader letters subsequently echoed this sentiment. These women were questioning, not their role or the suitability of their duties, but their education and their inability to perform their traditional role. Responses to these letters were sympathetic, but in the main they avoided the issue of whether the limiting nature of home life itself might not be at fault. Mrs. Lyman Abbott, editor of the column, intimated that if these women applied their educated minds to their tasks they could master and even lighten them, gaining some time to pursue their intellectual interests.

But some *Journal* writers as well as readers in these years began to suggest that there was a real and often stressful adjustment to be made after college. The most sympathetic and thoughtful of these articles was Katherine Roich's "The College-Bred Woman in her Home," which appeared in 1899. Roich opened by pointing to the restlessness or discouragement that came over young housewives recently out of college when they no longer had time of their own. She went on to expose the reality of domestic life for middle-class women:

> Often the whole day is spent in thinking and doing for others. . . . The character of her new work is such that there must often be much confinement, much physical weariness, much uninteresting repetition and monotony, and sometimes even drudgery.[18]

Roich went the farthest of any *Journal* writer in the 1890s decade in detailing the drawbacks of housekeeping as a way of life, and in pointing out the contrast with college life. In the end, however, Roich was only able to offer the same limited solution that Mrs. Lyman Abbott had offered earlier: to recognize that women's work is important though boring, to simplify one's life, and to use time intelligently in order to gain time for studies and interests outside the home.

If writers like Roich did not challenge the basic structures of middle-class lives, they at least recognized the gap between expectations created by higher education and the reality of domestic life, and they offered some sympathetic reflections about this gap. Some *Journal* writers and readers, then, began to conceive the problem of education vis-à-vis domesticity more broadly and more critically than did Bok.

Bok's tack was more consonant with the emerging consumer culture, and it was consonant as well with Knapp's. Bok expanded Knapp's earlier labor-saving focus into a whole philosophy of professionalizing housework. In an 1899 editorial Bok compared women's work to men's, asserting the notion that, while women were "naturally suited" for work in the home, this did not mean that their work was easier for them than business was for men:

> Just as more and more is constantly expected of a man in business by reason of keener competition and wider markets, so housekeeping is getting to be more and more complicated as the conditions of our social life change. The introduction of labor-saving devices does not simplify housekeeping any more than does the introduction of machinery simplify business. With easier and greater facilities the demand becomes greater, and responsibilities increase rather than decrease.[19]

Bok was more perceptive than many of his contemporaries and some historians when he recognized that housework was becoming more modern but not easier or less time-consuming, since standards for domestic life rose commensurate with new tools.[20] But Bok, of course, accepted and approved of this increasing complexity, and he did all he could in his magazine to promote the inevitability of this "progress." Much of Bok's *Journal* was devoted to touting the importance of just such progress.

Bok's *Journal* was also devoted to raising the status of domesticity. Bok suggested in the same 1899 editorial that men had made women feel that their work, while necessary, was hardly to be compared in importance with men's ventures.[21] Again, Bok was an astute observer of his culture. Recent studies reveal how housewifery was being devalued in these years even in the seemingly objective framework of the American census. Tracing the nineteenth-century evolution of views of housewifery, Nancy Folbre concludes that the concept of the unproductive housewife was a "by-product of a new definition of productive labor that valorized participation in the market and devalorized the non-market work central to many women's lives."[22] Bok approved of this cultural concept of the unproductive, unpaid housewife because it supported the gendered division of labor upon which clearly defined and separated gender roles were based. Therefore, even as he saw the negative effects of such devaluation on middle-class women's self-esteem, he could not and would not support any major change in the capitalist-patriarchal social order.[23]

Instead, Bok and other *Journal* writers offered several personal, privatized solutions to the reader, by which she could make her "position" more professional. She was to (1) learn as much as she could about her work in the home by studying domestic science and by reading the *Ladies' Home Journal;* (2) carefully pass that knowledge to her daughters and/or to any domestic help that she might have; and (3) raise the status of domesticity herself by performing her role proudly and by recognizing that her mundane tasks were part of a more worthwhile, integrated whole. As one contributor wrote: "[Contented women] know the right relations of things, and every one of them believes that the art of homekeeping is profession enough."[24]

Women were to invest housekeeping with the same qualities that distinguished a man's profession from a plain job: education, planning, training, the management of others, and a sense of mission. This last was summed up nicely by Bok when he exhorted women to focus on the attributes a good housewife brought to her work, including hospitality, tact, warmth, and love. The final detail was the appropriate professional title, and Bok was ready to supply that as well. In 1891 he urged women to transform themselves from "housekeepers" or "housewives" into "homemakers" who could legitimately claim a higher status.[25]

SHIRT-WAISTS WHICH ARE NOT IN THE SHOPS

Because Each One Has Been Specially Designed for the Journal by Emily Wight

THE designs for the shirt-waists which are given here have been made with an eye to simplicity and good taste. The front of the one of pale gray taffeta, shown in illustration, is covered with little puffs made by the odd arrangement of groups of tucks.

The one of spotted blue and white linen shot with silk is made with the right front crossing the left, and is bordered with a band of tucking which turns over and flares back into a wide collar. The belt and cuffs are tucked.

The blue Japanese silk waist is made with the fronts crossing surplice fashion, and is hooked invisibly down the left side. With it is worn a ribbon belt fastened with a bow at the side.

A FINE pin-checked pink gingham waist has the effect of a little jacket of the front with revers turning back. The vest front of the gingham has two rows of small pearl buttons, with narrow pink ribbon laced back and forth.

Pearl buttons are the essentials for the shirt-waist set shown in illustration. The little design is painted with oil paints and has the appearance of enamel. Some old-fashioned wire rings are used to hold the waist buttons in place, and for the

TO WEAR WITH A SHIRT-WAIST

sleeves two tiny bands of gray baby ribbon. One girl whom I know has painted herself a set of these buttons and fastens them in the front of her waist by running a white bonnet wire through the backs and twisting the ends so that it cannot slip out.

The linen lawn waist is made of a peculiar shade of deep old rose. The little yoke and sleeve tops are white, and the bands which form the trimming are covered with tiny bias frills of the lawn.

THE severely plain white waist is made with three stitched bands which extend down the front. The yoke back is made with three bands drawn down to the waist. The narrow belt is made of the same material as the waist.

The fullness in the waist of blue linen is drawn from the collar and shoulder seams to the waist both in the back and front. A broad band of lace insertion is let in between two rows of tucks just below the bust and around the sleeves.

The blue bayadère striped dimity has a yoke and upper sleeves of finely tucked white lawn showing above rows of tucks.

THE waist of white all-over tucking has a yoke of plain white lawn which fastens over the under part on the shoulder seam and down the side of the arm. The main part of the waist buttons invisibly down the centre of the front. The belt and cuffs are of white linen.

The shirt-waist of dotted tan-colored batiste is made with a yoke in the back and a slight fullness which is laid in plaits. In front three tabs extend over the yoke, each one being edged with three narrow folds of the material; the fullness is shirred under the ends of these tabs. The belt is a folded one of black satin fastened with three crystal buttons.

The shirt-waist of checked Madras is trimmed with stitched bands in white, curving from the shoulders and sleeves to the waist. The back has a yoke edged with a curved band. The cuffs and stock are white and the belt of steel-blue taffeta.

OF WHITE TUCKING

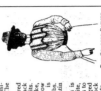

OF GRAY TAFFETA   *OF PINK GINGHAM*   *OF LINEN LAWN*   *IN PLAIN WHITE*

OF DOTTED LINEN   *OF JAPANESE SILK*

OF BLUE LINEN   *OF BLUE DIMITY*   *OF CHECKED MADRAS*

TAN-COLORED BATISTE

But as we have seen, Bok and some of his writers and readers disagreed about domesticity and its fulfilling nature, and a similar contrast emerges in the 1890–1900 discussion of suffrage. Although Bok would develop his opposition to the ballot for women more thoroughly later, early in his editorship he set the stage for his later aggressively negative stance. Bok's first mention of suffrage advanced the notion that the vote was irrelevant to most middle-class women's lives and that most women who had considered the issue at all did not want the vote.[26] Bok's subsequent references to woman's "real power" intimated that the ballot would be an empty attainment. An 1895 Parkhurst column, titled "Women Without the Ballot," made Bok's intimation explicit. "Women have," Parkhurst asserted, "a great many more rights than they are using."[27] Another writer, Lilian Bell, used sarcasm to convey a similar view of women's "readiness" for the vote: "Let them give us a vote if they will," she wrote. "I shall want at least three men to go with me to the polls—one to hold my purse, one to hold my gloves, and the third to show me how to cast my vote." Bell concluded matter-of-factly, "most of this talk about the new woman is mere nonsense."[28]

Bok undercut the notion that all of the talk was "mere nonsense," however, when he twice reported the outcome of *Journal* reader opinion polls. Bok conducted informal surveys of reader opinion about once a year. These two occasions, in November of 1891 and again in July of 1895, represent the only times he discussed specific results of his surveys in the magazine. He reported that in these two surveys a majority of readers had objected to the *Journal*'s negative stance on suffrage. This objection is important both because reader response to these surveys was substantial—over 1,000 readers in 1891, and 1,342 in 1895—and because it represents one of the few times when the reader's voice was heard in Bok's *Journal* on a substantive issue.[29] Simply by reporting this reader reaction, Bok presented and to some extent legitimized a view directly contradicting his own. This view complicated the monolithic character of the *Journal*'s stance on suffrage, and it suggests the breadth of popular support for suffrage by the late 1890s.

In a characteristically patronizing move, Bok "compromised" with his readers by announcing a new *Journal* column that would provide them with a civic education. Instead of supporting suffrage, Bok would respond to readers' obvious new interest in civic affairs by instructing them on the workings of local, state, and national government. Thereby did Bok coopt the disagreement of a substantial number of *Journal* readers. While readers could choose to ignore Bok's views on suffrage, to engage them directly and disagree with them, or simply not to buy the *Journal* at all, Bok could re-cast the "discussion" in such a way as to remove the subject of disagreement altogether. Bok's *Journal* utilized this approach to the question of women's suffrage for years, although the magazine did eventually engage the question directly again.

Positions on women's work for pay in Bok's *Journal* were more contradictory in these years. They were an interesting blend of explicit disapproval in editorials and feature articles and implicit support in how-to departments and some other articles. It is here that we see most clearly how even the most perfunctory, technical information can contribute to complicating the normative message of a magazine.

Complaining that "we hear about the 'Woman of Business' all the time," Bok asserted in 1893 that it was fine for a woman who was forced to earn money to go out of the home to work. But he was worried that the image of the working woman had begun to entice those who did not have to work. Bok argued that working conditions were poor, that special allowances could not be made for women, and that pay was low for female workers. Of course, similar observations were made by progressive activists of the day like Charlotte Perkins Gilman and Florence Kelley, who advocated thoroughgoing change in America's economic structures to address these problems. Bok's emphasis was very different, however, focusing on what he called the appeal of the home:

> The poorest, hardest-working woman in her home is a queen of independence compared to the woman in business, whether she be employee or employer. . . . The women in business to-day are the truest believers that the commercial world was never intended for their sex. The home has ever been woman's truest sphere and it will ever remain so. . . . There lies her greatest power, her surest influence, and there every true friend of her sex wishes her to remain unless circumstances force her out of it.[30]

Bok spoke more as the "true friend" of the other sex, however, when he responded to a male reader's question about competing with women in the workplace. Bok conceded the difficulty the young man faced in light of the fact that woman was the cheaper employee, but he urged his male reader to "go out and outdo her."[31] At least some of Bok's patronizing protection was therefore directly fueled by his concerns about women competing with men. The gendered division of labor could not be maintained if too many middle-class women went into the paid labor force. But Bok was not in general an outright alarmist about the issue.

The same could not be said for Adelaide Field, "An American Mother," who contributed a consistently conservative column appearing later in the 1890s. In April of 1900 Field's column damned "The American Woman in the Marketplace." Women in business were an evil influence, Field suggested, because they were derisive about "old-fashioned domesticity." Young women were being enticed by work for pay: "One dimpled, rose-lipped girl that I know insists on being a surgeon." "Working women's selfishness" explained the rapid increase in rates of divorce, the author asserted, as well as the greater number of childless homes which threatened the country with race suicide.

Field's diatribe ended with a final condemnation of and chilling explanation for the activities of women who work for pay:

> The American woman, like the American man, has gone down into the market-place. Like him, she has become crazed with the desire to gain money, social position and power. . . . But Nature is too strong for her. Until her rebellious soul escapes from the body which she has now she cannot deny that she was sent into the world to be a wife and mother. Her gropings, her made projects, her perpetual unrest, are simply the outcry of natural, noble instincts which she has strangled.[32]

Using words like "crazed," "rebellious," and "mad" put Field in the company of medical experts who, in the late nineteenth century, diagnosed active and/or dissatisfied women with a variety of new "illnesses." Thus did some elements of Bok's *Journal* situate the magazine in the "backlash" against middle-class white women's strides at the turn of the century. Women were deemed "sick" and prominent ministers and politicians claimed that the very survival of the Anglo-Saxon race was in question.

It is all the more striking, then, that the very issues of the *Journal* in which these negative references to women working for pay appeared also featured the following: Mrs. Lyman Abbott's report in the "Just Among Ourselves" column that women were constantly writing to ask how they might make some money for themselves; reader suggestions in the same column about interesting work for women, including piano-tuning and leather-tanning; a column on "Women's Chances as Bread Winners" that ran during the entire decade and highlighted occupations ranging from professional nursing to stenography to fashion designing; and another column, which ran from 1892 through the end of the decade, that instructed women on "The Art of Dressing for Business."[34]

Analyzing the entire *Journal* thus reveals a set of quite different and sometimes contradictory messages regarding women's work outside the home. A major reason for the range in message was that the trend under consideration was significant and growing. More and more women were going out of the home to work, and married women represented the fastest-growing segment of that group after 1880.[35] Middle-class women in particular were moving into what would become female-stereotyped jobs as teachers, office workers, librarians, nurses, social workers, and store clerks. Debate about women working raged in many periodicals of the day, including *Cosmopolitan, Scribner's,* the *North American Review,* and the *Forum.* Bok and his writers joined those producing other periodicals in their anxiety about such developments, even as the *Journal* simultaneously ran features that supported women in their new ventures.

Was this combination of images intentional? To the extent that Bok was both a cultural conservative and a businessman keen on making as much money as possible, the answer is yes. He knew that he had to meet reader demands in

I.—TO BECOME A TRAINED NURSE.

By Elizabeth Robinson Scovil.

SO many women have of late succeeded as trained nurses, that each year more attention is directed to the subject of nursing as a profession for women.

The question is constantly asked "How can I become a trained nurse?" To answer it and to afford further information that will be interesting to those who wish to take up the work is the purpose of this paper.

A letter addressed to the superintendent of any training school for nurses, and sent to a hospital in any large city will bring a speedy response. It should state that the writer wishes to enter the training school, and ask for the form of application. A circular will be sent containing questions to be answered by the applicant, and returned to the superintendent.

If the replies are satisfactory the applicant is accepted, usually for one month, on probation. During this time board and lodging are provided, and her washing is done in the hospital laundry, but she receives no other compensation.

If she proves intelligent, trustworthy and capable of receiving the necessary instruction, she is accepted as a pupil, and signs an agreement to remain in the school for two years, subject to its rules and requirements. She then assumes the uniform of the school and is given a cap, which only probationers are permitted to wear. It is a proud moment for the pupil nurse when she first puts on her cap and feels that she is fairly started in the career for which she has so ardently longed.

Some schools furnish a clinical thermometer, a pair of forceps and a pair of surgical scissors for each nurse. These are the property of the institution and must be replaced if broken or lost.

No fee is required for admission to an American hospital. In England, a lady probationer pays thirty pounds, about one hundred and fifty dollars, for the privilege of being trained as a nurse. In this country, after the month of probation, a pupil receives about ten dollars a month during the first year, and fourteen during the second year of the course.

Board and lodging are furnished free of expense, either in the hospital, or in the nurses' home adjoining it, and the necessary laundry-work is provided for.

Underclothing should be strong, plainly made, and plainly marked with the owner's name to insure its being returned from the wash. The pupil should bring two or three plain cotton dresses to wear in the wards during the probationary month. Six white aprons are usually lent by the school for this time, and given if the probationer is accepted. Should this not be the rule in the institution she selects, she should provide herself with

several large, plain, white aprons. A simple pin is the only jewelry that should be worn. The hours of duty are long; usually from seven A. M. to eight P. M. Each nurse has an hour off duty during the day, beside the time allowed for meals, one afternoon and one evening each week, and some time on Sunday. In most hospitals the nurses are able to attend service once in the day, if they wish to do so. A vacation of two weeks is given each year.

Practical instruction is given by the head nurse in the ward. The pupil learns a good deal from the physicians' and surgeons on their daily rounds. If she is a bright, intelligent woman she seeks information for herself and learns from a thousand sources. Theoretical instruction is given in classes by the superintendent. Often there is a course of lectures provided by the doctors connected with the hospital. Sometimes there is a special course of lessons in massage, which is very valuable, as a skillful masseuse commands a good price. There is always practical, or theoretical instruction in cookery for the sick. Many hospitals are fortunate enough to possess diet-kitchens where the nurses can learn to prepare invalid diet with the utmost delicacy and nicety.

In some hospitals, instruction is given in obstetrical work, but in many these cases are not received and the nurse must go elsewhere if she wishes to become proficient in this branch of nursing. There are institutions devoted specially to this class of cases, where the necessary knowledge can be obtained.

Examinations are held at stated intervals. If the pupil passes these successfully and goes through the two years with credit, she receives a diploma which certifies to the world that she is a trained nurse.

If her alma mater is a large hospital, where the wards are in charge of graduates as head nurses, she may be asked to remain in this capacity. If not, there is a wide opening for her outside its walls. Superintendents usually have more applications than they can fill for competent, trustworthy women to take positions of trust in other institutions. If the graduate prefers to nurse invalids in private families, she can command from fifteen to twenty dollars a week.

There is much discussion as to the comparative merits of large and small hospitals as training schools for nurses; each have their virtues and their defects. The wider range of experience in the large institution is counterbalanced by the personal interest and more careful instruction that is possible in the smaller one. When a woman intends to enter a training school she should send for circulars from several, and choose the one that she thinks is best suited to her needs. .

A list of a few hospitals, both large and small, where there are training schools, is subjoined:

Massachusetts General Hospital, Boston.
Boston City Hospital, Boston, Mass.
Bellevue Hospital, New York, N. Y.
New York Hospital, New York, N. Y.
St. Luke's Hospital, Chicago, Ill.
New Haven Hospital, New Haven, Conn.
Garfield Memorial Hospital, Washington, D. C.
Johns Hopkins Hospital, Baltimore, Md.
Maine General Hospital, Portland, Maine.
Newton Cottage Hospital, Newton, Mass.
Newport Hospital, Newport, R. I.

The following articles will appear in this series of "Women's Chances as Bread-Winners," in ensuing numbers: "Women as Telegraphers," by General Thomas T. Eckert, Vice-President of the Western Union Telegraph Company; "Women Behind the Counter," by Hon. John Wanamaker; "Women as Stenographers," by W. L. Mason, President of the Metropolitan Stenographer's Association of New York; "Women as Dressmakers," by Miss Emma M. Hooper; "Women on the Stage," by Mr. A. M. Palmer, of the Madison Square Theatre, New York; "Women as Artists," by General L. P. di Cesnola, President of the Metropolitan Museum of Art, New York; "Women as Doctors," by Dr. George F. Shrady, Editor of The Medical Record, of New York; "Women as Teachers, by Superintendent Jasper, of the New York City Public Schools; "Women as Type-Setters," by George F. Dumar, President of the Typographical Union, No. 6.

HINTS FOR MONEY MAKING GIRLS.

By Ruth Ashmore.

HUNDREDS of thousands of girls have a great desire to make a little money, and I don't know whether to call it a laudable one or not. I am not a believer in girls going out into the world to work unless it is absolutely necessary. But when it is then I want them to do it in the right way; I want them to think that every particle of work they do, is done not only for their own sakes, not only for their employers—it must be right and honest in the sight of God. A very clever woman not very long ago wrote an article about working women, and in it she used this beautiful quotation of Ruskin's:— "Queens you should always be. Queens to your lovers, to your husbands, to your sons; queens of a higher mystery to the world beyond." But she did not put the rest of the quotation, and in that lies the story of the non-success of many girls. This is it—" But, alas! you are too often idle and careless queens, grasping at majesty in the least things, while you abdicate in the greatest."

With only the hope of making money, your work will be worth little, and certainly not be worthy of consideration by noble minds or by the good God who watches over you day and night. You girls hurt yourselves, hurt your work, make it of less value and yourselves less respected because you so entirely draw the line at what you will and what you will not do. That which your hands find to do is the duty before you, and the woman who, employed in a counting-house, finds it but little trouble to keep her desk in order and, when she has time, to straighten up somebody else's who hasn't the time, is the woman whose work is going to be noted and counted as valuable. The woman who announcing that she must get work or starve, and who yet is not willing to be at her desk at eight o'clock in the morning, deserves to starve. The woman who knowing that for a certain number of hours she should be honor give her time to her employer, is but a poor worker when ten minutes after the hour finds her arriving, and five minutes before the hour to go away sees her getting her cloak ready and arranging for her out-door costume. The good workman doesn't drop the pen or the hammer at the stroke of the hour; he finishes first that which he is doing, for his heart is in his work, and that's the way it must be with you girls if you want to succeed and make even "a little money."

order to sell his magazine. He testified himself that the "breadwinner" and "dressing for business" columns, among others, had been created in direct response to reader interests.[36] Gender construction in Bok's *Journal* was, in short, fraught with internal contradictions and inconsistencies, because Bok himself had mixed intentions. Bok as a businessman responded to audience interests, but Bok as an editor promoted his own views. In the end he settled for reaching an enormous audience with messages, that, if one were paying attention, were decidedly mixed.

The discussion of marriage in Bok's *Journal* was less mixed, although Bok and his contributors recognized that middle-class marriage presented its difficulties. In the late nineteenth century marriage was a complicated institution. The companionate ideal was prominent, but divorce was still a largely unacceptable alternative when love failed; women's role was shifting in ways that to some at least, threatened marriage; men were working hard, some thought to the neglect of wives and children; and the money-based economy meant that the financial relation was a significant part of any marital relationship. Bok and his writers noted these complications, and they clearly viewed themselves as having an active role to play in negotiating the resulting difficulties.

Bok asserted once that too many writers were making marriage too much of a problem. He asked that marriage be left to the realm of emotions and to the heart instead of being made the subject of "mental study."[37] Bok's *Journal* was full, however, of just such "mental study," and much of it conveyed the impression that male-female relations in general were indeed troubled. Bok, like Knapp, assumed that men and women were meant to marry, and his *Journal* commented negatively on male-female relations only within the framework of this assumption. The activities of "advanced" women threatened seriously to weaken these relations, however.

Bok stated the problem clearly: "Whereas, only a few years back," he wrote in 1896, "one sex occupied a position above the other, the two are now side by side competing fiercely in every occupation, in every branch of life."[38] This created a real dilemma for men: could men live with strong, competitive women? A contributor, Amelia E. Barr, asserted that only the weakest men pretended to like the women called strong-minded. Barr went on to suggest the solution that society would probably see more and more frequently:

> Such women should evidently remain outside the realm of the home, for with their minds forever on some public "question," and their husbands and children neglected, they make a kind of wife that no mere flesh and blood man can tolerate.[39]

If these women did not decide to avoid marriage themselves, men might make the decision for them, Bok's *Journal* concluded. Another writer, John Lambert Payne, explained "Why Young Men Defer Marriage" in 1892, laying the blame at the feet of women who were being too independent. He theorized that women's greater opportunities for earning money were at least partly to blame, because they supported higher standards of living and raised material expectations regarding early married life.[40]

Recent studies of divorce at the turn of the century support part of Payne's analysis. Couples at the end of the century did tend to have higher material expectations. They therefore delayed marriage until they could afford a home of their own and the material belongings with which to equip it. They were also more likely to end a marriage if they were not satisfied with their standard of living.[41] But the extent to which women's paid work affected financial expectations within marriage is questionable. Payne's analysis is contradicted by evidence from social historians that demonstrates that women at the turn of the century, recognizing their lack of viable options in the work world, "preferred" the role of dependent housewife. As Elaine Tyler May writes, "As long as the economic system offered women satisfaction as consumers and frustration as producers, women would continue to look to the home for fulfillment and to men for support."[42]

In fact, instead of blaming working women for higher material expectations within marriage, one could reasonably blame the *Ladies' Home Journal* and other magazines like it. The magazine's thorough commercialism, combined with its images of the good homemaker, surely encouraged higher and higher material expectations on the part of its middle-class readers. The commercial ethos conveyed by magazines like the *Journal* probably contributed as much as anything did to promoting higher standards of living at the turn of the century.

But blaming women for the phenomenon of deferred marriage was convenient for Bok's *Journal,* as it had been convenient earlier for Knapp's to blame men. This pattern underscores the significance of the fact that, beginning in 1890, the *Journal* was a publication for women edited by a man. Bok could blame women easily simply because he was not a woman himself. Bok frequently preached to, chastised, and patronized his readers. Unfortunately it was this approach, as opposed to Knapp's sisterly tone, that became institutionalized in women's magazines at the turn of the century. This was just one of several patterns that began to inform women's magazines in the 1890s. These patterns would dominate women's magazines for much of the twentieth century.

Another pattern that would continue to characterize women's magazines was the *Journal*'s reflection on the nature of the male role. Bok took this rather sporadic feature of Knapp's *Journal* and made it much more regular and frequent. Commentary on the male role during Bok's early tenure demonstrates the attempt of Bok and his writers to rationalize the male role, to pick and choose between different cultural models of that role, and to educate women about the men they married and parented.

To the extent that Louisa's *Journal* had considered parenthood, it had focused mainly on the need to treat girls equally with boys, and on the desirability of training in domestic skills for boys as well as girls. There was virtually no discussion of fatherhood in the *Ladies' Home Journal* between 1883 and 1889. Bok's *Journal,* in contrast, commented on the nature of fatherhood frequently.

In "The Father's Domestic Headship," Parkhurst apologized for appearing to load all domestic responsibilities on women in his monthly column. He asserted that "sex is limitation" and claimed, therefore, that men in partnership with women have a crucial role to play in the home.[43] Parkhurst's discussion of the need to have the "moral head" of the family more involved at home points to the interaction of two dominant models of fatherhood identified by historians of the eighteenth and nineteenth centuries. The first of these is the preindustrial model of moral overseer. Fathers, who were generally farmers or artisans in these days, interacted frequently with their children, to teach them religious values, guide sons into a calling, and supervise the courtship and marriage of both sons and daughters; in short, they oversaw the moral development of their children. This model dominated until industrialization sent many men out to work.[44]

The second model, that of breadwinner, followed on the heels of industrialization, and it has dominated the mainstream culture to this day. Providing well for one's family became all-important as middle-class men increasingly went out to work and women increasingly took charge of the moral nurturing as well as caretaking of the children. The result was the individual father's virtual removal from the everyday care and supervision of his children. Parkhurst thus responded to the breadwinner model, that was dominant by the 1890s, by invoking the moral overseer role. Men must reassert their domestic authority, Parkhurst and other *Journal* writers declared, by reclaiming their God-given responsibility for moral leadership in the home.

Men had to tread carefully, however. "Henpecked" and "housekeeping" fathers were not good models for children nor desirable mates for women, but neither should men resort to tyranny.[45] The best way to achieve this important middle position between deference and tyranny was by attending regularly and carefully to the everyday tumult of family life. Frances Evans addressed the problem with a seagoing metaphor:

> The father is the captain of the family ship. He must prove his right to the title by keeping his weather eye open during the fogs and gales unavoidable in

the restless sea of his children's lives; otherwise he may be held responsible for wrecks.[46]

Therefore, while Bok and his writers would presumably hold women to first-mate's duty on the ship, they would at least try to chase the captain back on board, as well.

The *Journal*'s answer to troubled home lives was a variation on what one historian has termed "masculine domesticity." This ideology, which emerged at the end of the nineteenth century, asserted that men should spend more time at home and that they should be more attentive to their wives and children while in it.[47] Accompanying this notion in the *Journal* was the idea that men should spend less time at work. As Ruth Ashmore stated unequivocally in 1895, "men are slaves to money-making."[48] It was the husband's responsibility to provide well for his family, but Bok's early *Journal* regularly complained that men were going too far. Thus, while Bok prescribed a comparatively rigid and narrow domestic role for women, he made some attempt at balance by demanding men's greater allegiance to their children and their wives.

Bok urged men, through their wives, to go back home and to be more attentive and more pleasant in it, but he resolved these issues in his own life in a different way. In contrast to the picture he drew of the ideal husband, Bok was known by his family to be a cold, withdrawn husband to his wife, Mary Louise, a husband who spent most of his time at work. In addition, also in contrast to his image of the involved, nurturing father, he insisted that his sons be sent to boarding school at a very young age.[49] Bok's own life points to the danger of assuming any simple correspondence between magazine rhetoric and the ways in which real people negotiated their lives. It raises the possibility, in fact, that some magazine producers may have emphasized the very behaviors and values that were most troubled or troublesome in their own lives.

The *Journal* of the 1890s urged men back into the home rather than encouraging women to come out of it, but the magazine suggested that there was one important reason for women to leave the homefront regularly: to buy. Knapp's *Journal* grew out of the assumption that women are consumers; hence reading matter for women was surrounded by advertisements for products in which women were thought to have some interest. Knapp and her producers viewed consuming as one way for middle-class women to expand their activity and their autonomy. While they had begun to see women as the primary consumers in American culture, they did not view consuming as women's primary activity. Herein lies the critical shift over which Bok presided. The guiding principle of Bok's *Journal* comprised the twin notions that women were the primary consumers for their families and in the culture at large, and that women were primarily consumers. As a result of this shift, Bok and his contributors began to speak to the complexity of women's job as spender and saver, and, characteristically, to try to show women how to do it well.

In 1899, Helen Watterson Moody expounded on "What it Means to Be a Wife," capturing in one sentence a fundamental and important truth about middle-class marriage in the 1890s:

> When a woman marries she assumes two new sets of relations—those of sentiment, through which she becomes the loving, faithful companion of one man and the mother of his children, and the economic relation, through which she becomes one of the greatest conserving and distributing agents of the world.[50]

Moody, Bok, and other *Journal* writers in these years saw that much of the task of married middle-class people was to accommodate both the sentimental and the economic relations within marriage; significantly, they assigned much of the work of that accommodation to women.

The *Journal*'s commentary on women as money managers and spenders was markedly different from its discussion of other aspects of women's lives. Female independence and initiative were viewed as entirely compatible with financial management and consuming. On at least twenty-two different occasions in this decade Bok or a contributor noted that wives should receive an allowance, keep the family books, and make most of the family's spending decisions. Maria Parloa, in "Divisions of the Family Income," urged even brides-to-be to overcome their shyness about money matters and to initiate a prenuptial discussion about finances if their intended husbands did not. Every young couple needed to begin their life together knowing just what their means would be and what they would budget for various items.[51] Women were thinking more for themselves, Bok's *Journal* suggested approvingly in this context, and there was no more appropriate application for such thinking than to family financial matters.[52]

The marriage, the family, and the culture, the magazine suggested, would all benefit as woman became "one of the greatest conserving and distributing agents of the world." So, of course, would the *Ladies' Home Journal.* Money managers and smart consumers were just the right audience for a magazine driven by advertising, and the *Journal* was certainly such a magazine.

Indeed, the *Journal* expanded its function as a vehicle for advertising in its second decade. Advertising dictated the size of the 1890s *Journal;* the ratio of advertising to reading matter held steady at one column to three, but reading matter per issue increased or decreased depending on how many ads the business department had to run. Ads appeared earlier and earlier in the magazine, with the inside cover becoming a choice location. Ad-stripping, which Bok claimed to have originated, meant that the magazine's prime reading material was often carried over to the back, where it was surrounded by columns of advertising. *Journal* readers of the 1890s also got a strong signal about editorial priorities when they received their magazine in the mail and saw the condition of its pages. Until these years the *Journal*'s pages had all been unopened; that is, the reader had to detach each page from the next. Under Bok and Curtis's leadership, however, the magazine was sent with its advertising pages ready to read and its editorial pages left unopened.[53]

Advertisements in the 1890s became bigger, better-illustrated, and slicker in tone. Catchy names abounded, names like "Kantwearout" men's clothing, and "Waukenhose" hosiery for women. Ad copy began to exhort women to be modern, and to concern themselves with "fitting in": one advertisement, for Rubifoam tooth powder, asserted that "The NEW WOMAN, whatever costume she may wear, will be particular about her teeth."[54] Another, for a new sweeper, chided women, "Don't sweep the old way! The New Woman sweeps hard and soft carpets and bare floors with a Sweeperette."[55]

The recognition of women as consumers and the desire to capitalize on this recognition led directly to this type of exhortation. Advertisements echoed the condescending, exhortive tone found in Bok's writing and that of a number of *Journal* contributors. This was not an accident. Cyrus Curtis and Edward Bok wrote much of the advertising copy in these early days of the *Journal,* and Curtis especially helped to shape much advertising of the day in general.

As T. J. Jackson Lears asserts, advertisers like those in the late nineteenth-century *Ladies' Home Journal* increasingly emphasized conformity and feeling as opposed to autonomy and reason. They began to view potential consumers as fundamentally unthinking and impulsive. The use of half-truths and appeals to individual concerns about fitting in created a "world in which all overarching structures of meaning had collapsed, and there was 'nothing at stake beyond a manipulative sense of well-being.' "[56]

Lears suggests that this manipulative emphasis in advertising and the larger consumer culture which that advertising helped to shape required a favorable moral climate in which to thrive. He hypothesizes that the crucial moral change that helped to create this climate was a "shift from a Protestant ethos of salvation through self-denial toward a therapeutic ethos stressing self-realization in this world."[57] In characterizing this climate Lears attends briefly to advertising pitches directed to women, but he does not make gender central to his analysis. Close examination of the *Ladies' Home Journal* shows that certain attitudes toward women, perhaps in tandem with self-realization, played a critical role in the creation of the advertising ethos that emerged in the United States in the last decades of the nineteenth century.

The course of one long-running, lively ad campaign illustrates the approaches used by *Journal* advertisers and the way the substance of a major advertising campaign could contribute to the tone and content of a magazine. Pearline washing powder, a product manufactured by the James Pyle Company in New York and sold throughout the nation, was advertised in almost every is-

4.e. Look Around, Pearline.

Look Around

and see the women who are using Pearline. It's easy to pick them out. They're brighter, fresher, more cheerful than the women who have spent twice as much time in the rub, rub, rub, of the old way. Why shouldn't they be? Washing with **Pearline is easy.**

And look at the clothes that are washed with **Pearline.** They're brighter, and fresher, too. They haven't been rubbed to pieces on the washboard. They may be **old,** but they don't show it. For clothes washed with **Pearline** last longer.

Beware Peddlers and some unscrupulous grocers will tell you, "this is as good as" or "the same as Pearline." IT'S you an imitation, be honest—*send it back.* FALSE—Pearline is never peddled, if your grocer sends 317   JAMES PYLE, New York.

sue of the 1890s *Journal.* Pearline paid top dollar for its ads, which appeared on the magazine's back cover or on the popular housekeeping column page. The text of these advertisements ranged from instructive to exhortive, and, interestingly enough, they often featured a point of view that contradicted Bok's. It is impossible to guess whether readers believed what they read in Pearline ads, or whether they read the ads at all. But the fact that they were in the *Journal* and that the producer hoped to sell Pearline with certain messages tells us something important about the culture from which the advertisements came.

The notion that women were in competition with one another signals advertising's preoccupation with conformity, a preoccupation that regularly informed Pearline ads such as the one in figure 4.e from 1897.

Women were urged to conform by being modern as well, and other ads — such as the one in figure 4.f, which ran in the *Journal* in 1892—were even more explicit in their derision for the "old way."

Still other Pearline ads in the 1890s boasted of the product's liberating potential, highlighting more important things women might do with their time (see figure 4.g).

4.f. How it looks, Pearline.

How it looks, to the women who wash with Pearline (use with- out soap), when they see a woman washing in the old-fashioned way with soap — rubbing the clothes to pieces, rubbing away her strength, wearing herself out over the washboard! To these Pearline women, fresh from easy washing, she seems to "wear a fool's cap unawares." Everything's in favor of Pearline (no use soap)—easier work, quicker work, better work, safety, economy. There's not one thing against it What's the use of washing in the hardest way, when it costs more money?   489   James Pyle, New York.

Ads in this series also addressed the notion of women's expanded activity by noting Pearline's potential as a bicycle lubricant ("The best woman's bicycle tool-bag carries a little can or bottle of Pearline") and as a boon to club workers and to women running charitable events. This sales pitch demonstrates how efficiency, a notion that Bok emphasized for women, could be used to further one that he did not support, i.e., the expanded public activity of middle-class women.

In fact, advertisements for Pearline as well as for other products featured in the *Journal*'s pages, regularly contradicted Bok's editorial messages. This contradiction is striking since Bok at the least approved all advertisements; in many cases, he was closely involved in creating them. And this contradiction is important since it helped to complicate the message of the magazine, broadening the range of its commentary to reflect more realities of the day.

Hence the Rubifoam and Sweeperette ads with their positive references to the New Woman, a cultural ideal that Bok by turns derided or ignored, but that he always disliked. Similarly, Bok and his writers in editorial material argued against the Pearline advertisement notion that women were in competition with one another. Such competition, by Bok's lights, was a distinctly unfeminine mark of the new woman. Derision for the old-fashioned way also undercut Bok's regular references to the need to respect the past and to be knowledgeable about the way things were done in earlier generations.

But in one crucial way the advertisements' messages meshed with virtually all of the other messages in Bok's *Journal*. Common to Bok's preachy ed-

Instead
of Wasting

your time over a steamy, sloppy wash-tub, rubbing away with soap, why don't you use –Pearline? In the time that you'd save by it, you might be *reading, writing, sewing, playing, visiting, resting*, or doing anything else that's pleasant and profitable. Besides, you won't have that tired feeling that comes of the hard-working, old-fashioned way. That makes everything that you do, even the resting, uncomfortable. This slow, back-breaking, wearing way of washing with soap is a thing of the past. You'll wonder that you stood it so long, when you once see the easiness of **Pearline.** But beware of all sorts of washing powders— poor imitations of **Pearline.** They save some work, possibly, but think of the damage they may do. **Pearline** is the first and only washing compound. The women who have used it from the start will tell you that it's absolutely safe. And never so many women were using it as just now.

Why?

Ask some of the millions who use it. They'll tell you that with **Pearline** you can do the washing and cleaning with little or none of the rub! rub!! rub!!! — so necessary in "the old way," and so productive of that "tired feeling." They'll tell you they have used it for years — have found it always the same — always absolutely harmless — have failed to find anything to compare with it for easy, quick and satisfactory work. Just think of the saving at every point by avoiding this rubbing. Your most delicate laces and linens are washed without being torn to pieces, and wherever soap has been used, you'll find **Pearline** better in every way. **A luxury in the bath.** Hundreds of millions of packages used, and the consumption increasing; what better proof can we offer — only one: Get a package (every grocer has it) and try it according to the directions; without soap — without rubbing — with no help save clean water (hard or soft, hot or cold, it matters not) and you'll be convinced. You'll use **Pearline** until something better is discovered; there's nothing now known to equal it.

Beware of the imitations which peddlers and some unscrupulous grocers claim to be the "same as" or "as good as" **Pearline** — they are not.   Pearline is manufactured only by **James Pyle, New York.**

Hard Work or Easy Work, just as you choose. If you find it hard work, it's because you won't use PEARLINE. You'd rather waste your time and your strength with that absurd rubbing and scrubbing. Of course it's hard — that's why PEARLINE was invented — that's why PEARL-INE is a household word. You don't know how easy it can be, until you let PEARLINE do the work. Then house-cleaning slips right along. It is over before you know it. Not our word for it - ask some friend; if she is up to the times she uses PEARLINE; the brighter the woman the more uses she finds for PEARLINE.

Send it Back Peddlers and some unscrupulous grocers will tell you "this is as good as" or "the same as Pearl-ine IT'S FALSE—Pearline is never peddled, and if your grocer sends you something in place of Pearline, be honest—*send it back.* JAMES PYLE, New York.

itorials, service departments on dressing well for business, and advertisements for all sorts of products, were the themes that buying and consuming represented a natural way of life, that efficiency was an ideal to be sought above all others, and that intelligence equalled buying and using the right products. We see here the further elaboration of the commercial discourse that was initiated in Knapp's *Journal*. And this discourse was, of course, gendered. Specifically, then, women were the "natural" consumers, women valued efficiency in the home above all else, and intelligent women purchased the right products.

The fact that this gendered commercial discourse pervaded every aspect of Bok's *Journal* is significant; not only did this commercialism become difficult to escape, it also trivialized and coopted images that emphasized women's independence. It was not the traditional woman but the "New Woman" who would clean her teeth with Rubifoam tooth powder and use the Sweeperette broom.

We are left, therefore, with the question of how this gendered commercial discourse may have affected readers. The *Journal* under Bok continued Knapp's pattern of reflecting consciously and openly on matters of gender construction, reinforcing women's conscious reflection on their own gendered lives. And Bok's *Journal* presented women with several images of femininity, thereby validating at least a limited array of choices. But the *Journal* under Bok, instead of pointing out social constraints on middle-class women as Knapp's *Journal* had, discouraged women from recognizing constraints.

In fact, Bok's *Journal* itself became a constraining force as it redefined the parameters of gender discourse. Scholarly studies of advertising suggest that it is the subtle, matter-of-fact presentation of "reality" in advertising that gives it some power to influence. They point to the "power of frequently repeated media images and ideas to establish broad frames of reference, define boundaries of public discussion, and determine relevant factors in a situation."[58] The *Ladies' Home Journal* during Bok's early tenure established precisely this sort of framework. Commerce was framed in gendered terms in the magazine, and gender norms for women were framed in commercial terms. Hence the *Journal* established definite and influential parameters for both the conduct of commerce and the discussion of gender.

As a result, thoughtful and prescriptive discussions of gender were surrounded by advertisements. Advertisements themselves often conveyed gender prescriptions, and, as we have seen, they helped to make the consuming role for women appear natural. Editorial copy urged women to take charge of budgeting and spending. Nowhere else in the turn-of-the-century culture were notions about gender represented and discussed for such a huge audience; nowhere else were so many advertisers trying to get the attention of so many women. Gender construction for women and commercialism were thereby linked in a most profound yet perfunctory way in the commercial package that was the *Ladies' Home Journal* of the 1890s.

In addition to and in relation to this development, Bok and *Journal* advertisers presided over a critical cultural shift. They moved from representing consuming as an activity for middle-class women, the view that had prevailed in Knapp's *Journal,* to viewing women as the culture's primary consumers and women as primarily consumers. This shift was profoundly important in American culture. It is likely that readers of the day responded to this shift in a variety of ways, ranging from indifference to enthusiastic embrace. But it is the case that, over time, it would become virtually impossible to read the *Journal* or any other commercial women's magazine and not define oneself in some way as a "consumer." Here was the *Journal's* most significant locus of influence on both individual readers and the culture in general. This was the development that would outlast any specific message the *Ladies' Home Journal* carried.

5

Creating a Magazine for Men: Curtis Gets the *Post* and the *Post* Gets Lorimer, 1897–1900

By 1897 the *Ladies' Home Journal* had come far since its inauguration in 1883 as "sort of a ladies' journal." The magazine that Curtis, Knapp, and Bok had shaped and nurtured was a resounding success, with a well-established, large audience and a clear formula. The *Journal* and its producers had, in addition, played a key role in creating a sophisticated milieu of mass-circulation magazine publishing and in the joining of gender and commerce in the mass-circulation magazine forum.

Cyrus Curtis was not content to rest with this achievement, however, and he began to consider publishing "sort of a men's journal." Curtis's "pet idea to create a paper for men," as Bok put it, grew out of his conviction that the chief interest in a man's life was the fight for a living, and in Curtis's view that fight centered in the arena of business. Increasingly, earning a living for middle-class American men did touch on some phase of business; 50 percent of the total male labor force in 1910 described themselves as "businessmen."[1] Curtis accordingly planned loosely to aim his publication at the American man of business, targeting in particular the sons and husbands of *Journal* readers.

The years 1897 to 1900 saw Cyrus Curtis and the staff he would hire struggling to establish this new magazine for men, changing and fine-tuning its formula, and trying to distinguish it from other magazines of the day, particularly the *Ladies' Home Journal*. The creation of the *Journal,* as we have seen, represented the intersection of an early and relatively primitive mass culture and certain well-defined female gender norms. The creation of the *Saturday Evening Post* stood, in contrast, at the intersection of a more developed and more crowded mass market, and less explicit and more diffuse male gender norms. As a result, the identity of the *Post* proved to be comparatively difficult to establish and even harder to make commercially viable.

We see directly for the first time, then, major and negative ramifications of the gendered mass media milieu that Cyrus Curtis had a large part in shaping. Ironically, the creation and elaboration of the female-targeted *Journal* stood in the way of the success of the second major Curtis magazine. Both Cyrus Curtis and George Horace Lorimer, the editor he would hire, would grapple with the magazine's formula in this already-gendered commercial milieu. Above all, the magazines' producers would have to demonstrate how commercialism, already linked so closely and strongly to femininity, might also be linked to masculinity.

Curtis kept his eye open for the appropriate vehicle for his second magazine, and in 1897 an opportunity presented itself. A friend, Albert Smythe, owned a Philadelphia magazine called the *Saturday Evening Post.* As its masthead later proudly announced, the *Saturday Evening Post* had been founded as a newspaper in 1729, its original title being the *Pennsylvania Gazette.* It was sold in 1821 and under various owners throughout the nineteenth century it was published successively as the *Saturday Evening Post,* the *Daily Chronicle and Saturday Evening Post, Atkinson's Saturday Evening Post and Philadelphia News,* and finally as the *Saturday Evening Post* again.[2] Its lineage was distinguished: indirectly associated with Benjamin Franklin, an association Curtis and his editor would later exaggerate, the paper in one incarnation had published Edgar Allan Poe's "The Black Cat." Nathaniel Hawthorne, James Fenimore Cooper, and Harriet Beecher Stowe were among its other famous contributors.[3] The nineteenth-century *Post* was devoted to "Morality, Pure Literature, Foreign and Domestic News, Agriculture, Science, Art and Amusement," and at various times and under different owners it was touted as "A Mammoth Paper," "The Very Pearl of Literary Weeklies," and "The Great Family Paper of America."[4]

By 1895, the *Post,* despite its illustrious heritage, was faltering badly under weak leadership. Its sixteen newsprint pages were not illustrated, it no longer made any pretense at carrying the art, science, commercial, and political news it had once boasted of covering, and its fiction had sunk to the level of a penny weekly's. Curtis's friend, Smythe, died in August of 1897, leaving the periodical on the brink of bankruptcy. The *Post's* circulation numbered only 1,900, and it carried just one small column of advertising, which consisted mainly of patent-medicine announcements.[5] The executor of Smythe's business affairs, searching for a buyer, soon called on Curtis. Curtis stepped in and got himself a bargain, paying $1,000, $100 down, for the full rights to the *Saturday Evening Post.* For this token sum he bought a name and some associations that he hoped would attract both readers and advertisers.

Curtis put William George Jordan, formerly an assistant editor of the *Journal,* in charge of the new weekly. The 1897 issues were in large measure the old *Post* with the Curtis Publishing imprint on them, the first appearing on October 10, 1897. Jordan was not a strong editor, and he seemed headed for trouble working for Curtis, whose dictum regarding editors was "make good or hang yourself."[6] Fortunately, working under Jordan at the time was a young man named George Horace Lorimer. Lorimer had been a reporter in 1897 for the Boston *Herald* when, so the legend goes, the announcement came in over the press wire that Cyrus Curtis had bought the *Saturday Evening Post* and was looking for an editor. Less well known is the fact that Lorimer's father had not long before met Curtis and promoted his son as a prospective employee.[7] Young Lorimer soon wrote to Curtis, who came to Boston and hired him to serve not as editor but as "literary editor" of the new magazine.

Lorimer, who was thirty-one at the time, brought to the *Post* a lively and varied professional background. He was the son of a prominent actor turned evangelist, George Claude Lorimer, and he had passed his youth in Boston and Chicago. In contrast to Edward Bok's, Lorimer's had been a relatively comfortable and secure middle-class childhood, a fact that would bear quite directly on his editorship of the *Post.* In 1888, at the age of twenty-one, he left his family in Chicago to attend Yale, where he proved to be a rather aimless student. Back in Chicago for a visit, he met P. D. Armour, one of his father's wealthiest parishioners, who suggested that he could make the young Lorimer rich and happy in the meat-packing business. George Lorimer found this offer very attractive, and in spite of his parents' protests he left Yale for the business world. There he applied himself much more diligently than he had in college. Lorimer loved business, but he soon hankered to write about it more than to work at it. In 1896 he went east with his wife, Alma, to try his hand at newspaper work. After brushing up his writing skills at Colby College in Maine, he worked first at the Boston *Post* and then briefly at the *Herald,* where he learned about Curtis's acquisition of the *Saturday Evening Post.*

Lorimer might have felt qualified for the position as the *Post*'s editor-in-chief, but Curtis hired him to serve a secondary role and Lorimer seems to have been provisionally content. As it turned out, Jordan limped along for a year and a half, trying to "imitate some of the *Journal*'s sprightliness," but otherwise doing little to change the *Post.*[8] By the beginning of 1899 Curtis had run out of patience. He fired Jordan and sailed for Europe with the intention of enlisting the services of Arthur Sherburne Hardy, who had edited *Cosmopolitan Magazine* between 1893 and 1895. Curtis left Lorimer in charge, who later commented, "I had little money to spend and the paper had no reputation." What Lorimer did have, however, was an opportunity to prove his leadership capabilities.[9]

Lorimer dug up some old business fiction for the four issues he produced in Curtis's absence, and he instituted two new policies that quickly garnered some quality material for the periodical: he passed judgment on every submitted manuscript promptly, and he paid contributors upon acceptance. Curtis's meeting with Hardy never took place, and when he saw Lorimer's issues Curtis was impressed enough to give Lorimer the job of editor-in-chief, a position the editor would hold for thirty-eight years. Curtis raised Lorimer's salary from $40 to $250 per week, and, beginning with the March 17 issue of 1899, he gave free rein to Lorimer in the task of making the *Post* a vigorous weekly for men.[10]

Given the *Journal*'s quick success, some analysts have assumed that the same was true of the *Post.*[11] This was not the case. In January of 1898, six months after Curtis had acquired the magazine, it carried only nine advertisements, seven of them for the *Ladies' Home Journal.* By the end of 1900, three-

THE SATURDAY EVENING POST

FOUNDED, A.D. 1821

THE GREAT PIONEER FAMILY PAPER OF AMERICA

Vol. 77   PUBLISHED WEEKLY, AT 425 ARCH STREET   Philadelphia, Saturday, October 9, 1897   FIVE CENTS A COPY $2.00 A YEAR IN ADVANCE   No. 15

Entered at the Philadelphia Post-Office as Second-Class Matter

Copyright, 1897, by The Curtis Publishing Company

AS THE DAYS GO BY.

BY A. C.

Every day is a fresh beginning;
Every morn is the world made new;
You who are weary of sorrow and sinning,
Here is a beautiful hope for you.
A hope for me and a hope for you.

Yesterday now is a part of forever,
Bound up in a sheaf, which God holds tight.
With glad days, and sad days, and bad days
which never
Shall visit us more with their bloom and
their blight,
Their fullness of sunshine or sorrowful
night.

Let them go, since we cannot relieve them,
Cannot undo and cannot atone;
God in his mercy receive, forgive them;
Only the new days are our own;
To-day is ours, and to-day alone.

Every day is a fresh beginning;
Listen, my soul, to the glad refrain,
And spite of old sorrow and older sinning,
And puzzles forecasted and possible pain,
Take heart with the day, and begin again.

IN THE SHADOW.

BY N. S.

"O, that it was a night of sorrow and a dawn of hopelessness.

"Whatever Lili had done, I felt the hand of God was so heavy on her that it was not for me to judge her, though when I looked at the fur cloak and the jewels I knew something was amiss.

"I made coffee, but she could not drink it, and though her hands and head were as fire, she shivered as in an ague, and it was clear that fever burnt in her veins. At last, I know not how long first, she ceased to rock and sing; slowly, very slowly, she laid that piteous burden on her knees, and unwrapping a little shawl from about it, sat and gazed. Oh, but that was a moment never to be forgotten; a sight to make a strong man weep.

"There was silence, and then a long, long, wailing cry, and she fell forward senseless.

"I took it from her and laid it in the cradle it had so often gone to from my arms.

"And then I got Lili undressed, and saw on her shoulder a mark as of teeth of some beast, which had bruised and broken the skin. And as I lifted her into her bed, suddenly in my ear fell the deep solemn sound of a great bell tolling slowly; I had heard it once only before; it was the death knell of the family at the castle, and never was rung for any other reason than their passing away.

"Lili roused by it, but only to delirium; she raved incessantly though not violently, and from her talk I learnt little.

"O—, madame, my relief when I at length heard footsteps and Pierre entered with a young brother of my husband's. He hardly glanced at Lili when I bade him come to her, only saying to him-self:

"'She is dying, so is it best perhaps; so is it best.'

"And he had adored her!

"I had coffee hot, but Pierre drank raw brandy, and presently would have left the house in silence, but I would bear no more, and insisted that he fetch a doctor at once; he assented sullenly, and Jean, my husband's brother, stayed on, and from him I learnt all."

Widow Margot paused to dry her eyes and Lena's own were tear-dimmed as she thought of the tragic scenes these simple folks had gone through. Margot continued her tale, saying: ·

"Jean told me that in the terrible black storm a steamer ran into the yacht, and

Pierre with great difficulty brought her back to the harbor, for she was badly damaged. When, however, he got her in and could leave her in perfect safety, he and some others started to tell the Count, thinking it safer to go in a body, as the howling of wolves had been heard.

"They came first to Pierre's house, where he had promised them a supper and some good red wine, and found it as I did; but in the snow on the path leading towards the high road were foot-marks as of a woman and a man, who wore not the heavy boots of a country-man, though here and there the tracks of wolves, which I thought great dogs, had hidden them.

"Pierre had brought torches from the yacht, by whose light they saw these things; whether he suspected the truth none knew; but he pressed on, and at the main road found the marks of a sleigh, which had waited long, for the horses had pawed the snow and snatched at the branches.

"The other men fancied pursuit useless; they, too, began to suspect, but with bitter oaths Pierre ordered them to go on; and suddenly, where the road wound in a wide curve, they heard a horrible sound of snarling animals and a woman's cries for help.

"The moon had just shone out, and they saw clearly Lili against a tree, and standing before her Count Raymond, defending her against half-a-score of the great lean starving monsters; fur rugs and other things were scattered on the snow, and far away on the brow of the next hill, Jean caught a glimpse of the maddened horses flying with the sleigh and the rest of the pack in full pursuit.

"Just as they arrived Count Raymond, who was bleeding from half-a-dozen wounds, ran one wolf through the heart, but another sprang at his throat and a third seized Lili; but that pack of wolves, forewarned of a human foe, were cowardly at heart, and the sailors dashed at them furiously with their torches and thick sticks and beat off the unwounded ones, dashing out the brains of the others, and Pierre killed two with his knife. Without one word to Lili he knelt by Count Raymond, who had sunk down, and all the snow was red around him; but in Pierre's eyes gleamed such murderous hatred that Jean and another man drew near fearing he would use his knife once more. Count Raymond was helpless, but quite fearless; all he said was:

"'Pierre, I would have done you the cruellest wrong one man can do another, but God willed otherwise. I have suffered wrong by a fallen tree buried in snow, and the wolves were upon us at once.'

"Jean and the others strove to staunch the blood and give him brandy, but he said:

"'Leave me, my friends; it is useless.' "Then with a last effort he called Lili, and she came and knelt by him, and taking her hand he said firmly:

"'Pierre and all you others, listen. I swear that Lili is as pure as my own mother and sisters. I have respected the honor of those ornaments, and often brought her some trifle, a string of Venetian beads or coral ornaments, such as sailors bring from Mediterranean ports.'

"She was much delighted with a bunch of coral toys, a tiny Punchinello, a hand and other little charms, but one day came home crying because in her wandering they were lost.

"Pierre petted her tenderly and tried vainly to console her; but at last, smiling breaking through her tears, she demanded the permission to wear 'the watch, my grandmother's watch, to show madame.'

Lena expressed, of course, great interest and expected a common silver article of the turnip order, but to her surprise Lili danced up to her next day

but walked steadily and last by the dead body, for they dared not separate lest the pack should return after devouring the horses.

"Then they brought her home, and in the gray light she saw what they had missed, not far from the house; the little blue shoe of a baby showing from under the bushes, and with a heart-wrung cry she flung herself down and found all that remained of her boy.

"We only suppose she shut the door as she believed safely, but the wolves, hearing the child or the little dog, burst it open, the latch being old and worn; otherwise the little one, as she well knew, was quite safe till my return and would not have wakened."

Lena was crying openly by this time, and the widow Margot's tears fell fast.

"There is little more to tell, madame. It was, indeed, a day of mourning. At sunset the death-knell tolled once more, and we heard that the beautiful Julie, who loved her brother passionately, had passed away, giving premature birth to a child, which breathed but a few minutes and died too.

"Ah, since then the castle once so gay is as a tomb; the poor lady lives but to pray for her son's soul. She gives alms far and wide that all may join their prayers to hers that she may get that she may go to her with their grief.

"Pierre—well, madame, time dulls the keenest pain; he has grown to believe Lili was, as the count swore, still innocent, and he loves her still and is content in a fashion; at least, he complains not, and Lili—she is the only one, I think, who suffers not; behold her, madame, gay as a lark. She was long ill, but now—"

Lena looked out and saw the girl whose fatal beauty had brought such misery and sorrow, dancing gaily with some children singing the childish songs of the locality.

Setting to her little partner with dainty mincing steps, then he made her a rustic salute courtesying to the very ground and then with flying skirts dancing round once more in a ring with the romping happy little ones. Truly, her good angel had been near to petition that her senses should be thus clouded on that night of weeping.

Pierre became a hero in the estimation of Jack and Lena after this; his unconscious yet nobly chivalrous forgiveness of the girl-wife who had been so false to him touched the artist and his wife.

Lili took all Pierre gave, and for was content if trinket or dainty brought the laughter to her lips and won him a careless caress.

She occasionally remembered the lost jewels, which, as the Ainslies guessed, were given in simple faith to win intercession in heaven for the sin they had been used to bribe the foolish child to consent to.

Pierre could not bear to fancy her trifling even for those ornaments, and often brought her some trifle, a string of Venetian beads or coral ornaments, such as sailors bring from Mediterranean ports.

She was much delighted with a bunch of coral toys, a tiny Punchinello, a hand and other little charms, but one day came home crying because in her wandering they were lost.

Pierre petted her tenderly and tried vainly to console her; but at last, smiling breaking through her tears, she demanded the permission to wear "the watch, my grandmother's watch, to show madame."

Lena expressed, of course, great interest and expected a common silver article of the turnip order, but to her surprise Lili danced up to her next day

and proudly exhibited an old gold watch which had evidently been costly in its time.

With some curiosity Lena examined it. "Does it keep good time?" she asked. Lili looked wise and said, "No, madame, not it went to sleep when the grandmother did, and it has never awakened."

Jack, who had the watch in his hand, opened it and said carelessly, "An English watch; I wonder how the worthy old grandmother came by it."

He touched another spring and suddenly looked at it with much greater attention, and closing it, returned it to Lili, saying, as with sudden thought:

"Lili, the light will be just right in half-an-hour. Shall I finish your picture?"

Lili was delighted, and ran off to get ready, and Jack asked his wife with studied indifference if in all her gossip she had found out why Lili seemed to be of no relatives of her own, and who her mother was.

"Oh, yes, the mother was maid at the castle, and a valet fell in love with her and married her; they went away and took some sort of shop. A fever broke out and he died. And the mother, returned to the castle, brought—"

"Ask, Fanny, who owned the watch, who was she?"

"Oh, really, even my love of gossip did pursue the genealogy so far back," said Lena merrily. "You must ask Margot, if your curiosity exceeds mine, that is."

Jack turned the conversation, but before the day was spent hours older, question of Margot.

"The grandmother of Lili? Ah, monsieur, did I not tell you? We know not. Ah, it is a strange story."

Margot was polishing one of her most imposing brass pans, which already rivalled burnished gold, and pausing to hang it up, invited monsieur to sit down, while she shelled peas, and hear the tale.

Jack swung himself on to the broad window ledge, his eyes fixed on the comely black-eyed, buxom house-wife, who suited so well with her homely surroundings, the red-tiled floor, clean white tables, bright pans and well-washed china; but he hardly for once noted all these things, but thought only of what he was to hear.

"After all, monsieur," said Madame Margot, as the green peas fell quickly in her basin, "I only know what my brother told me, that there were storms, the like of which come not often, thanks to the blessed saints, and there were wrecks, oh, wrecks without number; and my father and others went out when the wind dropped a little to get anything they could. They were poor, see you, and wreckage belongs to all, does not monsieur agree?"

"Oh, perfectly, perfectly!" said Jack with a mental reservation—that he supposed they were a set of wreckers and smugglers.

Margot, however, continued, unconscious of his opinion, and explained that one morning clearly a very large vessel had been lost, for they found much broken timber and other things floating about; and at last, on some rocks well-known as most dangerous, they saw a little child bound to her by a shawl, and, miracle of miracles! it breathed; and the fishermen took it and did all they could to restore it, and after that was brought it home with all that was likely to be of value on the mother, and the good monks came from the monastery near and buried all the poor creatures.

and-a-half years after Curtis had acquired the *Post* and nearly two years after Lorimer had become its editor, the *Post* was costing the Curtis Publishing Company thousands of dollars a month. Its advertising had increased from 2 percent of its columns in 1898 to 5 percent in 1899 and 15 percent in 1900, but even 15 percent was still only half the advertising that the *Journal* had featured in its first issue in 1883. In addition, the *Post*'s circulation in 1899 was less than three hundred thousand, a level the *Journal* had surpassed some fifteen years earlier. Curtis had given full control to his new editor, Lorimer, who was exceptionally capable and efficient. Why, then, the struggle for this second Curtis magazine?

The reasons are several and overlapping, some obvious and some more subtle. One obvious reason is that Lorimer inherited a mess. Knapp started the *Journal* with a clean slate, and Bok inherited an established periodical with a strong formula and a solid circulation. The *Post,* in contrast, had already been struggling for years when Curtis bought it, and it was then put under the management of a weak editor. It is not clear why Curtis looked for an existing vehicle for his new magazine instead of simply starting fresh as he had with the *Journal.* He was certainly intrigued by the *Saturday Evening Post* heritage; that alone may have persuaded him to begin with an established though dying periodical. In any event, the *Post* had virtually no circulation base to begin with, and Curtis and Lorimer lost most of the small group of Philadelphia subscribers they had inherited when they began to modify the magazine. The weekly consisted of sixteen newsprint pages of mediocre short stories and unsigned columns, material mostly gathered from other periodicals. Curtis had bought the *Post* for its illustrious name, but that name was not the asset that Curtis had hoped it would be.

The nature of the magazine world contributed to their difficulties as well. Magazines at the turn of the century continued to be a growth industry. The years 1885 to 1905 saw remarkable industrial and financial expansion, and, except for 1893, those years were characterized by quite consistent prosperity. By far the quickest medium of the day to proliferate was magazines. In 1865 there had been one copy of a monthly magazine for every ten people; by 1905 there were three for every four people, or about four to every household.[12]

The greatest expansion came in the category of middlebrow magazines. Highbrow monthlies like the *Nation*, the *Century,* and *Harper's* cost thirty-five cents in the late 1890s, and they reached for the "only audience worth addressing . . . the thinking people."[13] In contrast, middlebrow magazines for women like the *Ladies' Home Journal, Good Housekeeping, McCall's,* and the *Delineator,* and the more general monthlies like *Cosmopolitan, Collier's, Munsey's,* and *McClure's* sold for the much lower price of ten cents.[14] In 1900 the circulation leaders—*Comfort, Ladies' Home Journal, Hearthstone,* and *Munsey's*— were either glorified mail order catalogues or middlebrow magazines costing ten cents. The lines of the magazine world were thus being drawn, with middle-class monthlies outnumbering and outselling both more and less expensive publications.

Curtis and Knapp had been able to establish the *Ladies' Home Journal* largely without professional notice, allowing them to experiment with the magazine's format and to test public reaction without much interference. Curtis had perhaps even less of a clear format in mind for the *Post* when he acquired it, and similar time for Curtis and Lorimer to try new ideas and to see how the public responded without critical examination would have been helpful. But from the day that Curtis purchased the *Post,* he and Lorimer faced skepticism from much of the publishing community. *Printer's Ink,* the primary journal of the publishing industry, was especially derisive about the new magazine's chances for success. Its writers suggested in the late 1890s that the weekly format was outdated, and that no publisher could produce a decent magazine and sell it for only five cents a copy. Besides, *Printer's Ink* editorialized, men already had plenty of magazines and newspapers to read.

The skepticism about the weekly format and decent quality proved relatively easy to dispel, but the last objection was more powerful. Did men have plenty of magazines and newspapers to read at the turn of the century? If they did, why did Curtis and Lorimer want to establish another publication intended for men?

The gender-related contours of the magazine world provide the answers to these questions. As I have noted, the world of nineteenth-century reading matter was already a world ordered to some extent by gender. Both books and magazines intended specifically for women and for boys and girls had begun to proliferate. But books and magazines targeted for these groups came out of an otherwise apparently genderless or gender-neutral context. This context was built around the assumption that men certainly were readers—readers of books, magazines, and newspapers. But these materials did not generally cater to men as men; instead they reflected the tendency to view the male as the norm. Consequently, much of the earliest conscious gender-targeting of print matter in the nineteenth century came from books and magazines designed expressly for women. As I have suggested earlier, the motivation was largely commercial. Women, given their status as potential consumers, were worth targeting in a special way.

Central to Curtis and Lorimer's aspiration for the *Saturday Evening Post* was the notion of making gender-targeting to men more explicit. It is no accident that it was the publisher of the *Journal* who sought to create a second gendered publication. If advertisers were so anxious to reach women with their messages, Curtis reasoned, surely they would welcome the opportunity to reach out consciously to men as well. And Curtis and Lorimer would provide the vehicle. They would prove to be somewhat ahead of their time in their conception of the new magazine, however. Advertisers and readers alike would echo the *Printer's Ink* view that men had enough to read already, and they would be slow to support the *Post.*

The *Journal* had a clear formula from the beginning, one that is striking in its breadth and simplicity: the magazine sought to speak to every major interest in a white middle-class woman's life. The formula that Curtis and Lorimer proposed for the *Post* was somewhat more narrow, and it appeared to be equally simple: to inspire and entertain middle-class men with discussions of and stories about their chief interest in life—work, especially business. But the beginnings of the two magazines were markedly different.

As we have seen, the *Journal* began almost accidentally, when three empty newspaper columns were filled at the last minute and advertisements geared for women were placed in proximity to those columns. Three aspects of this early phase of the *Journal* provide a clear contrast with the later fledgling *Post:* (1) there was an easily-identified range of interests known as women's interests, which could be gathered quickly and packaged neatly, first in a column, then on a page, then in a magazine; (2) advertisers were ready, even eager, to sell their products to women; and (3) women responded immediately and positively to the Curtises' column, page, and supplement, suggesting that there was indeed a demand for the new women's publication.

As I suggested earlier, Cyrus Curtis and Louisa Knapp Curtis built the *Journal* on the assumption that middle-class women shared a set of interests that could be contained in a single package, a package that in turn reflected women's circumscribed and prescriptive sphere. Cyrus Curtis had more difficulty determining a corresponding set of men's interests because, as I have already noted, there was no corresponding men's "sphere." Men's interests were more diffuse and were therefore significantly more difficult to package. Hence there were political magazines and nature magazines and sports magazines in which men were presumed to have an interest, but there were no magazines that attempted to speak to all of a middle-class man's interests.[15] Consequently, Curtis and the early editors of the *Saturday Evening Post* would wrestle with the magazine's range of content for years.

The second component contributing to the *Journal*'s success—the ready and willing group of advertisers to whom the *Journal*'s producers had catered—was also unavailable to Curtis and Lorimer. The concept of a men's general magazine was more difficult to link with commerce than the women's magazine had been. In large part this difficulty resulted from the work Curtis, Knapp, and Bok had done with the *Journal* and with the advertisers who had bought space in the magazine. They had helped to create an atmosphere in which women were seen not simply as consumers, but as *the* consumers. To suddenly suggest that men were consumers as well must have been alien to advertisers who were conditioned to focus in large part on women. In other words, there was no commercial superstructure of consumption for men to parallel that for women. Ironically, then, given their subsequent interest in men as consumers, the Curtis magazine producers had contributed directly to creating a milieu that by the turn of the century made it difficult to unite cultural constructions of masculinity with commerce.

This turn-of-the-century reality underscores the role that polarized, oppositional thinking played in conceptualizing gender; in this case, conceptualizing gender in relation to commercialism. In the space of ten to fifteen years, women had become known as the culture's primary consumers. Given the cultural tendency to polarize with regard to gender construction, the converse also became true, that is, that men were not the culture's primary consumers. Femininity and masculinity were preserved as polar opposites even in the face of denying potential profits from a new set of consumers. Men might have been responsible for buying some products, but advertisers and many magazine producers alike simply found women, given their role as primary consumers, the more compelling audience. Rather than seeing men as a different set of consumers with different interests, the commercial establishment polarized women and men as consumers and "not-consumers."

A powerful form of cultural hegemony was at work here. A gendered commercial world, in which women were central as active consumers, had taken shape; and at this time even Cyrus Curtis, who had been one of the primary shapers of gendered commerce in the 1880s, had relatively little power to affect it in the 1890s. The simplistic view that women were consumers reigned supreme. Curtis's lack of success demonstrates how pervasive and strong the cultural hegemony of woman-centered commerce had become.

There seemed to be no particular reason for middle-class men to read the *Post* at the turn of the century. They were used to reading gender-neutral or inclusive materials like newspapers and topical magazines, so middle-class men did not seem to "need" a gendered magazine the way women had needed the *Journal.* Above all, there was no parallel infrastructure for consuming among middle-class white men, that is, no parallel set of reasons to hear commercial messages and respond to them. Consequently, Curtis and Lorimer faced an uphill struggle in trying to create and sell their new magazine.

Lorimer regularly worked a fifteen-hour day, and he viewed himself as indispensable to every phase of the *Post* operation. Like Curtis and Bok, Lorimer was very much a part of the commercial side of the publishing/editing endeavor, once describing his job as the "business of buying and selling brains."[16] He ruled the *Post* organization with an iron fist, but he employed an informal management style that was very different from Bok's. The installation of a buzzer system in the new Curtis building in 1901 highlights this difference. It soon became a great honor to be "buzzed" by Bok, while Lorimer almost never used his own buzzer. Lorimer was more likely to be seen making the rounds of staff desks, stopping to inquire about some business detail, practicing an early version of management by walking around.[17] Workers described Lorimer's editorial style, however, as "benevolent despotism," and it is clear that he regulated more closely the material printed in the *Post* than Bok did the material placed in the *Journal*.[18]

Lorimer and Bok were different personalities as well. Bok was gregarious and arrogant, a relentless self-promoter. Lorimer, in contrast, was a man's man, with a sardonic sense of humor, an ambitious man who worked hard and played hard. As Jan Cohn suggests in *Creating America,* the *Post* was Lorimer, but Lorimer let the magazine stand for him, consciously refraining from promoting himself the way Bok did.[19] The differences between Bok and Lorimer serve as a caution against generalizing about media producers. If one were to study Bok alone, one might conclude that all male magazine producers were patronizing, publicity-seeking do-gooders who were bent on reforming both their readers and their culture. Bok and Lorimer shared a few attributes as editors, but Lorimer actually had more in common with Knapp as an editor than with Bok. We have seen that the gender of the editor is important in contrasting Bok's *Journal* with Knapp's. We will see the gender factor in evidence as well when we contrast Lorimer's *Post* with Knapp's *Journal.* But personality and temperament seemed to play an equally important part in determining an editor's approach.

Lorimer and Bok were never friends, and there actually soon developed something of a silent feud between the two editors. Bok was nervous about the acquisition of the *Post,* at first because it threatened to drain *Journal* resources, later because the magazine began to compete for acclaim and even for readers. He patronized the *Post* in print, referring to it as the *"Journal's* little brother" and entitling a description of the *Post's* difficult early years "The Story of a Singed Cat."[20] Lorimer for his part found Bok's self-promotion appalling, and he resented Bok's condescension toward the *Post* enormously. The two men dealt with their mutual dislike by staying as far away from each other as possible. "With regard to the *Ladies' Home Journal,"* wrote Lorimer at one point, "I am practically an outsider."[21]

In this strained environment Lorimer attempted to modernize the *Post,* to bring it up to par with the *Journal.* The heritage of the old *Post* certainly presented part of the difficulty in defining a new men's formula. Reflecting the gender inclusiveness of some nineteenth-century reading matter, the *Saturday*

Evening Post "reached for the whole man, in fact, for the whole family." In the latter half of the century its producers noted that "The *Post* is a family paper— [only] articles . . . calculated to enter the family circle can be admitted to its columns."[22] Unfortunately, the *Post* formula of the mid-to-late 1800s failed miserably in execution.

Thus, the *Post* that Lorimer inherited had a little something for everyone, with nothing of high quality. In 1897 it averaged twelve short stories of a moralistic and insipid nature per sixteen-page issue, with titles like, "For the Sake of Tom, a Story of Daffodil Time." The next most frequent offerings in the 1897 *Post* were articles about science or agriculture, which consisted of little more than quaint observations about natural phenomena. The magazine included a children's page, suggesting that it took its family mission seriously, and it regularly addressed women as well as men. There was a column called "Femininities. Masculinities." in this version of the *Post,* given to facts like "the population of the world averages 109 women to 100 men," and "one of the latest forms of gallantry on the Continent is to name one's bicycle after one's lady love."[23] The 1897 *Post* also featured a regular humor page. A typical exchange: " 'Marie, I thought your doctor told you that you were not strong enough to ride a bike?' 'Yes, but then I went to another doctor.' "[24] The quality of the *Post* had steadily declined over the last decades of the nineteenth century, diminishing what might have been an interesting contribution to the twentieth-century publishing world, a magazine that was explicitly gender-inclusive.

The magazine took on a new look and a slightly new tone in January of 1898, when Jordan tried to make the *Post* more of a Curtis publication. The humor page, children's page, and the "Femininities. Masculinities." column were gone, there were nine stories in each issue instead of twelve, and all material was signed. Biography became an important feature of the magazine under Jordan's editorship, appearing primarily in a column called "Men and Women of the Hour." The *Post* began to look more professional and its features were somewhat livelier. But despite Curtis's stated interest, Jordan did not even try to make it into a magazine especially for men.

Immediately upon assuming the editorship Lorimer began to beef up the *Post*'s editorial page, making it the center of the magazine. Lorimer's action was reminiscent of Bok's taking control of the *Journal*'s editorial page ten years earlier, but there were major differences. While Bok made his editorial page a coherent, organized letter, addressed to his readers in a self-consciously intimate tone and always signed, Lorimer presented a loosely constructed page featuring four or five short pieces on various topics, sometimes signed and sometimes unsigned, sometimes written by staff members, sometimes by himself. Lorimer's editorial page more closely resembled Knapp's, reflecting the flexibility and collegiality of both of their approaches.

Femininities.

Women of every rank go bareheaded in Mexico.

New Hampshire has three women treasurers of savings banks.

Speak with calmness on all occasions, especially in circumstances which tend to irritate.

If buttons or buttonholes are to be subjected to severe strain, add an extra layer of cloth when making the garment.

In the time of George III. it was the fashion for all the great Court ladies to take snuff. We read that Queen Charlotte herself was most particular as to the quality of her snuff.

Sixty thousand Italian ladies, led by the flower of the aristocracy of Rome, are petitioning the Chamber against divorce, which they contend is an offence against religion.

Pleasure has many definitions; but, very frequently, it consists of going somewhere, being perfectly uncomfortable all the time while there, and calling it "the best time you ever had."

A woman's club is being formed in Paris, whose object shall be social intercourse, afternoon tea, and gossip. Only the wives of members of men's clubs will be admitted into its sacred precincts.

In France it is forbidden under severe penalties for anyone to give infants under one year any form of solid food, unless such be ordered by written prescription signed by a legally qualified medical man.

Miss Passoe: "I accepted Dick Bradford last night." Miss Younge: "Yes, I expected it." "Why?" "Because, when I refused him, he said the next time he would propose to someone old enough to know her own mind."

A most objectionable custom, at present highly in vogue in smart society in Paris, is that of painting children's faces. Fashionable mothers paint their youngsters' cheeks and lips with the same hues that they wear themselves.

Cut glass will not look clear unless washed in very hot water, but does not require soap. If it is in any way blurred or tarnished, it must be cleaned with a soft brush dipped in whiting and then polished with a soft piece of newspaper; this gives it a brilliant, clear appearance; and no lint remains, as when rubbed with a linen towel.

In former times it was esteemed highly improper for single or unmarried persons to wear rings, "unless they were judges, doctors, or senators." For all but these dignitaries such an unwarranted ornament was considered an evidence of "vanity, levity, and pride," and was looked upon as a great piece of presumption on the part of the wearer.

The following dialogue is said to have taken place recently between a married couple on their travels:—"My dear, are you comfortable in that corner?" "Quite thank you, my dear." "Sure there's plenty of room for your feet?" "Quite sure, love." "And no cold air from the window by your ear?" "Quite certain, darling." "Then, my dear, I'll change places with you."

A new table ornament called the fairy flower has just been introduced. Electric wires run through the flowers like stems, which are attached to the plants, lighting the seemingly real leaves of tulips, roses white and red; and snowdrops and tiger lilies will shortly be produced. For dinner-table decoration the electricity can be secreted in a neat accumulator inside a flower pot, and will be charged from the main supply.

In China a woman is little more than a chattel. When a Chinese girl marries, she becomes, not the mistress of a household, but the servant of her mother-in-law. The men marry young, and it is the exception for a son to be single at the time of his mother's death. It is only when the mother-in-law becomes feeble and finally dies that the wife takes charge of the domestic arrangements, and then only if she be the wife of the eldest son.

Statistics show that the medical profession supplies 40 per cent of the male morphine users, which is the largest proportion, after which follow the men of leisure, 15 per cent; merchants, 6 per cent; while farmers, clergymen, and politicians occupy the lowest positions numerically on the list. Among the females addicted to the habit, the largest number, 45 per cent, are women of means, and these are followed in number by the wives of medical men, who make up 10 per cent of the list.

Here are some golden words for mothers: Never rub your eyes, nor allow your children to do so, from their cradles. Veils are bad for the sight, especially those spotted or covered with a pattern; so eschew veils when you can, or wear the softest, clearest net when obliged to do so. Pale blues or greens are the most restful wall-papers for the eyes, whereas red is exceedingly fatiguing. If the eyes be weak, bathe them in a basin of soft water, in which a pinch of table salt and a teaspoonful of ... to has been added.

Masculinities.

A man who has no one to tell his troubles to feels about as dismal as a woman who has no one to tell other people's troubles to.

Without the express consent of his wife no married Austrian subject can procure a passport for journeying beyond the frontier.

It was a very proper answer to him who asked why any man should be delighted with beauty, that it was a question that none but a blind man should ask.

"Yes, dear, I had to decline him, because I know he could never make me a happy woman." "Why do you think that?" "He told me he would never live beyond his income even for my sake."

The house of Voltaire, the celebrated infidel, who declared that Christianity would pass out of existence before the end of 100 years, is now used by the Geneva Bible Society as a repository for bibles.

A philosopher observes that there are two periods of life when a man looks to see if his hair is coming out—at twenty, when he inspects his upper lip; at forty, when he inspects the top of his head.

If a person is choking, break an egg as quickly as possible and give the white—do not beat it—and it will almost certainly dislodge the obstruction, whatever it may be, unless it is lodged in the windpipe.

A French inventor had attached a tiny incandescent lamp to an ordinary pencil, for use by reporters and others having to take notes at night. The battery is carried in the pocket, the wires passing down the sleeve.

"Yes, sir, I know one woman who can keep a secret." "Please explain." "My wife and I have been married for ten years now, and she has never yet consented to tell me how it is that she is always in need of money."

Daughter, reading letter: "But, pa dear, in this last word you put a letter too much. Pa, self-made, and not a bit of pride about him: 'Ave I, dear? Never mind; I dessay I've left one out in some other word, so that'll square it."

The Chinese believe there is a season for everything. In accordance with this belief, they think the opening year—the season when the peach petal bursts from the calyx—is the most auspicious season for forming matrimonial alliances.

In the ninth and tenth centuries the greatest kings and princes of Europe all wore wooden shoes—not wooden boots like those worn by some of the Germans, Hollanders, and Frenchmen of to-day, but wooden soles fastened to the feet with leather thongs.

"It's surprising how impracticable some very learned men are." "Yes; there's Professor Lingwist for example. He spent over half his life in acquiring fluency in nine or ten different languages, and then went and married a wife who never gives him a chance to get a word in edgeways."

"There is one satisfaction a bald-headed man can have," observes a physician, "and that is that there are hundreds of consumption. There seems to be some kind of connection between bald heads and sound lungs. If a man is prematurely bald it shows that there is something abnormal with him but it does not show that there is any trouble with his lungs."

Lorimer proceeded quickly to make the *Post* as masculine as he could. From the beginning he and Curtis were interested in reaching the American businessman. Historian Jan Cohn comments:

> Lorimer found the principal focus for the *Post* in the idea of business, and the intended audience in the businessman, especially the younger man out to make his way in an America Lorimer believed would discover and create itself through business in the century that lay ahead.[25]

Lorimer operated from a broad conception of the businessman, which included some professionals and lower-level workers like clerks and drummers, as well as the more obvious men of business in corporations and offices.[26]

Articles on business would soon be supplemented by biographical sketches and political and military features. This broadening occurred because Lorimer wanted to appeal to as many men as he could. He wrote to his friend Senator Albert Beveridge in 1899: "I'm beginning to see that the man of the day wants a variety, and we're trying to meet that demand by broadening our scope. I'd like an article from you about the everyday goings-on in Washington, one that will get young men interested in the way real government works."[27] Lorimer's desire to reach as broad a male audience as possible was entirely compatible with Curtis's own impulses.

While Curtis wanted a business magazine, he wanted even more a magazine that would appeal to many middle-class men, a mass-circulation magazine that the husbands of *Journal* readers would buy. And, of course, not all of those husbands were businessmen, even under Lorimer's broad definition. Curtis wanted a mass magazine, and if a magazine targeted only to businessmen would mean an exclusive or specialized magazine, he preferred seeing the magazine's formula broadened.

The *Post* evolution highlights a crucial facet of the male role: while work may be the central source of identity for almost all men—and sociologists, anthropologists, and historians agree that it is—the specialized nature of work as a source of identification means that it does not automatically link all men. In other words, men may share a common bond, namely the importance of work to their lives, but the very nature of men's work has as much potential to separate as it does to join them. For example, doctors and sales clerks share the general experience of working, but the specific natures of their jobs are very different. Therefore, when Lorimer tried to speak to one type of work, he effectively excluded others. Even business, with its rapid growth at the turn of the century, seemed to be too narrow a category to serve as the foundation of a mass-circulation magazine for men. Lorimer quickly adapted by addressing a constellation of men's interests rather than just one.

The fact that Lorimer chose to emphasize biography in his magazine for men is characteristic of his editorial style. An early Lorimer promotion for the *Post* suggested that much is to be learned between the lines of an autobiography as well as in the lines. More from an actual record of life than from deliberate and deadly attempts to tell the young man to be good and he will be happy.[28]

Lorimer as editor felt a duty to inspire his readers as well as to entertain, but he believed in the value of an indirect approach. Using biography as an indirect way to model appropriate behavior had several results: the magazine under Lorimer had a distinctly less preachy tone than did its earlier incarnations or Bok's *Journal;* famous businessmen, politicians, and writers—in general financially successful men—increasingly became the models for appropriate male behavior; and discussions of what it meant to be a good or real man were implicit rather than explicit. It is not the case that Lorimer was averse to moralizing: the *Post* regularly promoted its political and business-related views and attempted to influence readers' opinions in the realm of public issues. The *Post* therefore prescribed political and business views, but it avoided such prescription regarding men's personal lives.

While Bok engaged directly and often emotionally in gender-role prescription, Lorimer, the man's man, preferred to let the models whom he chose speak for themselves. This in part reflects Lorimer's aversion to editorial self-aggrandizement. It also reflects the difference in mission between the two magazines in these years. For while the *Post* aspired to some instruction, its more important goals were to entertain and inform. Lorimer's *Post* shared this general orientation with Knapp's *Journal.* In Bok's hands, however, the *Journal* had come to feature much more preaching, and Lorimer defined his magazine in conscious, purposeful contrast.

This raises the question of the possible impact of the editor's gender on gender construction as it was presented in the pages of a magazine. Evidence from Knapp's *Journal* and Lorimer's *Post* suggests that gender construction is more seamless and less intrusive when the editor and the targeted audience are of the same gender group. Gender expectations can be embodied more than explicitly discussed, and advice can be offered more sincerely. It is certainly the case that personality bears on this issue; hence Bok preached to men as well as to women when he had the opportunity. But the bulk of his discussion in the *Journal* was "man to woman," and it smacked always of condescension and moral judgment. Knapp's "woman to woman" and Lorimer's "man to man" discussions, to the extent that Lorimer held them, seemed much more natural and straightforward. The difference in tone between Bok's *Journal* on the one hand, and Knapp's *Journal* and Lorimer's *Post,* on the other, would have a long-term impact on the difference between women's and men's magazines in general. Lorimer was under pressure in these early years to convince readers of the worthiness of his style and tone, which would take some time. But in the long run they would appeal to a very large audience.

Thus Lorimer in 1899–1900 began to shape his version of a men's magazine, one that paralleled Bok's *Journal* with its explicit gender-targeting and broad set of offerings, but which revolved around a distinctly different set of interests and employed a distinctly different rhetoric. By the end of 1900 the *Post* featured a balance of political and military articles, biographical and autobiographical sketches, articles about business, and fiction. Another sign of the *Post*'s evolution under Lorimer is that contributions from women were halved each year between 1897 and 1900, falling from 40 percent to 20 percent to 10 percent; in 1900 women provided only about a third of the *Post*'s fiction, and virtually none of its nonfiction. Staffers and contributors to the *Post* by 1900 included Maurice Thompson, Fred Nye, Thomas B. Reed, Robert Ellis Thompson, Lynn Roby Meekins, Senator Albert J. Beveridge, and "Buffalo Bill" Cody.

Other magazines of the day reached out to men in ways similar to the *Post*. Two such publications were the *World's Work* and *McClure's*. These two magazines, along with the *Saturday Evening Post,* featured a new kind of realism that would distinguish the "modern" from the traditional magazine. This took the form of an emphasis on scientific objectivity in the *World's Work,* a monthly designed to inform men about both national and international affairs. Both the *World's Work* and *McClure's* made regular use of photographs, in the case of the first to provide authoritative evidence for assertions about people, places, and things, and in the case of the second to substantiate its muckraking accusations.[29]

The *Post*'s realism was conveyed, in contrast, through its particular folksy brand of common sense. Lorimer conveyed his tone through a steady stream of celebrity and political gossip, humorous anecdotes and aphorisms, and down home, boy-meets-girl romantic fiction.[30] He and Curtis also positioned the weekly *Post,* as compared with the monthly *World's Work* and *McClure's,* to compete more directly with daily newspapers. Accordingly, an 1898 prospectus for the *Post* noted, "a good magazine is a good newspaper in a dress suit."[31] In sum, the weekly *Post* was aimed in the marketplace of reading materials at the middle ground between the national monthlies and the local daily newspaper. The magazine thereby embodied the gendered assumption that men needed to keep up with current events.

Hence Curtis and Lorimer and some other magazine producers of the day began to establish newly gendered magazines consciously addressed to men. As I have suggested, this was a new and unpopular idea in the world of ungendered or female-targeted publishing. *Post* producers were, in these early years, actually unable to demonstrate to advertisers any compelling link between concepts of masculinity and commercialism. A gendered commercial milieu for men would take significantly longer to establish than it had for women.

It is also the case that in terms of their actual content, these magazines remained less gendered than women's magazines. Again, we see a polarizing pat-

When Buffaloes Roamed in Herds
HUNTING IN THE FAR WEST
By Colonel Wm. F. Cody

tern in masculine versus feminine content. The *Saturday Evening Post* did not comment explicitly on the nature or situation of the human male. The *Post* was a reflection of its editor, and as such the magazine embodied, more than it expressly considered, the male role. Accordingly, gender construction in the *Post* was a much more subtle enterprise than it was in the *Journal.*

But commentary on masculinity did exist in the *Post,* and we must not overlook it. The implicit nature of gender norms as presented in the *Post,* in fact, enhances the importance of the magazine as a medium for gender-related messages since it highlights fundamental and critical differences between constructions of femininity and masculinity. While womanhood demanded conscious definition and prescription, manhood demanded an equally real, if less overt set of definitions and prescriptions. Examining the *Post*'s more subtle consideration is central to understanding gender discourses and gender constructions at the turn of the century.

6

Speaking to and about Men: The Content of the *Post,* 1897–1900

The *Saturday Evening Post* between 1897 and 1900 was a complicated publication. It was a weak, dying magazine given new life upon Curtis's acquiring it; it was a fledgling commercial magazine under Lorimer's early editorial leadership; and it came to be a magazine intended for men but speaking to some women's interests as well. The *Post* reflected its time, even as it attempted to comment on and to shape it. Lorimer shared with Knapp the challenge of interpreting his own gender role, albeit less consciously, to members of his own gender group. He shared with Bok the challenge of reacting as a man to the changes occurring in the lives of middle-class women at the turn of the century.

The *Post*'s content focused on the public realm for the most part. Men were viewed primarily as breadwinners and as citizens concerned with public issues. Like Bok, Lorimer was informed by the concept of a clear division between public and private matters, but he employed that division very differently. Like Knapp, Lorimer believed that middle-class women had a right to expand their activity at the turn of the century. As a result, while he focused on public matters and on men mainly as public actors, Lorimer invited at least some women to join men in that public realm. The *Post*'s commentary on women between 1897 and 1900 was distinctly affirming and supportive of change.

Moreover, the *Post*'s commentary on women's lives in these years was direct and open, unlike its commentary on men. This contrast was a result largely of the fact that middle-class women who were seeking to improve their lot were working actively for change. In the main, middle-class men were simply seeking to preserve their power and privilege relative to women. Consequently, we see in the pages of the *Post* that men were defined less explicitly, that images of good men were conveyed most clearly in the magazine's fiction, and that the ideas the magazine did not contain were sometimes as important as those it did contain. We see, above all, the interactive nature of gender-role norms. Lorimer and his contributors were reacting to changes in women's lives in part by refining, slightly and subtly, images of masculinity.

Locating the *Post* in the gender culture of its early years is a necessary but difficult task. Our knowledge of interactive gender relations in the nineteenth century is still limited, as is our knowledge of ordinary men. Even when we know about the actual experiences of real men, their culturally "ungendered" nature often makes this information difficult to interpret. As Sigmund Freud once wrote, "masculinity is a term of no great clarity."[1] Some obvious changes were occurring in the lives of middle-class white men in these years. More and more men were coming to see themselves as businessmen, and the nation's economy was identified increasingly as industrial rather than agricultural.[2] Educational levels were rising steadily; by the turn of the century 7 percent of white men were attending college.[3] Middle-class men were experiencing an increasingly high standard of living, and many were expecting even better things for their sons and daughters.

Beyond these social facts historians disagree about the character of the middle-class male experience at the turn of the century. Historians of men's lives writing in the 1980s characterized this period as a time of a crisis of masculinity over the closing of the frontier, the rise of corporate capitalism, and changes in the female role. Early studies concluded that the role of the Victorian patriarch had been undercut by these broad social developments. The result was frustration and anger, according to these scholars, which was often vented in various forms of hypermasculinity: sports like boxing became increasingly popular, the Boy Scouts were formed to foster virility, male commentators prescribed women's behavior in advice literature and from pulpits, and huge numbers of middle-class men bonded and proved themselves in highly ritualized secret lodges and fraternities.[4]

This early assessment of a crisis of masculinity has the advantage of simplicity and inclusiveness, but more recent scholarship suggests that it glosses over the reality of men's lives. One historian argues, for example, that the distance between nineteenth-century men and women has been exaggerated, and that historians have neglected to recognize the rich and deep intimacies shared by nineteenth-century couples.[5] Another suggests, as I noted with respect to Edward Bok in chapter 4, that some men responded to perceived changes in women's role not by promoting hypermasculine or angry responses but by developing masculine domesticity as a gentler but still masculine alternative.[6] Other historians identify male responses to women ranging from antifeminist to masculinist to profeminist, as well as the tendency of turn-of-the-century men to cope with strains in their lives by compartmentalizing their public and private lives to a notable degree.[7]

In addition, recent scholarship has begun to provide evidence of an evolution in the middle-class male gender role over the course of the nineteenth century. The pre–Civil War years in this country were marked by significantly divergent concepts of masculinity.[8] Liberal abolitionist and conservative secessionist men alike enjoyed highly affectionate homosocial friendships, much like the ones Carroll Smith-Rosenberg has described for women of the day.[9] In contrast, lawyers in these years competed strenuously with one another and with men in other professions, celebrating political realism and physical courage.[10] Icons of the day included the stern Victorian patriarch, but also gentle ministers, tough cowboys, and even efficient male quilters.[11]

The Civil War was a time of major change in attitudes toward masculinity. Women began to take public leadership in these years on issues like suffrage, temperance, prostitution, and child welfare, hence demanding some new response from men. But even more significant for men were changes related to work and to leisure. As Clyde Griffen, editor of the essay collection entitled *Meanings for Manhood,* writes:

> Middle-class men after the Civil War moved toward an accommodation with the emerging world of a bureaucratized corporate capitalism—with its greater job security, consumer options, and leisure time in more comfortable homes—and simultaneously moved toward compensatory ideas and fantasies of male independence, adventure, and virility.[12]

The coupling of these largely contradictory notions—of business and adventure, of corporate capitalism and independence—informed the *Post* under Lorimer and supplied much of its content throughout his editorial tenure. As Anthony Rotundo observes, standards of masculinity in the late nineteenth century embraced the passion that earlier had been attributed to but quite consciously repressed in men. In the late 1800s the male body moved to the center of men's gender concerns; martial approaches to conflict were admired; and the competitive instinct in men was lauded.[13] The *Post* of these years embodied the tension of evolving male gender-role notions, but its content does not support the idea of a full-blown crisis of masculinity. Similarly, the editors of *Meanings for Manhood* conclude that the turn of the century signaled, not a crisis of masculinity, but rather a narrowing of the range of options for men.

Some men, like Edward Bok, were uncomfortable with this narrower range of options and with changes in norms for women. Bok reacted by castigating women who sought change and by creating a new alternative for men in the form of masculine domesticity. George Horace Lorimer, in contrast, was perfectly at home with the businessman/adventurer, corporate capitalist/independent actor model, and he promoted it without reservation or apology. This model of the "good man" suited his personality and it fit his own mix of life experiences. The content of the *Saturday Evening Post* between 1897 and 1900 reflected Lorimer's personal security, both as he conveyed this model positively to men, and as he supported changes in women's lives.

In fact, Lorimer's *Post* probably contributed further to the narrowing of men's options at the turn of the century. Carnes and Griffen write about magazines like the *Post*:

> Mass-circulation magazines carried . . . new expectations to middle-class readers everywhere; the expectations became a unifying national norm, cut-

ting across continuing variations in gender construction in occupational and other subcultures within this [middle] class. . . . Fewer alternative ways of defining masculinity were available, compared to the diversity of norms in the mid-nineteenth century.[14]

The *Post* was in the forefront of such magazines.

Like those of the *Journal,* the *Post*'s messages were various according to its different components. Lorimer and others spoke "man to man" in editorials. Fiction and biographical sketches gave readers accounts of individual lives and life experiences. Business, political, and social commentaries conveyed matter-of-fact information to readers. These components of the magazine differed also to the extent that they employed humor. Lorimer's editorials, some short stories, and some articles were humorous, while other fiction, prose pieces, and biographical sketches were more serious. The overall tone of the *Post* was less pedantic than Bok's *Journal,* however, and the magazine explicitly considered issues of gender only to the extent that those issues were part of the contemporary cultural debate.

In Knapp's *Journal* we saw the editor constructing her public self, and attempting to present images with which her readers could identify. In Bok's *Journal* we saw the editor working consciously to influence his female readers' gender construction. The pages of Lorimer's early *Post* reveal a secure man creating a magazine that he would have liked to read himself, attempting to influence the gender construction mainly of young men.[15] Even with pieces designed to instruct young men on gender-related matters, Lorimer downplayed the instruction. Gender construction for *Post* readers was a subtle matter of exposure to the implicit images of masculinity that the magazine presented. Gender construction in Lorimer's *Post* for men was much less conscious and reflective than in either Knapp's or Bok's *Journal* for women.

Determining the gender-related messages of the *Journal* is a relatively easy task, since discussion of roles was generally straightforward and direct. Analyzing the *Post*'s stance on the male role involves more inference. Fiction is important to an analysis of the *Post*'s gender-related notions because it often featured more explicit consideration of such matters than did *Post* nonfiction, and because fiction constituted at least half of any given issue of the *Post.* The importance of fiction in the *Saturday Evening Post* and the themes informing it reinforce the notion that men required gender construction just as women did—it was simply not as direct. Stories in the *Post* featured images of men that, while they were meant to entertain, were also meant to be either exemplary or cautionary. Significantly, when Lorimer could not locate the kind of fiction that he hoped would both interest and instruct, he wrote it himself.

Men in the *Post* of these years were viewed primarily as workers and as citizens acting mainly in the public sphere, but the rhetoric about appropriate goals and behaviors for men varied. Sometimes it featured the old-fashioned view that character and persistence made the man, and other times the notion that money and appearances were the real hallmarks of success.

As Jan Cohn's analysis of Lorimer's *Post* suggests, Lorimer and men like him were caught between nineteenth-century values developed in a producer society, and twentieth-century values revolving around the emerging consumer society.[16] Lorimer resolved several contradictions for himself by recreating the world of the American businessman in the *Saturday Evening Post*. Fiction, articles, and editorials spoke to and promoted the man of business, the model of which was the salesman. The salesman acted as neither the producer nor the consumer of America's goods, but as the distributor. An emphasis on distribution allowed Lorimer to emphasize at the same time both the nineteenth-century values of thrift and hard work, and the twentieth-century value of consumption for which his magazine stood.

Early and late, the few explicit articles instructing men on how to live well dealt almost exclusively with their work lives. A representative discussion is Maurice Thompson's 1899 editorial entitled "The New Outlook for Young Men." The piece focused solely on earning a living, and it suggested that with industrious effort any man could succeed. Thompson used a new phrase in his discussion, concluding that " 'Room at the top,' then, means room for the conscientious, persistent, cheerful plodder, as well as for the brilliant and lucky plunger who breaks the barriers half by accident."[17] Another article in 1899, called "Getting and Keeping a Business Position," commented that "a true young man, comprehending himself and having a proper self-respect, will understand that success is normal, failure abnormal."[18]

The *Post* placed itself in the American mainstream of advice to men when it touted what one historian calls the "myth of success," the belief that all men, exclusively by their own efforts, can make of their lives what they will.[19] The particular version of success promoted by the *Post* was the dominant model by the late nineteenth century, featuring an emphasis on materialism and getting ahead, and the attributes of initiative, aggressiveness, and competitiveness. Some articles in the *Post* paid lip service to character, decency, and honesty; but even these articles intimated that virtue would be rewarded with higher financial gains.

While the *Post* emphasized success and equated success with money, it also featured the significant contrasting theme of failure. In the September issue of 1899 there appeared a short, unsigned editorial piece called "Why Young Men Fail: A Clear Explanation by Shrewd Business Men." The article presented the usual admonitions to men to work hard and persist, but its emphasis on failure seemed to strike a raw nerve. This half-page article inspired a debate that went on in the *Post*'s pages for months, featuring both letters to the editor and commentary from *Post* writers. Reader letters ranged from the perfunctory to the pathetic. Here is a sample of the latter:

6.a. A Typical Early Lorimer Editorial Page.

THE SATURDAY EVENING POST

Philadelphia, July 9, 1898

The Boomerang of the Monroe Doctrine

THE essence of the Monroe Doctrine is the assumption by the United States that no European Power has any right to acquire new territory on this hemisphere, and that such acquisition would be a menace to our National peace and security. This position, according to the Monroe Doctrine, we should defend by force of arms, if necessary. Such is clearly the meaning of the honeyed words of diplomatic phrasing: "It is impossible, therefore, that we should behold such interposition, in any form, with indifference." The policy has been that we will tolerate no interference from European Powers in the political status or ownership of any State, colony or territory on this continent. For seventy-five years Uncle Sam has placed "Please Keep-Off-the-Grass" signs over all North and South America, and no island has been too small to escape the placard notice: "Private Grounds. No Trespassing Allowed. By Order of the Owner of Adjacent Property." The Powers of Europe have not agreed with Uncle Sam upon the question, and have several times approached it a warm argument with him...

Training Students to be Men

NOW that the graduate in his commencement oration has pointed out the course which the nation should pursue, the college student, as an institution, will sink into obscurity, for a while at least...

Loyal Americans in an Emergency

IN NOTHING is the majestic greatness of the American people more manifest than in the way the war tax has been received. It means an additional financial burden for practically every one in the land...

The Public Craving for Exciting News

THREE months ago, a story from the Klondike, a sensational speech, or a mysterious murder, would have achieved the distinction of a place on the first page of the newspapers, and have been eagerly devoured by their readers. But with the beginning of the war, the old run of news lost its flavor...

THE SECRETS OF BUSINESS SUCCESS

PRACTICAL TALKS BY PRACTICAL MEN

Why Some Men Fail in Business

IN THE course of an address before the St. Paul Credit Men's Association, a merchant of that city, referring to the classification of the causes of business failures in the United States and Canada, said...

From Victoria Cross to Music Hall

THE ingratitude of Republics has long been a favorite theme with writers living under a less enlightened form of Government than ours. But now a strange story comes from that monarchy which, by reason of its kinship to us, has most often felt privileged to exercise the brotherly right of criticism...

What Makes a Successful Merchant

WHAT is it to be a merchant? asks the Commercial Bulletin and Northwest Trade. The calibre of a man is best measured by his ability to endure against competition...

Enthusiasm in One's Business

A MAN can no more be successful in a business that he does not like than he can be happy with a wife whom he does not love, says the Furniture Journal...

Spurring a Man to Success

"THERE'S nothing like giving a boy a little encouragement once in a while," said a wealthy down-town merchant the other day...

To the Editor: I am a man of 43 who finds himself in an unexpectedly humble position. A man of some education, I have a loving wife and three fine children to support. I am struggling on basically the same clerk's salary that I first drew some 21 years ago, with little improvement over the years and little improvement in sight. My boss is as powerless as I to change my situation, since our business as a whole is struggling to survive. Signed, J. E. D., Detroit.[20]

The pathos of this letter comes from the fact that nowhere in the *Post* was there an explicit response, much less a sympathetic one. What "J. E. D." from Detroit says, but other *Post* commentators did not say, is that failure was not necessarily any given man's fault. Exigencies of the market were responsible for the relative success and failure of many turn-of-the-century men involved in commercial ventures, but many middle-class men were left wondering why they were not getting farther or were made to feel that they were to blame for their own misfortune. The discussion ran in the *Post*'s editorial columns well into the next year, with some *Post* writers and readers offering testimony about failure, but with more offering advice on how to avoid it. The debate culminated in a 1900 reader letter that accurately summarized more than nine months of discussion. Mr. Johnson of Tampa, Florida, had gleaned the following twenty-three "Rules for Success" from the pages of the *Post:*

1. Love Nature and listen to advice with an open heart. 2. Earn a little, spend a little less. 3. Hurry never. 4. Be cautious. 5. Keep your wits about you always. 6. Preserve and develop staying power. 7. Never misrepresent. 8. Place yourself in the other man's place. 9. Undertake one thing at a time. 10. Do it completely. 11. Explain things just as they are. 12. Never exaggerate. 13. Never avoid conversation. 14. Consider before speaking. 15. Control the body; force yourself to action; never idle. 16. Don't eat too much. 17. Be polite and kind, no matter to whom. 18. Carry out your plans and ideas yourself. 19. Have lots of nerve and grit. 20. Never fear anything. 21. Invite difficult things; don't shirk them. 22. Be earnest, punctual, ambitious, correct, contented. 23. Have a clear conscience.[21]

These rules offered by *Post* contributors and readers represent some of the most explicit gender construction to be found in the magazine's pages. The construction took two main forms in this discussion: control and compartmentalization. Male readers were to assume that they had control over their lives, and to exhibit self-control at every turn. Be cautious, develop staying power, consider before speaking, control the body, never fear anything, the magazine advised men. In short, constant vigilance with regard to one's behavior and body was required to succeed in a world where team effort and hierarchical structures were increasingly the norm.

Therefore, while female gender construction in the *Journal* revolved around connections to others and either rebelling against or accepting limitations imposed externally, male gender construction centered on autonomy and overcoming internal obstacles and limitation. Middle-class men had only themselves to blame if they did not achieve to their expectations. This brand of gender construction was, though subtle, also somewhat harsh. It emphasized men's autonomy and independence almost exclusively. Men faced the world alone and they had no one but themselves to blame if they failed. The *Post* also implied that gender for men, as for women, was a performative act. If one simply followed this script, and acted like a man, one would be a man.

In addition, men were encouraged implicitly to compartmentalize their lives, to separate work and love, public and private life. Hence the twenty-three rules had nothing to say about a man's personal or affective life. Little mention was made of expressing emotion of any kind, positive or negative, and there was little sense of men's potential for caring for those around them. Success equalled financial gain achieved through hard work; love and relationships were something quite apart from this central definition of a man's identity.

But Lorimer and his staffers assumed that marriage and children were indeed important to men, and they dealt with this notion and with its possible clash with work by going beyond compartmentalization to equate work with love.[22] George Horace Lorimer and others in the pages of the *Post* thus identified economic striving with love for their wives and children, a cultural pattern in the U.S. that has been obscured for years. The advent of the cash economy had the paradoxical effect of disassociating love from providing. As one analyst notes, in preindustrial days, "the reciprocal idea of conjugal love . . . grew out of the day-to-day cooperation, sharing, and closeness of the diversified home economy."[23] Men's role after industrialization centered increasingly on their breadwinner status. As men were more and more identified with work for pay, and women with nurturing in the home, love itself came to be seen increasingly as a female attribute. The definition of love shifted from a model of helping each other to a model of romantic expressions of affection. The result of women taking more and more responsibility for expressing loving feelings was a deep split between the cold, impersonal work world and the warm, nurturing home atmosphere. By the turn of the century many men were caught between these two worlds, believing that they were loving by providing for their wives and children, yet unable to express their feelings of love and affection in the open way that women did.[24]

The *Post* regularly reinforced the notion of a man's responsibility to, as the writer of the "success" letter had put it, his "loving wife" and "fine children." *Post* fiction especially linked providing well with loving well. Of thirty-seven lead short stories appearing between 1897 and 1900, seventeen were romances, three were business stories, and seventeen were adventure or action stories (see Methodological Note). Work was a major theme in twenty-five of the thirty-seven stories. *Post* fiction revealed the lives of men at all stages of work: law students and apprentices preparing for future jobs, clerks and shopkeepers beginning in humble circumstances, established professionals engrossed in their work, and old men dying and leaving their work to the next generation.

Short stories were a humanizing element in the early *Post,* often considering the impact of personal relationships on men's public lives. Lynn Roby Meekins' "The Assistant Boss: The Girl Who Managed a Political Campaign" tells the story of George Howe, one of the contenders for inheriting the political dynasty of a dying senator. The dying man's daughter eventually convinces her father's supporters to transfer their support to the young man. By the end of the story the young man has gained not only crucial political endorsements but the love of a good woman, the dying senator's daughter, who will run his campaign and "serve faithfully as a Congressman's wife" in the years to come.[25] This kind of support from home was seldom discussed in other parts of the early *Post,* and the contrast is significant: the young politician, while ultimately responsible for his own ideas and actions, was not alone.

Men in these short stories, as in other features of the *Post,* were viewed as controlling their work destinies and were measured in large part by their level of financial achievement. A variation on the theme of men controlling their work-fates and the importance of financial success appears in a story called "A Costly Triumph." The story's main character is a man named John Jardine, who at forty is still only a shop assistant. The reader is told that Jardine grew up poor; but the main reason for his lack of success, the story suggests, is his demeanor—John is solemn and stern and lacks the sociability and sense of humor that help a man move up in the world of business. Jardine's "Costly Triumph" involves his boss's frivolous daughter, whom Jardine loves. The daughter gets pregnant by a young man; Jardine, unable to express his true feelings for her and thus to marry her to give the child a name, uses a $5,000 inheritance he has just received to pay the young father to marry her. Despite the admitted strength of character that this action embodies, the writer concludes that Jardine is a failure, both because his sternness has cost him the woman he loves, and because it will keep him in the same financial position all of his working life.[26] This story is a striking illustration of the priorities of the *Post* in the late 1890s: men were to earn as much as they possibly could, and they needed strong social skills with which to succeed in the business world and in winning a desirable wife.

An early "action" story also illustrates the close identification of men with work. Herbert E. Hamblen's "His Last Run with the Limited: The Story of a Faithful Engineer" is the tale of a railroad engineer who prided himself on always bringing his train in on time. The story is almost a tall tale, as it makes Jake Woodford into a heroic figure who is good to his workers and who is as good at his work as anyone has ever been. The reader is regaled with the details of the troubles that beset Jake and his Limited on the day in question: water tanks are empty, fuel is missing, and switch operators are lax, all resulting in delays for the train. Knowing that his brakes are in bad condition, but determined to come in on time, Jake pushes the train to fifty miles per hour on its last leg of the day. At the station his brakes fail him and Jake and his crew and train all crash.

Revealing for the first time that Jake has a wife and children, Hamblen concludes his story in fine tall-tale fashion: "The radiant light has gone from the eyes of the widow and her orphans; but it is one of the valued traditions of the road to this day that Jake Woodford was the only man who never lost time with the Limited."[27] Stories like "His Last Run with the Limited" suggested in fantastic fashion the centrality of work to men's lives. While this story represents an extreme, early *Post* fiction over and over again featured heroes who unselfishly sacrificed for their work, for the honor of doing their jobs well.

Short stories in the early *Post* presented a more balanced view as well, however. Fiction in these years regularly featured some attention to the personal lives of its heroes, and consequently to both the need of men for relationships with women and the interaction of the home and the workplace. A love interest played a major part in twenty-five of the thirty-seven stories analyzed for this period, and it was the main plot line in twelve of the thirty-seven. Short stories in Lorimer's early *Post* about male–female relations often embodied this editorial comment from 1900: "Sometimes a man in love acts foolishly," the *Post* noted, "but all the same he is to be envied."[28] Fiction in these years featured bumbling men coming to realize just how much women could mean to them, and then trying to earn or win them. Most of these stories centered on courtship and ended with an agreement to marry or with the wedding itself. Stories discussing life beyond the altar featured a less rosy picture of love between men and women, however, focusing on financial difficulties and mismatched couples.

Editorial references to male–female relations were generally glib. The topic was a regular vehicle for joking commentary on the state of turn-of-the-century culture. But the particular nature of this commentary is revealing:

Woman is judged by her dress, man by his address.[29]

Honesty in business, constancy in love, and the front second-story room at the summer boardinghouse make up real success in life.[30]

Love in a cottage is all right, provided the cottage has gas, electric lights, steam heat, hot and cold water, baths, stationary washtubs, open plumbing, closets in every room, polished floors, new wall paper, fly screens, and servants who will stay.[31]

6.b. Post Short Stories Often Centered on Love-Work Conflicts.

Doctor Langdon's Dilemma
BETWEEN FRIENDSHIP AND LOVE
By Kate Erskine

These quips point to the preoccupation of many turn-of-the-century individuals with material goods and appearances. They highlight as well the difficulty that many couples were experiencing in reconciling their wants and their means. Above all, they underscore the fact that, to a great extent, an individual couple's level of material comfort rested on the man's ability to provide. As I pointed out earlier, women were responsible for the trappings of middle-class status, but it is also the case that class status relied at bottom on the earning capacity of men. The *Post* acknowledged this fact only in humorous terms like the ones noted here, evading any sort of straightforward reckoning with this responsibility.

Added to cultural pressures on men to succeed financially and to avoid failure were pressures to do so from within the marriage. This may help to explain the *Post*'s reticence about the male role and its flip treatment of marital relationships. As Anthony Rotundo demonstrates, two ideals of marriage circulated simultaneously in the late nineteenth century. The first featured the image of the male-dominated, hierarchical union, the second the union of two relatively equal companions. While the second ideal was in ascendance during the years in question, it had certainly not fully supplanted the first. This left both men and women confused about marital relations. It also left men in a difficult position; regarded negatively if they were domineering or tyrannical, they were also viewed negatively if they could not be models of strength and self-control.[32] Lorimer's early *Post* was subtly informed by the fear that men in intimate relations could not possibly measure up to all that was expected of them. Consequently, the serious discussion of such matters was simply seldom joined in the magazine.

One of the few relatively serious nonfiction considerations of the marital relationship in the *Post* during these years in fact criticized men for being poor husbands. Gertrude Atherton's "What Should be Done with a Husband?" also criticized women for being too dependent on men, asserting that a woman in marrying "agreed to make herself neither slave nor recluse." This promotion of female independence was carried to the point of advocating divorce: "If she cannot cure," Atherton concluded, "she should plainly say to her marital partner she will no longer endure."[33]

Viewing women's happiness and independence as important enough to warrant divorce is unusual for 1899, but it is in keeping with the rest of the *Post*'s issues-oriented rhetoric about women. The most extensive *Post* commentary on women's issues concerned higher education. Lorimer, as a "college man" himself, took such an education for men for granted. The explicit discussion of education for men in the *Post* of these years centered mainly on promoting higher education as a stepping stone to success, but it cautioned young men against becoming conceited about having higher than average education credentials.

The *Post* in these early years also took approving note of the fact that more and more women were attending colleges and universities. Parents were encouraged to send their daughters on to higher education, and the activities of college girls were occasionally reported. Charles Thwing, in a 1900 article called "Diverse Paths to Diverse Ends," challenged the notion that all women should be trained in colleges for the same role, advocating for women a flexible curriculum and freedom of choice equal to that of men.

> Education should not train women to become wives and mothers. Education should not train men to become husbands and fathers. Education is broader than either the nuptial or parental relationship. Education should be so broad and so high that one can enter into these domestic and other relations with fitness and ease. . . . One can trust a woman to select those studies which will make of her the best woman. She is to get herself ready for her work; God will find her work. Once ready . . . she is fitted to be the head of a home or of a school or of a hospital.[34]

Thwing's argument echoed Knapp's, as they both suggested that women should be free to choose where their primary activities in life would occur.

Another article, appearing in the first "College Man's Number" of the *Post* in October of 1899, put the issue in even clearer rights-based terms. "In all the colleges for women and the universities to which women are admitted," the *Post* asserted, "the rights of women to equal advantages with men and the necessity of higher education for women in their relations to the world have been dwelt upon, and back of this is the great popular sentiment in the homes of the country that the girls, having as bright faculties as the boys, ought to possess the same advantages for developing them." The piece went on to suggest that colleges and universities would do well to prepare for a constantly growing population of female students, predicting that "there will probably come a time when there will be in our colleges as many women as men."[35]

And women might well even head these institutions of higher education that young women attended. A paragraph in the column "Men and Women of the Hour" entitled "What Women are Doing for Women" observed that "there was a time when it was considered best to have a man—generally a doctor of divinity—at the head of a female college, but now most important women's colleges are headed by women."[36] The work of Alice Freeman Palmer, president of Wellesley, and of Mary Woolley, president of Mount Holyoke, was noted on several occasions, as were the achievements of scholars like Helen Bradford Thompson in psychology at the University of Chicago.

Post fiction affirmed women's access to higher education as well. Twelve of the thirty-seven stories analyzed for these years featured college-going or college-educated women, a disproportionately high number given the social context. Two stories made access to higher education for women a major theme, both comparing female to male students at the expense of men. In Maarten Maarten's "Some Women I Have Known," "John" is the only girl in a family with two older and two younger brothers. She is better at most things than her brothers are, especially schoolwork. Even though her mother and father worry about higher education de-sexing their already tomboyish daughter, John pursues her interest in mathematics to become an accounting expert. When her father dies unexpectedly, John is the only child capable of taking over his business.[37] "John" is, of course, an unusually masculine name for a woman, and one might surmise that the heroine could only succeed as a "man" in the world of business. But she attracts the love of a business colleague in spite of, and even because of, her unusual abilities. Her "masculine" capabilities, therefore, do not impede her fulfillment as a woman.

A similar heroine appears in Molly Elliot Seawell's "The Excellent Revenge of Eleanor." Seawell's story is a strong indictment of women's exclusion from higher education, demonstrating how a tutor's work is wasted on Eleanor's brother, a weak, uninterested student. Eleanor eavesdrops on the tutoring sessions from which she has been excluded solely because of her sex, studies on her own, and is soon an intellectual match for her brother's tutor. The tutor falls in love with Eleanor, and together they vow to encourage all of their children—daughters as well as sons—to pursue higher education.[38]

The *Post* between 1897 and 1900 was just beginning to consider other women's issues, but its earliest commentary in these areas signalled a supportive stance. In October of 1900, Lynn Roby Meekins, a regular contributor of editorials as well as short stories, thought the United States was backward with regard to women's suffrage. He asserted that the right of woman to vote "is conceded in every civilized land," and complained about the fact that most of the states had yet to pass laws permitting it.[39]

An indirect reference to women's paid work mirrors the stance of the magazine on education and suffrage. The October issue of 1899 featured an article by E. Benjamin Andrews, Chicago's Superintendent of Schools, entitled "The Attractions of Teaching." Andrews' article was addressed to men, and it noted the lively competition with women that male teachers faced in most school districts. But Andrews resisted the temptation to complain, even as women displaced some men:

> When one reflects on the increasing number of able women who, though well-to-do or having their support from others, demand to be usefully active, and on the increasing number of able women who have to earn their own bread, one must, apart from all gallantry, wish to keep open women's chance to compete for school principalships, as well as for all other positions which they can successfully fill.[40]

The *Post* also went beyond Bok's *Journal* to begin to speak in the broader terms of women's rights. A typical consideration of women's rights appeared in a November 1899 editorial by Thomas B. Reed:

> The equal rights of women have but just reached the region of possibilities. Men have only just left off sneering and have but just begun to consider. It needs no prophetic vision to see how cheap will appear the stock arguments for the subjection of women when shone upon by the light of trial. Every step of progress from the harem and the veil to free society and property-holding has been steadily fought by the vanity, selfishness and indolence . . . of mankind.[41]

Why was the *Post* so accepting of the expansion of women's activities? The answer lies in part in Lorimer's personality. Especially in comparison to Bok, Lorimer was secure in his own role. As a man's man he celebrated the masculine, and he saw no reason for men to change, but he was able to reach out from this secure position to support women's progress.

The context for this discussion is also important. The preoccupation with men's success and failure analyzed earlier was but one part of the *Post*'s overall emphasis on individualism. The magazine was located in the mainstream of American individualism, according to which rights are grounded in the individual and can only be infringed upon by the state in highly unusual circumstances.[42] Much of the *Post*'s discussion of women thus centered on the logical extension of individual rights to women, reflecting the magazine's commitment to justice and equity, at least for members of the native-born, white, middle class.[43]

The *Post*'s discussion of women's rights was thereby anchored firmly in the separation of the public and the private realm, with its focus directed almost exclusively on the public. While Knapp referred to the distinction between public and private only playfully, both Bok and Lorimer were grounded in the distinct and wide separation between the two realms. As we have seen, Bok invoked it to keep women in their place. Lorimer, in contrast, employed the division between public and private in order to make clear where men's rights and responsibilities lay—and, by extension, at least some women's as well.

In addition, Bok focused only on the disadvantages to the private realm of women being more active in the public, while Lorimer stressed only the advantages of women's more public activity for the public realm. Lorimer did not consider the impact of this activity on American homes and families, or on serious relationships between women and men. The result of both magazines' limited thinking, then, was only a partial consideration of the gender matters at hand. This partial consideration in later years reinforced the existing power relationships in ways that Lorimer may not have intended.

While Lorimer was refining his views and beginning to engage strong writers of the day, the *Post* as a commercial magazine was struggling. As I have suggested, the *Post*'s formula was not attractive to advertisers, and a significant number of the *Post*'s early commercial messages were limited to extolling the virtues of the *Ladies' Home Journal*. What little advertising the *Post* could attract was vague in its targeting, and it played little role in defining the magazine's tone.

The small numbers of advertisements that did appear in the early *Post* serve to demonstrate how advertisers might take a different tack in a magazine targeted to men instead of women, and how much the gendered commercial milieu and commercialized gender norms could inform one another. For example, Pearline, a longtime advertiser in the *Journal* and supporter in those pages of change in women's role, proclaimed in the 1900 *Post* that "Weak Women and Strong Men Use Pearline." This advertisement, which ran frequently in the *Post,* highlights the way advertisers sometimes tapped into a ready-made gender discourse in order to create attention-getting, snappy, and engaging slogans. "Weak women—strong men" was a culturally familiar, oppositional image that built on shared gender images in a cheap, shorthand way. This particular pitch did not run in the *Journal* because it was obviously more flattering to men than to women. It is not even clear what the intention of the advertisement was as it ran in the *Post;* did the manufacturer expect "strong" men to use Pearline washing powder? Or was it meant to flatter men into buying Pearline for their wives to use? What is clear, however, is that advertisements would eventually become part of the gendered commercial discourse. They also helped to further consumerism by conveying the notion that women and men use certain products because of the attributes they inherently possess.

The *Post* was more successful in attracting readers than advertisers in these years, and the question of the magazine's effect on these readers is a tantalizing one. As we have seen, the *Post*'s presentation of gender norms was very different from the *Journal*'s. It was subtle, consisting of implicit rather than ex-

DURING THE COMING YEAR
THE LADIES' HOME JOURNAL
WILL BE FIFTEEN YEARS OLD, AND THIS IT WILL CELEBRATE

By eclipsing all its former efforts. It will strive for two things: to make women happy in their homes and to help them in their lives. There will be a new, strong vitality in the magazine: new facilities will make new things possible. IN 1898 SUBSCRIBERS WILL SHARE IN THE JOURNAL'S BEST YEAR.

The most popular feature ever secured by the JOURNAL will consist of

The Inner Experiences of a Cabinet Member's Wife

As she writes them to her sister at home. They are the actual social experiences of a prominent Cabinet member's wife. For this reason the authorship will be withheld.

The most intimate peeps behind the curtain of high official and social life in Washington, written by one woman to another,—the wife of a Cabinet member to her favorite sister at home. Prominent in society, and a close friend of the President's wife, the President and the highest officials in the land, with the most brilliant women in Washington social life, figure familiarly in the scenes.

Through the "experiences" runs the strange romance of a beautiful Washington girl and a Lieutenant of the Army, into whose lives come the intrigues of one of the dangerously clever and beautiful women who infest the social life of the Capital. It will prove the most fascinating recital of politics, love, and the intrigues of high social and official life ever given publicly.

Ian Maclaren Will Write a Series of Articles

No writer of recent times has so endeared himself to thousands of people through his pen as has "Ian Maclaren," and in these "talks" on matters very close to the interests of every man and woman he will win even a stronger place in their affections.

The JOURNAL will have more stories during 1898 than in any previous year. There will be

Fully Thirty Bright, Live Stories During 1898

There will be two numbers entirely made up of stories.

The January issue will be made
A Midwinter Fiction Number
And the August issue, as heretofore,
A Midsummer Fiction Number
There will be stories, of course, in each number of the JOURNAL, but a larger proportion of them in these two issues.

Among the wealth of stories will be
Mark Twain's New Humorous Story
A Ghost Story by Marion Crawford
The First Story by Clara Morris
Mrs. Rollins' Quaint "Philippa" Stories
Several Stories by Mrs. Whitney

Following these will appear stories by
John Kendrick Bangs, Will N. Harben, Jeannette H. Walworth, Sophia Swett, and others

Hamlin Garland's New Novelette, "The Doctor"

The Romance of a Man Born to be "a Friend of All Women and a Friend of None"

A strong romance of a prosperous doctor, who believes himself born to be "a friend of all women and a lover of none." Two beautiful girls become his patients: one a girl of the slums; the other the daughter of a well-to-do home. The emotions awakened by each girl form the strong groundwork of a man's battle between feelings of undecided love and a yearning tenderness. Mr. William T. Smedley illustrates this story.

Two Romantic Episodes of Royal Exiles in America

Are told in two peculiarly fascinating articles:

When Louis Philippe
Taught School in Philadelphia

When the King of Spain
Lived on the Banks of the Schuylkill

By Camillus Phillips

The tale is told of how the future King of France played pedagogue in America's Capital to earn his living, and gives the famous answer of the haughty teacher to a slighted American lessee, Thomas Wiborg, when the Royal teacher sought his daughter's hand.

By William Perine

A fascinating story is this, when the real Napoleon's brother escaped from America, hoping that Napoleon himself would escape from St. Helena and join him. It is a picture of the life of a King and has two beautiful Princesses in our own land.

Ex-President Harrison on The Flag in the Home

It was General Harrison's idea that the stars and stripes should float over every school-house in America. Now, in a stirring article, he carries the idea farther, and shows why the flag should find a place over every fireside in our country.

John Philip Sousa, "The Great March King"

Whose soul-stirring marches every one knows, has composed a waltz for the JOURNAL, which he calls
The Lady of the White House
The complete composition will be published in an early copy of the JOURNAL.

In Needlework it Will Greatly Excel

Over any other year. With new arrangements, specially perfected, it will, in every issue, give one or more pages to the Newest Practical Embroidery, Knitting, Crocheting, Tatting, Drawn-Work, Patchwork—giving fresh ideas in every branch of Needlework.

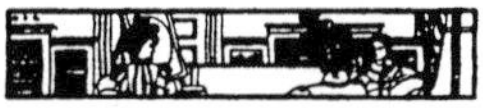

Fanny Crosby, "The Blind Singer"

Whose beautiful hymn, "Safe in the Arms of Jesus" and "Rescue the Perishing," have made her name beloved in thousands of households, has written a new hymn and a new song for the JOURNAL.

The Most Remarkable Sunday-School in the World

Is in America, the largest Sunday-School of one man, who to-day maintains it, now authoritatively described for the first time.

Mrs. Abbott's Peaceful Valley

Already so well received as showing the practical possibilities of happy village life, will run through several of the issues during 1898.

Mrs. Bottome's Popular Talks

Will continue through the year. A new departure will be Mrs. Bottome's series of "New Lines of Work for the Circles."

There will be a delightful series, the first article of which will present

The Anecdotal Side of Mrs. Cleveland

The closest friends of Mrs. Cleveland have here been combined to tell the brightest anecdotes of her tact and grace—stories and anecdotes which have never been told; and which show her as no sketch nor biography could possibly portray her. One sees Mrs. Cleveland in these pithy little stories with delightful unreserve. Following the article on Mrs. Cleveland will be presented

The Anecdotal Side of Mark Twain

The Anecdotal Side of Edison

In stories of his dry humor, and personal anecdotes which he has told to his intimate friends, heretofore not printed. A laugh is on every line.

Presenting stories of the wonderful wizard's strange life: his singular absent-mindedness: his forgetfulness of day or night or family.

The Anecdotal Side of the President

Those who know President McKinley best tell these stories in this article: stories which bring out his strong personality, and show the gentle side of his character which Mrs. McKinley knows so well. Each story is new.

Lilian Bell's Sparkling Letters From Europe

Commenced in the last October JOURNAL, will continue through several issues during 1898. Every line of these letters sparkles with Miss Bell's bright wit and clever piquancy. Miss Bell's letter from Paris, in the January JOURNAL, describes, with remarkable dash, French life as she sees it for the first time. Paris passes before one as if in a vitascope.

The Romantic Flavor of Life in Old New York

IN TWO FASCINATING ARTICLES, BY MRS. BURTON HARRISON

When Fashion Graced the Bowery
—when the famous New York street was a fashionable driveway, the centre of gayety and wealth, and a roadway of stately homesteads and farms.

With Washington in the Minuet
Will picture our first President in the graceful minuet with the Colonial maids and belles at the great Washington ball in New York City.

The Personal Side of Richard Wagner

SHOWING THE MAN BEHIND HIS WORK WITH TELLING FIDELITY

By Houston Stewart Chamberlain, Wagner's intimate friend, and who writes at the request and with the approval of Madame Wagner.

How his operas came into life: twenty-five years it took to write "Parsifal"; twenty-two years for "The Meistersinger." He finished "Lohengrin" in 1847, yet never heard the opera himself until fourteen years later. How and when he composed his great operas, his working hours, his dress, personal habits, religious views, business qualities, and domestic side.

Mrs. Rorer Will Begin Two New Series During 1898

See will open the year with a series of
New Cooking Lessons

Taking up branches of cooking entirely different from her series in the JOURNAL during 1897.
Cooking for the Sick and Convalescent.
Breakfast Foods and Cereals.
The Proper Cooking for the Family.
Thirty Soups Without Meat.
Forty Ways of Cooking Apples.
New Uses for the Chafing-Dish.
Forty Kinds of Sandwiches.
Twenty-five Simple Desserts for Every Stomach.

Mrs. Rorer will also begin a series of
Mrs. Rorer's Domestic Lessons

Do We Eat Too Much Meat?
What to Eat and Not Have Headache.
When Unexpected Company Surprises You.
The Best Food for a Growing Boy.
Light Refreshments for Evening Companies.
Fruits as Foods and Fruits as Poisons.
The Right Food for Different Men.
Food for Bloodless Girls.
The Table for Stout and Thin Women.
School Luncheons for Children.

Mrs. Rorer Writes for No Magazine but the JOURNAL

The JOURNAL'S Moderate-Cost Homes

Designed by Its Own Architect

Some New City and Country Houses for $1000, $1200 and $1500

Giving "Three Model $1000 Houses," "A $1200 City Brick House" and "An 8-Room $1500 House," after which will come "Three Model Small Churches"—one for $600, one for $1000, and one for $1500.

Also: "A Model Farmhouse With Barn and Out-buildings," and a remarkably practical article, showing how the plainest house can be made picturesque by remodeling the front door and a single window.

"The Most Successful Thing Ever Done by the JOURNAL"

Inside of a Hundred Homes

One one hundred views will be given in six issues. They show how the most tasteful homes in America

are furnished, and how much better taste will go than money. Hundreds of new ideas are presented.

The Social Side of the Home

Will be treated in an unusually complete series of articles.

How Entertaining on a Small Income
Can be done will be told in a special article.
Light Refreshments for Evening Companies
Novel Masquerade Parties for Children
Entertaining Children on Sunday Afternoon
Will give ideas to many a perplexed parent.
Will be given "Home Parties for Children"; "St. Valentine's Night Frolics"; "Literary and Musical Evenings"; "Porch and Garden Parties," and "The Newest Church Socials."

Beautifully Illustrated Articles

Will be a feature during the year, and treat of
A Charming American Avenue
A beautiful avenue, nestled away in the heart of New York State.
A Wonderful Little World of People
The life, customs and beliefs of the largest Shaker community in America.
A Race Which Lives in Mountain Coves
A strange people who live in the coves of the Tennessee mountains.
The Yearly Rose Upon the Altar
The beautiful custom of a community in the heart of Pennsylvania.
Easter in a Colored Convent
The beautiful ritual at Easter time in a colored convent.
The Flower Plains of California
The most striking pictures ever shown of these superb fêtes.

The Dainty Pixie and Elaine Stories

WILL CONTINUE THROUGH SEVERAL NUMBERS

To delight the children. No sweeter nor more wholesome stories have ever been told for children.

Fashionable Siberia
Correcting the popular impression that Siberia is only a land of cold, hardship and hunger.

THE PRICE REMAINS: ONE DOLLAR FOR AN ENTIRE YEAR

plicit messages and featuring virtually no outright discussion. Perhaps the most important and potentially influential feature of Lorimer's presentation of male gender norms was its consistency and relative simplicity. The *Post*'s central theme was that men are breadwinners and that men are the primary breadwinners for their families and within their culture. Lorimer spoke like a peer to his readers, and the messages of his *Post* were remarkably consistent from contributor to contributor and over the course of time. There were many fewer inconsistencies and contradictions in the magazine than there had been in Bok's *Journal,* and it featured much less flexibility than had Knapp's *Journal.* Around the breadwinning theme was built a cohesive, unified gender discourse that emphasized the public over the private, thinking and acting over feeling, autonomy over connections, and the importance of financial success.

Post readers may have been vulnerable to being influenced by this presentation of male gender norms because the message was simple and coherent, and because it was subtle and indirect. Gender construction in the *Post* was not a discussion to be joined, as it had been in Knapp's *Journal,* nor a matter of selecting from a range of images, as it had been in Bok's *Journal.* It was, instead, a process of being exposed to images of masculinity that were consistent with images presented to men earlier in American culture, but that were now more limited. It was a process of being exposed to coherent, limited images that were to be absorbed more than reflected upon.[44] Finally, it was a process of agreeing to some expansion of female boundaries, in order to avoid larger changes in the gendered status quo that might strip middle-class white men of some of the advantages of their social position.

It is apparent, then, that the issues of constraint and liberation are as relevant to considerations of men's gender construction as they are to women's. As we have seen, Knapp's *Journal* made middle-class women aware of some of the constraints they faced in American culture, although the solution offered—increased consumption—was inadequate. Bok's *Journal* de-emphasized constraint and even added to the mix the new constraint of defining women centrally as consumers.

The middle-class male position in American culture was, of course, very different from that of the female. The *Post* recognized men's relatively privileged position, and it was more focused on maintaining that position than on advocating change for men. Thus identifying the constraints on men or imposing further constraints on men was not the business of the *Post.* But the *Post* did add to the pressure on men that accompanied their privileged position as the culture's primary breadwinners. Emphasizing men's role as breadwinner preserved men's central identity and maintained the gendered division of labor upon which society was based. Coupled with the notion that men have full control over their lives, this emphasis on breadwinning put middle-class men under a great deal of pressure, however.[45] Men maintained their position of power, but in a culture with increasingly high material expectations they were in many cases set up to fail. And their relative lack of overt consideration of their gender construction left men virtually unable to sort out all these pressures. *Post* producers and readers alike were unable, then, to clearly analyze why so much tension accompanied discussions of masculinity in the late nineteenth and early twentieth century.

To the extent that they began to support the *Post* with their subscriptions, male readers of the magazine thereby colluded in further elaborating the cultural hegemony of a revised gender discourse at the turn of the century. The degree to which the *Post*'s gender discourse was also a commercial discourse was still very limited; it certainly did not parallel the *Journal*'s discourse about women as consumers to set men beside women as consumers in their own right. But the groundwork was being laid for a broader commercial discourse that would include an image of men that complemented the image of women as consumers. As we shall see, the *Post*'s discussion of men would play a crucial role in defining both a commercial gender discourse and a gendered commercial discourse.

7

The *Journal* is for Women and the *Post* is for Families: The Vicissitudes of the Curtis Magazines, 1900–1910

The Curtis publications in the early twentieth century were important social institutions as they reckoned with the contours of a gendered commercial milieu that had been created, in part, by their own publishers and editors. The *Post* was eventually forced to target women as well as men in order to attract the size of audience and number of advertisers Lorimer and Curtis sought. And the *Journal* tried unsuccessfully to broaden its audience to include substantial numbers of men. The experiences of the Curtis magazine producers in these years provide further evidence of the fact that gendered commerce had taken on a life of its own beyond the control of individual producers. The social history of the Curtis magazines—their staffing, their business tactics, their self-image, their readers' reactions—is a critical complement to the cultural history of the magazines' content in these years. We see real people with real power acting within and limited by real constraints.

The advertising campaign for the *Saturday Evening Post* around the turn of the century illustrates the evolution in the magazine's targeted audience. Promotions for the *Post* appeared in the *Journal* from the time of Curtis's acquisition of the magazine in 1897, but they began to appear more frequently in the second half of 1899. Early versions of these promotions, which were also featured in more expensive publications like *Scribner's* and the *Atlantic*, suggested that the *Post* was "the ideal reading for the up and coming man."[1] Promoters of the *Post* began to soften the masculine image of the magazine as early as March of 1900. That issue of the *Journal* featured an ad urging women to buy the *Post* "For Your Husband, For Your Son, For Your Family," emphasizing that the "family" would especially enjoy the *Post*'s fiction. In pitching the *Post* to the family, its promoters meant not that young children should be reading the magazine but that women as well as men would enjoy it. By July of 1901 the *Post* was described to female *Journal* readers as "The *Journal*'s Baby," and the promotion's accompanying invitation exclaimed, "We Want Every Woman to See It!"

In 1902 Curtis and Lorimer offered the first "Romance Number" of the *Saturday Evening Post*. Like the "College Man's Number" and the "Big Business Number," the romance version of the *Post* would begin to appear at least

THE SATURDAY EVENING POST

Established by Benjamin Franklin in 1728

HAS been regularly published for 172 years, and is now a weekly magazine of the highest grade (not a news weekly), and published by The Curtis Publishing Company, the owners of THE LADIES' HOME JOURNAL. It has a circulation of **200,000** copies weekly — that means **600,000** subscribers to the JOURNAL have not yet bought the POST.

Every reader of THE LADIES' HOME JOURNAL ought to have the POST, our weekly magazine, 24 to 32 pages every week, for only 5 cents the copy, or **$2.00** the year. Just as handsomely illustrated and printed as the JOURNAL, and costs but little — 5 cents the week of your dealer — and the best weekly magazine ever published.

FOR YOUR HUSBAND

An interesting series of papers by each of the following well-known public men, who write from knowledge gained on the inside of public affairs:

HONORABLE THOMAS B. REED
EX-SENATOR JOHN J. INGALLS
JUDGE NATH. C. SEARS,
On Practical Politics for Young Men

FOR YOUR SON

Business training, social and moral helps, by the best business men of this country. Papers by

ROBERT C. OGDEN, of Wanamaker's
ERSKINE M. PHELPS, of Phelps, Dodge & Palmer
WM. H. MAHER, of Maher & Grosh
GOVERNOR VOORHEES, of New Jersey
PRESIDENT PATTON, of Princeton
PRESIDENT HADLEY, of Yale
PRESIDENT BUTLER, of Colby
PRESIDENT THWING, of Western Reserve University
PRESIDENT BENJAMIN IDE WHEELER, of California University

FOR THE FAMILY

The best fiction in the world. These are among our contributors:

RUDYARD KIPLING
RICHARD HARDING DAVIS
IAN MACLAREN
F. HOPKINSON SMITH
S. R. CROCKETT
A. T. QUILLER-COUCH

THE best editorial writers in the country are engaged for the POST. Every number full of personal sketches, and our " Publick Occurrences " keep you fully informed.

We have spent money liberally to make the best weekly this country has ever had — and it is worthy the special attention of every reader of THE LADIES' HOME JOURNAL. We want every JOURNAL reader to know of our weekly.

For One Dollar it will be sent every week for five months — or for $2.00 every week for a year. This is our special rate to all Journal readers. Newsdealers all have it. Try a copy.

THE CURTIS PUBLISHING COMPANY
PHILADELPHIA

7.b. The Midwinter Romance Number.

Ch e
MIDWINTER
ROMANCE
NUMBER

annually after 1902, but the significance of this first edition lies in its specific content. For although the January 25, 1902, issue of the *Post* was billed as a special romance number on the cover, its reading material was much the same as that for any issue, with the usual mix of nonfiction and action and love stories. There was, however, one distinguishing feature of this particular issue: it contained twice as much advertising directed to women as did a normal issue of the *Post*. Over 60 percent of the romance number's advertising pages were for household products or women's and children's clothing.

The character of this first romance number demonstrates that the *Post* between 1900 and 1910 was consciously trying to attract women readers, and that advertising played a central role in determining the slant of the magazine. In the later years of this decade the *Post* by necessity evolved from a men's magazine to a family magazine, reaching out eventually to an extremely large audience. The early twentieth-century *Post* would retain its masculine tone and many of its masculine interests, but it would broaden to address some women's interests more directly and bill itself as a gender-inclusive magazine, thereby attracting lucrative amounts of female-targeted advertising.

The reason for this broadening is clear. The state of affairs at the beleaguered *Post* was tersely summarized at the top of a 1900 Lorimer memorandum to his staff: "We need women."[2] Despite Lorimer's editorial successes, the *Post* was still struggling financially at the turn of the century. Circulation remained under 400,000, far below what Curtis and Lorimer had hoped it would be by then, and by the end of 1901 Curtis Publishing had lost over a million dollars on the *Post*. National advertisers were still reluctant to purchase space in this magazine for men, since men were not viewed as major consumers of nationally marketed goods.

By the end of 1900 the ratio of advertising to other columns in the *Post* was 18 percent. However, as the percentage rose, making the *Post* more the commercial magazine that Curtis and Lorimer envisioned, the character of the advertising seemed to undermine the other part of the *Post*'s mission: to serve middle-class men. For as advertising gradually increased in the *Post,* the category of advertising that emerged as the most important was household products. In the years 1899 and 1900, ads for food and cleaners accounted for an average of 25 percent of the *Post*'s total advertising, with entertainment following at about 15 percent and education or self-improvement at about 10 percent. As the *Post*'s advertising base finally began to establish itself, it actually did not appear to be very different from that of the *Ladies' Home Journal,* despite the *Post*'s very different targeted audience. Therefore, even when the *Post* was at its most masculine in tone and content, a full 25 percent of its advertising was for female-targeted household products. Unable to attract enough male-targeted advertising to succeed as a big-time commercial venture, Lorimer out of necessity manufactured a major identity change for the *Post.*

By 1908 Lorimer was boasting about the gender mix of the *Post*'s audience, asking, "Who says that the *Saturday Evening Post* is a magazine for men only?" and declaring, "we number women readers not by tens but hundreds of thousands."[3] As the magazine broadened its content and continued its promotional campaign aimed at women readers, the circulation of the magazine grew dramatically. Fifty-five thousand readers were added to the magazine's circulation list late in 1902 and early in 1903, by far the fastest rise in *Post* circulation figures to that point.

And advertisers began to jump on the bandwagon. As Edward Bok later put it, "advertisers were chary . . . but they thought they would 'try it for an issue or two.' "[4] Advertisements as a proportion of total *Post* pages, which ranged from twenty-four to thirty-two in number, increased from an average of three pages to an average of five. Household advertisements helped to fuel this increase, growing from 25 to 30 percent of the *Post*'s total advertising, and representing its most elaborate and expensive ads. Other categories grew significantly in these years as well. Entertainment- and work-related products would vie over the course of the decade for second place in terms of percentage of overall advertising, and education and self-improvement advertisements were another major source of revenue for the *Post*. Household advertisements, however, carried the magazine during its lean earliest years, gave it major support in becoming a commercial magazine around 1902 and 1903, and continued to constitute its largest single category of advertising throughout the first decade of the twentieth century. These ads, which were geared almost exclusively to women, therefore constituted the commercial backbone of the *Post* during its critical early years of growth.

The *Post* might have succeeded without female-targeted advertising; other magazines targeted more exclusively to men with less advertising were succeeding. But the *Post* would not have been the circulation-leader that Curtis and Lorimer wanted. They were not willing to sacrifice their vision of a circulation-leader to preserve their mission of targeting middle-class men.

The nature of the gendered commercial milieu of the day thereby in effect dictated the target audience of the *Saturday Evening Post*. Women were viewed as the primary consumers in the culture; in order to make it big with a commercial magazine, then, women had to constitute at least some of the magazine's primary audience. Curtis and Lorimer's process of defining the *Post* is instructive as it demonstrates the limited power any one or even several representatives of the "capitalist patriarchy" might wield. Neither advertisers nor readers behaved in quite the ways that the *Post*'s producers initially hoped they would. Gendered commerce, as it had taken shape by the turn of the century, was beyond the control of even Curtis and Lorimer, who were among the most savvy and influential magazine producers of their day.

The experience of the Curtis Publishing producers highlights the reality that "the market" is made up of individual producers and consumers, and that no individual has unlimited power within that market. It puts a human face on the entity to which we sometimes attribute virtually total control. Further complicating the picture, to the extent that consumers had participated in the creation of the gendered commercial milieu, they aided in the creation of an entity beyond the control of any given individual or set of individuals. Curtis and his editors were central to the developing contours of early mass-circulation magazine publishing, but those contours evolved in directions not always amenable to their desires, namely, to create one mass-circulation magazine aimed at women and another aimed at men.

Curtis and Lorimer could not have been pleased with this situation. It cost Curtis huge sums of money. Centrally defined by work as he was, Lorimer must have experienced great frustration when readers and advertisers did not behave in ways he hoped they would. But both Lorimer and Curtis must have been consoled by the huge leaps in circulation and advertising revenue that soon resulted from changing the *Post*'s formula. For business people concerned with financial success, this was more important than preserving the magazine's original target audience.

Edward Bok, who would attempt a parallel broadening of the *Journal* in these years, would not have the same consolation of increased circulation and advertising revenue. Bok attempted to speak to men as well as to women in order to make the *Journal* an even bigger seller. The *Journal* was the top-selling magazine in the country in these years, and its advertising revenues outstripped any other periodical's. But Bok could see that a magazine targeting only one gender group had, by definition, a limited audience. In addition, his targeted audience—women—was of relatively lower status than men. Woman's position as the primary consumer in American culture could not compensate completely for this lower status. Bok may also have grown tired at this point of the lampooning that he suffered for years as a result of serving as the male editor of a women's magazine. For example, early in Bok's career Eugene Field facetiously linked the young editor with Miss Lavinia Pinkham, granddaughter of Mrs. Lydia Pinkham, of patent-medicine fame. Bok's series of celebrity columns entitled "Unknown Wives of Well-Known Men" and "Clever Daughters of Clever Men" prompted commentators to respond with proposed alliterative columns like "Homely Husbands of Wonderful Wives" and "Exhilarated Editors of Marvelous Magazines."[5] Finally, competition from the growing *Post,* and his consolidation of the *Journal*'s gains in the late nineteenth century, led Bok to seek a male audience in addition to the female in the early 1900s.

Later Bok made explicit an assumption that seems to have guided the *Journal*'s editorial content as early as 1900. He wrote:

> It is a question, however, whether the day of the women's magazine, as we have known it, is not passing. . . . The interests of women and of men are being brought closer with the years, and it will not be long before they will entirely merge. This means a constantly diminishing necessity for the distinctly feminine magazine.
>
> Naturally, there will always be a field in the essentially feminine pursuits which have no place in the life of a man, but these are rapidly being cared for by books, gratuitously distributed and issued by the manufacturers of dis-

tinctly feminine domestic wares; for such publications the best talent is being employed, and the results are placed within easy reach of women, by means of newspaper advertisement, the store-counter, or the mails. These will sooner or later—and much sooner than later—supplant the practical portions of the woman's magazine, leaving only the general contents, which are generally interesting to men and to women.[6]

It is clear that Bok was still informed in these years by the notion of separate spheres; there would always be, in his view, some "feminine pursuits which have no place in the life of a man." But he was also of the opinion that women and men shared some interests that a magazine like the *Journal* could address. One suspects that this opinion grew stronger as the *Post* succeeded in attracting both men and women. While Bok's *Journal* of the early twentieth century continued to feature the same practical columns and articles that it had from the start, it also purposefully directed its attention to men as well as to women. Articles proliferated on success versus failure for the American man. The *Journal* considered the nature of twentieth-century fatherhood, and the advantages of the "strenuous life." Columns such as "The Problems of Young Men" and "Questions Men are Asking" were continued from the 1880s, and about one-fifth of Bok's editorials during the first decade of the twentieth century were addressed primarily to men.

But Bok did not succeed in broadening the audience for the *Journal* in any significant way. From the beginning of Bok's tenure male readers had had a limited but regularly expressed voice in the magazine. One or two general letters to the editor from men appeared in most issues of the *Journal* between 1889 and 1895 or so. Yet by the late 1890s letters from men were very rare. Even the most controversial articles—among them articles discussing venereal disease and the importance of honest discussions with children about sex—prompted no male response. The *Journal* remained a magazine for women despite Bok's desires and predictions.

The *Journal* became the first American magazine to reach a circulation of a million in February of 1903, and it ran upwards of a million dollars' worth of advertising per year. The *Post* moved into position to overtake the *Journal* at the end of the first decade of the century, when its circulation also surpassed a million and its advertising revenues went over the million-and-a-half dollar mark. By 1910 the *Post* enjoyed a mixed readership by gender while the *Journal* remained a magazine read primarily by women. This contrast eventually allowed the *Post* to outstrip its sister publication in both circulation and advertising revenues. The *Post* boomed during the years of World War I, reaching the unheard-of circulation figure of two million by the war's end. In the period between the wars, the *Post* outsold all other American magazines in advertising (over thirty million dollars in revenues in 1922), and it stayed at the top of the Ayer's circulation list for many years. The *Journal*'s "baby" therefore outgrew its "mother" to become the most popular and the most financially successful magazine in the United States.[7]

Why the successful broadening for the *Post* and not for the *Journal*? The reasons range from those specific to these magazines and their producers to those that are broader and more reflective of early twentieth-century culture in general. Central to the magazines' different experiences was the fact that the *Journal* was an established magazine, which from its inception had a clear, female-targeted audience. Broadening that audience some twenty years after the magazine's founding was much more difficult than for the younger and less identity-bound *Post*. In addition, the *Post* was struggling commercially as a men's magazine, making cross-gender development essential, while the *Journal* was clearly succeeding as a women's magazine. Also, the articles and editorials addressed to men in the *Journal* featured the same style and tone as those addressed to women, which meant that the magazine's actual content changed only in a minor way. The themes considered were, for the most part, those that the magazine had featured for the benefit of women for years. Perhaps most importantly, Curtis and Bok made no serious attempts to advertise the *Journal* as a magazine for men to parallel the *Post*'s promotion as a magazine for women. The *Post* would have been an ideal, cheap vehicle for such a campaign, but there was none. Curtis may not have supported Bok's interest in broadening the *Journal*'s audience, or Lorimer may not have felt comfortable running such a campaign in his *Post*. It might well have confused male readers of the *Post* to have the *Ladies' Home Journal* pitched to them as yet another "new" magazine for men.

Campaigns for the *Post* in the *Journal*'s pages did not seem problematic for *Journal* readers, and it is indeed the case that women began to read the *Post* in significant numbers in the early 1900s. One reason for women's crossover to the *Post* may lie in the contrasting tones of the two magazines. It seems that Bok's preachy, moralistic style was less inviting to men than Lorimer's more open, less judgmental style was to women. One is then led to ask why women would tolerate Bok's preaching when men were not willing to do so. Women may simply have been more accustomed to this style or, even if they disliked it, liked the magazine for its fiction, features, and advertisements. This does not preclude the possibility, however, that women found the *Post*'s less judgmental style equally appealing, and it is likely that the *Post*'s broadening in audience succeeded in part because of the more open tone it employed.

Perhaps even more significant is the stigma that would have accrued in this period to a man reading a women's magazine. While these are not fairly described as years of a masculinity crisis, it is the case that a heightened sensitivity and concern about effeminate or sissified boys and men characterized the early twentieth century. From Freudian analyses of childhood to the creation of the Boy Scout organization to new attention to homosexuality, these years saw a rigidifying of the male role. In an increasingly gender-targeted publishing world, men were not likely to seek out a magazine that had for years been targeted to women. Its gender-specific name alone was probably sufficient to guarantee that men would avoid reading it, at least openly.

We have seen the agency of producers in trying to wrestle with the contours of gendered commerce, and the agency of readers who bought and read whichever magazine attracted them, regardless of producers' desires. But there is little evidence that consumers tried to alter this relationship between gender and commerce, or that they objected to it in any substantive way. A lone reader in a letter to the editor in Knapp's magazine had suggested that women try to simplify their lives. But this reader's message was lost in the *Journal*'s promotion of consumption, and its encouragement of higher material standards of living. Simplifying life either did not occur to other readers, or it did not move them sufficiently to write to the *Journal,* or the increasingly consumption-oriented magazine did not print the letters. In any event, first the *Journal* and then the *Post* promoted consumption, and individual readers appear to have accepted, even embraced, this emphasis.

There is little evidence of substantive opposition to the gendering of commerce at the cultural level either. Rosalind Williams notes the creation in 1891 of the Social League of Shoppers in New York, a group that staged shopper boycotts in attempts to prevent the exploitation of workers.[8] But organizations like this in the United States were rare and short-lived, and they did not address the bond between gender and commerce. A Frenchman, Charles Gide, suggested at the turn of the century that this very theme should inform the work of the consumer cooperatives that had proliferated in France. He regarded "feminism and the consumer movement as natural allies."[9]

But in neither France nor the United States did significant feminist analyses of consumption arise, much less hold sway. Consumption became bound up with gender norms in a pervasive and most appealing way. Significant critical analyses would not emerge until much later in the twentieth century, long after the gender–commerce relationship had been established and solidified.

The *Journal* and the *Post* continued to be unevenly gendered texts in the first decade of the twentieth century, the *Journal* more consciously gendered, the *Post* much less so. The *Journal* was as mixed in its messages about women as it had been in Bok's early tenure, but it still centered primarily on women and their interests. The magazine was edited by a condescending man who promoted conservative views, but it also featured a range of views and images in its articles, fiction, and advertising. Although both women and men wrote for the *Journal* between 1900 and 1910, as they would continue to do over the course of the century, feminine gender construction in the *Journal* was conscious, direct, and often very prescriptive. This gender construction was somewhat removed from readers since the *Journal's* editor was a man and it was a slick, modern magazine. The peer to peer intimacy of gender construction in Knapp's *Journal* found no place in Bok's *Journal* of the early 1900s.

The *Post* as a gendered text is an interesting case in light of the fact that the magazine was increasingly targeted to women as well as to men. The *Post* in this period continued to implicitly embody more than explicitly discuss masculinity in most editorials and articles. Some articles addressed female gender norms openly, and short stories centered more consciously on gender norms for both men and women. Given these characteristics, one must conclude that the *Post* was a gender-inclusive rather than a gender-neutral text. Although it embodied the cultural stance of male as norm, and thus generally refrained from explicit discussions of masculinity, the *Post* implied masculine norms and explicated feminine ones. As we have seen, it also began to target both men and women readers out of necessity.

Characterizing the Curtis publications in gender terms is therefore much more complicated than simply describing a women's magazine and a men's magazine. The *Journal* was a magazine for women and a thoroughly feminine text, to the extent that it discussed women's gender construction regularly and directly. But it was edited by a man and many of its contributors were men. The *Post* increasingly targeted women as well as men, and its content became increasingly gender inclusive as well. Lorimer remained a "man's man," however, and the content of the magazine continued to embody gender more than it commented directly on it.

This pattern ultimately allowed the *Post* to become central to American culture, the beloved text of men, women, and even children, for decades. Bok had been right to worry about the *Post*. While the *Journal* was limited to the "specialized" audience of middle-class women, the *Post* would come to speak to and symbolize the whole of American mainstream society.

Before this could happen to the *Post*, however, commercial gender norms would have to be refined to incorporate masculinity as well as femininity. Analyzing and comparing the content of the *Journal* and the *Post* between 1900 and 1910 reveals two very different discourses, to which we will turn in chapter 8. But there was complete agreement between the two Curtis publications on the relative roles that women and men should play in the early twentieth-century commercial milieu. This agreement signalled the cementing of a longlasting and pervasive relationship between gender and commerce, a relationship that rested on norms for masculinity as well as for femininity.

8

Oppositions and Overlaps in Views of Women and Men: The Content of the *Journal* and the *Post* Compared, 1900–1910

The *Journal* and the *Post* were by the first decade of the twentieth century established and influential social institutions in American popular culture. The *Journal* took a twenty-fifth "birthday bow" in 1908, and both magazines ran photographs in this decade of the Curtis Publishing Company building, which was completed in 1910. The *Post* had become a widely known institution by this time as well, Curtis having developed a network of hundreds of "*Post* boys" who sold and delivered the magazines in towns and cities all over the United States. These boys were urged in the *Post* to greater and greater heights of selling success. One inspiring model was Willie Fugate of New Mexico, who lived on the Santa Fe Railroad line: "We have more coyotes than people here," Willie reported, "but I think I can jump that order [from 125] to 200 copies a week when the travel gets a little heavier."[1]

Both the *Journal* and the *Post* had found their niche in American culture, and they were decidedly different cultural texts, featuring different rhetoric, different tones, and some different focuses. But the two magazines agreed on the cultural and economic equation that would give substance and durability to the union between gender and commerce in the twentieth century. Women should consume, and men should earn to support that consumption, the Curtis magazines declared. The agreement on this equation in the midst of the two periodicals' many disagreements is striking. The women should consume, men should earn equation set the tone for these two magazines in subsequent years, and it helped to shape both commerce and gender norms in American culture for years.

Despite the fact that the *Post* evolved into a gender-inclusive magazine, it remained sufficiently dominated by a male oriented style and interests to provide a clear contrast with the *Journal*. Both magazines continued to comment explicitly on women's role during these years, giving special attention to the question of the New Woman. In 1904, fifteen years after Knapp had virtually dismissed the separate spheres metaphor, Bok was still invoking it emphatically:

155

THE LADIES' HOME JOURNAL

REGISTERED IN UNITED STATES PATENT OFFICE

VOLUME XXV, NUMBER 12 · PHILADELPHIA, NOVEMBER, 1908

Our Birthday Bow

WOMAN at twenty-five is in the flush of her young womanhood ; a man at twenty-five is just beginning life. This magazine feels like a man. Twenty-five years is not a long time for a periodical to learn wisdom ; it is even less of a period for an editor to get well-fitted to his work. It takes a long time to feel ourselves competent, if we ever do!

So, on our twenty-fifth birthday, we hope that the unstinted confidence and success meted out to us by the public have made us humble and grateful rather than boastful and forgetful. If anything were needed to keep us from being boastful it is the incontrovertible fact, incessantly faced each day, that it is so much easier to make a success than it is to hold it.

The twenty-five years gone by have been full of the hardest kind of work: that kind of work we shall not have to repeat. But no success comes without bringing in its train grave new problems and a recognition of new and untried responsibilities. The work simply changes: lessens it does not.

If the success of this magazine has been without precedent so have been the problems that such a success brings. And because they have no precedent they must be worked out on absolutely new and individual lines. We do not always choose the wisest solutions:

human judgment is human and not infallible, no matter how honest may be the spirit back of it. We simply do our best: none can do more. We take our work seriously, but never ourselves, and so we preserve a healthy equilibrium. We acknowledge the mistakes of the past, a legion of them. Our only wish is that they were not so many. And yet it is only through mistakes that real lessons are taught and learned. Costly as experience always is it is cheap if its lessons are heeded.

In the next twenty-five years we shall continue to make mistakes. All we can hope for is not to make the same mistakes over, and to ask your patience with our new errors. It is that unswerving patience, indulgence and leniency that have made this birthday possible for us. For this our gratitude is not to be conveyed by word. The heart that is full cannot speak — only by action. And thus we shall hope to speak. Direct from full hearts, we say the simple — and so often pitiably-inadequate — words: Thank you.

For the future we ask: Patience as we go forth on untried paths. We shall try to act on what the wit said: "Be good, but don't overdo it." By some we shall probably be considered bad, but believe us we shall not be all bad. We shall be neither as good as we are thought to be, nor as bad as we are painted. We shall just be normal, full of good intentions, full of shortcomings, hoping and believing, however, that "the best is yet to be."

DRAWN BY C. M. RELYEA

The Journal's New Home

The Imposing New Building for The Curtis Publishing Company, Upon Which Work Will Soon be Started. It Will Take Two Years to Erect It. When Finished it Will be the Largest and Best-Equipped Publishing Building in the United States

The Location of the New Building

IT MAY very truly be said that the most famous spot in America has been chosen for the new home of THE LADIES' HOME JOURNAL. An entire city block has been taken: from Sixth Street to Seventh, and from Walnut Street to Sansom, in the centre of the business and financial district of Philadelphia—the very site, in fact, chosen some years ago for the new United States Mint, but abandoned because of the high value of the ground. For the Curtis Building thirty-six estates were purchased at a cost of more than $1,175,000.

The new building will face on two public parks. One is Independence Square, the other Washington Square. Both are historic. In Independence Square stands the most precious building in the United States: the old State House, better known as Independence Hall, because it was there that the Declaration of Independence was adopted and formally read to thousands of patriots a few days later. The hall still contains the Liberty Bell, which was rung so joyfully on the memorable Fourth of July in 1776. It was here that the Constitution of the United States was ratified, here that the new nation had its Capital, here that the first Supreme Court sat, here that George Washington was inaugurated for his second term as President, and John Adams for his first term.

Long before this, however, the building was well known as the scene of many ceremonial gatherings. For instance, the King's birthday was celebrated there; when a new commander-in-chief of the royal troops in the Colonies reached Philadelphia a splendid banquet was prepared there; the arrival of a new Governor was made the occasion of a brilliant parade, followed by a dinner at the State House; after the Revolutionary War Lafayette was honored with a reception there, and Abraham Lincoln once raised a flag over the hall—indeed, after he was assassinated his body lay in state there.

The State House was also virtually the first home of a public library in Philadelphia. Benjamin Franklin and some of his friends had founded a library of sorts were using a room in a private dwelling when permission was obtained to remove the books to the State House. The Library Company is still in existence.

Washington Square is sacred ground because it was the burial place of many American soldiers who died in the war for independence. More than two thousand bodies were laid there.

The Contents of This Number

What the New Building Will be Like

THE new building will, in its architecture, enter directly into the spirit of its historic surroundings. It will, in a general way, follow the beautiful simple Colonial lines of Independence Hall, and thus be built of red brick with white marble trimmings. The front of the building will be on Sixth Street, facing Independence Square, and will be two hundred and thirty-seven feet long. The south side of the building will be on Walnut Street, facing Washington Square, and will be two hundred and forty feet long—only one-half of the block being built up at first. The building will be nine stories high, have a total height of one hundred and eighty feet, and will have a total inside floor space of eleven acres. It will be solely and exclusively occupied by The Curtis Publishing Company.

The front entrance to the building will be singularly impressive. The columns you see in the picture will be 32 feet, 6 inches high, and 3 feet 6 inches in diameter, and made of solid marble. These columns will support a balcony promenade 124 feet long and 9 feet wide, which will blossom with the green of the evergreen and bay tree. Ten steps, 55 feet long, will ascend to the front door, which will be of bronze in a Colonial design.

The magnificent first floor of the building, which of itself is 18 feet high, will be finished chiefly in marble. On the entire centre wall facing the main entrance will be an impressive decorative painting over 12 feet high and nearly 40 feet wide, by Edwin A. Abbey, the designer of the famous Holy Grail decorations in the Boston Public Library. This superb painting will strike the artistic keynote to the building, and will, of itself, make it a Mecca for strangers.

One of the chief features of the building, outside of its strictly business side, will be the upper two floors, which will be entirely given over to the comfort of the employees. There will be three distinct dining-rooms, one for every day; a fully-equipped kitchen the size of a hotel kitchen; an art gallery containing hundreds of interesting paintings, which the public will be welcome to view at any time; two large rest-rooms and reading-rooms for the girl employees; a modern-equipped hospital and retiring-room, and on top of the roof a glass-covered promenade, 130 feet long, will be constructed for noon exercise—open in summer and closed in winter, with a mammoth fireplace and comfortable lounging corners.

Another "Rough Rider" Wins Out

WILLIE FUGATE is a twelve-year-old boy living in a town of 200 inhabitants in the Pecos River Valley, New Mexico, on the line of the Santa Fe Railroad. He had a bronco, but had grown tired of riding "bareback" and wanted a saddle. He read of a boy in an Eastern town having made money by selling

THE SATURDAY EVENING POST

and wrote for information. His neighbors did not know much about THE POST and he sold only two copies out of the ten received. Most of the trains stop at Willie's town for water and he wandered down to the station "to see the train come in." When he saw a number of passengers step out of the train a thought struck him. Mounting a pile of ties, he announced in a loud voice: "You won't have a chance to get any more reading matter for 250 miles—you'd better get a copy of this week's SATURDAY EVENING POST." In about two minutes he had sold the other eight copies and could have sold a dozen more. That night he wrote for 50 copies for next week and sold every one.

During the next month he sold over 400 copies and bought "not only a dandy saddle but a blanket." Since then he has sold an average of about 125 copies a week and each month won one of the cash prizes offered to the boys who do good work. He writes: "We have more coyotes than people here, but I think I can jump that order to 200 copies a week when the travel gets a little heavier."

Any Boy Out of School During Vacation Can Earn Money

selling THE POST. We send the first week's supply free. This provides capital for the following week. Write for the TEN FREE COPIES to-day. DON'T BE AFRAID TO TRY IT. If 6000 other boys are making money by this plan you can do the same.

NEXT MONTH $250 in Extra Cash Prizes will be Given to Boys Who Do Good Work

Address Boy Department, The Curtis Publishing Company, 445 Arch Street, Philadelphia, Pa.

> In all this talk of which we hear so much about the "broadening of woman's sphere" we seem to forget that in the home itself, over which woman reigns and in which she is supreme, lie the parts of our entire social order: political, religious and industrial. There is not a branch of our living that does not directly come out of the home and is not influenced by it. When a woman speaks of her home as being narrow she does not mean so much . . . that her home is narrow, as she does that she herself has made it narrow.[2]

Bok updated the ideology of the Cult of True Womanhood as an alternative to New Womanhood in the early twentieth century by further elaborating on his notion of professional housewifery. Bok's emphasis on True Womanhood exemplifies how he circumscribed the *Journal*'s discussion of gender during these years. He completely ignored the ideology of Real Womanhood to which Knapp had subscribed, with its emphasis on women's need to learn to provide for themselves and their right to increased public activity. He focused instead on the image of the New Woman, which was fraught with contradictions and seemed extreme to many.[3] Bok's ideal woman was the sophisticated homemaker, and the ideal homemaker was a dietician, financier, employer (of servants), teacher, artist, and "social economist."[4] In Bok's view, the good woman of the early twentieth century adapted her household work to technological change but shunned public activity as much as possible.

From the beginning of his editorial tenure (and in direct contrast to Knapp) Bok had opposed women's clubs, an arena of public life that engaged thousands of middle-class women by the turn of the century.[5] At his most supportive he set restrictive standards for club participation, suggesting that women should belong to only one club and should always put their work in the home before their club activities. And while Knapp had affirmed the range of endeavors undertaken by women's clubs, Bok had a clearly prescribed agenda for those women who did join clubs. He asserted in 1903 that clubs after twenty years were still "stumbling," messing about with mediocre political, cultural, and literary pursuits. Why not focus, Bok asked repeatedly, on more worthwhile endeavors like beautifying the landscape or fostering "pretty towns" by offering awards for redecorating? His suggestions ranged from the banal to the absurdly sentimental. An example of the latter was his idea for mothers' clubs to erect monuments celebrating motherhood. It is perhaps not surprising that a man who frequently tried to put women on a pedestal would assume that they might wish to put themselves there.[6]

In any case, Bok's campaign was wrongheaded in the eyes of many of his readers. His comments about women's clubs seriously angered a significant number of *Journal* subscribers. Bok himself noted later that thousands of club women, many of them readers of the *Journal,* signed petitions calling for Curtis to discharge his anticlub editor.[7] In 1905, after the *Journal* published an inflammatory article on clubs by Grover Cleveland, who accused club women of being antifamily and even anti-American, a prominent women's club went so far as to organize a boycott against the magazine. Bok undercut that effort by threatening to sue the club for violating the Sherman Act, but the magazine lost hundreds of subscribers in this period.[8] This flap illustrates how far Bok was willing to go in pressing his conservative views, even at the risk of seriously alienating many of his readers. It also illustrates how entrenched middle-class women's clubs had become by the first decade of the twentieth century, and it highlights readers' agency in responding to stances taken by magazines as well. Bok's opposition to women's clubs quite possibly had the paradoxical effect of giving club members and their work together renewed vitality.

The *Journal* between 1900 and 1910 voiced regular and vociferous opposition to women's suffrage as well. In 1905 Grover Cleveland considered the issue in an article entitled "Would Woman Suffrage Be Unwise?" and he concluded that it most assuredly would be. Women, he asserted, were illogical, impractical, unbusinesslike, and stubborn. They were, on the other hand, intuitive, sympathetic, trustful, charitable, thoughtful, and loving. The former qualities, Cleveland thought, made women unfit for public life, while the latter made their refining, elevating influence crucial to the men who appropriately did the voting for their families.[9]

To Bok's credit, however, he began to broaden the *Journal*'s sights on this and other issues in 1910 by instituting a column called "Both Sides of Live Questions." The column featured the views of prominent figures of the day on controversial questions, and its first installment focused on women's suffrage. On the "pro" side, Jane Addams argued in a now-famous passage that the "municipal housekeeping" duty of women required that they be able to vote:

> [I]t is necessary that woman shall extend her sense of responsibility to many things outside of her own home if she would continue to preserve the home in its entirety. . . . [Women] simply want an opportunity to do their own work and to take care of those affairs which naturally and historically belong to women, but which are constantly being overlooked and slighted in our political institutions.[10]

The Reverend Lyman Abbott echoed Grover Cleveland's inflammatory rhetoric in his argument against suffrage in the next issue of the *Journal,* but the debate format provided some balance. More than anything else, presenting both sides of the matter was probably a signal of Bok's reluctant admission of the likelihood of women winning the right to vote in the twentieth century.

Bok's *Journal* was more supportive of women's higher education, and the *Journal* between 1900 and 1910 featured some innovative analyses of women's college life. The photographic essay or "pictorial" made its first appearance in the pages of the *Journal* in 1901 with a double-page spread of halftones illustrating "What a Girl Does at College." Vassar, Wellesley, and Barnard

THE LADIES' HOME JOURNAL

Vol. XXII, No. 6   PHILADELPHIA, MAY 1905   Yearly Subscription, One Dollar
Single Copy, Fifteen Cents

The Clevelands' Home at Princeton, New Jersey

Woman's Mission and Woman's Clubs

By Grover Cleveland, Ex-President of the United States

"I am Persuaded that There are Woman's Clubs Whose Objects and Intents are Not Only Harmful, But Harmful in a Way that Directly Menaces the Integrity of Our Homes"

Mr. Cleveland

Mrs. Cleveland

8.e. Details from *Journal* Pictorial "What a Girl Does At College."

women were pictured in groups wearing shirt-waists (suitable collegiate attire), playing basketball, and rowing. Pictorials gave new punch to the *Journal*'s discussion of women's higher education. Suddenly *Journal* readers could actually see women participating in college activities, a development in popular magazines of the day to which historians have given short shrift.[11] Women in these and other photographs were not arbiters of major social change, however. Like many magazines in the early twentieth century, Bok's *Journal* accepted and even promoted women's higher education, but it stopped short of supporting meaningful change in women's lives that might result from such education.[12]

Most *Journal* discussions of the college curriculum for women centered on domestic science, the appropriate training for future professional housewives. Bok continued to proclaim the benefits of the domestic science course for every middle-class woman. A new development in these years was that Bok became the butt of jokes in other magazines for his relentless championing of domestic science training.[13]

The *Post* was actually among those magazines, poking fun at domestic science courses directly and at Bok indirectly. A 1906 issue, for example, featured a poem by Elsie Duncan Yale entitled "The Song of the Scientific Housewives," which lamented the passing of old-fashioned cooking (see figure 8.f).

In other contexts the *Post* took women's higher education seriously, but its frequent digs at domestic science exemplify the *Post*'s regular use of humor. There is little use of a light tone or humor in Bok's *Journal*, partly because Bok himself appears to have possessed no sense of humor, and partly because of perceived differences between the audiences for the two magazines. Many contributors to American popular culture at the turn of the century, especially men, assumed that a sense of humor was a masculine trait.[14] Accordingly, the *Post* employed a light tone and relied frequently on humor, and it placed a high value on a man's having a sense of humor. This identification of humor with men was carried further by both the *Post* and the *Journal* to suggest that, to the extent that humor was a masculine trait, it was distinctly unfeminine.

The *Journal,* while it never employed the *Post*'s pervasive humorous tone, did run a humor column for a brief time. Beginning in 1905, "That Reminds Me" appeared at the front of the magazine, featuring some jokes similar to those appearing in the *Post*'s pages (see figure 8.g). In January of 1907, however, Bok reported that he was receiving many letters from readers opposed to the column. Some readers saw no reason for it, Bok testified, while others objected to the specific content of some jokes. The column was discontinued soon thereafter, the episode apparently supporting the notion that women, at least those reading the *Journal,* indeed did not have a sense of humor.[15]

THE SONG OF THE SCIENTIFIC HOUSEWIVES

By Elsie Duncan Yale

Before we learned to do things right we always used to cook
Without so much as peeping at a dietetic book,
But this is not the way at all, as science has made plain,
And now, as we prepare the meals, we murmur this refrain:
"There's nitrogen, and hydrogen, a small per cent. of fat,
The carbo-hydrates, gluten, starch—remember all of that;
The right proportion must be found in every meal each day,
For 'tis the only accurate and hygienic way."

Pa used to plead for pork and beans, the children called for cake,
The boarders begged for pumpkin pie whenever we would bake.
We used to try to please them all, in our misguided way,
But now, as we prepare the meals, beneath our breath we say:
"There's nitrogen, and hydrogen, a small per cent. of fat,
The carbo-hydrates, gluten, starch—remember all of that;
The right proportion must be found in every meal each day,
For 'tis the only accurate and hygienic way."

Pa hopes in vain for ham and eggs; the children can't have pie;
The boarders one and all have left—we often wonder why.
We steadfastly decline to do the way we know is wrong,
And as we cook the daily meals we hum the well-known song:

8.g. The *Journal*'s Short-Lived Humor Column.

THAT REMINDS ME

Bright Things of All Times that People Have Laughed Over

She was a Chosen One

TWO very nice little girls had a quarrel one day. "Anyhow," said one to the other, who was an adopted child, "your parents are not real." Whereupon the other little girl retorted: "I don't care, my papa and mamma picked me out. Yours had to take you just as you came."

Not in Her Class

AFTER preaching a sermon on the fate of the wicked an English clergyman met an old woman well known for her gossiping propensities, and he said to her: "My good dame, I hope my sermon has borne fruit. You heard what I said about the place where there shall be wailing and gnashing of teeth?"

"Yes," she replied, "but as to that, if I 'as anything to say it be this: Let 'em gnash their teeth as has 'em — I ain't."

Easy — When She Knew the Facts

WHEN preparing his parishioners for the solemn ordinance of confirmation an old clergyman found among them one old woman so excessively ignorant and stupid that for some weeks prior to the time he was obliged to have her come to his house every day in order to instruct and catechize her. At length he began to hope that his time, patience and zeal had not been entirely bestowed in vain, a few bright flashes of understanding having burst from the old dame's clouded intellect. "Now, my good friend," said the worthy pastor, just previous to the commencement of the ceremony, "as this is the last moment in which I shall have an opportunity of conversing with you, let me ask, do you thoroughly understand and believe all the articles of your Christian faith?"

"Ay, yes, sir, thank'ee," replied his venerable pupil with a simper, and dropping one of her best courtesies, "I does indeed, now; and, thank God, I heartily renounces them all."

Which Would You Rather Be?

IF AN editor makes a mistake he has to apologize for it, but if a doctor makes a mistake he buries it. If an editor makes one there is a lawsuit, swearing and the smell of sulphur, but if a doctor makes one there is a funeral, cut flowers and a smell of varnish.

A doctor can use a word a yard long without knowing what it means, but if an editor uses it he has to spell it. Any old college can make a doctor. You can't make an editor: he has to be born.

A Cause for Thanks

IN THE audience at a lecture on China there was a very pious old lady who was slightly deaf. She thought the lecturer was preaching, and every time he came to a period she would say "Amen!" or some other pious exclamation. The people in the audience, which was composed mostly of the village church members, knew she was being reverent and did not even smile when she exclaimed, until finally the lecturer mentioned some far-off city in China, saying, "I live there." At this point clearly and distinctly could be heard the old lady, saying, "Thank God for that."

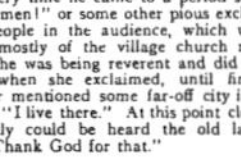

He was Served Accordingly

AT A MEN'S café one night a young American — a barber — fell in with an Englishman. The latter was berating the Yankees for doing all manner of business in their shops and not following the better English plan of sticking to one branch. The next day he swaggered into the barber-shop to be shaved. The barber gave his face an extra good soaping and left him, at the same time seating himself to read. The Englishman kept quiet for a few minutes, when, seeing his attendant reading, he blurted out, "Why don't you shave me, sir?" "You will have to go up the street for your shave," quietly replied the barber. "We only lather here."

An Eye-Opener

A CHILD of strict parents, whose greatest joy had hitherto been the weekly prayer-meeting, was taken by his nurse to the circus for the first time. When he came home he exclaimed: "Oh, mamma, if you once went to the circus you'd never, never go to prayer-meeting again in all your life."

His Sister's Ingratitude

THERE'S my sister, had a bracelet on her birthday from her beau.
"Twenty pearls," he said, "are in it — one for every year, you know."
I said: "Better make it thirty!" (thought she'd like the extra pearls).
Crickey! but I caught it later! There's no gratitude in girls!

Would Have Been More Considerate

AN ANTIQUARY one day visited Westminster Abbey, and found a stonecutter at work in the little cloisters, recutting the name of Wilson, the great tenor of Shakespeare's day.

The antiquary began to tell the stonecutter about Wilson, how he had been Shakespeare's friend, and Ben Jonson's, and Kit Marlowe's, and how all these men loved and honored him.

The stonecutter, looking up from his work, frowned and shook his head. "I wish, sir," he said, "we'd knowed he was such a swell afore we run that drainpipe through him."

Pat was Not Glad

A FINE, robust soldier after serving his country faithfully for some time became greatly reduced in weight, owing to exposure and scanty rations, until he was so weak he could hardly stand. Consequently, he got leave of absence to go home and recuperate. He arrived at his home station looking very badly. Just as he stepped off the boat one of his old friends rushed up to him and said: "Well, well, Pat, I am glad to see you're back from the front."

Pat looked worried and replied: "Begorra, I knew I was getting thin, but I nivver thought you could see that much."

The Ethics of Laps

A GIRL recently sent this extraordinary request to the editor of her church paper:

"Do you think it is right for a girl to sit in a man's lap, even if she is engaged?"

The editor answered her question thus:

"If it were *our* girl and *our* lap, yes; if it were *another* fellow's girl and *our* lap, yes; but if it were *our* girl and *another* fellow's lap, *never!* NEVER! NEVER!"

A la Mode

"WHICH is the first and most important sacrament?" asked a Sunday-school teacher of a girl preparing for confirmation.

"Marriage," was the prompt response.

"No, baptism is the first and most important sacrament," the teacher corrected.

"Not in our family," said the pupil haughtily; "we are respectable."

Why He Joined the Sunday-School

"TOMMY," said a young lady visitor at his home, "why not come to our Sabbath-school? Several of your little friends have joined us lately."

Tommy hesitated a moment. Then suddenly he exclaimed: "Does a red-headed kid by the name of Jimmy Brown go to your school?"

"Yes, indeed," replied the new teacher.

"Well, then," said Tommy, with an air of interest, "I'll be there next Sunday, you bet. I've been layin' for that kid for three weeks, and never knew where to find him."

Too True

"WOMAN is not only barbarous — she is illogical and inconsistent as well," remarked a man of letters. "I was walking in the country one day with a young woman. In a grove we came upon a boy about to shin up a tree. There was a nest in the tree, and from a certain angle it was possible to see in it three eggs.

"'You wicked little boy,' said my companion, 'are you going up there to rob that nest?'

"'I am,' the boy replied.

"'How can you?' she exclaimed. 'Think how the mother will grieve over the loss of her eggs.'

"'Oh, she won't care,' said the boy. 'She's up there in your hat.'"

The Contents of This Number

Not that Time

ON A COLD, stormy night a man was hastening home with his overcoat buttoned up to his neck. He was rather anxious to know what time it was, but he was too lazy to unbutton his coat in order to get at his watch.

Just then he saw a well-dressed man coming in the distance, and he remarked to himself:

"I'll ask this gentleman the hour of the night, and so save myself the trouble of unbuttoning my coat."

"Sir, do you know what time it is?" he asked.

The stranger paused, and removed his right glove, unbuttoned his overcoat from top to bottom, unbuttoned his undercoat, and finally pulled out his watch, while the cool wind beat against his unprotected chest.

Holding up the watch so that the light would shine on it he scrutinized it an instant, and as he passed on said, "I do."

It was Up to the Bachelor

AN OLD bachelor, who lives in the suburbs of a Southern city, hires a colored man to clean up his room, fill the lamp, and perform like services. A few days ago the colored domestic, who had been using his employer's blacking, said:

"Boss, our blackin' am done out."

"What do you mean by saying 'our blacking'?" growled the sordid employer; "everything belongs to me. I want you to understand that nothing belongs to you."

The terrified darky apologized and promised to remember. On the following Sunday the bachelor happened to meet the colored menial, accompanied by a chocolate-colored female pushing a baby-carriage.

"Was that your baby in that carriage?" he asked next day at his house where he was entertaining quite a number of his friends.

"No, boss, dat's not our chile; dat's your chile. I'se nebber gwine to say nuffin belongs to me no moah."

Natural Philosophy

EARLY in the morning session, when the pupils were feeling bright and happy, the teacher thought it a good plan to give them sentences to correct, both as to grammar and sense. She accordingly wrote on the blackboard: "The hen has four legs. He done it." Thoughtful little Ignatius, at the foot of the class, pondered deeply, and at the end of the fifteen minutes' time allowed for correction he wrote: "*He* didn't done it: God done it."

A Lasting Invention

A NUMBER of men on the street were having a discussion as to who was the greatest inventor. Some said Edison, some Watt, some Morse, some one and some another. Finally a pawnbroker got in a word, and said:

"Vell, chentlemens, dose vas gread peoples, but I tells you dot man vot invented interest vas no slouch."

All for Her Sake — as Usual

THE colored sexton of a wealthy church had a very stylish mulatto wife. Finding his domestic income not quite equal to his expenses he decided to apply for an increase in salary. So he wrote a letter to the committee in charge with this explanation at the close: "It's mighty hard to keep a sealskin wife on a muskrat salary."

An Eye for Business

THE boy of the family, the smart little son of an editor, had just passed his ninth birthday, and delighted in stirring things up whenever he found a chance. On his way to school one day he popped into a hardware store.

"Say, mister," he called out, "do you keep knives?"

"Oh, yes," replied the storekeeper, "we've kept them for years."

"Well," returned the boy, starting for the door, "just advertise, and then you won't keep them so long."

Failed to Attract

THE best efforts to make a home attractive sometimes fail.

Recently a district visitor in the slums of a large city asked the wife of a notorious drinker why she did not keep her husband from the public-house.

"Well," she answered, "I 'ave done my best, ma'am, but he will go there."

"Why don't you make your home look more attractive?"

"I'm sure I've tried 'ard to make it 'ome-like, ma'am," was the reply. "I've took up the parlor carpet and sprinkled sawdust on the floor, and put a beer barrel in the corner. But, lor', ma'am, it ain't made a bit of difference!"

The case of the *Post* complicates this generalization, however. Since the *Post* did not change its light tone and regular use of humor even as it broadened to try to reach more women, female readers of the *Post* were addressed in the same light way as were male readers. Quips and jibes pervaded the magazine, from its editorials to its articles and much of its fiction, and the fact that the *Post* was able to attract and to hold many women readers suggests that women were not as delicate on the matter of humor as many had supposed.

Cristanne Miller's recent analysis of language in women's and men's magazines of the mid-1980s suggests that women's magazines may continue to stereotype women in similar ways. She notes that while both female and male speech patterns depend on context—audience, class, situation, etc.—women's speech tends to be oversimplified in women's magazines. The language of women's magazines seems to be designed to create anxiety, Miller notes, and it is more earnest and directive than the language in men's magazines. Men's magazines feature a friendly, lighter tone. Miller writes: "No doubt because men's magazines do not assume that their readers need serious help, the tone is less earnest than in women's magazines."[16] Miller concludes that women's magazines are problematic because they foster the myth that women have a single way of talking, and because they present women as earnest but not serious users of the language.

But Miller's analysis suffers since she offers no criticism of men's magazines. Her unilateral criticism of women's magazines undercuts the positive functions of women's magazines, functions that are revealed by explicit comparison of women's and men's magazines like the *Journal* and the *Post*. It is indeed the case that the *Journal* under Bok was more earnest and pedantic than Lorimer's *Post*. But for all its heavy-handedness, Bok's *Journal* did feature serious and straightforward consideration of critical issues. In contrast, the *Post* employed a playfulness that allowed *Post* writers to allude to certain issues without actually analyzing them or considering them in any thoughtful way. To the extent, then, that it had featured comparable consideration without preaching, as well as a friendly, sometimes playful tone, Knapp's *Journal* was actually the most positive model of the various incarnations of the two magazines.

The *Post* between 1900 and 1910 continued to view American middle-class women as a group undergoing significant and positive change, still framing its discussion largely in the context of individual rights. A recent analysis of Lorimer's *Post* asserts that Lorimer was "anything but a supporter of feminism," but a close reading of his magazine suggests that this characterization sells Lorimer short.[17] Lorimer's *Post* aggressively endorsed the cause of woman's suffrage, for example, presenting the vote for women as both inevitable and just. In 1910, the *Post* cited the fact that women constituted almost half of the voting stockholding membership of the Pennsylvania Railroad. If more than 26,000 women were able to vote responsibly in this complicated business setting, the *Post* asked, were not American women as a group ready for the ballot?[18] In 1909 the magazine noted that the Chicago Superintendent of Schools, the manager of 6,100 teachers, was a woman. Men were willing to entrust this kind of crucial responsibility to a woman, the *Post* commented dryly, but would "consider the country in peril" if she could vote.[19]

The *Post* took a similarly affirmative view of women's work for pay, beginning the 1900-1910 decade with a ringing endorsement of just such work. Lorimer, in a 1901 editorial entitled "What the Century has Done for Women," announced that

> no lesson that the nineteenth century taught us is more directly impressive than its exhibition of the unused resources which it brought into use . . . [that is] the great increase of women's activity during the past century.[20]

Lorimer went on to observe that women by the end of the nineteenth century had been counted among the ranks of professionals in science, law, medicine, business, philosophy, and "social reform of every kind," concluding on this overly optimistic but decidedly progressive note:

> In a word, woman is now allowed to make what she will out of her own life, and to work out any kind of power that is in her, as she never was before; and she has laid us all under obligation by the splendid use she has made of her new opportunity.[21]

The magazine in these years asserted that the main impediment to women working in the early twentieth century was the American culture itself. In a July 1910 piece entitled "The New Woman and Her Ways—The Woman Farmer," University of Chicago alumna Maude Radford Warren detailed the reasons that more and more single women were turning to farming for their life's work. These included the high cost of city living, the burnout factor for teachers, low pay, and the low cost of educational opportunities at agricultural colleges and universities.[22] In Warren's view, women were suited to the profession of farming by virtue of their patience, their attention to small detail, and, interestingly, their superior buying and selling skills. But the cultural attitude toward women was still the major—and the negative—motivator for such women. Warren concluded:

> Above all, smarting as she does under the injustice of the wage scale, accustomed in the city to do man's work at woman's wages, she finds her greatest argument in the fact that Mother Earth is no respecter of persons or of sexes, and on the farm she will not be fined because she is a woman.[23]

A later Warren article went even farther, calling for deep and fundamental change. In "Petticoat Professions—New Women in Old Fields," Warren expressed the hope that her work and the work of writers like her would inspire the culture to take women seriously as workers and to accommodate their needs. Warren's conclusion suggests the sacrifice that female professionals of the day were making, and it is full of pathos in light of what we know about the limited results of that sacrifice. "Perhaps it is not a Utopian dream," Warren wrote hopefully, "that the professional woman of today is blazing a trail for that possible woman who, in a readjusted world, may have not only a profession but a husband and children too."[24]

Building on its earlier support of the extension of individual rights to women, some *Post* writers began to examine the implications of such rights for home life. They came to the advanced conclusion that someday women might "have it all." But as it had been in its early years, the *Post*'s progressive view of women would be overshadowed by the magazine's more conventional view of the male role.

The consideration of marital relations in both magazines reflects the contradictions inherent in late nineteenth-century marriage norms. Romantic love was the basis for marriage, but the notion of love as a mysterious force made feelings grown dull or lost over time with one partner virtually impossible to revive. Furthermore, divorce was not sanctioned as a solution to the problem of "marital disaffection."[25] The producers of the *Journal* and the *Post,* like their turn-of-the-century readers, were caught in a time when the reality of marital difficulties was beginning to be openly acknowledged. But the only viable alternative for respectable members of the middle class was to try to conform to wifely and husbandly roles as much as possible. Not surprisingly, the *Journal* blamed men for the troubled state of many marriages, while the *Post* tended to blame women.

Some of the most striking commentary on male–female relations in the *Journal* of these years came from a new feature, the personal confession. Such pieces, contributed anonymously but in all likelihood produced by the *Journal*'s usual stable of writers, began to appear with regularity after 1903. One suspects that these sensational accounts were instituted in the hopes of attracting more readers after the *Journal*'s circulation had topped a million and had begun to plateau. Such titles as "Why I Have Not Become a Mother—A Wife's Frank Statement of Her Reasons for Not Having any Children" and "My Experiences in Wanting to be Beautiful" were designed to stimulate interest in a magazine that by then was well-established and quite staid.

One 1908 confession story, entitled "Why I Would Not Marry My Husband Again, As Told by a Wife and Written for the Consideration of a Few Husbands," was a stinging attack on husbands' treatment of wives. This wife would not marry her husband again because she did not love him enough after "my suffering in silence, my meekness under injustice, my bearing patiently with slights and disagreeable habits and selfishness."[26] The author had a number of serious and specific complaints about her husband, including the fact that he had no idea what it took for her to accomplish all the domestic work for which she was responsible. Moreover, he gave her none of the appreciation that she and other women craved. This woman's most serious complaint was that her husband was "less polite to me than to any other woman of his acquaintance. He uses a special tone of voice that says 'Well, well, hurry up!' which I have heard hundreds of husbands use when speaking to their wives."[27]

This melodramatic account and others like it signal the tension of a culture that is increasingly open about problematic relations, but still has no viable safety valve in separation or divorce. These accounts were entirely compatible with Bok's earnest and pedantic tone, although they contributed a new element of sensationalism to the magazine. They provided, in effect, the female confessional complement to Bok's male sermonizing. A new female voice was therefore added to the *Journal* in these years, but it was a voice that emphasized women's vulnerability, emotionalism, and neediness. Bok's *Journal* continued to promote the idea that middle-class women need help, and that men were largely to blame for marital tensions.

Lorimer's *Post* responded to the cultural tension between men and women in an equally characteristic way, featuring an almost exclusively flippant treatment of male–female relations. Marriage and courtship provided much of the grist for the *Post*'s joke mill, especially after the institution in 1902 of an editorial page column called "Poor Richard Junior's Philosophy." From the start the column was dominated by jokes related to gender. Regarding men, for example: "Rivalry is the spice of love."[28] On women: "No woman ever marries her ideal, for all women respect godliness and all love a dash of the Old Nick."[29]

The *Post*'s explicit discussion of male–female relations therefore continued to be glib in these years, but it would be a mistake to assume that the *Post* did not take such relations seriously nor value them highly. The *Post* simply commented on these issues in a more roundabout way than did the *Journal*. For example, it is impossible to discuss the treatment of love in the *Post* without considering the magazine's position on men's work. Men were defined in the pages of the *Post* primarily in terms of the work they did, but this definition was also bound up with the primacy of love relationships.

In spite of the broadening of the *Post*'s format, the magazine continued to run numerous articles on business, and its editorials as well as its short stories frequently featured a business or work-related theme. The *Post*'s view of men as workers in these years built on that first introduced between 1897 and 1900, and it can be summed up in the homily appearing in a 1903 issue: "Formerly it was, Be good! Now it is, Make good!"[30] As they had been earlier, men in the *Post* were defined and judged more by their activity than by their character, and that activity was almost always work-related.

The *Post*'s representation of work issues for men raises the critical question of life cycle vis-à-vis gender construction. Especially in its fiction, the *Post* spoke to the nature of work for men in terms of its differing demands across the man's life cycle. There was no comparable discussion in either the *Post* or the *Journal* of women's paid work cycle, but there was a parallel life cycle for women: women's life stages were defined by marriage and children, consisting of premarriage, which might include college attendance and/or a brief period of work for pay; the married and child-bearing/rearing years; and life after the children are grown and the husband dies. Women, as they went through these stages, were represented as recreating themselves at each stage, working to be the best women they could be.

Men too were always recreating themselves, underscoring the fact that gender is an ever-evolving construct.[31] While the center of that evolution for women was marriage and the family, the center of it for men was work. Heroes of *Post* stories between 1900 and 1910 grappled with the difficulties of starting out as a worker, tangled with knotty problems of integrity in and devotion to various professions once established, and coped with the pain of aging and becoming a less vital and productive worker.[32]

Representing the early stage of a man's work cycle was H. K. Webster's "The Matter with Carpenter. A Story of the First Year Out of College." Carpenter (we never learn his given name) is a brand-new design engineer who is finding it difficult to adjust to life after graduation. His work is much more challenging and trying than textbook exercises, his boss is harder to get along with than his teachers, and thoughts of the "girl" back at school are distracting the young man. Given an especially difficult designing assignment, Carpenter throws himself into it, forgetting his complaints and problems. He finally produces the right design, and he is then able to turn his attention to the girl again. The message of the story is that compelling, fulfilling work is essential to a man's sense of well-being; and only after such work is under way is a man able to focus on and be happy with the personal side of his life.[33]

Representing the other end of the work career is a poignant Jack London story, "A Piece of Steak." Tom King is a forty-year-old boxer with a wife and two small children to support. As he has aged, his ability to win and therefore to earn money has declined. "A Piece of Steak" focuses on a particular night when Tom must fight after a week of not eating meat, the family's grocer having finally refused to extend any more credit. Tom kisses his wife and goes to the match, where the only strategy he can use is to try to tire his opponent by taking punch after punch, then to strike back with a couple of well-placed, mighty blows. The aging fighter does take the punches from his opponent,

A PIECE OF STEAK By Jack London

ILLUSTRATED BY GEORGE GIBBS

"Good Luck, Tom. You Gotter Do 'Im"

8.i. Illustration for A Piece of Steak.

A Living Wonder of White Flesh and Stinging Muscle

"Youth incarnate," a "living wonder of white flesh and stinging muscle." But at the point when he needs to be the aggressor his tired, malnourished body simply gives out.[34]

The story does not end in the ring, however. We see Tom in the locker room, too ashamed to go home to his equally hungry, equally beaten-down wife. He holds his head in his hands, remembering the sight early in his own career of an older, beaten opponent holding his head in the locker room in much the same way. "A Piece of Steak" highlights the emphasis that men placed on their own physicality, even though the fighter is of a lower class than Lorimer's mainly middle-class readers. As historian Anthony Rotundo points out, stories that featured working-class heroes like Tom King were especially popular at the turn of the century and in the early twentieth century, because men were noticeably anxious about their "softening" in these years.[35]

The story resonates as well with the fear that informed much of Lorimer's early *Post,* the fear that men would not measure up to their task as sole providers for the family. Fiction dealing with the middle of the male work cycle makes this consideration even more explicit. Men are shown being forced to make difficult decisions about their work lives, choosing to testify against new corporate owners, for example, or taking the risk of buying out the boss in a small business.[36] Men had to cope with circumstances beyond their control in these short stories, yet they were held solely responsible for their success or failure and for their families' relative comfort. Bok, even as he urged men to spend good time in the home, shared this view of men's solitary responsibility: "I want every young fellow," he once wrote, "to feel that, to a large extent, he stands alone for himself in the world. Counsel he may seek and should seek, but the action is his, and his alone."[37]

In staking out this territory so clearly and exclusively for themselves, men like Bok and Lorimer and their readers were left with a heavy load of responsibility and pressure.[38] One might think that women could have provided aid and comfort to men in this situation, but the *Post* in these years suggested that women were too often a distraction, and worse, that their attitudes only added to the burdens men were carrying. Thus *Post* stories focusing on the middle years of men's careers showed men having to cope regularly with their wives' worries and objections. Men spent much of their time trying to convince women of the validity of their actions.

A series of stories contributed by Rupert Hughes in 1910 spoke most clearly to this theme. The hero of these stories, which included "The Hireling" and "The Heart Mender," is a physician in his mid-thirties named Merrill. A single man, Dr. Merrill grapples in both of these stories with the competing demands of professional and personal life. In "The Hireling," Merrill courts a younger woman named Enid Layton, a woman who finds him attractive but who resents the time he spends with his patients. After being left at a party by herself for the third time, Enid protests. "I am attentive, Enid," Merrill pleads in response. "Surely you don't ask me to neglect my duty?" Merrill is called away during a fourth social engagement with Enid to make a house call, and he saves another woman from death while her grateful young lover hovers close by. As a result of abandoning Enid once again, Merrill loses her. But his professional integrity, and all that it means to Merrill, remain intact.[39]

"The Heart-Mender" shows Merrill in competition with a local minister for the love of another woman, the beautiful but ill Fanny Protheroe. An interesting theme in the story involves the notion that men can be best friends at the same time that they are ardent competitors. But the main point is that Merrill once again is torn between professional and personal demands. Too busy to court Fanny with the same attentiveness as Reverend Findley does, Merrill is running a close second to his friend when Fanny suffers a serious physical setback. Merrill not only works like a demon to save her "for Findley's sake"; he also overcomes the incompetence of Findley's awkward medical assistance to perform a heroic operation that pulls Fanny back from the brink of death. The story ends with Findley and the girl happy in each other's arms, and with Merrill, alone once more, gazing at the mountains and feeling "their profound respect" for his work.[40]

Again and again, men in *Post* stories were forced to choose work over their personal relationships and/or to fight resistance and complication from women along the way. Women in many *Post* short stories seemed not to understand, to sympathize with, or to respect the nature of specific demands that work made upon men. They were also unable to see the larger picture until men made it clear to them. These stories were informed by a deep sense of injustice and frustration on the part of men.

Echoing this exasperation was a 1905 Lorimer editorial entitled "When the Honeymoon Wanes." Lorimer asserted that too many brides were pressuring their husbands to shirk their duties, and he chided such women sarcastically: "'Dear' ought not to come home early; 'dear' ought not to forget all about the business. The honeymoon vacation is over; life has begun." Lorimer advised young wives to let their husbands stay at work as long as they needed to in order to "get ahead," and he urged them to share in their husbands' work interests as often as possible.[41] The intensity and regularity of this theme in the *Post* suggests its importance to men like Lorimer and others who contributed to the magazine. Taken in toto, these stories and editorials constituted a cry from men to women, a cry to women to recognize and respect the centrality of work to men's identity. Work for middle-class men was not only an economic necessity but an ego-bound necessity as well.

Problematic relations between men and women could therefore be blamed at least in part on women's failure to understand men's need to work hard, according to the *Post*. Carrying this logic farther, Lorimer's magazine in these years suggested that the answer to marital tensions lay precisely in hard work. In 1905 Lorimer drew from a collection of the unconscious humor of schoolchildren this amusing observation: "The marriage customs of the ancient Greeks were that a man had only one wife, and it was called monotony." Lorimer went on to treat the question seriously, to assert that monotony in marriage is easily joked about but is "an increasingly prolific source of unhappiness." Interestingly, the editor in this case laid most of the blame for this state of affairs at the feet of men. Too many husbands did not communicate after marriage and did not take their marital commitment seriously enough.[42]

Lorimer's answer was simple: men should work harder at their jobs. Men would be energized and invigorated by serving their families more diligently, Lorimer asserted, and he cited as evidence this testimony from one of the best-known theatrical personages of the day:

"To tell the truth," confessed Tyrone Power, "family and poverty have done more to support me than I have done to support them. . . . When on the eve of despairing, they have forced me, like a coward in the corner, to fight like a hero, not for myself, but for my wife and little ones."[43]

Continuing in these years to equate breadwinning with loving, Lorimer concluded that men should find happiness in serving the family, thereby obtaining the "precious satisfactions which drive out monotony."[44]

Taken together, the *Post* and the *Journal* embody a conflict that has characterized much of twentieth-century gender culture regarding work and love. For at the same time that Lorimer was advocating more work for men as a way to rejuvenate their marriages, Bok and other *Journal* writers were continuing to question the role that work played in early twentieth-century men's lives. Objections were frequently cast in terms of short-changing the family. In an editorial entitled "Is the Game Worth the Candle?" Bok wrote, "it is a lamentable pity that it can be so truthfully said of the average American man immersed in business affairs that he sees so little of his children."[45] In one of the *Journal*'s few direct references to class, Bok characterized this as a middle-class situation, asserting that mechanics in American society were better off than professionals or businessmen since they saw more of their children and wives. Bok went on to ask if "all this commercial strife" was worth the price of children being strangers to their fathers, concluding that men must certainly be the culture's wage-earners, but that men must also know when to stop working.[46]

Similarly, Theodore Roosevelt's commentary on men's lives in the *Journal* expressed concern over the "mad pursuit of trifles" that he feared was taking the place of more worthy work in the lives of many middle-class men. What Roosevelt meant by "worthy work" involved two areas: civic activity and the family. Roosevelt on several occasions in the *Journal* called men to turn from excessive materialism to a more altruistic service of country, and Roosevelt himself was regularly pictured in the magazine as an actively engaged father.[47] In 1904 the antisuffrage *Journal* ran a political advertisement for "Theodore Roosevelt, the Man" ostensibly to convince women to exert their influence on men. Roosevelt, the ad boasted, had by his "grit, patriotism, integrity and culture set the standard of the new man—the rounded strong man." In order to be a good citizen, the advertisement suggested, a man had to be a family man as well as a good breadwinner, a man who upon coming home from work rushed first to the nursery to be with his little ones; in short, a man like Theodore Roosevelt.[48]

The *Journal* was promoting a balance in men's lives, not campaigning for men to give up work or to modify their goals and behaviors in any extreme way. Nevertheless, there is still a significant gap between the positions of the *Post* and the *Journal,* at least at the level of rhetoric. Both magazines recognized

The President and His Family Starting on a Ride

The American Woman as a Mother

By Theodore Roosevelt

With Photographs Taken by Mr. Arthur Hewitt with the Permission of the President

This address was delivered by President Roosevelt before the tional Congress of Mothers, at Washington, in March last. a reprint, made by permission of the President, is from an torized official copy of the address.   THE EDITORS.

IN OUR modern industrial civilization there are many and grave dangers to counterbalance the splendors and the triumphs. It is not a good thing to see cities grow at disproportionate speed relatively to the country ; for the small landowners, the men who own their little homes, and therefore to a very large extent the men who till farms, the men of the soil, have hitherto le the foundation of lasting national life in every State ; , if the foundation becomes either too weak or too ow, the superstructure, no matter how attractive, is in :inent danger of falling

But far more important than the question of the occupation of our citizens is the question of how their family life is conducted. No matter what that occupation may be, as long as there is a real home and as long as those who make up that home do their duty to one another, to their neighbors and to the State, it is of minor consequence whether the man's trade is plied in the country or the city, whether it calls for the work of the hands or for the work of the head.

But the Nation is in a bad way if there is no real home, if the family is not of the right kind ; if the man is not a good husband and father, if he is brutal or cowardly or selfish ; if the woman has lost her true sense of duty, if she is sunk in vapid self-indulgence or has let her nature be twisted so that she prefers a sterile pseudo-intellectuality to that great and beautiful development of character which comes only

to those whose lives know the fullness of duty done, of effort made and self-sacrifice undergone.

In the last analysis the welfare of the State depends absolutely upon whether or not the average family, the average man and woman and their children, represent the kind of citizenship fit for the foundation of a great nation ; and if we fail to appreciate this we fail to appreciate the root mortality upon which all healthy civilization is based.

No piled-up wealth, no splendor of material growth, no brilliance of artistic development, will permanently avail any people unless its home life is healthy, unless the average man possesses honesty, courage, common sense and decency, unless he works hard and is willing at need to fight hard ; and unless the average woman is a good wife, a good mother, able and willing to perform the first and greatest duty of womanhood, able and willing to bear and to bring up as they should be brought up, healthy children.

The President and His Four Boys

lutions were diametrically opposed. Men should work less, said the *Journal*, while the *Post* told men to work more.

Underlying the rhetoric of both magazines, however, were the assumptions that middle-class women and men should and would marry, that women were responsible for the business of love in intimate relationships, and that men were responsible for providing well for their wives and children. In fact, until very recently in this century there has been basic agreement on the neat cultural and economic equation that women are nurturers and lovers while men are bread-winners.[49] One reason for the tenacity of this equation is that in magazines like the *Journal* and the *Post*, both sides of this equation were joined and given force by powerful commercial considerations. Women were the primary consumers of the culture, and they nurtured and showed love by consuming well for their families; men had the potential to be consumers in their own right, but their far more important function was to provide well for their families so that their wives could consume well. And, of course, in the increasingly sophisticated commercial milieu of the early twentieth century, consuming well meant consuming more.

The Curtis publications were most alike in their combination of gender norms and commercial messages. The *Journal* in these years continued to be the successful, thoroughly commercial publication it had always been, while the *Post* began to catch up and eventually to surpass it. By 1910, 40 percent of the *Journal* and 50 percent of the *Post* consisted of advertisements. Articles and editorials in both magazines supported women's right to autonomy with regard to family spending and the expansion of women's consumption. In addition, the specific character of their advertising in this decade linked gender and con-sumption in some new ways.

A Bok editorial in 1901 claimed that women often worked outside the home because men were not generous enough with the household allowance.[50] It was embarrassing for women to have to ask for money, Bok asserted, an opin-ion echoed with force in a 1907 confession article, "Twenty Years' Humilia-tion with My Husband, As Told by the Wife." The anonymous writer confessed that she and her husband had never discussed "the financial question" before marriage. Given her husband's insensitivity to her needs and to those of the household, this woman subsequently spent twenty years being humiliated by having to ask for money. To make matters worse, her husband thought of him-self as a generous and thoughtful man and frequently bragged about the way he provided for his family. One such bragging session finally precipitated this out-burst from his wife: "You haven't been just, and I am sick and tired of asking for every cent I want to spend. A share of your income should be mine by right, and not by courtesy."[51] This author and other *Journal* writers encouraged women to take responsibility for the family finances and to initiate frequent talks about such matters.

The *Post* agreed that women were too often forced into false economy by "cheap, stingy husbands," and lauded women for their economic savvy. A 1909 editorial defended the "Prodigal Daughters of Eve" against accusations of tendencies to extravagance among middle-class women of the day:

> We read periodically that spendthrift wives are ruining men. In making over father's old pants for Tommy—after only ten hours or so of light, congenial exercise in the kitchen—they will throw away half a pound of very good cloth and then spend eighty or ninety cents buying new cloth for a Sunday shirt-waist. Such is the riotous life of a large majority of American wives.[52]

It was entirely consistent with the mix in the *Post* of these years, however, that the magazine also regularly shared tips and wisdom on precisely how sellers might tease and tantalize women shoppers. Women were capable of resisting temptation and therefore should be trusted with the family purse strings, the *Post* suggested; they were at the same time fair game for the "businessmen" to whom Lorimer's magazine was still targeted.

The *Post* ran a number of articles on selling to women between 1900 and 1910, all of them promoting the best ways to manipulate women into buying. A single instance is a 1907 piece by Joseph Smith entitled "Getting On in the World. Steps and Missteps on the Road to Fortune—The Feminine Mind." Smith, a dry goods salesman, noted that three-quarters of American retail purchases were made by women; hence smart businessmen must appeal to them. Smith addressed in particular the question of pricing as it related to selling to women, noting the need for careful comparison pricing and clear statements on what women would save, since the feminine mind was weak on abstractions and arithmetic. The answer, Smith proposed, was to give the feminine mind concrete facts and definite prices.[53]

Isaac Marcosson in 1910 echoed the importance of catering to women shoppers, and he noted other attributes of female consumers. Marcosson observed that the wife shopped for the whole family and that she was therefore an essential audience for advertising and in-store promotional campaigns. A woman did not know just what she wanted but wanted to see what was offered and to have the leisure to pick and choose. Marcosson's advice on attracting women and enticing them to buy covered a wide range: put stores in proximity to theaters; provide free bus rides to the store; place appealing items on the main floor; and offer fashionable merchandise. Marcosson even suggested providing free child care to shoppers. The owner/manager of a department store could never rest easy, Marcosson concluded. The need for vigilance was the price merchants had to pay for women's trade.[54]

Thus the *Post* treated women's ability to handle family finances with respect, but at the same time it encouraged businessmen to do anything they had to in order to convince women to buy. Advertising in the *Journal* and the *Post* embodied this same combination. Advertisements in the *Journal* continued to be more progressive than much of the rest of the magazine, but they raised to new heights the practice of coopting images of independent women in order to sell things. The "New Woman" rode a Columbia bicycle, cooked with Gold Medal Flour, and cleaned with the Hoover Electric Sweeper. The years 1900 to 1910 also saw a substantial increase in cosmetics advertising, which began to appeal to women's anxieties: "Are you as pretty as you should be?" one asked. These advertisements served as the foundation for the boom in cosmetics advertising that would occur later in the twentieth century.[55]

Advertisements in the *Post* catered in these years to women more often than to men, and household ads continued to be the largest single category of advertising in the *Post*. Another important feature of *Post* advertising in these years was that almost all of it was clearly targeted to one gender or the other. Between 1900 and 1910, *Post* advertising broadened to include more products intended for men. This was a major new development in advertising and magazine history, which was made possible by the developing national production of some items thought to be of importance to men, and encouraged by the presence of a forum like the *Post*. Earlier general magazines like the *Atlantic* and *Scribner's* predated the development of national markets for male-oriented products and settled for smaller audiences and fewer advertisements, and more focused periodicals for men like *Field and Stream* tended to carry a narrow range of advertising closely related to editorial content.

Business-related machines and books, clothing, opportunities for education and self-improvement, and even some foods were advertised to men increasingly in the early twentieth-century *Post* (see figure 8.k). Perhaps most significant, in terms of visual impact and long-term relationship to the magazine, were the advertisements for automobiles that began to appear in 1903. Fords, Oldsmobiles, Columbias, and Wintons were regularly advertised in the *Post* in the 1900–1910 period, with lavish illustrations designed to entice first-time car buyers.

Most of the automobile advertisements were targeted to men, and most *Post* ads in general were targeted either to men or to women (see figures 8.l and 8.m). But the mix of the *Post*'s audience provided for some limited but interesting crossover in advertisement targeting. An ad in 1905 pictured a smiling woman in the driver's seat of a new Oldsmobile, with this caption: "Makes everyone your neighbor—the Oldsmobile has endeared itself to the feminine heart just as it has established itself in the business world."[56] And crossover in the other direction in the *Post* is illustrated by an ad for Pompeiian Face Cream, which in 1908 urged men to convince their wives of the benefit to women of

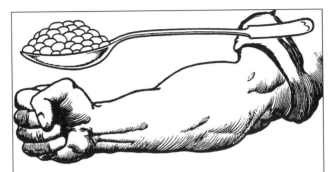

Eat Beans for
Strength!

ONCE a week, at least. Beans, as you know, are among the most *nourishing* of all foods.

Great Tissue-formers, — fine Muscle-makers!

Rich in Nitrogen and Proteid,— two of the most expensive and necessary factors in food.

Beans contain 23 to 25 per cent. of Nitrogenous Proteid, while Beefsteak contains only 20 per cent., and Bread 7½ per cent.

Beans *used* to be comparatively *indigestible.*

Because, as ordinarily treated and cooked, they were so dense-fibred that the juices of the stomach could not *penetrate* them sufficiently to fully *digest* them.

* * *

But *that* is all changed now, since the *"Snider-Process"* of treating and cooking Pork & Beans was invented.

Snider Beans are rendered *porous* and *absorbent* by this Process so that the Digestive Juices of the Stomach can fully enter, and act on, them while they remain firm, cheesy, and toothsome.

They are mellow, fine-textured, and deliciously flavored with that *seven*-spiced Tomato Catsup which has made the name of "Snider" famous.

Just get a tin of "Snider-Process" Pork & Beans *to-day*, and try them.

Your money back from the Grocer if *you* do not find them the *best* you've ever eaten.

This advertisement is your authority for the refund.

The T. A. Snider Preserve Co., Cincinnati, U.S.A.

8.l. Columbia.

The detailed refinements and
luxury of Columbia motor cars
distinguish them among other
high grade automobiles.

Painting by George Gibbs

THE COLUMBIA MOTOR CAR COMPANY
Station 104-A, HARTFORD, CONNECTICUT
Licensed under Selden Patent.

using the cream. A later ad suggested that the cream was beneficial even to men (see figures 8.n and 8.o).

In the crossover ads, and in the ads catering specifically to men, we see the roots of the view of men as consumers in their own right. The later twentieth century would witness the increasing targeting of men in general publications

8.m. Going Like the Wind.

Going Like The Wind

yet gliding along so smoothly that only the rapidly moving panorama, the exhilarating
breeze and the surprised faces of those you pass tell you
how fast when riding in

The Winton

like the *Post* as well as the rise of even more consciously commercial magazines intended only for men, like *True* and *Playboy.*

Most *Post* advertisements in this period, however, continued to target
women and to assume that women were the primary consumers for the family.
A major function of *Post* advertisements seemed to be to expose men to the
same messages as women were exposed to, perhaps in an indirect attempt to
educate men about women's role as consumer. A 1903 Pearline campaign in
the *Post,* for example, featured an angle that never appeared in the *Journal*:
"Pearline makes washing a woman's work. . . . It saves at every point coarse
things easily washed by delicate women."[57] Appealing to the male ego by emphasizing women's weakness, the campaign also legitimized women's active
consumerism, in this case referring to the fact that the purchase of a certain
product would make the woman's job more manageable. Curtis and Lorimer

Your Wife?

Is she as fair and fresh as the day you were married? If not, it is probably because she neglected to care for her skin. Household and social cares, and family duties incident to the rearing of children, have left lines on her face and robbed her of the bloom of her youth.

She can regain much of her youthful charm, and your daughters also can discover how to outwit Father Time, if you will call their attention to this advertisement and ask them to write for our 16-page illustrated booklet. We send it with our free sample. Either fill out coupon yourself *now* before you lay this magazine aside, or call it to the attention of the other members of your family.

POMPEIAN
Massage Cream

It Gives a Clear, Fresh Velvety Skin

Wrinkles and crow's-feet are driven away, sallowness vanishes, angles are rounded out and double-chins reduced by its use. Thus the clear, fresh complexion, the smooth skin and the curves of cheek and chin that go with youth, may be retained past middle age by the woman who has found what Pompeian Massage Cream will do.

This is not a "cold" or "grease" cream. The latter have their uses, yet they can never do the work of a massage cream like Pompeian. Grease creams fill the pores. Pompeian Massage Cream cleanses them by taking out all foreign matter that causes blackheads, sallowness, shiny complexions, etc. Pompeian Massage Cream is the largest selling face cream in the world, 10,000 jars being made and sold daily.

Test It With Free Sample

Also our illustrated book on Facial Massage, an invaluable guide for the proper care of the skin. 50 cents or $1.00 a jar, sent postpaid to any part of the world, on receipt of price, if your dealer hasn't it.

Remarkable Popular Song Offer: We'll send postpaid for only 6c. in loose stamps (not stuck to the paper) the present popular success of New York, " I Don't Want No Imitation Man " (a most laughable song story of the girl who advertised for the 18-karat man, but got an imitation of the genuine brand), by Frederick Hamill, and more catchy and tuneful than any of his successes. This song doesn't cost you 25c., because we bought the copyright for the benefit of our patrons. Offered now for the first time.

Man use Pompeian at home or at the barber's. It prevents soreness after shaving and gives a clear, healthy glow to the skin.

The Pompeian Mfg. Co., 49 Prospect Street, Cleveland, O.

Pompeian Massage Soap is appreciated by all who are particular in regard to the quality of the soap they use. For sale by all dealers—25c a cake; box of 3 cakes, 60c.

Cut out along dotted line, fill and mail, or send postal today

Pompeian Mfg. Co.
49 Prospect St.
Cleveland, Ohio

Gentlemen :—
Please send, without cost to me, one copy of your book on facial massage and a liberal sample of Pompeian Massage Cream.

Name

Address

8.p. Pro-phy-lac-tic.

ran advertisements for household products for the simple reason that such contracts were the most frequently available in the first decade of the twentieth century. But the result of their running so many household ads in a magazine catering to men as well as to women was the creation of a consumer world in microcosm, a world where buying was presented to both women and men as a legitimate and essentially feminine activity.

8.q. Ads Presented Women as the Primary Shoppers
for Their Families.

This creation of a consumer-oriented world is the crucial function that the
Journal and the *Post* shared. The differences in rhetoric and content between
the two magazines were real and significant; as I have suggested, several of
these differences represent gender-based conflicts and ways of stereotyping
women and men that continue to characterize our culture today. But both magazines embodied and reinforced a more unified, larger view of life that had a

profound impact on American popular culture as well. In this view, women were responsible for love, a notion clearly consistent with nineteenth-century ideals. New by the end of the first decade of the twentieth century was the idea that women demonstrated this love in large part by consuming well, by choosing, buying, using, and helping family members use the right products in the right ways. Men were responsible for providing well, a complementary notion, and again, one consistent with the nineteenth century. This notion was refined by the *Journal* and the *Post* between 1900 and 1910 to suggest that men show love by providing both financial and moral support for women's consumer activity. Hence men were to give up control over the way some money was spent, and to give women freedom to do their job of spending.

Giving up control over some money did not signify a major shift in marital power relations, however. Emphasizing women's exclusive responsibility for loving and encouraging their ever-expanding consumption masked women's economic dependence on men, and their subordinate position in the gender hierarchy.[58] Emphasizing breadwinning and supporting women's consumption in turn masked men's emotional dependence on women; it also allowed men to undervalue the services they received from women in the home.[59] The magazines' prescription for marital financial arrangements did not give women more power or free men from their position as sole breadwinners. It worked instead to maintain largely traditional gender roles.

By 1910, then, the framework for a powerful cultural hegemony was firmly in place. Magazines like the *Journal* and the *Post* were gendered texts that served as forums for commercial messages as well as for both direct and indirect gender norms. The gender norms themselves were convincingly commercialized, with women centrally defined as consumers and men centrally defined as breadwinners. The equation at the level of individual relationships was complete (women consume, men earn), as was the relationship at the cultural level (commerce is gendered, gender is commercialized).

To the extent that they supported the *Journal* and the *Post* and their advertisers with their subscriptions and purchases, women and men alike colluded in the creation and sustaining of this powerful, hegemonic relationship between gender and commerce. As I have suggested earlier, for many readers this was probably a relatively safe "deal," if a process this subtle can be described in such terms. Women gained some tangible expansion in activity and responsibility, and they avoided confronting the larger and more threatening reality of a biased labor market and an unfair division of labor. Men preserved most of the benefits of their position, and they avoided confronting the extreme pressures that accompanied their exclusive responsibility for breadwinning. What both women and men gave up was the opportunity to consider the cultural issues of love and money separately, and to negotiate meaningful change in the gendered division of labor.

As we have seen, the cultural hegemony of the mutually reinforcing relationship between gendered commerce and commercialized gender was strong enough by the turn of the century to prevent producers like Curtis, Bok, and Lorimer from reshaping its contours to any significant degree. Gramsci's model of the "historical bloc" had been created and solidified by then, as producers, advertisers, and readers agreed that consuming and earning were gendered activities running along certain lines. The Curtis publishers and editors suffered a loss in pride when they tangled with this cultural hegemony of gender and commerce. But readers were in the end much more seriously limited by the creation of this discourse to which they themselves had contributed. Readers lost the very ability to define themselves in terms of gender apart from commercial rhetoric and considerations. *Journal* readers were, by 1910, consumers. *Post* readers were either breadwinners or consumers. Important lines for the consideration of gender had been drawn, lines that would not waver for many years.

In the late 1880s Louisa Knapp had encouraged women to do "cheerfully and well the work that comes to her hand, whether it be with a pen, a surgeon's knife, a dentist's drill, a pair of scissors or a broom." She had also urged women to further consumption as an appropriate expansion of their activity.[60] Unfortunately, as the publishing world grew more sophisticated and the gendered commercial milieu took shape, women's consuming was reinforced and emphasized while flexibility regarding other activities was not. Both gender construction and the shape of commerce were irrevocably altered.

Epilogue

Examining the roots of mass-media development as exemplified by the early *Journal* and the *Post* has revealed a bond between gender and commerce that was complex and powerful. The gender–commerce bond was complex insofar as it took different forms vis-à-vis femininity and masculinity. As I have shown, the link between commerce and femininity was forged early, and it was strong from the start. In Louisa Knapp's *Journal,* which became a national powerhouse, both editorial material and advertisements conveyed the notion of consuming as a central activity for middle-class women. And this image of women as people who can and should consume evolved and became stronger in two distinct and significant ways under Bok's editorship: first, women not only could consume, but they were fundamentally defined as consumers; and second, by definition, consumers were women.[1]

The bond between commerce and masculinity was negotiated later, and differently. Women were already established as the culture's primary consumers. Consequently, the bond forged between masculinity and commerce was relatively weak. In the main it took the form of urging men to earn enough money to supply not only necessities but also luxuries for their families; secondarily it targeted men directly for advertising messages that touted a relatively limited range of consumer goods. This complicated gender–commerce bond, with its different relationships to femininity and masculinity, is characterized by the same differential relationship today. Despite the fact that most women work outside the home for pay, women are still viewed as the culture's primary consumers, and they are viewed only secondarily as breadwinners.[2] Men continue to be viewed as the culture's primary breadwinners, although they consume a larger share of commercial goods now than they did at the turn of the last century.

The hegemony that resulted from producers, advertisers, and readers collaborating to connect gender and commerce has proven to be both extremely strong and very resilient over the course of the twentieth century. A significant legacy of the *Ladies' Home Journal* and the *Saturday Evening Post* was their support for a gender-segmented consumer culture. The Curtis magazines contributed substantially to the parallel gender differentiation in the content of mass-circulation American magazines, a general development that has affected a major portion of the twentieth-century magazine market. Patterns noted in the *Journal* and the *Post* reappeared frequently in the top-selling mass-circulation

189

magazines over the course of the twentieth century. This was in part because the *Journal* and the *Post* were influential models and in part because the factors that shaped the *Journal* and the *Post* shaped later magazines as well.[3]

Indeed, many magazines repeated the *Journal*'s success. American mass-circulation women's magazines have been relatively easy to establish and relatively long-lived. Women's magazines have consistently ranked among the nation's top-selling magazines, with a few titles appearing repeatedly, including the *Ladies' Home Journal, Woman's Home Companion, McCall's,* and *Good Housekeeping.* In any given year, titles targeted for women have represented from four to six of the top ten circulating magazines in the United States. Most of these top sellers followed the *Journal* formula until the 1950s, when the women's market expanded to include the supermarket magazines, specifically *Woman's Day* and *Family Circle,* both of which were in the top twelve in 1990. Commercial magazines targeted for women have had huge circulations for much of the twentieth century, with commensurate advertising revenues.

The pool from which advertisements could be drawn was not unlimited, however, because of the rigid gender targeting of the genre. During the middle decades of the twentieth century, other women's magazines followed the *Journal*'s early lead to try to broaden their images, out of a similar combination of pecuniary motive and a sense that the future of women's magazines was questionable. For example, in 1945 *McCall's,* under the editorship of Otis Wiese, made a conscious effort to appeal to middle-class men and children as well as women. According to Theodore Peterson, "the new editorial pitch was based on what Wiese called 'togetherness'—a family's living not as isolated members but as a unit sharing experiences."[4] The policy failed as a device to attract readers; more importantly, it failed also to attract any new, male-oriented advertising. For the reasons noted earlier in discussing the *Journal*'s attempt to create crossover—the problems of tone, format, lack of interest from men, and the stigma of men reading women's publications—there has been no significant crossover or broadening in audience by gender for a women's magazine in the United States.

Producers of men's magazines faced a different limitation: the small number of nationally marketed male-targeted goods, significantly smaller than the number targeted for women. This restriction, combined with assumptions about the male sex role, has led to two approaches in the twentieth-century world of commercial magazines for men: special-interest magazines created specifically to draw large numbers of specialized advertisements, and general magazines like the *Post,* which, as we have seen, broadened its focus to speak to women as well. Because of their very nature, most of the magazines in the first category have not been among the top sellers in America, but a brief glance at *Playboy*—a highly successful special-interest magazine—is in order.

Since the founding of *Field and Stream* in 1895, commercial magazines for men have frequently focused on a special interest like sports, woodworking, or financial matters. In 1952 a young man named Hugh Hefner decided that there was a place on the men's market for a new special interest magazine. Hefner commented later:

> The most popular men's magazines of the time were the outdoor-adventure books—*True, Argosy* and the like. They had a hairy-chested editorial emphasis with articles on hunting, fishing, chasing the Abominable Snowman over Tibetan mountaintops. . . . *Esquire* had changed its editorial emphasis after the War, eliminating most of the lighter material—the girls, cartoons, and humor. So the field was wide open for the sort of magazine I had in mind.[5]

Playboy's special interest—sex—was different, but it was its combination of sex and higher-quality advertising that most distinguished it from earlier men's magazines. From the start, Hefner recognized the importance of upscale advertising to the well being of his magazine; in fact, he borrowed money to run it without advertising until 1954, when his circulation was high enough to attract the kind of advertising he wanted. Instead of selling muscle creams and cheap sex aids, as had earlier "girlie" magazines, *Playboy* featured a multitude of advertisements for liquor, cigarettes, clothing, cars, stereos, soaps and colognes, and other products identified primarily with men. Able to attract a wide-ranging and stable group of advertisements over the years, *Playboy* worked its way up the circulation chart to the number eleven spot in 1980, and it still ranked within the top twenty in 1990.

Other magazine producers have overcome the limitation of the men's market by broadening their publications to appeal to women, the pattern first demonstrated by the *Saturday Evening Post.* Several major twentieth-century magazines followed the *Post*'s example, including *Collier's, Cosmopolitan,* the *American Magazine,* and the *Farm Journal and Farmer's Wife.* Each of these magazines began in the late nineteenth or early twentieth century as a men's magazine, and after broadening to include women, each placed among the top ten circulators in either 1920 or 1940, or both. Of course, many factors and circumstances combined to make these magazines commercially successful; gender crossover is but one. But the fact that through 1960 all of the top ten circulating magazines were either family or women's magazines does support the notion that advertising to women was crucial to the biggest mass-circulating magazines. Crossover therefore contributed in a significant way to the commercial success of some of the most important twentieth-century magazines.

Not all successful "family" magazines started as publications for men. Perhaps the most popular family magazine of all, *Life,* was targeted to both men and women from its founding in 1936. Clare Boothe Luce originally conceived the idea for an American picture magazine to parallel the popular French magazine *Vu*. Her husband, Henry Luce, gave substance to the idea, considering it to be a family magazine from its early days, but only after toying with the notion of establishing a women's magazine. "In the end," Luce said later, "we decided that the plain fact was as a group of general news journalists, we were not really very deeply interested in the matter of a woman's magazine. And so, however attractive the possibilities might have been from a publishing standpoint, we decided to forget it."[6]

Although Luce may have decided not to cater exclusively to women, he remained highly conscious of the women's market. In the summer before *Life*'s first issue appeared, Luce was sent a thirty-four page list of advertisers committed to buying space. Historian of *Life* Loudon Wainwright reports: "Some of the accounts were Zenith Radio, Seagram's Crown Whiskey, Maxwell House Coffee, United Air Lines, Four Roses Whiskey, General Motors. Luce replied that he thought the list was 'fine except for perhaps a little too much liquor. I like Wrigley's and Maxwell,' he said, 'and would like to see a few more female advertisements.' "[7] Attracting female-targeted advertising and women readers, Luce knew, was good business.

Although not all family-oriented magazines broadened from men's magazines, all of the biggest ones from quite early in the century ran huge numbers of gender-targeted advertisements. Cyrus Curtis, as we have seen, was one of the pioneers who demonstrated what came to be a basic principle of publishing: a publisher could lose millions of dollars on circulation by selling a magazine at less than production cost and still reap millions of dollars in profit from advertising. The *Post* issue dated December 6, 1929, was a monument to this policy. Theodore Peterson described it as follows: "Weighing nearly two pounds, the 272-page magazine contained enough reading matter to keep the average reader occupied for twenty hours and twenty minutes. From the 214 national advertisers appearing in it, Curtis took in revenues estimated at $1,512,000."[8] Similarly, a single issue of *Life* in October 1960 carried $5 million worth of advertising. Such huge advertising revenues were common among the big magazines of the 1950s and 1960s, magazines such as *Life,* the *Post,* and *Look,* which all appeared among the top ten circulators in 1960.

But the days of such huge circulations and huge revenues for these magazines were numbered, because of a single invention: television. The dependence of general family-oriented magazines on very large audiences and on very large profits from advertising made them extremely vulnerable to the threat presented by the rise of television as an entertainment and commercial medium.[9] Other factors, such as the political mood of the 1960s and various managerial mistakes, played some role in the demise of the "giants," but the overwhelming factor seems to have been competition from television for the attention of former readers and, even more, for the advertising dollar. The *Post* died in 1969, and *Look* and *Life* in 1972. Even where there was still audience interest, the magazines became too expensive to produce when advertising was increasingly difficult to attract.[10]

Family magazines were not the only magazines vulnerable to television's inroads on advertising. Since the founding of the *Journal* in 1883, women's magazines had been heavily dependent on advertising revenues, and that dependence only increased as the century wore on. For instance, the October 1946 issue of the *Ladies' Home Journal* was 246 pages long and brought in over $2 million from 334 advertisers.[11] Women's magazines to the present have enjoyed circulation figures and advertising revenues as high as any. Why, then, did mass-circulation women's magazines not succumb to the financial difficulties presented by shifts from magazine to television advertising?

The answer is complicated. Some women's magazines did succumb, most notably the Crowell Company's *Woman's Home Companion.* But others have thrived: the *Journal, McCall's,* and *Good Housekeeping* have all recently published their centennial issues. One major reason for the success of these and other women's magazines is that the genre could play as both "general interest" and "special interest." Advertisers chose television over general magazines because television could reach "everyone." There was no basis on which general magazines could compete; television could reach a large audience more efficiently and effectively. But the breadth of television advertising worked in favor of women's magazines, at least to the extent that those magazines were able to refer to television advertisements in their own pages ("as seen on television") and to scale back their expectations for share of revenue. For there was still a place in the culture for a national forum that would guarantee a more targeted audience, in this case, women.

And women's magazines as a genre adapted to the smaller amounts of advertising that they were able to attract. Magazine sizes were cut back and circulations reduced, and the top sellers sharpened their images somewhat to give clearer audience definitions to advertisers. Hence *Good Housekeeping* and the *Journal* began to cater to the older woman, whereas *Redbook* and *McCall's* catered to the younger. Middle-class women's magazines have had to lower their sights in terms of audience share and advertising revenue in order to stay in business, but stay in business they have.

The magazine market overall is characterized today more by fragmentation than by concentration. Special interest magazines have proliferated, and there are no "giants"; over 3,000 publications fight for space on newsstands today. Almost 500 magazines were launched in 1988 alone.[12] Magazines in the late twentieth-century United States cater to all but the poorest economic groups, different racial and ethnic groups, adolescents and children, and readers with interests as wide-ranging as computer hacking, weaving, and the circus. Gender concerns continue to inform these magazines; many of them are targeted to either men or women, and those that are gender-inclusive or gender-neutral tend to feature advertising that is geared especially for both sexes or to one sex or the other. As disparate in content as they are, these magazines share in helping to create what Roland Marchand has called a "community of discourse," in this case a commercial community of discourse.[13]

The early *Journal* and the *Post* therefore played a significant role in shaping what has become a thoroughly gender-segmented magazine market. But the influence of these magazines and others like them did not stop there. Commercial magazines like the Curtis publications modelled the gender–commerce connection for subsequent forms of popular culture, including radio, film, and television.

While some popular trends seem to have moved from the lower economic classes upward (for example, attendance at taverns and night clubs) and some seem to have evolved on several fronts at once (such as the targeting of cosmetics advertising to working-class and middle-class women at roughly the same time in American culture), the popularization of the gender-commerce bond seems to have been more of a top-down phenomenon.[14] It was, after all, grounded in having the means to buy, which by definition included only the upper and the middle classes at the turn of the last century. As commerce increasingly featured the extension of credit, and as the middle class expanded over the course of the twentieth century, more and more Americans were exposed to the gender–commerce connection. Television was the great equalizer, extending its largely gender-segmented, advertising-driven messages to most Americans by the 1960s. Popular culture as a whole today is both pervasively gendered and pervasively commercial, and gender and commerce continue to inform and to reinforce each other. The commercial community of discourse is, therefore, a gendered discourse as well. We are women and men who buy and use, no matter what our means, geographic location, or access.

I have argued in this study that the gender–commerce bond of the late nineteenth century and early twentieth century was largely positive for producers of commercial products like magazines and for advertisers, and largely negative for readers and consumers. What is the significance of this bond today? What are its ramifications in the late twentieth century?

We can begin by asserting the importance of popular culture, of which gendered magazines constitute only one part. As Pam Gilbert and Sandra Taylor write in *Fashioning the Feminine,* "culture is a struggle for meaning as society is a struggle for power."[15] Righting the structural inequities that oppress women and people of color in our society is critical, but so is grappling with the media through which so many of our norms are conveyed. And popular culture, which appears so intransigent and resistant to change, is precisely the site where at least some of us must focus our energies because it is here—in magazines, films, music, and television, and the advertising that drives them—where most

Americans get both their entertainment and their information. Todd Gitlin, in his article "Who Communicates What to Whom and Why About Communications Research," urges scholars to recognize our responsibility to examine popular culture and then to propose change in clear, accessible, action-oriented prose.[16]

This task is a delicate one for, as Michael Schudson suggests, it is not easy to navigate between the poles of piety in condemning lowbrow popular culture on the one hand, and sentimentality about popular culture and its audiences on the other. Scholars have traditionally pursued the first course, dismissing commercial popular culture (as opposed to folk culture) as trashy and unworthy of study, or casting it as a malevolent agent of mass deception.[17] More recently, Schudson asserts, we have seen a new appreciation of popular culture; this new validation has too often, however, been combined with an overly celebratory view of popular culture and its audiences.[18] The danger in this attitude lies in the tendency to "romanticize and sentimentalize audiences as they exist in inhumane social conditions."[19] In other words, it is possible both to de-emphasize the negative effects that some elements of popular culture may have on consumers, and to overestimate the audience's ability to decode popular culture messages. Neither extreme does justice to the complexities of popular culture.

Looking at the roots of mass media provides the sort of evidence that allows for a more complex analysis. For example, it is the case that a specific group of historical agents, as opposed to vague, distant "market forces," helped to create the gender–commerce bond that has informed so much of twentieth-century popular culture. And the interactions of these agents were complicated, uneven, and sometimes unpredictable. Cyrus Curtis, Edward Bok, and George Horace Lorimer all promoted women's spending and men's earning because it was good business; they illustrate clearly the expected pattern of male capitalists seeking to exploit women for financial gain. But Louisa Knapp Curtis encouraged this relationship as well, because consuming appeared to her to be a truly useful and liberating new activity for women. Her participation in laying the foundation for the gender–commerce bond both foreshadowed and influenced the tacit approval of female readers who supported the *Journal* with their subscriptions and their purchase of products advertised in its pages. Knapp could not foresee the results of emphasizing consuming, nor could readers and consumers. Looking at the early days of these magazines thus throws into relief the decisions that real men and women made, some of them decisions that have shaped the ways we have thought about both gender and commerce ever since.

In addition, focusing on the early days of the *Journal* and the *Post* has demonstrated the very real influence of the historical conditions within which the magazines were founded. Gender analysis of both a women's and a men's magazine has revealed that a nineteenth-century gendered division of labor—

consuming for women and earning for men—was institutionalized in magazines conceived primarily as vehicles for advertising. The context for this development was the turn-of-the-century white, androcentric, and patriarchal culture; the consuming/earning pattern institutionalized in these middle-class magazines helped to maintain the male-dominated status quo throughout most of the twentieth century.[20]

Further, an "historical bloc" coalesced around this combination of commercialized gender and gendered commerce, featuring the all-important though relatively intangible approval of readers and consumers in addition to producers and advertisers. Over time, however, as these patterns became less new and more established, audience reactions were more mixed. Advertising became increasingly condescending, evolving from the early view that consumers might be influenced by flattery but were still shrewd, to the view that consumers were rushed, overgrown children who were ruled by their largely irrational impulses.[21] Magazines themselves were increasingly advertising-driven, which circumscribed their editorial content to an even greater extent than previously. In addition, the commercial market grew and became more complicated, further widening the gap between advertisers and producers on the one hand, and consumers and readers on the other. The result was the development among consumers and readers of what Antonio Gramsci called a "contradictory consciousness" that mixed "approbation and apathy, resistance and resignation."[22]

A critical component of this contradictory consciousness is one that critics of popular culture have often ignored and that has been underscored by examining the early *Journal* and the *Post*: consuming was—and is—a largely pleasurable experience, at least for those with some disposable income. Buying products and using them is often fun; reading about products and about using them can also be pleasurable. In addition, in the early years of the mass media middle-class women did indeed gain some autonomy through increased consumption, giving them further cause to support gendered commerce. Thus it is the case that many readers and consumers in the past saw, and many consumers today see, little reason to change the gendered, commercial contours that characterized popular culture in the past and continue to characterize it today.

Analyzing the *Journal* and the *Post* has revealed two additional pieces of evidence that shed light on contemporary popular culture: (1) the pairing of certain gender norms gave them particular force; and (2) gender is constructed in popular culture differently for women and for men. The two Curtis magazines were in many respects quite different from each other, but their main messages were neatly complementary: women consume and men earn to support that consumption. At the same time the magazines conveyed the idea that while both women and men are gendered beings, women need to and should attend more consciously to their gender construction, and that women therefore should be taught certain relevant skills.

The conscious construction of womanhood has characterized women's magazines throughout the twentieth century, and it is on this score that they have been judged harshly by a number of critics. It is no accident that the book that helped to launch the women's movement beginning in the 1960s was grounded in an angry attack on middle-class women's magazines. Betty Friedan's *The Feminine Mystique,* published in 1963, criticized women's magazines for helping to create and promulgate the "problem that has no name." Friedan, in her thoroughly white, middle-class analysis suggested that the post World War II era had seen the rise of a "feminine mystique," whereby women were fulfilled only in their domestic service to others. And magazines were one of the major purveyors of this mystique: "In the magazine image," Friedan wrote, "women do no work except housework and work to keep their bodies beautiful and to get and keep a man."[23] Friedan's analysis was largely ahistorical. For example, she simplistically painted the decades of the 1930s and 1940s as a time of significantly greater independence for women than were the 1950s and 1960s. But she did point accurately to woman's role as consumer as a source of false autonomy: "She was free to choose automobiles, clothes, appliances, supermarkets," Friedan wrote. "She had everything that women ever dreamed of."[24] Friedan recognized that defining women primarily as consumers was limiting and even insulting. The close relationship between women's magazines and advertising meant that women's world was defined in terms of their place in the home and the products used therein. Friedan quoted a male editor of a large women's magazine in the 1950s:

> Our readers are housewives, full time. They're not interested in national or international affairs. They are only interested in the family and the home. They aren't interested in politics, unless it's related to an immediate need in the home, like the price of coffee. Humor? Has to be gentle, they don't get satire. Travel? We have almost completely dropped it. Education? That's a problem. Their own education level is going up. They've generally all had a high school education and many, college. They're tremendously interested in education for their children—fourth-grade arithmetic. You just can't write about ideas or broad issues of the day for women. That's why we're publishing 90 per cent service now and 10 per cent general interest.[25]

As the study of the *Ladies' Home Journal* has demonstrated, the foundation for this condescending, even misogynist attitude toward women lay at least in part in the reliance of magazine editors on large amounts of gender-targeted advertising.

Naomi Wolf updates Friedan's critique for the 1990s, locating in contemporary women's magazines major support for what she calls "the beauty myth." As women have gained more rights and expanded their activities in contemporary society, Wolf argues, images of beauty have become increasingly rigidified and restricted. Standards of attractiveness have literally constricted women: whereas models a generation ago weighed eight percent less than the average American woman, today they weigh twenty-three percent less.[26] Women must starve themselves even to approach socially sanctioned standards of attractiveness, and they spend billions of dollars on products and tools to make themselves "naturally" beautiful. Standards of beauty have paralleled changes in consumption patterns for women during this century. Just as the notion that women could be consumers evolved into the notion that women are consumers, so did the notion that women can use cosmetics to beautify themselves evolve into the notion that women are constituted by the appearance they create for themselves with these products.[27] And women's magazines are prime conveyors of these messages.

But Wolf, unlike Friedan, does not condemn women's magazines altogether. Wolf points out that women's magazines have been important repositories of female culture in American society for years. She argues that magazines for younger and older women are the only products of popular culture that take women's concerns seriously, that change with women's reality, and that are mostly written by women about women's issues. Unfortunately, however, serious content in women's magazines is paid for with advertisements for "beauty trappings" and household products. Wolf suggests that women's magazines have done more to popularize feminist ideas in American society than any other medium, but that they are split between their (moderate) feminism and their heavy reliance on ads that perpetuate traditional, confining images of femininity.[28] Again we see the limiting, constraining nature of the gender–commerce bond. Femininity continues to be defined by what women buy; and commerce continues to rely on the shorthand of gender norms in order to sell products.

This strong bond between femininity and commerce as well as a certain underestimation of women have led most analysts of popular culture to exhibit more concern over the messages of women's magazines than the messages of those that target men. Naomi Wolf, for example, suggests that women are more vulnerable to magazine messages than are men because women are more "isolated" and "sequestered" and therefore more dependent on cultural models.[29] But my case study of the *Ladies' Home Journal* and the *Saturday Evening Post* demonstrates that magazines for both women and men were pervaded by images of appropriate gender ideals and behaviors; they were merely presented differently for women than for men. Women's activities were circumscribed in these magazines, while a broader range of public activity was endorsed for men. But women were encouraged actively to consider and construct their own gendered being, while men's gender construction as presented in the pages of the *Post* came closer to unconscious indoctrination. In addition, women could cross over to read a men's publication, giving them a valuable dual vision, and men could not. Finally, a contemporary critic suggests that magazines targeted for men present patriarchy and male domination as natural, so men find the domination and exploitation of women not only expected, but demanded by the culture.[30] A more complete view of gendered magazines must take these patterns into account.

Thus it appears that both women's magazines and men's magazines have their strengths as well as their weaknesses. And the weaknesses stem in large part from their advertising-driven, circulation-seeking natures. Would it be possible to communicate about gender in commercial popular culture in a more constructive and positive way? The story of one American women's magazine suggests that it is indeed possible.

Ms. magazine was founded in 1972 as a magazine for women with an explicitly feminist stance and an implicitly disapproving view of traditional women's magazines. Gloria Steinem reported later that "when *Ms.* began, we didn't consider *not* taking ads. The most important reason was keeping the price of a feminist magazine low enough for most women to afford. But the second and almost equally important reason was providing a forum where women and advertisers could talk to each other and improve advertising itself. After all, it was (and still is) as potent a source of information in this country as news or TV and moving dramas."[31]

Steinem and her staff used two main approaches with regard to advertising in a conscious attempt to break the link between advertisements and editorial content. They solicited advertisements from makers of products used by women but traditionally advertised to men, including cars, credit cards, insurance, and sound equipment. And they sought the best ads for traditional "women's products" such as food, clothes, and shampoo, but they refrained from providing the traditional supporting editorial copy, that is "how-to" articles on using the products.[32] But the *Ms.* staff's idealistic hope that advertisers would see how these new ways of doing business would benefit them—by finding a new growth market for products traditionally aimed at men, and by reaching women in a forum that was not swamped with hundreds of ads for similar women's products—was soon dashed. Advertisers did not want to tout untraditional products or products that had to stand alone without explicit editorial support. They wanted to conduct business as usual, even in the face of evidence that consumers were receptive to these changes. As Steinem writes, "That's why I spent more time persuading advertisers than editing or writing for *Ms.* and why I ended up with an unsentimental education in the seamy underside of publishing that few writers see (and even fewer magazines can publish)."[33]

The dilemma for *Ms.*, then, was as follows: the magazine implicitly and sometimes explicitly eschewed the traditional women's magazine formula; but at the same time, to remain a vital mainstream magazine for women, it needed the advertising that had become so bound up with that formula as to be indistinguishable from it. *Ms.* strayed farther and farther from its original tone and purposes in an attempt to become commercially viable. By the 1980s, under different ownership and management, *Ms.* was running both editorial and advertising copy that looked very much like that which the earlier version of the magazine had criticized so vigorously.

But the *Ms.* story does not end there. In October 1989 Dale Lang, owner of *Working Mother* and *Working Woman,* purchased *Ms.* In response to requests from the original *Ms.* staff, reader letters, and his own conviction that *Ms.* "would benefit his other magazines by blazing a trail," Lang agreed to try an ad-free, reader-supported *Ms.*[34] This reincarnated version of *Ms.* was editorially free enough to run Steinem's article entitled "Sex, Lies & Advertising," revealing the problematic aspects of the advertisement-media relationship. The magazine is a bimonthly now, thoroughly centered on women's concerns, concerns which are defined very differently by *Ms.* than by other magazines for women. International news, politics, economic issues, abortion, lesbian rights, the environment, health, generational similarities and differences, prose and poetry by women of all colors and classes, concerns of disabled women, rape, battered women's shelters; all these topics and more find their way into the pages of *Ms.* today, without the very real fear of economic reprisal that haunted the magazine in earlier days. A recent article in *Newsweek* entitled "Sisterhood is Profitable: A Resurrected *Ms.* Succeeds Without Ads" suggests that the magazine is indeed healthy, even thriving in the 1990s.[35]

Ms. has done nothing less dramatic than to disrupt the pattern established by Cyrus Curtis and Louisa Knapp Curtis in 1883. The relationship between advertising and editorial content has become so close that Steinem and others agree that advertisers act as one of the primary censors in our culture.[36] The only recourse for *Ms.* was to eschew advertising altogether. As observers of the commercial popular culture we need to work to separate gender from advertisement-driven commerce wherever possible. This is particularly critical as we consider children and adolescents, whose worlds are already commercial and gendered to an almost overwhelming degree. The recent introduction into our nation's schools of "news shows" supported by commercials is a particularly pernicious form of exploiting children for profit. These "newscasts" with commercial breaks—like the *Ladies' Home Journal* a century before—were conceived primarily to deliver an audience to advertisers. Whether the advertisement is for Pearline washing powder or Stridex medicated pads, the result is the same: furthering the gendered commercial discourse and further defining gender in commercial terms.

This leads to the question of whether it is possible to have commerce without gender. A highly gendered and gender-polarized society such as the late twentieth-century United States supports popular culture products whose appeal rests on simplistic gender images and norms. Since the turn of the last century, gender has provided an easy shorthand for advertisers and purveyors of popular culture, a language that carries numerous subtle cultural cues in a few words or a single image. Who is speaking, what they say, with what kind of authority they speak, what they look like, how they use their bodies, how they are depicted using or benefiting from a product, how much power they hold; all these ideas and more can be communicated swiftly and effectively by exploiting longstanding, conventional gender stereotypes. This reliance on simplistic stereotypes characterizes advertising, the media, and the gender-segmented popular culture milieu as a whole.

Defining gender in terms of polar, complementary oppositions is a powerful means of supporting a male-dominated and male-centered culture. As we have seen, the women consume/men earn equation has been a mainstay in popular culture for much of the twentieth century. Other complementary gendered equations have become central in popular culture as well: women consume beauty and household products, while men consume large-ticket items like stereos and cars; and, most importantly, women are objects and men are (at best) the appreciators of those objects, and (at worst) the exploiters of those objects.

Polarized gender norms are problematic in many ways: they limit both women and men, forcing them into categories of ideas and behaviors that are artificial and often unsuitable; they pit women and men against each other, preventing the sort of shared consciousness that would allow for deeper understandings and change; and, above all, they perpetuate androcentrism as they set the feminine off as the opposite of the masculine, and then privilege the masculine. This polarization works quite subtly in the transitional culture of the late twentieth century. Society makes an almost infinite number of options available but then "communicates that the individual's adequacy as a man or a woman depends on the selection of a limited subset of those options."[37] Popular culture operates in countless ways to dictate and limit women's and men's behavior, appearance, attitudes, sexuality, work, and leisure activities.

Only as we chip away at rigid and polarized standards of gender-appropriate ideas and behaviors can we hope to see commerce become less reliant on polarized gender stereotypes. We can help to break the grip of the gender–commerce connection on popular culture by teaching ourselves and our young people to read the media more carefully, and by educating for thoughtful and creative gender construction. We can do much more to educate for critical social literacy, or what Michael Schudson has called "significant response."[38] We can teach people beginning at young ages and regularly thereafter to "read" the media, and to deconstruct what they read, hear, and see. We can bring new texts into our classrooms, and be better prepared to talk through the texts that have already made their way into our living rooms.[39] It is critical for us to convey to young people the fundamental idea that they are the makers of their own meaning and that they can and should read all the texts they encounter thoughtfully and critically. It is the case that popular culture as it exists provides spaces for alternative gender constructs; as Lorraine Gamman and Margaret Marshment put it, the "contradictions of capitalism and patriarchy allow space for disturbances of dominant meanings in the mainstream, with results that may not be free of contradictions, but which do signify shifts in regimes of representation."[40] We need to locate these spaces and to use them creatively. We can also support the positive alternative images and products that exist now—such as *Ms.*, some programming on public television, and some films—and urge the development of more.

Finally, we must also educate for thoughtful gender construction. We are all constructed beings, and those constructs in our culture center on gender; we are enculturated to have a gendered personality and a gendered body, and to practice heterosexuality and abhor homosexuality.[41] The keys to gender construction in our culture are its pervasiveness and its subtlety. As young children we learn through subtle cues, and we internalize them so that we construct ourselves in the culture's image. Through this process of enculturation we become "cultural natives" who cannot distinguish between "reality and the way the culture construes reality."[42] The key to disrupting patterns of gender construction, therefore, is to encourage both women and men to be cultural observers as well as cultural natives, to make them aware of the norms to which they have been exposed and of how they might change them.

This skill of cultural observation is important for children and young adults, but it is also important for established adults. As we have seen, the *Ladies' Home Journal* and the *Saturday Evening Post* were magazines for adults that both embodied and affected the turn-of-the-century discussion of gender. In effect, they each contributed only half of a conversation: the *Journal* urged conscious gender construction but circumscribed women's activities, while the *Post* supported unlimited activities for men but ignored the need for conscious gender construction. What we need to do today is to move beyond these half conversations to engage in a richer and more equitable dialogue. We must work to make the broadest possible range of attitudes, activities, and role models available to both women and men, and to teach both women and men the importance of thoughtful and flexible gender construction. And we must separate this dialogue about gender from the realm of commerce whenever we can. Perhaps then we can begin to realize a more equitable and less conflicting culture.

METHODOLOGICAL NOTE

The purpose of my study was to tell the story of the *Ladies' Home Journal* and the *Saturday Evening Post* as both commercial and cultural enterprises. Given the scarcity of extant corporate records for the Curtis Publishing Company, I relied mainly on secondary sources for the commercial part of the story. Jan Cohn (*Creating America*) and Salme Steinberg (*Reformer in the Marketplace*) make good use of the few business records for the Curtis Publishing Company scattered around the country; James Wood (*The Curtis Magazines*) worked for the *Post* at one time and therefore had access to some company records now unavailable. I supplemented the published business-related observations of these writers and of Edward Bok by reading the private papers of Cyrus Curtis, Edward Bok, and George Horace Lorimer, all held by the Historical Society of Pennsylvania. Mrs. A. Margaret Bok, daughter-in-law of Edward Bok, of Rockport, Maine, was most helpful in supplementing my scanty knowledge of Louisa Knapp Curtis and in commenting on family matters in general.

This study attempted to go beyond traditional content analysis of popular magazines by doing the following: (1) analyzing the content of the magazines in the context of what is known about the magazines' producers; (2) carefully attending to any evidence regarding the readers themselves and their actual and possible responses to the magazines; (3) analyzing the content of the magazines over a period of several years; and (4) paying careful attention to all parts of the magazines.

I therefore surveyed every issue of the *Ladies' Home Journal* in its entirety between December 1883 and December 1910, for a total of over 300 issues; and every issue of the *Saturday Evening Post* in its entirety between October 1897 and December 1910, for a total of over 600 issues. I closely analyzed each nonfiction item pertaining in some way to gender roles. Since the *Journal*'s nonfiction was in general very direct regarding gender roles and thus yielded an abundance of material, I analyzed one short story in every fourth issue of the monthly, for a total of 64 stories. Fiction was much more important to the *Post,* constituting half of each issue, and was the place where gender relations were most often considered, so I analyzed one short story in every fourth issue of the weekly, for a total of 132 stories. I read in each magazine the first short story that was not part of a continuing serial.

NOTES

INTRODUCTION

1. LaRue Brown to Dorothy Kirchway, n.d. [Spring 1915] [38], quoted in Ellen K. Rothman, *Hands and Hearts: A History of Courtship in America* (New York: Basic Books, Inc., 1984), p. 202.

2. See, for example, Michele Barrett, "Ideology and the Cultural Production of Gender," in Judith Newton and Deborah Rosenfelt, eds., *Feminist Criticism and Social Change* (New York: Methuen, 1985); Bonnie J. Fox, "Selling the Mechanized Household: 70 Years of Ads in *Ladies' Home Journal*," *Gender and Society* 4 (March 1990): 25–40; Erving Goffman, *Gender and Advertisements* (New York: Harper & Row, 1979); Gloria Steinem, "Sex, Lies & Advertising," *Ms.* (July/August 1990): 18–28; Penny Belknap and Wilbert M. Leonard II, "A Conceptual Replication and Extension of Erving Goffman's Study of Gender Advertisements," *Sex Roles* 25 (1991): 103–118; Gaye Tuchman et al., eds., *Hearth and Home: Images of Women in the Mass Media* (New York: Oxford University Press, 1978); Betty Friedan, *The Feminine Mystique* (London: Penguin Books, 1982); Steve Craig, *Men, Masculinity and the Media* (Newbury Park: SAGE Publications, 1992); Rosalind H. Williams, *Dream Worlds: Mass Consumption in Late Nineteenth-Century France* (Berkeley: University of California Press, 1982); Marjorie Ferguson, *Forever Feminine* (London: Heinman Press, 1983); Janice Winship, *Inside Women's Magazines* (New York: Pandora Press, 1987); Naomi Wolf, *The Beauty Myth: How Images of Beauty Are Used Against Women* (New York: Anchor Books, 1991); Jean Kilbourne, "The Child as Sex Object: Images of Children in the Media," *Challenging Media Images of Women* 3 (Summer 1991): 1–2, 6; and bell hooks, *Sisters of the Yam: Black Women and Self-Recovery* (Boston: South End Press, 1993), especially the Preface.

3. For a discussion of cultural hegemony as theorized by Antonio Gramsci, see T. J. Jackson Lears, "The Concept of Cultural Hegemony: Problems and Possibilities," *American Historical Review* 90 (June, 1985): 567–593. Lears defines cultural hegemony as the "spontaneous consent given by the great masses of the population to the general direction imposed on social life by the dominant fundamental group," p. 568.

4. Linda K. Kerber, "Separate Spheres, Female Worlds, Woman's Place: The Rhetoric of Women's History," *The Journal of American History* 75 (June 1988): 17.

5. The concept of the "private sphere" is also complicated by the fact that many women worked for pay inside the home, by taking in boarders, for example.

6. See for example, "Forum: Beyond Dichotomies," *Gender and History* 1 (Autumn 1989): 291–329.

7. Joan W. Scott, "Gender: A Useful Category of Historical Analysis," *American Historical Association* 5 (December 1986): 1053–1075; see also, Scott, *Gender and the Politics of History* (New York: Columbia University, 1988).

8. Bryan D. Palmer, *Descent into Discourse: The Reification of Language and the Writing of History* (Philadelphia: Temple University Press, 1990), p. xiv.

9. Louise A. Tilly, "Gender, Women's History, and Social History," *Social Science History* 13 (Winter 1989): 452. See also the debate on theory centering on book reviews and responses by Joan Scott and Linda Gordon in *Signs* 15 (Summer 1990): 848–860.

10. Palmer, *Descent into Discourse*, p. xiv.

11. Craig, *Men*, p. xi.

12. Denise Riley, *"Am I that Name?" Feminism and the Category of "Women" in History* (Minneapolis: University of Minnesota Press, 1988), p. 2.

13. Ibid.

14. See, for example, institutional histories of magazines and producer biographies: Walter Davenport and James C. Derieux, *Ladies, Gentlemen and Editors* (New York: Doubleday & Co., Inc., 1960); Frank Luther Mott, *A History of American Magazines, 1885–1905* (Cambridge: Harvard University Press, 1957); Richard Ohmann, "Where Did Mass Culture Come From? The Case of the Magazines," *Berkshire Review* 16 (1981): 85–101; Ernest Schell, "Edward Bok and the *Ladies' Home Journal*," *American History* (February 1982): 16–29; Salme Harju Steinberg, *Reformer in the Marketplace: Edward Bok and The Ladies' Home Journal* (Baton Rouge: Louisiana State University Press, 1979); and James P. Wood, *The Curtis Magazines* (New York: Ronald Press, 1971). Studies focusing almost exclusively on editorial content include Judith Leverett Dye, *For the Instruction and Amusement of Women: The Growth, Development, and Definition of American Magazines for Women, 1780–1840*, University of Pennsylvania dissertation, 1974; Marjorie Ferguson, *Forever Feminine: Women's Magazines and the Culture of Femininity* (Exeter, New Hampshire: Heineman Ed. Books, 1983); Theodore Greene, *American Heroes: The Changing Models of Success in American Magazines* (New York: Oxford University Press, 1970); Kathryn Shevelow, *Women and Print Culture: The Construction of Femininity in the Early Periodical* (London: Routledge, 1989); and Christopher Wilson, "The Rhetoric of Consumption: Mass-Market Magazines and the Demise of the Gentle Reader, 1880–1920," in Richard Wightman Fox and T. J. Jackson Lears, eds., *The Culture of Consumption: Critical Essays in American History, 1880–1980* (New York: Pantheon Books, 1983). Studies focusing on advertising include Penny Belknap and Wilbert M. Leonard, "A Conceptual Replication and Extension of Erving Goffman's Study of Gender Advertisements," *Sex Roles* 25 (1991): 103–118; and Bonnie J. Fox, "Selling the Mechanized Household: 70 Years of Ads in *Ladies' Home Journal*," *Gender and Society* 4 (March 1990); 25–40. And the focus on periodical fiction is represented by Martin Martel and George McCall, "Reality-Orientation and the Pleasure Principle: A Study of American Mass-Periodical Fiction

(1890–1955)," in Lewis Dexter and David Manning White, *People, Society, and Mass Communications* (Glenco, Illinois: Free Press, 1964); and Maureen Honey, ed., *Breaking the Ties That Bind: Popular Stories of the New Woman, 1915–1930* (Norman, Oklahoma: University of Oklahoma Press, 1992). Studies that go beyond the single-genre approach include Jan Cohn, *Creating America: George Horace Lorimer and the Saturday Evening Post* (Pittsburgh: University of Pittsburgh Press, 1989); Cristanne Miller, "Who Talks Like A Woman's Magazine? Language and Gender in Popular Women's and Men's Magazines," *Journal of American Culture* 10 (Fall 1987): 1–9; and Mary Ellen Waller (Zuckerman), *Popular Women's Magazines, 1890–1917* (Columbia University Dissertation, 1987).

15. Elizabeth Fox-Genovese, quoted in Ava Baron, ed., *Work Engendered: Toward a New History of American Labor* (Ithaca: Cornell University Press, 1991), p. 21.

16. T. J. Jackson Lears in his analysis of the notion of cultural hegemony explores the relevant concept of the "historical bloc," i.e., the "world view that appeals to a wide range of groups within the society." The magazine producers were attempting to create such a historical bloc. See Lears, "The Concept of Cultural Hegemony," p. 571.

17. See Janet Steele, "The Nineteenth Century *World* versus the *Sun:* Promoting Consumption (Rather than the Working Man)," *Journalism Quarterly* 67 (1990): 592; and Stuart Ewen, *Captains of Consciousness: Advertising and the Social Roots of the Consumer Culture* (New York: McGraw-Hill Book Co., 1976).

18. Craig, *Men, Masculinity, and the Media,* p. xxi.

19. See Robert G. Kelly, "Literature and the Historian," *American Quarterly* 26 (1974): 141–59; and Jay E. Mechling, "Advice to Historians on Advice to Mothers," *Journal of Social History* 9 (Fall 1975): 44–63. This study, because it focuses on the Curtis magazines that were mainstream bestsellers, focuses by definition on middle-class white American women and men. I hope that future studies will tell the equally significant story of smaller periodicals differentiated by race as well as by class and gender.

20. Pam Gilbert and Sandra Taylor, *Fashioning the Feminine: Girls, Popular Culture and Schooling* (Australia: Allen & Unwin Pty Ltd, 1991), p. 10.

21. Rosalind Williams, *Dream Worlds,* especially chapter 1.

22. Denise Riley, *Am I That Name?,* p. 96.

23. Craig, *Men, Masculinity, and the Media,* p. xii.

24. Michael Schudson, "The New Validation of Popular Culture: Sense and Sentimentality in Academia," *Critical Studies in Mass Communication* 4 (1987): 51–52.

25. Carl F. Kaestle, "History of Readers," in Kaestle et al., *Literacy in the United States* (New Haven: Yale University Press, 1991), p. 36.

26. Ibid, pp. 39–49.

27. Ibid, p. 50.

28. Janice Radway suggests, for example, that female readers of romance novels read them for escape, both figuratively and literally. The literal escape is the women's removal from the demands of their lives, i.e., "I am not available to anyone while I am reading." See Janice Radway, *Reading the Romance: Women, Patriarchy, and Popular Literature* (Chapel Hill: University of North Carolina Press, 1984), especially chapter 3.

29. Kaestle, "History of Readers," in Kaestle et al., *Literacy in the United States,* p. 50. See also Gilbert and Taylor, *Fashioning the Feminine,* p. 20.

30. Kaestle, "History of Readers," in Kaestle, et al., *Literacy in the United States,* p. 51.

31. Ibid.

32. See Kaestle, et al., *Literacy in the United States,* in particular the essays "The History of Readers" and "Standardization and Diversity in American Print Culture, 1880 to the Present."

33. Kaestle, "History of Readers," pp. 36–37.

34. Clifford Geertz, cited in S. Elizabeth Bird, *For Enquiring Minds: A Cultural Study of Supermarket Tabloids* (Knoxville: University of Tennessee Press, 1992), p. 3.

35. David Paul Nord suggests that the formulae of popular culture vehicles like magazines emerge in the "contention between consumers and producers, whose interests and whose preferences are not [necessarily] the same." David Paul Nord, "An Economic Perspective on Formula in Popular Culture," *Journal of American Culture* 3 (Spring 1980): 17.

36. T. J. Jackson Lears, "Some Version of Fantasy: Toward a Cultural History Of American Advertising, 1880–1930," *Prospects* 9 (1984): 376.

37. For a discussion of sustaining male hegemony see Harry S. Brod, *The Making of Masculinities: The New Men's Studies* (Boston: Allen & Unwin, Inc., 1987), especially the Introduction, pp. 1–20.

38. For a relevant discussion see Arlie Hochschild, *The Second Shift: Working Parents and the Revolution at Home* (New York: Avon Books, 1989).

39. For a useful discussion of the importance of mass media analyses to cultural history, see David Paul Nord, "Intellectual History, Social History, Cultural History . . . and Our History," *Journalism Quarterly* 67 (Winter 1990): 645–648.

CHAPTER 1

1. Edward Bok, *A Man From Maine* (New York: Charles Scribner's Sons, 1923), pp. 94–95.

2. Ibid, p. 45.

3. James Playsted Wood, *The Curtis Magazines* (New York: The Ronald Press Co., 1971), p. 6.

4. Louisa's birthdate was never published accurately. The only published description of her life was her daughter, Mary Louise's, sketch of her in *Notable Women of Pennsylvania*, which gave her birth year as 1855; *Notable Women of Pennsylvania* (Philadelphia: Pennsylvania Publishing, 1952), pp. 254–256. According to Louisa's application for membership in the Daughters of the American Revolution, however, she was born on October 24, 1851. D.A.R. application from the personal collection of A. Margaret Bok.

5. Lynn Weiner, *From Working Girl to Working Mother: The Female Labor Force in the United States, 1820–1980* (Chapel Hill: University of North Carolina Press, 1985), pp. 4 and 29.

6. Louisa and her sisters were "full-grown" when her family moved from Newburyport to Boston, and they therefore, according to Mary Louise's sketch of her mother, "looked about for something to do." One sister taught piano at the Perkins Institute for the Blind, while Louisa became private secretary to Howe. *Notable Women of Pennsylvania*, p. 255.

7. Bok, *A Man*, p. 74.

8. Wood, *Curtis Magazines*, p. 7.

9. *Ladies' Home Journal*, November 1893, p. 13. Hereafter cited as *LHJ*.

10. Bok, *A Man*, p. 92.

11. Ibid.

12. The Curtises bought out the advertising manager's share in the supplement and within a year the Curtises were sole owners of the *Ladies' Home Journal*. Bok, *A Man*, p. 95.

13. Maris Vinovkis and Gerald F. Moran, "The Great Care of Godly Parents: Early Childhood in Puritan New England," *Monographs of the Society for Research in Child Development* 50 (Serial No. 211): 32–37.

14. William F. Gilmore, *Reading Becomes a Necessity of Life: Material and Cultural Life in Rural New England, 1780–1835* (Knoxville: University of Tennessee Press, 1989), pp. 43–49.

15. Linda K. Kerber, *Women of the Republic: Intellect and Ideology in Revolutionary America* (Chapel Hill: University of North Carolina Press, 1980), p. 235.

16. James Hart, *The Popular Book: A History of America's Literary Taste* (New York: Oxford University Press, 1963), p. 86.

17. On children's books see Elizabeth Segel, "And the Twig is Bent: Gender and Childhood Reading," in Elizabeth A. Flynn and Patrocinio P. Schweickart, eds., *Gen-*

der and Reading: Essays on Readers, Texts, and Contexts (Baltimore: Johns Hopkins University Press, 1986), pp. 165–186. On the proliferation of women's books and materials see Madonne M. Miner, "Guaranteed to Please: Twentieth-Century American Women's Bestsellers," in Flynn and Schweickart, eds., *Gender and Reading,* pp. 187–211; Nina Baym, *Women's Fiction: A Guide to Novels By and About Women in America, 1820–1870* (Ithaca: Cornell University Press, 1978); Ann Douglas, *The Feminization of American Culture* (New York: Basic Books, 1978); Mary Kelley, *Private Woman, Public Stage: Literary Domesticity in Nineteenth-Century America* (New York: Oxford University Press, 1984); and Barbara Welter, "The Cult of True Womanhood: 1820–1860," *American Quarterly* XVIII (Summer 1966): 151–174.

18. Kate Sanborn, ed., *Our Famous Women* (Hartford: A. D. Worthington & Co., 1886), pp. 633–634.

19. Barbara Sicherman, "Sense & Sensibility: A Case Study of Women's Reading in Late-Victorian America," in Cathy N. Davidson, ed., *Reading in America: Literature and Social History* (Baltimore: Johns Hopkins University Press, 1989), p. 201.

20. Ibid, p. 202. For a similar argument see Janice Radway, *Reading the Romance: Women, Patriarchy, and Popular Literature* (Chapel Hill: University of North Carolina Press, 1984), especially chapter 3.

21. Jennifer Monaghan, "Literacy Instruction and Gender in Colonial New England," in Davidson, ed., *Reading in America,* p. 74.

22. Kathryn Shevelow, "Fathers and Daughters: Women as Readers of the *Tatler,*" in Flynn and Schweickart, *Gender and Reading,* pp. 107–123, especially pp. 121–122.

23. Carl Kaestle et al., *Literacy in the United States: Readers and Reading Since 1880* (New Haven: Yale University Press, 1991), pp. 4 and 51.

24. See Kelley, *Private Woman, Public Stage.*

25. Judith Leverett Dye, *For the Instruction and Amusement of Women: The Growth, Development, and Definition of American Magazines for Women, 1780–1840* (University of Pennsylvania Dissertation, 1977), chapter 2; and John Tebbel and Mary Ellen Waller-Zuckerman, *The Magazine in America, 1741–1990* (New York: Oxford University Press, 1991), p. 35.

26. *Godey's* was edited by Hale until her retirement in 1877, and maintained its circulation level until then despite its waning literary quality. The magazine died twenty years later in the face of competition from cheaper imitators like *Peterson's* and *Demorest's.* See Paul N. Boyer, "Sarah Josepha Hale," in *Notable American Women* (Cambridge: Harvard University Press, 1970), pp. 113–114.

27. Ruth Schwartz Cowan, *More Work for Mother: The Ironies of Household Technology from the Open Hearth to the Microwave* (New York: Basic Books, Inc., 1983), pp. 47–65.

28. Wells, *Revolutions,* pp. 107–109 and 121–124. Mary Ellen Waller (Zuckerman) asserts the need women in the late nineteenth century had for new "reliable prescriptive manuals." See Waller (Zuckerman), *Popular Women's Magazines, 1890–1917* (Columbia University Dissertation, 1987), p. 43. On mother-daughter relationships see Linda W. Rosenzweig, *The Anchor of My Life: Middle-Class American Mothers and Daughters, 1880–1920* (New York: New York University Press, 1993).

29. See Elaine Abelson, *When Ladies Go A-Thieving: Middle-Class Shoplifters in the Victorian Department Store* (New York: Oxford University Press, 1989); Cindy Sondik Aron, *Ladies and Gentlemen of the Civil Service: Middle-Class Workers in Victorian America* (New York: Oxford University Press, 1989); and Stuart M. Blumin, "The Hypothesis of Middle-Class Formation in Nineteenth-Century America: A Critique and Some Proposals," *American Historical Review* 90 (April 1985): 299–338.

30. Abelson, *When Ladies Go A-Thieving,* p. 15.

31. Daniel Horowitz, *The Morality of Spending: Attitudes Toward the Consumer Society in America, 1875–1940* (Baltimore: Johns Hopkins University Press, 1985), pp. xxv–xxvii.

32. Alfred D. Chandler, *The Visible Hand: The Managerial Revolution in American Business* (Cambridge: Harvard University Press, 1977), pp. 289–291.

33. Ibid, p. 289.

34. Richard Ohmann, "Where Did Mass Culture Come From? The Case of the Magazines," *Berkshire Review* 16 (1981): 93.

35. Chandler, *The Visible Hand,* p. 290.

36. Tebbel and Waller-Zuckerman, *The Magazine in America* (New York: Oxford University Press, 1991), p. 142.

37. See Salme Harju Steinberg, *Reformer in the Marketplace: Edward Bok and the Ladies' Home Journal* (Baton Rouge: Louisiana State University Press, 1979), p. xii. For a useful analysis of views of women as consumers, see Michael Schudson, *Advertising, The Uneasy Persuasion: Its Dubious Impact on American Society (New York: Basic Books, 1984),* chapter 5; see also Waller (Zuckerman), Popular Women's Magazines, pp. 135–144.

38. Quoted in Waller (Zuckerman), *Popular Women's Magazines,* p. 144.

39. Edward Bok, *The Americanization of Edward Bok: The Autobiography of a Dutch Boy Fifty Years Later* (New York: Charles Scribner's Sons, 1923), p. 105.

40. Theodore Peterson, *Magazines in the Twentieth Century* (Urbana: University of Illinois Press, 1964), pp. 140–142, 201–206, 215–217.

41. Walter D. Fuller, *The Life and Times of Cyrus H. K. Curtis (1850–1933)* (New York: The Newcomen Society of England, American Branch, 1948), p. 28.

42. Ralph M. Hower, *The History of an Advertising Agency, N. W. Ayer & Son at Work, 1869–1949* (Cambridge: Harvard University Press, 1949), pp. 115–119.

43. *Ladies' Home Journal,* May 1889, p. 10.

CHAPTER 2

1. Nancy Theriot, *The Biosocial Construction of Femininity: Mothers and Daughters in Nineteenth-Century America* (Westport: Greenwood Press, 1988), p. 2.

2. Ibid, especially pp. 7–19, 133–150.

3. Ibid.

4. *Ladies' Home Journal,* February 1887, p. 5. Hereafter cited as *LHJ.*

5. Ibid.

6. Ibid. For information on middle-class women's wardrobes, see Ruth Schwartz Cowan, *More Work for Mother: The Ironies of Household Technology from the Open Hearth to the Microwave* (New York: Basic Books, Inc., 1983), pp. 64–65.

7. Sketch of Phelps by Elizabeth T. Spring, in Kate Sanborn, ed., *Our Famous Women* (Hartford: A. D. Worthington & Co., 1886), pp. 560–565.

8. Penina M. Glazer and Miriam Alter, *Unequal Colleagues: The Entrance of Women Into the Professions, 1890–1940* (New Brunswick & London: Rutgers University Press, 1987), pp. 10–11.

9. Mary Catherine Bateson, *Composing a Life* (New York: The Atlantic Monthly Press, 1989), pp. 9–10.

10. *LHJ,* February 1887, p. 5.

11. Ibid.

12. *LHJ,* February 1887, p. 5, reprinted from the New York *Journalist.* This article was the only biographical sketch of the editor published during Knapp's tenure, and her death in 1910 was noted in a single paragraph on the editorial page of the *Journal.* There is no record of Louisa Knapp's work in standard biographical sources. Knapp's granddaughter-in-law, A. Margaret Bok, was most helpful in providing a sketch written by Mary Louise Curtis Bok about her mother, which appeared in *Notable Women of Pennsylvania.* Otherwise, information about Knapp comes from family reminiscences, from Edward Bok's published writing and A. Margaret Bok's letters to the author.

13. Judith Butler, *Gender Trouble: Feminism and the Subversion of Identity* (New York: Routledge, 1990), especially pp. 24–25, 33, 115 and 134–141.

14. Ibid.

15. *LHJ*, June 1888, p. 10. Using reader letters as evidence is not without its disadvantages; letters are only selectively reprinted in magazines, we know little about their composers, and their very authenticity can always be challenged. But their value outweighs these disadvantages. Letters to the editor, especially in the early *Ladies' Home Journal*, featured a variety of voices (suggesting their authenticity), and a significant portion of the magazine was devoted to such letters each month (suggesting their representative character). The historian of gender and reading must utilize any evidence available about the all-important and often-elusive reader response.

16. *LHJ*, September 1884, p. 4.

17. In this last year Edward Bok, later the magazine's editor, gradually became involved with the management of the *Journal*. This may well explain the increase in contributions from men, given the significant increase in male contributions under his subsequent sole leadership.

18. See Michael Schudson, *Discovering the News* (New York: Basic Books, Inc., 1978), for a fine discussion of "objectivity" and the development of what our society currently considers to be "newsworthy."

19. Women's history, as it values the contributions of women, calls for this new perspective on at least some of the content of women's magazines. For example, if clubwork was an important arena for vital civic contributions from women, then reports on club activities which appeared in magazines like the *Journal* are as newsworthy as the business analyses which appeared in magazines like the *Saturday Evening Post*. Perhaps more so even, given the overall benefit to the community or nation, as documented by historians of women like Karen Blair. See Karen H. Blair, *The Clubwoman as Feminist: True Womanhood Redefined, 1868–1914* (New York: Holmes & Meier Publishers, Inc., 1980).

20. The *Journal* under Knapp assumed that women want and need to reflect on and learn about gender role configurations and issues; recent scholarship supports the notion of such a propensity in women, at least in comparison to men. See Carol Gilligan, *In a Different Voice: Psychological Theory and Women's Development* (Cambridge, Massachusetts: Harvard University Press, 1982), and Lynn Mikel Brown & Carol Gilligan, *Meeting at the Crossroads: Women's Psychology and Girls' Development* (Cambridge, Massachusetts: Harvard University Press, 1992); Lillian B. Rubin, *Intimate Strangers: Men and Women Together* (New York: Harper & Row, 1983); Elinor Lenz and Barbara Myerhoff, *The Feminization of America: How Women's Values are Changing Our Public and Private Lives* (New York: St. Martin's Press, 1985), especially chapters 3 and 11; and Carol Tavris, *The Mismeasure of Woman: Why Women are not the Better Sex, the Inferior Sex, or the Opposite Sex* (New York: Simon & Schuster, 1992), especially chapter 7.

21. *LHJ*, December 1884, p. 4.

22. *LHJ*, December 1887, p. 10.

23. *LHJ*, June 1888, p. 10.

24. Salme Harju Steinberg, *Reformer in the Marketplace: Edward W. Bok and the Ladies' Home Journal* (Baton Rouge, Louisiana: Louisiana State University Press, 1979), p. 4.

25. Richard Ohmann, "Where Did Mass Culture Come From? The Case of the Magazines," *Berkshire Review* 16 (1981): 91.

26. Frances Cogan, *All-American Girl: The Ideal of Womanhood in Mid-Nineteenth-Century America* (Athens, Georgia: University of Georgia Press, 1989), p. 4.

27. *LHJ*, October 1886, p. 6.

28. Ibid.

29. Ibid.

30. *LHJ*, February 1884, p. 4.

31. *Historical Statistics of the U.S. Department of Commerce,* 1976, p. 379.

32. Barbara Miller Solomon, *In the Company of Educated Women: A History of Women and Higher Education in America* (New Haven: Yale University Press, 1985), p. 64.

33. *LHJ*, March 1887, p.8.

34. *LHJ*, July 1888, p. 20.

35. Ibid.

36. *LHJ*, May 1988, p. 3.

37. *LHJ*, February 1889, p. 10.

38. Mary Louise Curtis Bok, "Louisa Knapp Curtis," *Notable Women of Pennsylvania*, p. 256.

39. *LHJ*, April 1887, p. 17.

40. *LHJ*, July 1884, p. 2.

41. *LHJ*, March 1887, p. 13.

42. *LHJ*, June 1887, p. 2.

43. *LHJ*, October 1887, p. 8.

44. Patricia Branca's study of Victorian England highlights similar difficulties. Branca's chapter on "The Modern Homemaker," for example, illuminates the middle-class housewife's struggle to meet increasingly high standards of living with her husband's wage. Rising costs and constant innovation, coupled with a limited income, meant that women had to choose between appliances and other household conveniences and to opt only for the "most economical and practical of novelties." See Branca, *Silent*

Sisterhood: Middle-Class Women in the Victorian Home (London: Croom Helm, 1975), p. 53 and all of chapters 3 and 8. There are no published studies for the United States to parallel Branca's. Daniel Horowitz in *The Morality of Spending: Attitudes Toward The Consumer Society in America, 1865–1940* (Baltimore: Johns Hopkins University Press, 1985) offers some useful information garnered from nineteenth-century studies of household budgets, but it only pertains to working-class families.

45. *LHJ*, April 1884, p. 4.

46. *LHJ*, June 1884, p. 4.

47. Carl Degler, *At Odds: Women & the Family from the Revolution to the Present* (New York: Oxford University Press, 1980), p. 152; and Sheila Rothman, *Woman's Proper Place: A History of Changing Ideals and Practices, 1870 to the Present* (New York: Basic Books, Inc., 1978), p. 16.

48. See Cowan, *More Work For Mother,* chapter 1, and Strasser, *Never Done,* chapter 2.

49. *LHJ*, May 1885, p. 4.

50. See Strasser, *Never Done,* chapter 2.

51. *LHJ*, January 1886, p. 6.

52. Karen Lystra, *Searching the Heart: Women, Men, and Romantic Love in Nineteenth-Century America* (New York: Oxford University Press, 1989), p. 128.

53. *LHJ*, March 1887, p. 7.

54. *LHJ*, July 1885, p. 4. The perception that more women were remaining unmarried was accurate; as Carl Degler shows, the cohort of women born between 1860 and 1880 (the oldest of whom would be among the younger of the *Journal's* readers in the mid-to late 1880s) had the highest proportion of never-married women: about 10 percent of these women never married.

55. *LHJ*, February 1885, p. 4.

56. *LHJ*, July 1887, p. 2.

57. See Blanche Wiesen Cook, *Eleanor Roosevelt, Volume One, 1884–1933* (New York: Viking Press, 1992), p. 24. For an important discussion of these issues in the contemporary United States, see Marcia Millman, *Warm Hearts and Cold Cash: The Intimate Dynamics of Families and Money* (New York: Free Press, 1991).

58. *LHJ*, December 1887, p. 4.

59. Ibid.

60. For a discussion that links the historical and contemporary economic position of American middle-class wives, see Nancy Folbre, "The Unproductive Housewife: Her Evolution in Nineteenth-Century Economic Thought," *Signs* 16 (1991): 463–484.

61. *LHJ*, July 1886, p. 6.

62. *LHJ*, March 1888, p. 10.

63. *LHJ*, December 1887, p. 10.

64. Ibid.

65. *LHJ*, June 1886, p. 6.

66. *LHJ*, April 1888, p. 9.

67. *LHJ*, December 1883, p. 16.

68. *LHJ*, September 1887, p. 16.

69. *LHJ*, August 1890, p. 4.

70. *LHJ*, April 1888, p. 15.

71. For a discussion of this issue see Elizabeth Bird, *For Enquiring Minds: A Cultural Study of Supermarket Tabloids* (Knoxville: University of Tennessee Press, 1992), p. 110.

72. Michael Schudson, *Advertising, The Uneasy Persuasion: Its Dubious Impact on American Society* (New York: Basic Books, Inc., 1984), p. 238.

73. Ibid.

74. The price also doubled, causing a noticeable drop in subscriptions.

75. Mary Louise Curtis Bok, *Notable Women of Pennsylvania*, p. 256.

76. Bok, *A Man*, p. 76.

77. The exceptions were Gertrude Battles Lane, who edited the *Woman's Home Companion* between 1912 and 1941, and Beatrice Gould, who, with her husband, Bruce, coedited the *Ladies' Home Journal* from the mid-1930s to 1950.

CHAPTER 3

1. *Ladies' Home Journal*, January 1890, p. 8. Hereafter cited as *LHJ*.

2. *LHJ*, June 1890, p. 24.

3. *LHJ*, April 1890, p. 8.

4. Edward Bok, *The Americanization of Edward Bok: The Story of a Dutch Boy Fifty Years Later* (New York: Charles Scribner's Sons, 1923), pp. 160–161.

5. Cristanne Miller, "Who Talks Like a Women's Magazine? Language and Gender in Popular Women's and Men's Magazines," *Journal of American Culture* 10 (Fall 1987): 1–9.

6. Bok, *Americanization,* p. 1.

7. Ibid, p. 115.

8. Ibid, p. 28.

9. See, for example, the full-length treatment of such public discourse by Barbara Ehrenreich and Deirdre English, entitled *For Her Own Good: 150 Years of the Experts' Advice to Women* (New York: Anchor Books, 1979).

10. See Ehrenreich and English, *For Her Own Good;* David G. Pugh, *Sons of Liberty: The Masculine Mind in Nineteenth-Century America* (Westport, Connecticut: Greenwood Press, 1983), especially chapter 2; and Carroll Smith-Rosenberg, "The Hysterical Woman: Sex Roles and Role Conflict in Nineteenth-Century America" and "The Abortion Movement and the AMA, 1850–1880," in *Disorderly Conduct: Visions of Gender in Victorian America* (New York: Alfred A. Knopf, 1985).

11. Edward Bok, *Twice Thirty: Some Short and Simple Annals of the Road* (New York: Charles Scribner's Sons, 1925), p. 373.

12. Christopher Wilson, *The Labor of Words: Literary Professionalism in the Progressive Era* (Athens, Georgia: University of Georgia Press, 1985), pp. 40–46.

13. Ibid, p. 47.

14. Ibid, pp. 40–62.

15. Bok, *Americanization,* p. 179.

16. Ibid, pp. 162–163.

17. Ibid, p. 316.

18. *LHJ,* April 1890, p. 8.

19. *LHJ,* August 1895, p. 12.

20. Bok, *Americanization,* p. 179.

21. See especially Christopher Wilson, "The Rhetoric of Consumption" in Richard Wightman Fox and T. J. Jackson Lears, eds., *The Culture of Consumption: Critical Essays in American History, 1880–1980* (New York: Pantheon Books, 1983), pp. 44, 61; Stuart Ewen proposes a similar notion in *Captains of Consciousness* (New York: Pantheon Books, 1979).

22. Miller, "Who Talks Like a Women's Magazine?"

23. Bok, *Americanization,* p. 174.

24. Ibid.

25. Ibid, p. 169.

26. Ibid, p. 170.

27. *LHJ*, June 1895, p. 33.

28. Bok, *Americanization*, pp. 174–175.

29. *LHJ*, April 1894, p. 14.

30. Steinberg, *Reformer*, p. 10.

31. Ibid, p. 3.

32. Ibid, pp. 6–7.

33. Ibid, p. 7.

34. *LHJ*, April 1891, p. 10.

35. Steinberg, *Reformer*, p. 6.

36. *LHJ*, June 1891, p. 10; see also April 1893, p. 14; December 1896, p. 14; and July 1899, p. 21.

37. "Side-Talks with Boys" first appeared in the October 1891 issue, p. 14; "Problems of Young Men" in September 1894, p. 10; and "What Men are Asking" in January 1897, p. 28.

38. Steinberg, *Reformer*, p. 12.

39. *LHJ*, July 1893, p. 14.

40. *LHJ*, October 1890, p. 8.

41. *LHJ*, November 1893, p. 14.

42. Steinberg, *Reformer*, p. 28.

43. Ibid, p. 14.

44. Bok, *Americanization*, p. 453.

CHAPTER 4

1. John Fiske, *Television Culture* (London: Methuen Press, 1987), p. 20.

2. Edward Bok, *The Americanization of Edward Bok: The Story of a Dutch Boy Fifty Years Later* (New York: Charles Scribner's Sons, 1923), p. 162.

3. For a discussion of these contested images see Kathy Peiss, "Making Faces: The Cosmetics Industry and the Cultural Construction of Gender, 1890–1930," *Genders* (Spring 1990): 152–153; and Carroll Smith-Rosenberg, "New Woman as Androgyne," in Smith-Rosenberg, *Disorderly Conduct: Visions of Gender in Victorian America* (New York: Oxford University Press), 1985.

4. *Ladies' Home Journal,* March 1890, p. 8. Hereafter cited as *LHJ.*

5. *LHJ,* May 1891, p. 10.

6. *LHJ,* January 1891, p. 10.

7. *LHJ,* January 1892, p. 12.

8. Ibid.

9. *LHJ,* February 1895, p. 15.

10. *LHJ,* January 1895, p. 13.

11. *LHJ,* April 1891, p. 27.

12. Ibid.

13. *LHJ,* June 1895, p. 14.

14. *LHJ,* April 1895, p. 15.

15. Ibid.

16. *LHJ,* May 1900, p. 6.

17. *LHJ,* March 1894, p. 20.

18. *LHJ,* July 1899, p. 14.

19. *LHJ,* April 1899, p. 20.

20. Ruth Cowan in *More Work for Mother* suggests that historians like Carl Degler and Alice Kessler-Harris have assumed that housework became easier in the nineteenth century. See Cowan, *More Work for Mother: The Ironies of Household Technology from the Open Hearth to the Microwave* (New York: Basic Books, Inc., 1983), note 1, p. 235. It is also important to acknowledge Susan Kleinberg's point that new household tools were not reaching the working-class at all in this period. We must remember that Bok was addressing middle-class *Journal* readers, not all women or all households. See Kleinberg, "Technology and Women's Work: The Lives of Working-Class Women in Pittsburgh, 1870–1900," *Labor History* 17 (1976): 58–72.

21. *LHJ,* April 1899, p. 20.

22. Nancy Folbre, "The Unproductive Housewife: Her Evolution in Nineteenth-Century Economic Thought," *Signs* 16 (Spring 1991): 481.

23. For a relevant discussion see Bonnie J. Fox, "Selling the Mechanized Household: 70 Years of Ads in *Ladies' Home Journal,*" *Gender & Society* 4 (March 1990): 24–40.

24. *LHJ,* December 1896, p. 15.

25. *LHJ,* February 1891, p. 14. For a discussion of the term "homemaker," see Glenna Matthews, *"Just a Housewife": The Rise and Fall of Domesticity in America* (New York: Oxford University Press, 1987), pp. xvi–xvii.

26. *LHJ,* February 1891, p. 12.

27. *LHJ,* June 1895, p. 15.

28. *LHJ,* June 1896, p. 12.

29. See *LHJ,* November 1891, p. 12, and *LHJ,* July 1895, p. 6.

30. *LHJ,* April 1893, p. 18.

31. *LHJ,* May 1895, p. 16.

32. *LHJ,* April 1900, p. 19.

33. For examples of such over-reactions, see Elaine Abelson, *When Ladies Go A-Thieving: Middle-Class Shoplifters in the Victorian Department Store* (New York: Oxford University Press, 1989); Barbara Ehrenreich and Deirdre English, *For Her Own Good: 150 Years of the Experts' Advice to Women* (New York: Anchor Books, 1979); and, for a semi-autobiographical account, see Charlotte Perkins Gilman, *The Yellow Wallpaper* (Old Westbury, New York: The Feminist Press, 1973). For the more contemporary version see Susan Faludi, *Backlash: The Undeclared War Against American Women* (New York: Crown Publishers, Inc., 1991).

34. See Mrs. Lyman Abbott's report on page 32 of the February 1893 issue of the *Journal;* for an example of the "Women's Chances as Bread-Winners" column see the *Journal* of January 1891, p. 4; and for an example of the "Art of Dressing for Business" column see the *Journal* of February 1894, p. 21.

35. Alice Kessler-Harris, *Out to Work: A History of Wage-Earning Women in America* (New York: Oxford University Press, 1982), chapter 5.

36. *LHJ,* March 1895, p. 10.

37. *LHJ,* April 1895, p. 14.

38. *LHJ,* May 1896, p. 14.

39. *LHJ,* June 1894, p. 4.

40. *LHJ,* September 1892, p. 4.

41. See May, *Great Expectations,* and Griswold, "Divorce and the Legal Redefinition of Victorian Manhood," and *Family and Divorce in California.*

42. May, *Great Expectations,* p. 155.

43. *LHJ,* November 1895, p. 15.

44. Joseph H. Pleck, "American Fathering in Historical Perspective," in Michael S. Kimmel, ed., *Changing Men: New Directions in Research on Men and Masculinity* (Newbury Park, California: *SAGE* Publications, 1987), pp. 84–89.

45. *LHJ*, February 1890, p. 32.

46. *LHJ*, May 1889, p. 30.

47. Margaret Marsh, "Suburban Men and Masculine Domesticity, 1870–1915," *American Quarterly* 40 (June 1988): 165–186.

48. *LHJ*, January 1895, p. 16.

49. Interview with A. Margaret Bok, June 1989, Camden, Maine.

50. *LHJ*, March 1899, p. 26.

51. *LHJ*, February 1898, p. 13.

52. Ibid.

53. Salme Harju Steinberg, *Reformer in the Marketplace: Edward W. Bok and the Ladies' Home Journal* (Baton Rouge, Louisiana: Louisiana State University Press, 1979), p. 19.

54. *LHJ*, April 1896, p. x; see Roland Marchand, *Advertising the American Dream: Making Way for Modernity, 1920–1940* (Berkeley: University of California Press, 1985), p. xxi, for a discussion of the bias toward modernity in early advertising.

55. *LHJ*, August 1895, p. 27.

56. T. J. Jackson Lears, "From Salvation to Self-Realization: Advertising and the Therapeutic Roots of the Consumer Culture, 1880–1980" in *The Culture of Consumption: Critical Essays in American History, 1880–1980* (New York: Pantheon Books, 1983), pp. 2–38, 19.

57. Ibid., p. 4.

58. Marchand, *Advertising the American Dream*, p. xix.

CHAPTER 5

1. Peter Gabriel Filene, *Him/Her/Self: Sex Roles in Modern America* (New York: Harcourt Brace Jovanovich, 1974), p. 73.

2. James Playsted Wood, *The Curtis Magazines* (New York: The Ronald Press Co., 1971), p. 33.

3. Ibid, pp. 33–34.

4. Ibid.

5. Ibid, p. 37.

6. Edward Bok, *A Man From Maine* (New York: Charles Scribner's Sons, 1923), p. 149.

7. Jan Cohn, *Creating America: George Horace Lorimer and the Saturday Evening Post* (Pittsburgh: University of Pittsburgh Press, 1989), p. 26.

8. Wood, *The Curtis Magazines,* p. 38.

9. John Tebbel, *George Horace Lorimer and the Saturday Evening Post* (Garden City, New York: Doubleday and Company, Inc., 1948), p. 20.

10. Wood, *The Curtis Magazines,* p. 45.

11. See, for example, Salme Harju Steinberg, *Reformer in the Marketplace: Edward W. Bok and the Ladies' Home Journal* (Baton Rouge, Louisiana: Louisiana State University Press, 1979), p. 8.

12. Richard Ohmann, "Where Did Mass Culture Come From? The Case of the Magazines," *Berkshire Review* 16 (1981): 90–91.

13. Frank Luther Mott, *A History of American Magazines, 1885–1905* (Cambridge: Harvard University Press, 1957), p. 251.

14. Ohmann, "Where Did Mass Culture Come From?" p. 90.

15. John Tebbel and Mary Ellen Waller-Zuckerman, *The Magazine in America, 1741–1990* (New York: Oxford University Press, 1991), p. 282.

16. Tebbel, *George Horace Lorimer,* p. 20.

17. Ibid, pp. 210–212.

18. Christopher P. Wilson, *The Labor of Words: Literary Professionalism in the Progressive Era* (Athens, Georgia: The University of Georgia Press, 1985), p. 54.

19. Cohn, *Creating America,* p. 16.

20. Tebbel, *George Horace Lorimer,* pp. 210–212.

21. George Horace Lorimer letter to Adelaide S. Neall dated 29 December 1908, Neall Scrapbook, Historical Society of Pennsylvania.

22. Wood, *The Curtis Magazines,* p. 35.

23. The *Saturday Evening Post,* 23 October 1897, p. 5. Hereafter cited as *SEP.*

24. Ibid, p. 8.

25. Cohn, *Creating America,* p. 30.

26. Ibid, p. 31.

27. George Horace Lorimer letter to Albert Beveridge dated 5 June 1899, Lorimer file, Historical Society of Pennsylvania.

28. Tebbel, *George Horace Lorimer,* pp. 109–110.

29. Christopher Wilson, "The Rhetoric of Consumption: Mass Market Magazines and the Demise of the Gentle Reader, 1880–1920," in Richard W. Fox and T. J. Jackson Lears, eds., *The Culture of Consumption: Critical Essays in American History, 1880–1980* (New York: Pantheon Books, 1983), pp. 50–53.

30. Ibid, p. 59.

31. *Saturday Evening Post* Prospectus, v. 170, 28 May 1898, p. 8.

CHAPTER 6

1. Quoted in Robert W. Connell, "A Whole New World: Remaking Masculinity in the Context of the Environmental Movement," *Gender and Society* 4 (December 1990): 453.

2. *Historical Statistics of the United States, Colonial Times to 1970* (U.S. Department of Commerce, Bureau of Census, 1975), p. 383.

3. Ibid.

4. Peter Gabriel Filene, *Him/Her/Self: Sex Roles in Modern America,* 2d ed. (Baltimore: Johns Hopkins University Press, 1986); Joe Dubbert, "Progressivism and the Masculinity Crisis," and Jeffrey Hantover, "The Boy Scouts and the Validation of Masculinity," both reprinted in Elizabeth Pleck and Joseph Pleck, eds., *The American Man* (Englewood Cliffs, New Jersey: Prentice-Hall, 1980).

5. Karen Lystra, *Searching the Heart: Women, Men, and Romantic Love in Nineteenth-Century America* (New York: Oxford University Press, 1989), Introduction and chapters 2, 5, 6, 7, and 8.

6. See Margaret Marsh, *Suburban Lives* (New York: Rutgers University Press, 1990), p. xiv.

7. See Michael S. Kimmel, "Men's Responses to Feminism at the Turn of the Century," *Gender and Society* 1 (September 1987): 261–283; and Peter N. Stearns, *Be a Man! Males in Modern Society* (New York: Homes and Meier Publishers, Inc., 1979), pp. 39–110.

8. Clyde Griffen, "Reconstructing Masculinity from the Evangelical Revival to the Waning of Progressivism: A Speculative Synthesis," in Clyde Griffen and Mark Carnes, *Meanings for Manhood: Constructions of Masculinity in Victorian America* (Chicago: University of Chicago Press, 1990), p. 185.

9. Ibid, p. 186.

10. Ibid, p. 188.

11. For a fascinating account of the life of one early nineteenth-century man that provides evidence for diverse gender norms for men, see Karen V. Hansen, "I Helped Put in a Quilt: Men's Work and Male Intimacy in Nineteenth-Century New England," *Gender and Society* 3 (September 1989): 334–354.

12. Griffen, "Reconstructing Masculinity," p. 191.

13. Anthony Rotundo, *American Manhood: Transformations in Masculinity From the Revolution to the Modern Era* (New York: Basic Books, 1993), p. 222.

14. Griffen, "Reconstructing Masculinity," p. 198.

15. Jan Cohn, *Creating America: George Horace Lorimer and the Saturday Evening Post* (Pittsburgh: University of Pittsburgh Press, 1989), pp. 11–12.

16. Ibid, pp. 12–13.

17. *Saturday Evening Post,* 15 July 1899, p. 46. Hereafter cited as *SEP.*

18. *SEP,* 4 November 1899, p. 1.

19. Richard Weiss, *The American Myth of Success: From Horatio Alger to Norman Vincent Peale* (Urbana: University of Illinois Press, 1988), pp. 1–4; see also Rotundo, *American Manhood,* especially chapter 8; and John Cawelti, *Apostles of the Self-Made Man: Changing Concepts of Success in America* (Chicago: University of Chicago Press, 1965), p. 4.

20. *SEP,* 14 July 1900, p. 12.

21. *SEP,* 24 March 1900, p. 871.

22. Lystra, *Searching the Heart,* p. 133. For a relevant discussion see Rotundo, *American Manhood,* pp.167–169, 176–191.

23. Mary Ryan, quoted in Francesca Cancian, *Love in America: Gender and Self-Development* (New York: Cambridge University Press, 1987), p. 16.

24. Stearns, *Be a Man!,* p. 39.

25. *SEP,* 8 April 1899, pp. 645–646.

26. *SEP,* 20 November 1897, pp. 6–7.

27. *SEP,* 27 August 1898, pp. 1–2.

28. *SEP,* 29 December 1900, p. 14.

29. *SEP,* 23 June 1900, p. 1206.

30. Ibid.

31. *SEP,* 22 September 1900, p. 12.

32. Rotundo, *American Manhood*, p. 130.

33. *SEP*, 25 March 1899, p. 611.

34. *SEP*, 10 February 1900, p. 718.

35. *SEP*, 21 October 1899, p. 330.

36. *SEP*, 14 July 1900, p. 13.

37. *SEP*, 17 June 1899, pp. 1–3.

38. *SEP*, 13 January 1900, pp. 604–606.

39. *SEP*, 20 October 1900, p. 12.

40. *SEP*, 14 October 1899, p. 269.

41. *SEP*, 18 November 1899, p. 394.

42. Elizabeth Fox-Genovese, *Feminism Without Illusions: A Critique of Individualism* (Chapel Hill: University of North Carolina Press, 1991), p. 7.

43. This commitment extended basically to native-born American Caucasians. Lorimer's *Post* became increasingly anti-immigration over these years, and seldom reached out to African Americans or other minority groups.

44. For a similar characterization of male adolescent literature see Kimberly Reynolds, *Girls Only? Gender and Popular Children's Fiction in Britain, 1880–1910* (Philadelphia: Temple University Press, 1990), especially pp. xv–xxi, 37–38, and 51–61. On page 37, Reynolds reports that British boys at the turn of the century were "directed away from the kind of reading matter which explored the uncertain worlds of emotions and relationships."

45. For a discussion parallel to this one, see Rotundo, *American Manhood*, chapter 8.

CHAPTER 7

1. *Ladies' Home Journal*, July 1899, p. 29.

2. George Horace Lorimer memorandum dated 17 February 1900, Lorimer Scrapbook, Historical Society of Pennsylvania.

3. *Saturday Evening Post*, 20 June 1908, p. 1.

4. Edward Bok, *A Man From Maine* (New York: Charles Scribner's Sons, 1923), p. 161.

5. Edward Bok, *The Americanization of Edward Bok: The Autobiography of a Dutch Boy Fifty Years Later* (New York: Charles Scribner's Sons, 1923), p. 190.

6. Bok, *A Man From Maine*, p. 161.

7. Theodore Peterson, *Magazines in the Twentieth Century* (Urbana: University of Illinois Press, 1964), p. 13.

8. Rosalind H. Williams, *Dream Worlds: Mass Consumption in Late Nineteenth-Century France* (Berkeley: University of California Press, 1982), p. 303.

9. Ibid, p. 307.

CHAPTER 8

1. *Saturday Evening Post,* 18 February 1905, inside cover. Hereafter cited as *SEP.*

2. *Ladies' Home Journal,* January 1904, p. 16. Hereafter cited as *LHJ.*

3. See note 3 in chapter 4.

4. *LHJ,* February 1910, p. 5.

5. See Karen J. Blair, *The Clubwoman as Feminist: True Womanhood Redefined, 1864–1914* (New York: Holmes & Meier Publishers, Inc., 1980); Theodora Penny Martin, *The Sound of Our Own Voices: Women's Study Clubs, 1860–1910* (Boston: Beacon Press, 1987); and Anne Firor Scott, *Natural Allies: Women's Associations in American History* (Urbana: University of Illinois Press, 1991), especially chapters 5–7.

6. *LHJ,* September 1903, p. 16.

7. Edward Bok, *A Man From Maine* (New York: Charles Scribner's Sons, 1923), pp. 299–300.

8. Ibid.

9. *LHJ,* October 1905, pp. 7–8.

10. *LHJ,* January 1910, p. 21.

11. *LHJ,* December 1901, pp. 4–5; see Neil Harris, "Iconography and Intellectual History: The Half-Tone Effect," in John Higham and Paul Conklin, eds., *New Directions in American History* (Baltimore: Johns Hopkins University Press, 1979), pp. 196–211.

12. Lynn D. Gordon, "The Gibson Girl Goes to College: Popular Culture and Women's Higher Education in the Progressive Era, 1890–1920," *American Quarterly* 39 (Summer 1987): 226.

13. Bok discussed the lampooning activity in general in his autobiography with some bravado, but an undercurrent of bitterness informs these passages. See Edward Bok, *The Americanization of Edward Bok: The Autobiography of a Dutch Boy Fifty Years Later* (New York: Charles Scribner's and Sons, 1921), chapters 7 and 8.

14. Alfred Habegger, *Gender, Fantasy and Realism in American Literature* (New York: Columbia University Press, 1982), p. 117 and chapters 12–17. See also two early

collections of women's humor: Kate Sanborn, ed., *The Wit of Women* (New York: Funk and Wagnalls, 1885); and Martha Bensley Bruere and Mary Ritter Beard, *Laughing Their Way* (New York: Macmillan Company, 1934).

15. *LHJ,* January 1907, p. 14.

16. Cristanne Miller, "Who Talks Like a Women's Magazine? Language and Gender in Popular Women's and Men's Magazines," *Journal of American Culture* 10 (Fall 1987): 3.

17. John Tebbel and Mary Ellen Waller-Zuckerman, *The Magazine in America, 1741–1990* (New York: Oxford University Press, 1991), p. 176.

18. *SEP,* 1 January 1910, p. 18.

19. *SEP,* 21 August 1909, p. 18.

20. *SEP,* 19 January 1901, p. 12.

21. Ibid.

22. *SEP,* 30 July 1910, p. 8.

23. Ibid.

24. *SEP,* 5 November 1910, p. 20.

25. Karen Lystra, *Searching the Heart: Women, Men, and Romantic Love in the Nineteenth Century* (New York: Oxford University Press, 1989), p. 206.

26. *LHJ,* August 1908, p. 4.

27. Ibid.

28. *SEP,* 20 April 1907, p. 18.

29. *SEP,* 29 November 1902, p. 12.

30. *SEP,* 17 October 1903, p. 12.

31. Tim Carrigan et al., cogently criticize "male role" literature for implying that "once a man has been socialized to his role, that is more or less the end of it." The same criticism can be extended to female role literature. See Carrigan et al., in Harry Brod, ed., *The Making of Masculinities: The New Men's Studies* (Boston: Allen & Unwin, 1987), p. 97.

32. Almost three-quarters of the ninety-eight *Post* stories analyzed for the 1900–1910 period featured a work-related theme.

33. *SEP,* 26 March 1904, pp. 6–7, 27–28.

34. *SEP,* 20 November 1909, pp. 6–8, 43–45.

35. Anthony Rotundo, *American Manhood: Transformations in Masculinity From the Revolution to the Modern Era* (New York: Basic Books, 1993).

36. See Will Payne's "The Troublesome Truth," *SEP,* 23 April 1904, pp. 12–13, 32; and William Hamilton Osborne's "The Golden Chain," *SEP,* 20 January 1906, pp. 4–5, 24.

37. Edward Bok, *Successward: A Young Man's Book for Young Men* (New York: Fleming H. Revell Co., 1896), p. 21.

38. For a relevant discussion see Ava Baron, "The Masculinity of Production: The Gendering of Work and Skill in U.S. Newspaper Printing, 1850–1920," in Dorothy O. Helly and Susan M. Reverby, eds., *Gendered Domains: Rethinking Public and Private in Women's History* (Ithaca: Cornell University Press, 1992), p. 288; see also Rotundo, *American Manhood,* especially chapter 8.

39. *SEP,* 22 January 1910, p. 7–9, 30–31.

40. *SEP,* 18 June 1910, pp. 16–18, 58–60.

41. *SEP,* 20 May 1905, p. 14.

42. Ibid.

43. Ibid.

44. Ibid.

45. *LHJ,* April 1902, p. 16.

46. Ibid.

47. *LHJ,* May 1906, p. 27; July 1906, p. 17.

48. *LHJ,* November 1904, p. 49.

49. Francesca Cancian, *Love in America: Gender and Self-Development* (New York: Cambridge University Press, 1987), especially chapters 1–5, 11.

50. *LHJ,* March 1901, p. 16.

51. *LHJ,* September 1907, p. 25.

52. *SEP,* 31 July 1909, p. 16.

53. *SEP,* 2 March 1907, p. 16.

54. *SEP,* 20 March 1910, p. 12.

55. See Kathy Peiss, "Making Faces: The Cosmetics Industry and the Cultural Construction of Gender, 1890–1930," *Genders* 7 (Spring 1990): 143–169.

56. *SEP,* 25 February 1905, p. 27; for an excellent analysis of women and driving see Virginia Scharff, *Taking the Wheel: Women and the Coming of the Motor Age* (New York: The Free Press, 1991).

57. *SEP,* 3 January 1903, p. 17.

58. Rachel T. Hare-Mustin and Jeanne Marecek, *Making a Difference: Psychology and the Construction of Gender* (New Haven: Yale University Press, 1990), p. 187.

59. Nancy Folbre, "The Unproductive Housewife: Her Evolution in Nineteenth-Century Economic Thought," *Signs* 16 (1991): 469.

60. *LHJ,* October 1886, p. 6.

EPILOGUE

1. Mary Ellen Waller (Zuckerman) identifies this shift as the evolution from "housewife as producer" to "housewife as consumer." See Waller (Zuckerman), *Popular Women's Magazines, 1890–1917* (Columbia University Dissertation, 1987), p. 3.

2. John Tebbel and Mary Ellen Waller-Zuckerman, *The Magazine in America, 1741–1990* (New York: Oxford University Press, 1991), pp. 268–269.

3. See Waller (Zuckerman), *Popular Women's Magazines,* p. 9.

4. Theodore Peterson, *Magazines in the Twentieth Century,* 2d ed. (Urbana: University of Illinois Press, 1964), p. 204.

5. Hugh Hefner, quoted in Thomas Weyr, *Reaching for Paradise: The Playboy Vision of America* (New York: Times Books, 1978), p. 3.

6. Henry Luce, quoted in Loudon Wainwright, *The Great American Magazine: An Inside History of Life* (New York: Alfred A. Knopf, 1986), p. 6.

7. Ibid, p. 42.

8. Peterson, *Magazines in the Twentieth Century,* p. 23.

9. See especially A. J. van Zuilen's *The Life Cycle of Magazines: A Historical Study of the Decline and Fall of the General Interest Mass Audience Magazine in the U.S. During the Period 1946–1972* (Vithoorn, Netherlands: Graduate Press, 1977).

10. The only major general-interest magazine left among the top ten in 1990 was *Reader's Digest.* Founded in 1922, the *Digest* has always been something of an anomaly. The reprinting function of the magazine has given it an extremely low production overhead, allowing it to remain above the fray of competition with television. Pale imitations of the *Post* and *Life* were later resurrected, but they have had a negligible effect on American popular culture.

11. Peterson, *Magazines in the Twentieth Century,* p.23.

12. Tebbel and Waller-Zuckerman, *The Magazine in America,* p. 371.

13. Roland Marchand, *Advertising the American Dream: Making Way for Modernity, 1920–1940* (Berkeley: University of California Press, 1985), p. xx.

14. On nightlife and class, see Christine Stansell, *City of Women: Sex and Class in New York, 1789–1860* (Urbana: University of Illinois Press, 1987), chapter 9; and Lewis A. Erenberg, *Steppin' Out: New York Nightlife and the Transformation of American Culture, 1890–1930* (Westport, Conn.: Greenwood Press, 1981). On the marketing of cosmetics see Kathy Peiss, "Making Faces: The Cosmetics Industry and the Cultural Construction of Gender, 1890–1930," *Genders* 7 (Spring 1990): 143–169.

15. Pam Gilbert and Sandra Taylor, *Fashioning the Feminine: Girls, Popular Culture and Schooling* (Australia: Allen & Unwin Pty Ltd, 1991), p. 7.

16. Todd Gitlin, "Who Communicates What to Whom and Why About Communications Research," *Critical Studies in Mass Communication* 7 (1990): 185–196.

17. Michael Schudson, "The New Validation of Popular Culture: Sense and Sentimentality in Academia," *Critical Studies in Mass Communication* 4 (1987): 52.

18. Ibid, p. 51.

19. Ibid, p. 64.

20. Thus a major question of gender history is partially answered, the question that Mark Carnes and Clyde Griffen suggest: gender history must ask why "male dominance [has] remained essentially intact despite . . . many transformations." See Carnes and Griffen, *Meanings for Manhood: Constructions of Masculinity in Victorian America* (Chicago: University of Chicago Press, 1990), p. 7.

21. See T. J. Jackson Lears, "The Concept of Cultural Hegemony: Problems and Possibilities," *American Historical Review* 90 (June 1985): 577.

22. Ibid, p. 570.

23. Betty Friedan, *The Feminine Mystique,* 20th anniversary edition (New York: W. W. Norton & Co., Inc., 1983), p. 18.

24. Waller, *Popular Women's Magazines,* pp. 1–3.

25. Friedan, *The Feminine Mystique,* p. 37.

26. Naomi Wolf, *The Beauty Myth: How Images of Beauty are Used Against Women* (New York: Anchor Books, 1992), p. 184.

27. See Peiss, "Making Faces," pp. 143–169.

28. Wolf, *The Beauty Myth,* p. 70.

29. Ibid, p. 58.

30. On women's double vision and its value, see Rachel T. Hare-Mustin and Jeanne Marecek, *Making a Difference: Psychology and the Construction of Gender* (New Haven: Yale University Press, 1990), p. 187. On boys' limited range of reading which parallels men's see Elizabeth Segel, " 'As the Twig is Bent . . .': Gender and Childhood Reading," in Elizabeth A. Flynn and Patrocinio P. Schweickart, *Gender and Reading:*

Essays on Readers, Texts, and Contexts (Baltimore: Johns Hopkins University Press, 1986), pp. 165–186; and Kimberly Reynolds, *Girls Only? Gender and Popular Children's Fiction in Britain, 1880–1910* (Philadelphia: Temple University Press, 1990), pp. xv–xxi, 51–61. On male domination as it is nurtured by the media, see Steve Craig, ed., *Men, Masculinity, and the Media* (Newbury Park, Cal.: SAGE Pubs., 1992), p. 3.

31. Gloria Steinem, "Sex, Lies & Advertising," *Ms.* (July/August 1990): 18–28, p. 19.

32. Ibid.

33. Ibid, p. 20.

34. Ibid, p. 25.

35. Lydia Denworth, "Sisterhood is Profitable," *Newsweek* (August 26, 1991): 60.

36. See Steinem, "Sex, Lies & Advertising," and Wolf, *The Beauty Myth,* pp. 77–84.

37. Sandra Bem, *The Lenses of Gender: Transforming the Debate on Sexual Inequality* (New Haven: Yale University Press, 1993), p. 152.

38. Schudson, "The New Validation," p. 66.

39. On bringing texts like soap operas and romance novels into the classroom, see Gilbert and Taylor, *Fashioning the Feminine,* especially the Introduction.

40. Lorraine Gamman and Margaret Marshment, *The Female Gaze: Women as Viewers of Popular Culture* (Seattle: The Real Comet Press, 1989), p. 4.

41. Bem, *The Lenses of Gender,* chapter 5, especially p. 153.

42. Ibid, pp. 140–141.

BIBLIOGRAPHY

BOOKS

Abelson, Elaine S. *When Ladies Go A-Thieving: Middle Class Shoplifters in the Victorian Department Store.* New York: Oxford University Press, 1989.

Anthony, Edward. *This is Where I Come In.* Garden City, New York: Doubleday, 1960.

Aron, Cindy Sondik. *Ladies and Gentlemen of the Civil Service: Middle-Class Workers in Victorian America.* New York: Oxford University Press, 1987.

Atwan, Robert. *American Mass Media: Industries and Issues.* 2d ed. New York: Random House, 1982.

Atwan, Robert, Donald McQuade, and John W. Wright. *Edsels, Luckies, and Frigidaires: Advertising the American Way.* New York: Dell Publishing Co., 1979.

Bagdikian, Ben H. *The Media Monopoly.* 3d ed. Boston: Beacon Press, 1990.

Banner, Lois W. *American Beauty.* New York: Alfred A. Knopf, 1983.

———. *Women in Modern America: A Brief History.* 2d ed. New York: Harcourt Brace Jovanovich, 1984.

Baron, Ava, ed. *Work Engendered: Toward a New History of American Labor.* Ithaca: Cornell University Press, 1991.

Bateson, Mary Catherine. *Composing A Life.* New York: The Atlantic Monthly Press, 1989.

Baughman, James L. *Henry R. Luce and the Rise of the American News Media.* Boston: Twayne, 1987.

Bem, Sandra Lipsitz. *The Lenses of Gender: Transforming the Debate on Sexual Inequality.* New Haven: Yale University Press, 1993.

Benson, Susan Porter. *Counter Cultures: Saleswomen, Managers, and Customers in American Department Stores, 1880–1940.* Urbana: University of Illinois Press, 1986.

Berger, Peter, and Thomas Luckmann. *The Social Construction of Reality.* Garden City, New York: Doubleday, 1966.

Bernard, Jessie. *The Female World*. New York: MacMillan Publishing Co., Inc., 1981.

———. *The Future of Marriage*. New York: The World Publishing Company, 1972.

Berry, Mary Frances. *The Politics of Parenthood: Child Care, Women's Rights, and the Myth of the Good Mother*. New York: Viking, 1993.

Bird, S. Elizabeth. *For Enquiring Minds: A Cultural Study of Supermarket Tabloids*. Knoxville: University of Tennessee Press, 1992.

Birken, Lawrence. *Consuming Desire: Sexual Science and the Emergence of a Culture of Abundance, 1871–1914*. Ithaca: Cornell University Press, 1988.

Blair, Karen J. *The Clubwoman as Feminist: True Womanhood Redefined, 1868–1914*. New York: Holmes & Meier, 1980.

Blair, Walter, and Hamlin Hill. *America's Humor From Poor Richard to Doonesbury*. New York: Oxford University Press, 1978.

Bledstein, Burton J. *The Culture of Professionalism: The Middle Class and the Development of Higher Education in America*. New York: Norton Press, 1976.

Bloomfield, Maxwell. *Alarm and Diversion: The American Mind Through American Magazines, 1900–1914*. New York: Basic Books, 1967.

Bok, Edward. *The Americanization of Edward Bok: The Autobiography of a Dutch Boy Fifty Years Later*. New York: Charles Scribner's Sons, 1923.

———. *Dollars Only*. New York: Charles Scribner's Sons, 1926.

———. *A Man From Maine*. New York: Charles Scribner's Sons, 1923.

———. *Successward: A Young Man's Book for Young Men*. New York: Fleming H. Revell Co., 1896.

———. *Twice Thirty: Some Short and Simple Annals of the Road*. New York: Charles Scribner's Sons, 1925.

———. *Why I Believe in Poverty as the Richest Experience That Can Come to a Boy*. New York: Houghton Mifflin, 1915.

Boydston, Jeanne. *Home and Work: Housework, Wages, and the Ideology of Labor in the Early Republic*. New York: Oxford University Press, 1990.

Boyer, Paul. *Purity in Print: The Vice-Society Movement and Book Censorship in America*. New York: Charles Scribner's Sons, 1968.

———. *Urban Masses and Moral Order in America, 1820–1920*. Cambridge: Harvard University Press, 1978.

Branca, Patricia. *Silent Sisterhood: Middle Class Women in the Victorian Home*. London: Croom Helm, 1975.

Brantlinger, Patrick. *Bread and Circuses: Theories of Mass Culture as Social Decay.* Ithaca: Cornell University Press, 1983.

Brenton, Myron. *The American Male.* Greenwich, Conn.: Fawcett Pubs., 1966.

Britain, Arthur. *Masculinity and Power.* New York: Basic Blackwell, 1989.

Brod, Harry, ed. *The Making of Masculinities: The New Men's Studies.* Winchester, Mass.: Allen & Unwin, Inc., 1987.

Brown, Bruce W. *Images of Family Life in Magazine Advertising, 1920–1978.* New York: Praeger Publishers, 1981.

Brown, Lyn Mikel, and Carol Gilligan. *Meeting at the Crossroads: Women's Psychology and Girls' Development.* Cambridge: Harvard University Press, 1992.

Burdette, Clara, ed. *Robert J. Burdette: His Message.* Pasadena, Cal.: The Clara Vista Press, 1922.

Burstyn, Joan. *Victorian Education and the Ideal of Womanhood.* London: Croom Helm, 1980.

Butler, Judith. *Gender Trouble: Feminism and the Subversion of Identity.* New York: Routledge, 1990.

Cancian, Francesca M. *Love in America: Gender and Self-Development.* New York: Cambridge University Press, 1987.

Carnes, Mark, and Clyde Griffen, eds. *Meanings for Manhood: Constructions of Masculinity in Victorian America.* Chicago: University of Chicago Press, 1990.

Carroll, Berenice. *Liberating Women's History.* Urbana: University of Illinois Press, 1976.

Cawelti, John. *Apostles of the Self-Made Man: Changing Concepts of Success in America.* Chicago: University of Chicago Press, 1965.

Chafe, William. *The American Woman: Her Changing Social, Economic, and Political Roles, 1920–1970.* New York: Oxford University Press, 1972.

———. *Women and Equality: Changing Patterns in American Culture.* New York: Oxford University Press, 1977.

Chandler, Alfred D. *The Visible Hand: The Managerial Revolution in American Business.* Cambridge: Harvard University Press, 1977.

Chase, Edna Woolman. *Always in Vogue.* Garden City, New York: Doubleday & Co., Inc., 1954.

Chenoweth, Lawrence. *The American Dream of Success: The Search for the Self in the Twentieth Century.* N. Scituate, Mass.: Duxbury Press, 1974.

Chodorow, Nancy. *The Reproduction of Mothering: Psychoanalysis and the Sociology of Gender.* Berkeley: University of California Press, 1978.

Christian-Smith, Linda K. *Becoming a Woman Through Romance.* New York: Routledge, 1990.

Clifford, Edward Clark, Jr. *The American Family Home, 1800–1960.* Chapel Hill: University of North Carolina Press, 1986.

Clinton, Catherine. *The Other Civil War: American Women in the Nineteenth Century.* New York: Hill and Wang, 1984.

Cogan, Frances B. *All-American Girl: The Ideal of Real Womanhood in Mid-Nineteenth Century America.* Athens: University of Georgia Press, 1989.

Cohn, Jan. *Creating America: George Horace Lorimer and the Saturday Evening Post.* Pittsburgh: University of Pittsburgh Press, 1989.

Cott, Nancy F. *The Bonds of Womanhood: "Woman's Sphere" in New England, 1780–1835.* New Haven: Yale University Press, 1977.

———. *The Grounding of Modern Feminism.* New Haven: Yale University Press, 1987.

———. *A Woman Making History: Mary Ritter Beard Through Her Letters.* New Haven: Yale University Press, 1991.

Covert, Catherine L., and John D. Stearns, eds. *Mass Media Between the Wars: Perceptions of Cultural Tension, 1918–1941.* Syracuse: Syracuse University Press, 1984.

Cowan, Ruth Schwartz. *More Work for Mother: The Ironies of Household Technology from the Open Hearth to the Microwave.* New York: Basic Books, Inc., 1983.

Craig, Steve, ed. *Men, Masculinity, and the Media.* Newbury Park, Califorina: SAGE Pubs., 1992.

Curtis Publishing Company. *Selling Forces.* Philadelphia, 1913.

Darnton, Robert. *The Kiss of Lamourette: Reflections in Cultural History.* New York: W. W. Norton, 1990.

Davenport, Walter, and James C. Derieux. *Ladies, Gentlemen and Editors.* New York: Doubleday and Co., Inc., 1960.

Davidson, Cathy N. *Reading in America: Literature and Social History.* Baltimore: Johns Hopkins University Press, 1989.

Degler, Carl N. *"At Odds": Women and the Family from the Revolution to the Present.* New York: Oxford University Press, 1989.

D'Emilio, John, and Estelle B. Freedman. *Intimate Matters: A History of Sexuality in America.* New York: Harper & Row, Pubs., 1988.

Diebold, Elizabeth, Marie Wilson, and Idelisse Malavé. *Mother Daughter Revolution: From Betrayal to Power.* Reading, Mass.: Addison Wesley, 1993.

Douglas, Ann. *The Feminization of American Culture.* New York: Alfred A. Knopf, 1977.

Drewry, John E. *Some Magazines and Magazine Makers.* Boston: The Stratford Co., 1924.

Dubbert, Joe. *A Man's Place: Masculinity in Transition.* Englewood Cliffs, New Jersey: Prentice-Hall, Inc., 1979.

DuBois, Ellen Carol. *Feminism and Suffrage: The Emergence of an Independent Women's Movement in America, 1848–1869.* Ithaca: Cornell University Press, 1978.

———. *Feminist Scholarship: Kindling in the Groves of Academe.* Urbana: University of Illinois Press, 1985.

Dudden, Faye. *Serving Women: Household Service in Nineteenth-Century America.* Middletown, Conn.: Wesleyan University Press, 1983.

Dye, Judith Levitt. *For the Instruction and Amusement of Women: The Growth, Development and Definition of American Magazines for Women, 1780–1840.* University of Pennsylvania Dissertation, 1974.

Ehrenreich, Barbara. *The Hearts of Men: American Dreams and the Flight from Commitment.* Garden City, New York: Anchor Books, 1983.

Ehrenreich, Barbara, and Deirdre English. *For Her Own Good: 150 Years of the Experts' Advice to Women.* New York: Anchor Books, 1979.

Ellis, Leonard. *Men Among Men: An Exploration of All-Male Relationships in Victorian America.* Ph.D. Dissertation, Columbia University, 1982.

Elshtain, Jean Bethke. *Public Man, Private Woman: Women in Social and Political Thought.* Oxford: Martin Robertson, 1981.

Entrikin, Isabelle Webb. *Sarah Josepha Hale and Godey's Lady's Book.* Lancaster, Penn.: Lancaster Press, 1946.

Epstein, Barbara Leslie. *The Politics of Domesticity: Women, Evangelism and Temperance in Nineteenth-Century America.* Middletown, Conn.: Wesleyan University Press, 1981.

Epstein, Cynthia Fuchs. *Deceptive Distinctions: Sex, Gender and the Social Order.* New Haven: Yale University Press, 1988.

Erenberg, Lewis. *Steppin' Out: New York Nightlife and the Transformation of American Culture, 1890–1930.* Westport, Conn.: Greenwood Press, 1981.

Evans, Sarah. *Liberty's Daughters.* New York: The Free Press, 1989.

Ewen, Stuart. *Captains of Consciousness: Advertising and the Social Roots of the Consumer Culture.* New York: McGraw Hill, 1976.

Ewen, Stuart and Elizabeth. *Channels of Desire: Mass Images and the Shaping of American Consciousness.* New York: McGraw Hill, 1982.

Faludi, Susan. *Backlash: The Undeclared War Against American Women.* New York: Crown, 1991.

Faragher, John Mack. *Women and Men on the Overland Trail.* New Haven: Yale University Press, 1979.

Farrar, R. T., and J. D. Stevens. *Mass Media and the National Experience.* New York: Harper & Row, 1971.

Ferguson, Marjorie. *Forever Feminine: Women's Magazines and the Cult of Femininity.* Exeter, New Hampshire: Heinemann Educational Books, 1983.

Filene, Peter Gabriel. *Him/Her/Self: Sex Roles in Modern America.* New York: Harcourt Brace Jovanovich, 1974.

Fish, Stanley. *Is There a Text in the Class? The Authority of Interpretive Communities.* Cambridge: Harvard University Press, 1980.

Fishburn, Katherine. *Women in Popular Culture: A Reference Guide.* Westport, Conn.: Greenwood Press, 1982.

Flexner, Eleanor. *Century of Struggle: The Woman's Rights Movement in the U.S.* Cambridge: Harvard University Press, 1975.

Flynn, Elizabeth A., and Patrocinio P. Schweickart, eds. *Gender and Reading: Essays on Readers, Texts, and Contexts.* Baltimore: Johns Hopkins University Press, 1986.

Fox, Richard Wightman, and T. J. Jackson Lears, eds. *The Culture of Consumption: Critical Essays in American History, 1880–1980.* New York: Pantheon Books, 1983.

Fox, Stephen. *The Mirror Makers: A History of American Advertising and Its Creators.* New York: William Morrow & Co., 1984.

Frankel, Noralee, and Nancy S. Dye. *Gender, Class, Race, and Reform in the Progressive Era.* Lexington: The University Press of Kentucky, 1991.

Frankfort, Roberta. *Collegiate Women: Domesticity and Career in Turn-of-the-Century America.* New York: New York University Press, 1977.

Frederick, Christine. *Selling Mrs. Consumer.* New York: The Business Bourse, 1929.

Friedan, Betty. *The Feminine Mystique.* New York: W. W. Norton & Co., 1963.

Fuller, Walter D. *The Life and Times of Cyrus H. K. Curtis (1850–1933).* New York: The Newcomen Society of England, American Branch, 1948.

Geertz, Clifford. *The Interpretation of Cultures.* New York: Basic Books, 1973.

Gerzon, Mark. *A Choice of Heroes: The Changing Faces of American Manhood.* Boston: Houghton Mifflin, 1982.

Gilbert, Pam, and Sandra Taylor. *Fashioning the Feminine: Girls, Popular Culture and Schooling.* Australia: Allen & Unwin Pty Ltd, 1991.

Gilligan, Carol. *In a Different Voice: Psychological Theory and Women's Development.* Cambridge: Harvard University Press, 1982.

Gilligan, Carol, Janie Victoria Ward, and Jill McLean Taylor, eds. *Mapping the Moral Domain: A Contribution of Women's Thinking to Psychological Theory and Education.* Cambridge: Harvard University Press, 1988.

Gilman, Charlotte Perkins. *Women and Economics.* New York: Harper & Row Publishers, 1966.

Gilmore, David D. *Manhood in the Making: Cultural Concepts of Masculinity.* New Haven: Yale University Press, 1990.

Gilmore, William J. *Reading Becomes a Necessity of Life: Material and Cultural Life in Rural New England, 1780–1835.* Knoxville: University of Tennessee, 1989.

Gingrich, Arnold. *Nothing But People.* New York: Crown, 1971.

Ginzberg, Lori D. *Women and the Work of Benevolence: Morality, Politics, and Class in the Nineteenth Century U.S.* New Haven: Yale University Press, 1990.

Glazer, Penina, and Miriam Slater. *Unequal Colleagues: The Entrance of Women Into the Professions, 1890–1940.* New Brunswick, New Jersey: Rutgers University Press, 1987.

Goffman, Erving. *Gender Advertisements.* Cambridge: Harvard University Press, 1979.

Goldin, Claudia Dale. *Understanding the Gender Gap: An Economic History of American Women.* New York: Oxford University Press, 1990.

Gordon, Linda. *Woman's Body, Woman's Right: Birth Control in America.* New York: Grossman Publications, 1976.

———. *Heroes of Their Own Lives: The Politics and History of Family Violence.* New York: Penguin Books, 1989.

Gordon, Michael, ed. *The American Family in Social-Historical Perspective.* New York: St. Martin's Press, 1973.

Gordon, Suzanne. *Prisoners of Men's Dreams: Striking Out for a New Feminine Future.* Boston: Little, Brown and Company, 1991.

Goulart, Ron. *The Assault on Childhood.* London: Victor Collancz, Ltd., 1970.

Goulden, Joseph C. *The Curtis Caper.* New York: Putnam, 1965.

Green, Harvey, with Mary-Ellen Perry. *The Light of the Home: An Intimate View of the Lives of Women in Victorian America.* New York: Pantheon Books, 1983.

Green, Martin. *The Great American Adventure.* Boston: Beacon Press, 1984.

Greene, Theodore. *American Heroes: The Changing Models of Success in American Magazines.* New York: Oxford University Press, 1970.

Griffith, Sally Foreman. *Home Town News: William Allen White and the Emporia Gazette.* New York: Oxford University Press, 1989.

Grossberg, Michael. *Governing the Hearth: Law and the Family in Nineteenth-Century America.* Chapel Hill: University of North Carolina Press, 1985.

Gutman, Herbert J. *Work, Culture and Society in Industrialized America.* New York: Vintage, 1977.

Habegger, Alfred. *Gender, Fantasy and Realism in American Literature.* New York: Columbia University Press, 1982.

Hagan, Kay Leigh, ed. *Women Respond to the Men's Movement: A Feminist Collection.* San Francisco: Pandora, 1992.

Halttunen, Karen J. *Confidence Men and Painted Women: A Study of Middle-Class Culture in America, 1830–1870.* New Haven: Yale University Press, 1982.

Hare-Mustin, Rachel T., and Jeanne Marecek. *Making a Difference: Psychology and the Construction of Gender.* New Haven: Yale University Press, 1990.

Harris, Barbara J. *Beyond Her Sphere: Women and the Professions in American History.* Contributions in Women's Studies, No: 4. Westport, Conn.: Greenwood Press, 1978.

Hart, James D. *The Popular Book: A History of America's Literary Taste.* New York: Oxford University Press, 1950.

Hayden, Dolores. *Redesigning the American Dream: The Future of Housing, Work, and Family Life.* New York: W. W. Norton, 1984.

Helly, Dorothy O., and Susan M. Reverby, eds. *Gendered Domains: Rethinking Public and Private in Women's History.* Ithaca: Cornell University Press, 1992.

Higham, John, and Paul Conklin. *New Directions in American Intellectual History.* Baltimore: Johns Hopkins University Press, 1979.

Hochschild, Arlie. *The Second Shift: Working Parents and the Revolution at Home.* New York: Avon Books, 1989.

Hoggart, Richard. *The Uses of Literacy.* London: Chatto and Windus, 1957.

Honey, Maureen. *Breaking the Ties that Bind: Popular Stories of the New Woman, 1915–1930.* Norman: University of Oklahoma Press, 1992.

――――. *Creating Rosie the Riveter: Class, Gender, and Propaganda During World War II.* Amherst: University of Massachusetts Press, 1984.

Horowitz, Daniel. *The Morality of Spending: Attitudes Toward the Consumer Society in America, 1875–1940.* Baltimore: Johns Hopkins University Press, 1985.

Hower, Ralph M. *The History of an Advertising Agency, N. W. Ayer & Son at Work, 1869–1949.* Cambridge: Harvard University Press, 1949.

Hudson, Liam, and Bernardine Jacot. *The Way Men Think: Intellect, Intimacy and the Erotic Imagination.* New Haven: Yale University Press, 1991.

Hummel, Michael Dennis. *The Attitudes of Edward Bok and the 'Ladies' Home Journal' Toward Women's Roles in Society, 1889–1919.* North Texas State University Dissertation, 1952.

Jackson, Kenneth T. *The Crabgrass Frontier.* New York: Oxford University Press, 1985.

Janeway, Elizabeth. *Man's World, Woman's Place: A Study in Social Mythology.* New York: William Morrow and Co., 1971.

Kaestle, Carl F. *Pillars of the Republic: Common Schools and American Society, 1780–1860.* New York: Hill and Wang, 1983.

Kaestle, Carl F., and Maris A. Vinovskis. *Education and Social Change in Nineteenth-Century Massachusetts.* New York: Cambridge University Press, 1980.

Kaestle, Carl F., Helen Damon-Moore, Lawrence C. Stedman, Katherine Tinsley, and William Vance Trollinger, Jr. *Literacy in the United States: Readers and Reading Since 1880.* New Haven: Yale University Press, 1991.

Kaschak, Ellyn. *Engendered Lives: A New Psychology of Women's Experience.* New York: Basic Books, 1992.

Kelley, Mary. *Private Woman, Public Stage: Literary Domesticity in Nineteenth-Century America.* New York: Oxford University Press, 1984.

Kelly, Joan. *Women, History and Theory.* Chicago: University of Chicago Press, 1984.

Kelly, R. Gordon. *Mother Was a Lady: Self and Society in Selected American Children's Periodicals, 1865–1890.* Westport, Conn.: Greenwood Press, 1974.

Kerber, Linda K. *Women of the Republic: Intellect and Ideology in Revolutionary America.* Chapel Hill: University of North Carolina Press, 1980.

Kessler-Harris, Alice. *Out to Work: A History of Wage-Earning Women in America.* New York: Oxford University Press, 1982.

――――. *A Woman's Wage: Historical Meanings and Social Consequences.* Lexington: The University Press of Kentucky, 1990.

Kimmel, Michael S., ed. *Changing Men: New Directions in Research on Men and Masculinity*. Newbury Park, Cal.: SAGE Pubs., 1987.

Lamont, Helen Otis, ed. *A Diamond of Years: The Best of the "Woman's Home Companion."* Garden City, New York: Doubleday, 1961.

Lane, Ann J. *Mary Ritter Beard: A Sourcebook*. New York: Schocken Books, 1977.

―――. *To Herland and Beyond: The Life and Work of Charlotte Perkins Gilman*. New York: Pantheon Books, 1990.

Leach, William. *Land of Desire: Merchants, Power, and the Rise of a New America*. New York: Pantheon Books, 1993.

Lears, T. J. Jackson. *No Place of Grace: Antimodernism and the Transformation of American Culture*. New York: Pantheon Books, 1981.

Lerner, Gerda. *The Creation of Feminist Consciousness from the Middle Ages to 1870*. New York: Oxford University Press, 1993.

―――. *The Creation of Patriarchy*. New York: Oxford University Press, 1986.

―――. *The Majority Finds Its Past: Placing Women in History*. New York: Oxford University Press, 1979.

Lewis, Jane, ed. *Labour and Love: Women's Experience of Home and Family, 1850–1940*. Oxford: Basil Blackwell Ltd., 1986.

Lystra, Karen. *Searching the Heart: Women, Men, and Romantic Love in Nineteenth-Century America*. New York: Oxford University Press, 1989.

Macleod, David I. *Building Character in the American Boy: The Boy Scouts, YMCA, and Their Forerunners, 1870–1920*. Madison: University of Wisconsin Press, 1983.

Mallon, Isabel. *The Business Girl in Every Phase of Her Life*. Philadelphia: Curtis Publishing Co., 1898.

Marchand, Roland. *Advertising the American Dream: Making Way for Modernity, 1920–1940*. Berkeley: University of California Press, 1985.

Margolis, Maxine. *Mothers and Such: Views of American Women and Why They Changed*. Berkeley: University of California Press, 1984.

Marsh, Margaret. *Suburban Lives*. New York: Rutgers University Press, 1990.

Martin, Theodora Penny. *The Sound of Our Own Voices: Women's Study Clubs, 1860–1910*. Boston: Beacon Press, 1987.

Matthaei, Julie A. *An Economic History of Women in America: Women's Work, the Sexual Division of Labor, and the Development of Capitalism*. New York: Schocken Books, 1982.

Matthews, Glenna. *"Just a Housewife": The Rise and Fall of Domesticity in America.* New York: Oxford University Press, 1987.

———. *The Rise of Public Woman: Woman's Power and Woman's Place in the United States, 1630–1970.* New York: Oxford University Press, 1992.

May, Elaine Tyler. *Great Expectations: Marriage and Divorce in Post-Victorian America.* Chicago: University of Chicago Press, 1980.

Miller, Jane. *Seductions: Studies in Reading and Culture.* Cambridge: Harvard University Press, 1991.

———. *Women Writing About Men.* New York: Pantheon Books, 1986.

Millman, Marcia. *Warm Hearts and Cold Cash: The Intimate Dynamics of Families and Money.* New York: Free Press, 1991.

Mitchell, Juliet, and Ann Oakley. *What is Feminism? A Re-Examination.* New York: Pantheon Books, 1986.

Mott, Frank Luther. *A History of American Magazines, 1885–1905.* Cambridge: Harvard University Press, 1957.

Motz, Marilyn Ferris. *True Sisterhood: Michigan Women and Their Kin, 1820–1920.* Albany: SUNY Press, 1983.

Naether, Carl A. *Advertising to Women.* New York: MacMillan Pub. Co., 1928.

Newton, Judith, and Deborah Rosenfelt, eds. *Feminist Criticism and Social Change.* New York: Methuen, 1985.

Nicholson, Linda J. *Gender and History: The Limits of Social Theory in the Age of the Family.* New York: Columbia University Press, 1986.

O'Neill, William. *Divorce in the Progressive Era.* New Haven: Yale University Press, 1967.

Ortner, Sherry B., and Harriet Whitehead, eds. *Sexual Meanings: The Cultural Construction of Gender and Sexuality.* New York: Cambridge University Press, 1981.

Ownby, Ted. *Subduing Satan: Religion, Recreation, and Manhood in the Rural South, 1865–1920.* Chapel Hill: University of North Carolina Press, 1990.

Paine, Fred K., and Nancy E. Paine. *Magazines: A Bibliography For Their Analysis, with Annotations and Study Guide.* Metchuen, New Jersey: Scarecrow Press, 1987.

Palmer, Bryan D. *Descent Into Discourse: The Reification of Language and the Writing of Social History.* Philadelphia: Temple University Press, 1990.

Papashvily, Helen Waite. *All the Happy Endings: A Study of the Domestic Novel in America, the Women Who Wrote It, the Women Who Read It, in the Nineteenth Century.* New York: Harper and Row, 1956.

Peiss, Kathy. *Cheap Amusements: Working Women and Leisure in Turn-of-the-Century New York.* Philadelphia: Temple University Press, 1986.

Peterson, Theodore. *Magazines in the Twentieth Century.* Urbana: University of Illinois Press, 1964.

Pleck, Joseph and Elizabeth. *The American Man.* Englewood Cliffs, New Jersey: Prentice-Hall, Inc., 1980.

Pope, Daniel. *The Making of Modern Advertising.* New York: Basic Books, 1983.

Presbey, Frank. *The History and Development of Advertising.* Garden City, New York: Doubleday & Co. Inc., 1929.

Pugh, David G. *Sons of Liberty: The Masculine Mind in Nineteenth-Century America.* Westport, Conn.: Greenwood Press, 1983.

Radway, Janice A. *Reading the Romance: Women, Patriarchy, and Popular Literature.* Chapel Hill: University of North Carolina Press, 1984.

Raphael, Ray. *The Men From the Boys: Rites of Passage in Male America.* Lincoln: University of Nebraska Press, 1988.

Reynolds, Kimberley. *Girls Only? Gender and Popular Children's Fiction in Britain, 1880–1910.* Philadelphia: Temple University Press, 1990.

Rhode, Deborah L., ed. *Theoretical Perspectives on Sexual Difference.* New Haven: Yale University Press, 1990.

Riley, Denise. *"Am I That Name?" Feminism and the Category of 'Women' in History.* Minneapolis: University of Minnesota Press, 1988.

Rodgers, Daniel T. *The Work Ethic in Industrial America, 1850–1920.* Chicago: University of Chicago Press, 1978.

Roman, Leslie, and Linda Christian-Smith, eds. *Becoming Feminine: The Politics of Popular Culture.* London: The Falmer Press, 1988.

Roosevelt, Theodore. *The Strenuous Life: Essays and Addresses.* New York: The Century Co., 1900.

Rosaldo, Michelle, and Louise Lamphere. *Woman, Culture, and Society.* Stanford: Stanford University Press, 1974.

Rose, Phyllis. *Parallel Lives: Five Victorian Marriages.* New York: Random House, 1983.

Rosenberg, Rosalind. *Beyond Separate Spheres: The Intellectual Roots of Modern Feminism.* New Haven: Yale University Press, 1982.

———. *Divided Lives: American Women in the Twentieth Century.* New York: Hill and Wang, 1992.

Rosenzweig, Linda W. *The Anchor of My Life: Middle-Class American Mothers and Daughters, 1880–1920.* New York: New York University Press, 1993.

Ross, Ishbel. *Crusades and Crinolines: The Life and Times of Ellen Curtis Demorest and William Jennings Demorest.* New York: Harper & Row, 1963.

Rothman, Ellen K. *Hands and Hearts: A History of Courtship in America.* New York: Basic Books, 1984.

Rothman, Sheila M. *Woman's Proper Place: A History of Changing Ideals and Practices, 1870 to the Present.* New York: Basic Books, 1978.

Rotundo, E. Anthony. *American Manhood: Transformations in Masculinity From the Revolution to the Modern Era.* New York: Basic Books, 1993.

Rourke, Constance. *American Humor: A Study of the National Character.* Garden City, New York: Doubleday & Co., Inc., 1931.

Rowbotham, Judith. *Good Girls Make Good Wives: Guidance For Girls in Victorian Fiction.* New York: Basil Blackwell, 1989.

Rowell, George P. *Forty Years an Advertising Agent.* New York: MacMillan Pub. Co., 1906.

Rubin, Lillian. *Intimate Strangers: Men and Women Together.* New York: Harper & Row, 1983.

Russett, Cynthia Eagle. *Sexual Science: The Victorian Construction of Womanhood.* Cambridge: Harvard University Press, 1989.

Ryan, Mary P. *Cradle of the Middle Class: The Family in Oneida County, New York, 1790–1865.* New York: Cambridge University Press, 1981.

———. *Womanhood in America: From Colonial Times to the Present.* New York: Franklin Watts, Inc., 1975.

———. *Women in Public: Between Banners and Ballots, 1825–1880.* New York: Cambridge University Press, 1992.

Sanborn, Kate. *Our Famous Women.* Hartford, Conn.: A. D. Worthington & Co., 1886.

Scharf, Lois. *To Work and To Wed: Female Employment, Feminism and the Great Depression.* Westport, Conn.: Greenwood Press, 1980.

Schiller, Dan. *Objectivity and the News: The Public and the Rise of Commercial Journalism.* Philadelphia: University of Pennsylvania Press, 1981.

Schudson, Michael. *Advertising, The Uneasy Persuasion: Its Dubious Impact on American Society.* New York: Basic Books, 1984.

———. *Discovering the News: A Social History of American Newspapers.* New York: Basic Books, 1978.

Scott, Anne Firor. *The Southern Lady: From Pedestal to Politics, 1830–1930.* Chicago: University of Chicago Press, 1970.

———. *Natural Allies: Women's Associations in American History.* Urbana: University of Illinois Press, 1991.

Scott, Joan W. *Gender and the Politics of History.* New York: Columbia University Press, 1988.

Scott, Joan W., and Louise Tilly. *Women, Work and Family.* New York: Oxford University Press, 1978.

Segal, Lynn. *Slow Motion: Changing Masculinities, Changing Men.* New Brunswick, New Jersey: Rutgers University Press, 1990.

Shevelow, Kathryn. *Women and Print Culture: The Construction of Femininity in the Early Periodical.* London: Routledge, 1989.

Shi, David E. *The Simple Life: Plain Living and High Thinking in American Culture.* New York: Oxford University Press, 1985.

Shiach, Morag. *Discourse on Popular Culture: Class, Gender, and History in Cultural Analysis, 1730 to the Present.* Stanford: Stanford University Press, 1989.

Shorter, Edward. *The Making of the Modern Family.* New York: Basic Books, 1975.

Sklar, Kathryn Kish. *Catharine Beecher: A Study in American Domesticity.* New York: W. W. Norton & Co., 1973.

Spain, Daphne. *Gendered Spaces.* Chapel Hill: University of North Carolina Press, 1992.

Spindler, Michael. *American Literature and Social Change: William Dean Howells to Arthur Miller.* Bloomington: Indiana University Press, 1985.

Stage, Sarah. *Female Complaints: Lydia Pinkham and the Business of Women's Medicine.* New York: W. W. Norton & Co., 1979.

Stansell, Christine. *City Of Women: Sex and Class in New York, 1789–1860.* Urbana: University of Illinois Press, 1987.

Stearns, Peter N. *Be a Man! Males in Modern Society.* New York: Holmes & Meier Pubs., Inc., 1979.

Steinberg, Salme Harju. *Reformer in the Marketplace: Edward W. Bok and The Ladies' Home Journal.* Baton Rouge, La.: Louisiana State University Press, 1979.

Strasser, Susan. *Never Done: A History of American Housework.* New York: Pantheon Books, 1982.

———. *Satisfaction Guaranteed: The Making of the American Mass Market.* New York: Pantheon Books, 1989.

Sullivan, Mark. *The Education of an American.* New York: Doubleday, Doran & Co., Inc., 1938.

Sutherland, Daniel E. *Americans and Their Servants: Domestic Service in the U.S., 1880–1920.* Baton Rouge, La.: Louisiana State University Press, 1981.

Tavris, Carol. *The MisMeasure of Woman: Why Women Are Not the Better Sex, the Inferior Sex, or the Opposite Sex.* New York: Simon & Schuster, 1992.

Tavris, Carol, and Carole Offir. *The Longest War: Sex Differences in Perspective.* New York: Harcourt Brace Jovanovich, 1977.

Tebbel, John. *George Horace Lorimer and the Saturday Evening Post.* Garden City, New York: Doubleday & Co., Inc., 1948.

———. *The Media in America.* New York: Thomas Y. Cromwell, 1974.

Tebbel, John, and Mary Ellen Waller-Zuckerman. *The Magazine in America, 1741–1990.* New York: Oxford University Press, 1991.

Terhune, Mary Virginia [Marion Harland]. *Marion Harland's Autobiography: The Story of a Long Life.* New York: Harper & Bros., 1910.

Theriot, Nancy M. *The Biosocial Construction of Femininity: Mothers and Daughters in Nineteenth-Century America.* Westport, Conn.: Greenwood Press, 1988.

Thurston, Carol. *The Romance Revolution: Erotic Novels for Women and the Quest for a New Sexual Identity.* Urbana: University of Illinois Press, 1987.

Tompkins, Jane P., ed. *Reader-Response Criticism: From Formalism to Post-Structuralism.* Baltimore: Johns Hopkins University Press, 1980.

Trachtenberg, Alan. *The Incorporation of America: Culture and Society in the Gilded Age.* New York: Hill & Wang, 1982.

Tuchman, Gaye, Arlene K. Daniels, and James Benet, eds. *Hearth and Home: Images of Women in the Mass Media.* New York: Oxford University Press, 1978.

Walker, Nancy A. *A Very Serious Thing: Women's Humor and American Culture.* Minneapolis: University of Minnesota Press, 1988.

Waller (Zuckerman), Mary Ellen. *Popular Women's Magazines, 1890–1917.* Columbia University Dissertation, 1987.

Waring, Marilyn. *If Women Counted: A New Feminist Economics.* New York: Harper & Row, 1988.

Weibel, Kathryn. *Mirror, Mirror: Images of Women Reflected in Popular Culture.* Garden City, New York: Doubleday Anchor Press, 1977.

Weiner, Lynn Y. *From Working Girl to Working Mother: The Female Labor Force in the United States, 1820–1980.* Chapel Hill: University of North Carolina Press, 1985.

Weiss, Richard. *The American Myth of Success: From Horatio Alger to Norman Vincent Peale.* Urbana: University of Illinois Press, 1988.

Wells, Robert V. *Revolutions in Americans' Lives: A Demographic Perspective on the History of Americans, Their Families and Their Society.* Westport, Conn.: Greenwood Press, 1982.

Weyr, Thomas. *Reaching for Paradise: The Playboy Vision of America.* New York: Times Books, 1978.

White, Cynthia L. *Women's Magazines, 1693–1968.* London: Michael Joseph, 1970.

Wiebe, Robert. *The Search for Order, 1877–1920.* New York: Hill & Wang, 1967.

———. *The Segmented Society: An Introduction to the Meaning of America.* New York: Oxford University Press, 1975.

Wilkinson, Rupert. *American Tough: The Tough-Guy Tradition and American Character.* New York: Harper & Row Publishers, 1986.

Williams, Raymond. *The Long Revolution.* New York: Columbia University Press, 1961.

Williams, Rosalind H. *Dream Worlds: Mass Consumption in Late Nineteenth-Century France.* Berkeley: University of California Press, 1982.

Williamson, Judith. *Consuming Passions: The Dynamics of Popular Culture.* New York: Marion Boyars, 1986.

Wilson, Christopher P. *The Labor of Words: Literary Professionalism in the Progressive Era.* Athens: University of Georgia Press, 1985.

Wilson, Margaret Gibbons. *The American Woman in Transition: The Urban Influence, 1870–1920.* Westport, Conn.: Greenwood Press, 1979.

Winship, Janice. *Inside Women's Magazines.* London: Pandora Press, 1987.

Wolf, Naomi. *The Beauty Myth: How Images of Beauty Are Used Against Women.* New York: Anchor Books, Doubleday, 1992.

Wolseley, Roland P. *The Changing Magazine: Trends in Readership and Management.* New York: Hastings House, Pub., 1973.

Wood, James P. *The Curtis Magazines.* New York: Ronald Press, 1971.

Woodward, Helen R. *The Lady Persuaders.* New York: Ivan Ohlensky, Inc., 1960.

———. *Through Many Windows.* New York: Harper & Bros., 1932.

Wyllie, Irvin G. *The Self-Made Man in America: The Myth of Rags to Riches.* New York: The Free Press, 1966.

Ziff, Larzer. *The American 1890s: Life and Times of a Lost Generation.* New York: Viking, 1966.

Zuilen, A. J. van. *The Life Cycle of Magazines: A Historical Study of the Decline and Fall of the General Interest Mass Audience Magazine in the U.S. During the Period 1946–1972.* The Netherlands, Ulthorn: Graduate Press, 1977.

ARTICLES

Allen, Frederick Lewis. "Fifty Years of Scribner's Magazine." *Scribner's* 191 (January 1937): 20–21.

Badaracco, Claire. "Alternatives to Newspaper Advertising, 1890–1920: Printers' Innovative Product and Message Designs." *Journalism Quarterly* 67 (Winter 1990): 1042–1050.

Baron, Ava. "The Masculinization of Production: The Gendering of Work and Skill in U.S. Newspaper Printing, 1850–1920." In Dorothy O. Helly and Susan M. Reverby, eds. *Gendered Domains: Rethinking Public and Private in Women's History.* Ithaca: Cornell University Press, 1992, pp. 277–288.

Barrett, Michele. "Ideology and the Cultural Production of Gender." In Judith Newton and Deborah Rosenfelt, eds. *Feminist Criticism and Social Change.* New York: Methuen, 1985.

Belknap, Penny, and Wilbert M. Leonard. "A Conceptual Replication and Extension of Erving Goffman's Study of Gender Advertisements." *Sex Roles* 25 (August 1991): 103–118.

Bloch, Ruth. "Untangling the Roots of Modern Sex Roles: A Survey of Four Centuries of Change." *Signs* 4 (1978): 237–252.

Blumin, Stuart M. "The Hypothesis of Middle-Class Formation in Nineteenth-Century America: A Critique and Some Proposals." *American Historical Review* 90 (April 1985): 299–338.

Bok, Mary Louise Curtis. "Louisa Knapp Curtis." In *Notable Women of Pennsylvania.* Philadelphia: Pennsylvania Publishing, 1952.

Boydston, Jeanne. "To Earn Her Daily Bread: Housework and Antebellum Working-Class Subsistence." *Radical History Review* 35 (1986): 7–25.

Boyer, Paul. "Sarah Josepha Hale." In *Notable American Women.* Vol. 2. Cambridge: The Belknap Press, 1971, pp. 110–114.

Butler-Flora, Cornelia. "The Passive Female: Her Comparative Image by Class and Culture in Women's Magazine Fiction." *Journal of Marriage and the Family* 33 (August 1971): 435–444.

Cancian, Francesca M., and Steven L. Gordon. "Changing Emotion Norms in Marriage: Love and Anger in U.S. Women's Magazines Since 1900." *Gender and Society* (September 1988): 308–342.

Cohn, William. "Popular Culture and Social History." *Journal of Popular Culture* 11 (Summer 1977): 167/29–179/41.

Curti, Merle. "The Changing Concept of 'Human Nature' in the Literature of American Advertising." *Business History Review* 41 (Winter 1967): 335–357.

Dalton, Kathleen. "Why America Loved Teddy Roosevelt, or, Charisma Is in the Eyes of the Beholders." In Robert Brugger, ed. *Ourselves/Our Past: Psychological Approaches to American History.* Baltimore: Johns Hopkins University Press, 1981.

Damon-Moore, Helen, and Carl F. Kaestle. "Gender, Advertising, and Mass-Circulation Magazines." In Carl F. Kaestle, Helen Damon-Moore, Lawrence C. Stedman, Katherine Tinsley, and William Vance Trollinger, Jr. *Literacy in the United States: Readers and Reading Since 1880.* New Haven: Yale University Press, 1991, pp. 245–271.

———. "Surveying American Readers." In Carl F. Kaestle, Helen Damon-Moore, Lawrence C. Stedman, Katherine Tinsley, and William Vance Trollinger, Jr. *Literacy in the United States: Readers and Reading Since 1880.* New Haven: Yale University Press, 1991, pp. 180–203.

Degler, Carl. "What Ought To Be and What Was: Women's Sexuality in the Nineteenth Century." *American Historical Review* 30 (December 1974): 1467–1490.

"Dialogue: Six (Or More) Feminists in Search of a Historian." *Journal of Women's History* 1 (Fall 1989): 134–146.

DuBois, Ellen, MariJo Buhle, Temma Kaplan, Gerda Lerner, and Carroll Smith-Rosenberg. Symposium—"Politics and Culture in Women's History: A Symposium." *Feminist Studies* 6 (Spring 1980).

Faderman, Lillian. "Lesbian Magazine Fiction in the Early Twentieth Century." *Journal of Popular Culture* (Spring 1978): 800–817.

Filene, Peter Gabriel. "In Time of War." In Elizabeth and Joseph Pleck, eds. *The American Man.* Englewood Cliffs, New Jersey: Prentice-Hall, 1980, pp. 321–335.

Folbre, Nancy. "The Unproductive Housewife: Her Evolution in Nineteenth-Century Economic Thought." *Signs* 16 (1991): 463–484.

Folbre, Nancy, and Heidi Hartmann. "The Rhetoric of Self Interest and the Ideology of Gender." In Arjo Klamer, D. McCloskey, and R. Solow, eds. *The Consequences of Economic Rhetoric.* New York: Cambridge University Press, 1988, pp. 184–206.

"Forum: Beyond Dichotomies." *Gender and History* 1 (Autumn 1989): 291–329.

Fowler, Nathaniel C. "Reaching the Men Through the Women." *Printer's Ink* 5 (22 July 1891).

Fox, Bonnie J. "Selling the Mechanized Household: Seventy Years of Ads in *Ladies' Home Journal.*" *Gender and Society* 4 (March 1990): 25–40.

Gitlin, Todd. "Who Communicates What to Whom, in What Voice and Why, About the Study of Mass Communication?" *Critical Studies in Mass Communication* 7 (1990): 185–196.

Gordon, Lynn D. "The Gibson Girl Goes to College: Popular Culture and Women's Higher Education in the Progressive Era, 1890–1920." *American Quarterly* 39 (Summer 1987): 211–230.

Gordon, Michael. "The Ideal Husband as Depicted in the Nineteenth-Century Marriage Manual." In Elizabeth and Joseph Pleck, eds. *The American Man.* Englewood Cliffs, New Jersey: Prentice Hall, 1980, pp. 145–157.

Griffen, Clyde. "Reconstructing Masculinity From the Evangelical Revival to the Waning of Progressivism: A Speculative Synthesis." In Clyde Griffen and Mark Carnes, *Meanings for Manhood: Constructions of Masculinity in Victorian America.* Chicago: University of Chicago Press, 1990, pp. 183–204.

Griswold, Robert L. "Law, Sex, Cruelty, and Divorce in Victorian America, 1840–1900." *American Quarterly* 38 (1986): 721–745.

Hall, Stuart. "Culture, the Media and the 'Ideological Effect.' " In James Curran, Michael Gurevitch, and Janet Woollacott, eds. *Mass Communication and Society.* London: Edward Arnold in Association with the Open University Press, 1977.

Hansen, Karen V. "Helped Put in a Quilt: Men's Work and Male Intimacy in Nineteenth-Century New England." *Gender and Society* 3 (September 1989): 334–354.

Hantover, Jeffrey P. "The Boy Scouts and the Validation of Masculinity." In Elizabeth and Joseph Pleck, eds. *The American Man.* Englewood Cliffs, New Jersey: Prentice Hall, 1980, pp. 285–301.

Harrison, James B. "Review Essay/Men's Roles and Men's Lives." *Signs* 4 (Winter 1978): 324–336.

Hartmann, Heidi. "Capitalism, Patriarchy, and Job Segregation by Sex." *Signs* 1 (Spring 1976): 162–174.

Hodge, Carl. "For Men Only." *Magazine Industry* 1 (Winter 1950): 13.

Honey, Maureen. "Images of Women in *The Saturday Evening Post,* 1931–1936." *Journal of Popular Culture* 10 (Fall 1976): 352–358.

Howard, Judith A., and Carolyn Allen. "The Gendered Context of Reading." *Gender and Society* 4 (December 1990): 534–552.

Inglis, Ruth A. "An Objective Approach to the Relationship Between Fiction and Society." *American Sociological Review* 3 (1938): 526–531.

Johns-Heine, Patricke, and Hans Gerth. "Values in Mass Periodical Fiction, 1921–1940." *Public Opinion Quarterly* 13 (Spring 1949): 105–113.

Katz, Michael B. "Social Class in North American Urban History." *Journal of Interdisciplinary History* 11 (Spring 1981): 579–605.

Kelly, R. Gordon. "The Social Construction of Reality: Implications for Future Directions in American Studies." *Prospects: The Annual of American Culture Studies* 8 (1983): 49–58.

Kerber, Linda. "Separate Spheres, Female Worlds, Woman's Place: The Rhetoric of Women's History." *The Journal of American History* 75 (June 1988): 9–39.

Kesselman, Amy. "The 'Freedom Suit': Feminism and Dress Reform in the United States, 1848–1875." *Gender & Society* 5 (December 1991): 495–510.

Kilbourne, Jean. "The Child as Sex Object: Images of Children in the Media." *Challenging Media Images of Women* 3 (Summer 1991): 1–2, 6.

Kimmel, Michael S. "Men's Responses to Feminism at the Turn of the Century." *Gender and Society* 1 (September 1987): 261–283.

Kleinberg, Susan J. "Technology and Women's Work: The Lives of Working-Class Women in Pittsburgh, 1870–1900." *Labor History* 17 (1976): 58–72.

Leach, William R. "Transformations in A Culture of Consumption: Women and Department Stores, 1890–1925." *The Journal of American History* 71 (September 1984): 319–342.

Lears, T. J. Jackson. "The Concept of Cultural Hegemony: Problems and Possibilities." *American Historical Review* 90 (June 1985): 567–593.

———. "From Salvation to Self-Realization: Advertising and the Therapeutic Roots of the Consumer Culture, 1880–1930." In Richard Wightman Fox and T. J. Jackson Lears, eds. *The Culture of Consumption: Critical Essays in American History, 1880–1980.* New York: Pantheon Books, 1983, pp. 3–38.

———. "Some Versions of Fantasy: Toward a Cultural History of American Advertising, 1880–1930." *Prospects* 9 (1984): 349–405.

Lerner, Gerda. "Reconceptualizing Differences Among Women." *Journal of Women's History* 1 (Winter 1990): 106–122.

Long, Elizabeth. "Women, Reading, and Cultural Authority: Some Implications of the Audience Perspective in Cultural Studies." *American Quarterly* 38 (Fall 1986): 591–612.

Lowenthal, Leo. "Biographies in Popular Magazines." Reprinted in William Peterson, ed. *American Social Patterns.* Garden City, New York: Doubleday & Co., Inc., 1956, pp. 63–118.

Marsh, Margaret. "Suburban Men and Masculine Domesticity, 1870–1915." *American Quarterly* 40 (June 1988): 165–186.

———. "From Separation to Togetherness: The Social Construction of Domestic Space in American Suburbs, 1840–1915." *American Quarterly* 40 (June 1988): 165–186.

McGovern, James R. "The American Woman's Pre-World War I Freedom in Manners and Morals." In Jean Friedman and William Shade, eds. *Our American Sisters*. Boston: Allyn & Bacon, Inc., 1973, pp. 239–250.

———. "David Graham Phillips and the Virility Impulse of Progressives." *New England Quarterly* 39 (1966): 334–355.

Mechling, Jay E. "Advice to Historians on Advice to Mothers." *Journal of Social History* 9 (Fall 1975): 44–63.

Miller, Cristanne. "Who Talks Like a Women's Magazine? Language and Gender in Popular Women's and Men's Magazines." *Journal of American Popular Culture* 10 (Fall 1987): 1–9.

Morris, Meaghan. "Banality in Cultural Studies." *Discourse* 10 (1988): 3–29.

Nichols, William. "Changing Attitudes Toward Poverty in the *Ladies' Home Journal*, 1895–1919." *American Studies* 5 (Spring 1964): 3–16.

Nord, David Paul. "An Economic Perspective on Formula In Popular Culture." *Journal of American Culture* 3 (Spring 1980): 17–31.

———. "Intellectual History, Social History, Cultural History . . . and Our History." *Journalism Quarterly* 67 (Winter 1990): 645–648.

———. "Working-Class Readers: Family, Community, and Reading in Late Nineteenth-Century America." *Communication Research* 13 (April 1986): 156–181.

Ohmann, Richard. "Where Did Mass Culture Come From? The Case of the Magazines." *Berkshire Review* 16 (1981): 85–101.

Peiss, Kathy. "Making Faces: The Cosmetics Industry and the Cultural Construction of Gender, 1890–1930." *Genders* 7 (Spring 1990): 143–169.

Peterson, Theodore. "Edward Bok and the American Dream." *Emory University Quarterly* 21 (Fall 1965): 207–216.

Pleck, Joseph H. "American Fathering in Historical Perspective." In Michael S. Kimmel, ed. *Changing Men: New Directions in Research on Men and Masculinity*. Newbury Park, Cal.: SAGE Pubs., 1987, pp. 83–97.

———. "The Male Sex Role: Definitions, Problems and Sources of Change." *Journal of Social Issues* 22 (Summer 1976): 155–164.

Radway, Janice. "Reading is Not Eating: Mass-Produced Literature and the Theoretical, Methodological, and Political Consequences of a Metaphor." *Book Research Quarterly* (Fall 1986): 7–29.

Ribuffo, Leo P. "Jesus Christ as Business Statesman: Bruce Barton and the Selling of Corporate Capitalism." *American Quarterly* 33 (Summer 1981): 206–221.

Rosenberg, Charles E. "Sexuality, Class and Role in Nineteenth-Century America." In Elizabeth and Joseph Pleck, eds. *The American Man*. Englewood Cliffs, New Jersey: Prentice-Hall, 1980, pp. 219–254.

Rothenberg, Paula. "The Construction, Deconstruction, and Reconstruction of Difference." *Hypatia* 5 (Spring 1990): 42–51.

Rotundo, E. Anthony. "Body and Soul: Changing Ideals of American Middle-Class Manhood, 1770–1920." *Journal of Social History* (Summer 1983): 21–38.

Schudson, Michael. "The New Validation of Popular Culture: Sense and Sentimentality in Academia." *Critical Studies in Mass Communication* 4 (1987): 51–68.

Scott, Joan W. "Gender: A Useful Category of Historical Analysis." *American Historical Review* 91 (December 1986): 1053–1075.

———. "Women in History." *Past and Present* 101 (November 1983): 141–157.

Searles, Patricia, and Janet Mickish. "A Thoroughbred Girl: Images of Female Gender Roles in Turn-of-the-Century Mass Media." *Women's Studies* 10 (1984): 261–281.

Segel, Elizabeth. " 'As The Twig is Bent' . . . . : Gender and Childhood Reading." In Elizabeth A. Flynn and Patrocinio P. Schweickart, eds. *Gender and Reading: Essays on Readers, Texts, and Contexts*. Baltimore: John Hopkins University Press, 1986, pp. 165–186.

Seidel, Joan M. "Consumer's Choices: A Study of Household Furnishing, 1880–1920." *Minnesota History* (Spring 1983): 183–197.

Sicherman, Barbara. "Sense and Sensibility: A Case Study of Women's Reading in Late-Victorian America." In Cathy N. Davidson, ed. *Reading in America: Literature and Social History*. Baltimore: Johns Hopkins University Press, 1989, pp. 201–225.

Smith, Daniel Scott. "Family Limitation, Sexual Control, and Domestic Feminism in Victorian America." In Nancy Cott and Elizabeth Pleck, eds. *A Heritage of Her Own*. New York: Simon & Schuster, 1979, pp. 222–245.

Smith-Rosenberg, Carroll. "The Female World of Love and Ritual: Relations Between Women in Nineteenth-Century America." In Nancy Cott and Elizabeth Pleck, eds. *A Heritage of Her Own*. New York: Simon & Schuster, 1979, pp. 311–342.

———. "The Hysterical Woman: Sex Roles and Role Conflict in Nineteenth Century America." *Social Research* 39 (Winter 1972): 652–678.

Stearns, Peter N., and Carol Z. "Emotionology: Clarifying the History of Emotions and Emotional Standards." *American Historical Review* 90 (October 1985): 813–836.

Steele, Janet. "The Nineteenth Century *World* versus the *Sun:* Promoting Consumption (Rather Than the Working Man)." *Journalism Quarterly* 67 (1990): 592–600.

Tilly, Louise A. "Gender, Women's History, and Social History." *Social Science History* 13 (Winter 1989): 439–462.

Vanek, Joann. "Time Spent in Housework." In Nancy Cott and Elizabeth Pleck, eds. *A Heritage of Her Own.* New York: Simon & Schuster, 1979, pp. 499–506.

Vogel, Lise. "Telling Tales: Historians of Our Own Lives." *Journal of Women's History* 2 (Winter 1991): 89–101.

Waller-Zuckerman, Mary Ellen. "Marketing the Women's Journals, 1873–1900." In William J. Hausman, ed. *Essays in Business and Economic History.* 2d series, vol. 18 (Fall 1989): 99–108.

———. "Old Homes in a City of Perpetual Change: The Women's Magazine Industry, 1890–1917." *Business History Review* (Fall 1989): 715–756.

Welter, Barbara. "The Cult of True Womanhood: 1820–1860." *American Quarterly* 18 (Summer 1966): 151–174.

Wilson, Christopher P. "The Rhetoric of Consumption: Mass-Market Magazines and the Demise of the Gentle Reader, 1880–1920." In Richard W. Fox and T. J. Jackson Lears, eds. *The Culture of Consumption: Critical Essays in American History, 1880–1980.* New York: Pantheon Books, 1983, pp. 41–64.

Wood, Gordon S. "Intellectual History and the Social Sciences." In John Higham and Paul Conklin, eds. *New Directions in American Intellectual History.* Baltimore: Johns Hopkins University Press, 1979, pp. 27–41.

MAGAZINES

The *Ladies' Home Journal,* all issues from December 1883 through December 1910.

The *Saturday Evening Post,* all issues from October 1897 through December 1910.

MANUSCRIPT SOURCES

Bok, Edward. Papers. Historical Society of Pennsylvania, Philadelphia.

Bok, A. Margaret. Letters to author. December 1986 and February 1987.

Bok, Mary Louise Curtis. Papers. Historical Society of Pennsylvania, Philadelphia.

Curtis, Cyrus. Papers. Historical Society of Pennsylvania, Philadelphia.

Neall, Adelaide S. Papers and Scrapbooks. Historical Society of Pennsylvania, Philadelphia.

INDEX

Abbott, Mrs. Lyman, 59, 74, 86
Ad-stripping, 99
Advertising: sexism in, 2; need a forum for, 3; development of, 23–24; manufacturers and, 23–24; agencies for, 23–24; women and, 24, 180–187; N. W. Ayer Agency and, 27; first issue *Journal* and, 35; *Journal* readers and, 50; for Castoria, 54; superstructure and infra-structure for, 54–55, 116–117; national in *Journal*, 77, 99–107; John Adams Thayer as manager, 77; ad-stripping, 99; Pearline Soap and, 100–106; gender construction and, 102–107; the *Post* and, 115–117, 141–150; men and, 180–187; television and, 192–195; *Ms.* Magazine and, 199; and censorship, 200
Age, 7
Alcott, Louisa May, 30
"All About the Home," 69
All-American Girl, 38–39
American Magazine, 191
The Americanization of Edward Bok, 62
Andrews, E. Benjamin, 140
Anticipatory production, 65
Argosy, 191
Armour, P. D., 111
Atherton, Gertrude, 137–138
Atlantic, 73, 145
Ayer, N. W., 27

Barr, Amelia E., 95
Bateson, Mary Catherine, 31–32

Beauty Myth, The 197
Beauvoir, Simone de, 8
Beecher, Henry Ward, 63
Bell, Lilian, 91
Beveridge, Albert, 121, 123
Bicycle, 119
Biography, 119, 121
Blatch, Harriet Stanton, 41
Bok, Edward: hired as *Journal* editor, 56–60; as *Journal* editor, 59–79; on superiority of male editors, 59–62; and view that women need help, 62; as a preacher, 64; as stock-holder in Curtis Publishing Co., 78; marries Mary Louise Curtis (Knapp), 79; as businessman, 81; and narrowing options for men, 129; and male readers, 150–151; and domestic science, 163–164; as a male capitalist, 195
Bok, William, 62
Books for women, 20
Borden, 23
Boston, 73, 111
Boston *Herald*, 110
Boston *Post*, 110
Bottome, Margaret, 74
Boy Scouts, 128
Brooklyn, 62
Boys' and mens' education, 138
Brown, LaRue, 1
Burdette, Robert J., 35, 83–84
Business: and the *Post*, 109, 169; and George Horace Lorimer, 111, 121, 129; businessmen, 131, 178; in *Post* fiction, 139

257

49–50; Bok's view of, 95–96; and divorce, 95–96; work and, 134; *Post* and, 136–138, 169; ideals of, 137; Edward Bok's *Journal* and, 168–169
Marshment, Margaret, 202
Masculine domesticity, 98
Masculinity, 8
Mass media, 109
May, Elaine Tyler, 96
McCall's, 24–25, 190–193
McClure, S. S., 64
McClure's, 114, 123
Meanings for Manhood, 129
Meekins, Lynn Roby, 123, 139
Men: history of, 3, 128–130; as norm, 8; and maintaining status quo, 8, 11–12, 127; as providers, 12, 134–136; and *Journal*, 74, 96–99; as fathers, 97–98; masculine domesticity and, 98, 128; as readers, 115–116; and public realm, 127; as culturally ungendered, 128; heightened sensitivity about, 153; work and, 170–177; magazines and, 190–191; and *Playboy*, 190–191.
"Men and Women of the Hour" column, 119
Men, Masculinity, and the Media, 8
Michigan, 86
Middle Class: magazines for, 6–7, 116, n19, 207; defined, 23; and women's advancement, 62; as *Journal* audience, 38, 73–74; Edward Bok attempts to educate, 63–64; Lorimer and, 111; gender-commerce bond and, 194; white, androcentric, patriarchal, 196
Miller, Cristanne, 165
Milwaukee, 73
Money, 49
Mother-daughter relationships, n28, 211
Ms., 199–200
Muckraking, 123
Munsey, Frank, 64
Munsey's, 114

Nation, The, 114
Netherlands, 62
New Woman, 159
Newspaper: *Journal* founded as supplement to, 1; only medium available besides magazines, 54; George Horace Lorimer and, 111; *Saturday Evening Post* and, 123
Newsweek, 200
New York City, 42, 100
New York Star, 63
North American Review, 93
Nye, Fred, 123

Page, Walter Hines, 64
Palmer, Alice Freeman, 139
Palmer, Bryan, 5
Parkhurst, Charles, 84–85, 91, 97
Patent medicine advertising, 110
Pennsylvania Railroad, 167
Peterson, Theodore, 190–191
Phelps, Elizabeth Stuart, 31
Philadelphia, 19, 34, 46
Pinkham, Lavinia, 150
Pinkham, Lydia, 150
Playboy, 190–191
Poe, Edgar Allan, 110
Portland, Maine, 15
Postal Mailing Act of 1879, 26
Poverty, 37
Power, Tyrone, 176
Printer's Ink, 115–116
Professionalism: defined, 31–32; flexibility and, 31–32; Louisa Knapp Curtis and, 31–32; and readers of the *Journal*, 38
Prostitution, 129
Provider role, 8, 12
Public realm, 127
Publisher: see Cyrus H. K. Curtis
Pulitzer Prize, 62

Race, 7
Race suicide, 92